The Arabic Language and National Identity

The Arabic Language and National Identity

A Study in Ideology

YASIR SULEIMAN

Georgetown University Press
Washington, D.C.

For Tamir and Sinan

Georgetown University Press, Washington, D.C.

10 9 8 7 6 5 4 3 2 1 2003

This volume is printed on acid-free offset book paper.

First published in the United Kingdom by Edinburgh University Press.

Typeset in Goudy by
Koinonia, Manchester, and
printed and bound in Great Britain by
The Cromwell Press, Trowbridge, Wilts

Library of Congress Cataloging-in-Publication Data

Suleiman, Yasir.
The Arabic language and national identity : a study in ideology /
Yasir Suleiman.
p. cm.
Includes bibliographical references and index.
ISBN 0-87840-395-7 (pbk.)
1. Arab nationalism. 2. National characteristics, Arab. 3. Arabic language—Political aspects. 4. Arabic language—Social aspects. 5. Language and culture—Arab countries. I. Title. DS63.6.S94 2003
320.54'089'927—dc21
2002151195

Contents

Acknowledgements

This book builds on research I have carried out over the past decade. Many people have helped me during this period, not all of whom I can acknowledge here. I would however like to express my thanks to Ramzi Baalbaki, Youssef Choueiri, Rachid El-Enany, Ronak Husni, Emad Saleh, Muhammad Shaheen and Iman Soliman for their help in securing some of the works upon which this book is based. Ramzi Baalbaki's help in securing some of Kamal Yusuf al-Hajj's publications was crucial in expanding my discussion of Lebanese nationalism. I am particularly grateful to him.

I am also grateful to Bill Donaldson, Carole Hillenbrand, Ibrahim Muhawi and Bill Roff for reading the entire manuscript and making many valuable comments. Their perceptive remarks have improved the manuscript on all fronts. I am also indebted to Ivor Normand, my copy-editor, for his meticulous reading of the text. Needless to say, the responsibility for any remaining errors is entirely mine.

In carrying out the research for this book, I have benefited from a number of small grants from the British Academy, the Carnegie Trust for the Universities of Scotland and the Royal Society of Edinburgh. I am grateful for this financial assistance, which enabled me to visit a number of libraries in the Middle East and elsewhere.

I cannot fully acknowledge the contribution of my family to this project. As usual, Shahla has been a tower of strength. She pursued references for me on her trips to the Middle East. She has also ensured that our two sons, Tamir and Sinan, were kept busy. Her computing expertise got me out of trouble on several occasions. For all this, I want to thank her.

Finally, Tamir and Sinan were the real power behind this book. Their interest in it was enormous. They asked the real questions: What is nationalism? What has language got to do with nationalism? And why is nationalism so important as to make a father devote so much time away from his family to studying it? To them, I owe a debt of gratitude for showing understanding and patience.

1

The Arabic Language and National Identity: Aims and Scope

1. AIMS OF THE STUDY: THE DISCIPLINARY CONTEXT

Nationalism is a thriving field of study in which a variety of disciplines participate. Historians, political scientists, sociologists, social anthropologists, social psychologists, political geographers and others have all delved into different aspects of this field. This reflects the complexity and the elasticity of the phenomena of nationalism and of the durability of the interests they generate across disciplinary boundaries. It must, however, be said that this multiplicity of theoretical perspectives has generated a corresponding multiplicity of discourses, none of which can claim the prerequisite universality necessary to allow us to talk about a *theory of nationalism* with any confidence. Broadly speaking, what we have so far are two types of study. First, there are those that seek to generalize out of a limited evidential base by proposing a set of explanatory ideas which can then be tested against further data outside the base in question. These studies are then refined, extended or restricted both empirically and theoretically, but they can never completely escape the limitations inherent in their empirical sources or the theoretical perspectives which inform them. And there is no reason why they should. What we have here, therefore, are restricted *approaches* to the study of nationalism, not a theory of nationalism or theories of nationalism, although the term "theory" is used in this sense from time to time. A paradigm example of this is Gellner's modernist or functionalist approach, which is best suited to the study of the rise and development of nationalism in industrialized societies, or, it may be argued, just to a sub-set of these societies. The present study of the Arabic language and national identity does not belong to this genre in the study of nationalism.

The second type of approach is restricted to a particular nationalism, dealing with it in isolation or in relation to other interacting or comparable nationalisms. The study of Arab, Turkish, Greek or other named nationalisms exemplifies this approach. The interest of the researcher here is to describe and explain the observed phenomena by utilizing the insights of studies of the first type. Additionally, studies of this second type may serve as test cases for the insights generated by general approaches. They define the empirical limits of these general studies or circumscribe their excessive explanatory claims.

Progress in the study of nationalism requires the two types of study. It is impossible to imagine that general approaches to the study of nationalism can be conducted in an empirical vacuum, or that studies of specific nationalisms can proceed without any recourse to theoretical insights. The present study belongs to the second type of approach. It aims to provide a reading of a limited site of nationalist discourse – that pertaining to the Arabic language and national identity – as a contribution towards a general understanding of the phenomenon of nationalism in the Arab Middle East. This study will also contribute to the understanding of the phenomenon of nationalism in its language-related dimension. A prime example of this kind of study is Joshua Fishman's pioneering monograph *Language and Nationalism* (1972) which, unfortunately, hardly figures in standard works on nationalism even when language is directly invoked.

The study of nationalism in the Arab Middle East has made great strides in the last few decades. First, advocacy in favour of a particular nationalism or the apologetic defence of it gave way to a more objective outlook. This danger of confusing the subjective with the objective is particularly present when the nationalist turns into a student of nationalism, thus producing a discourse which aims to (1) valorize the status quo, (2) sanction and instigate a particular brand of nationalist behaviour, or (3) convert the decision-makers in a centre of political power to a particular nationalist cause. Second, description in the study of the topic under investigation has increasingly given way to a more analytical and explanatory orientation. This has in turn led to an increased sophistication in the standard of argumentation and counter-argumentation. It has also led to the development of a sharper interest in cross-cultural comparisons, at least in the regional context. Third, the study of nationalism in the Arab Middle East has sought to extend its disciplinary scope beyond its traditional domain of history and politics, although it continues to be dominated by historians and political scientists. Anthropologists and sociologists have participated from the edges in a way which has enhanced our understanding of the social processes involved in the internalization, negotiation and contestation of national identities. Fourth, some students of nationalism in the Middle East have sought to widen the kinds of data which can be subjected to study and analysis. The call to use newspaper articles and other kinds of non-orthodox materials, for example graffiti, in the study of nationalism represents a bold attempt at trying to reshape the scope within which this enterprise has hitherto been conducted.

But there are also glaring weaknesses, the most prominent of which is the reluctance to take the study of nationalism in the Arab Middle East into the wider cultural arena of literary production, the arts, film, music, sports, tourism, festivals, school textbooks, architectural styles, naming practices, maps, stamps and other media of symbolic expression. There is perhaps a feeling among historians and political scientists that data from these domains are fickle and subject to deliberate manipulation. Moreover, scholarly tradition considers the above media of symbolic expression to fall at the margin of the scope of history and politics, which thus far have dominated the study of nationalism in the Arab Middle East. This problem, however, is not entirely the making of the historians or the political scientists. It is also partly the responsibility of specialists in the above domains of inquiry, who have done very little to show how their disciplines can inform the study of nationalism. Considerations of academic worth are central here. For example, it is unlikely that any serious literary critic would consider the study of the interaction between nationalism and literature to be the kind of material from which scholarly reputations are made. A study of this kind would be considered more relevant to an understanding of social and political history than to the study of literature in its creative mode. The same ethos may also apply in art history, architecture, music and film studies. Falling between disciplines with different intellectual agendas, some nationalist phenomena in the Arab Middle East have been left out of consideration, thus curtailing our understanding of nationalism in this important part of the world.

Another glaring gap in the study of nationalism in the Arab Middle East is the absence of a serious study of the most important of all systems of functional and symbolic expression: language. It is indeed remarkable that, to the best of my knowledge, a study of this kind has not been produced, not even in Arabic, although limited studies touching on aspects of language and nationalism do exist (see Bengio 1998, Chejne 1969, Holes 1993, Mazraani 1997 and Suleiman 1993, 1994, 1996b, 1997, 1999b, 1999d). I say this because of the centrality of language in articulations of nationalism in the Arab Middle East. This is true of Arab nationalism in the nineteenth and twentieth centuries. It is also true of Egyptian and Lebanese nationalism in the first half of the twentieth century and beyond (see below). This lacuna is all the more glaring because, when set in a comparative regional context, the study of language and nationalism in the Arab Middle East deserves greater attention. Witness the enormous interest in this subject in Turkish nationalism and Hebrew nationalism, which have succeeded in promoting themselves as paradigm cases against which other nationalisms may be judged.

The responsibility for this lacuna does not belong to the historians or political scientists alone, although so far they are the ones who have dominated the study of nationalism in the Arab Middle East. A historian or political scientist is aware of the functional and symbolic roles of language, but does not usually study language *per se* or in any of its hyphenated modes. In a world of disciplinary specialization, this is regarded as the task of the linguist. But linguists are hemmed in by the imperatives of their discipline. They tend to be interested in the theoretical foundations of linguistics or the generation of descriptive studies for individual languages or portions of languages. Hyphenated approaches such as psycho-linguistics or socio-linguistics (henceforth "sociolinguistics") answer to two masters, which tend to pull them in different directions and, more often than not, assign those who profess expertise in them to the margins of the parent disciplines.

The closest approach to a linguistics-related field of study which can investigate the question of language and national identity is sociolinguistics, provided we conceive of this discipline as being "*essentially about identity*, its formation, presentation and maintenance" (Edwards 1988: 3). But this discipline is handicapped in a number of ways in its treatment of Arabic. First, Arabic sociolinguistics tends to be interested in the functional capacity of the language rather than in its symbolic connotations. By treating the language as a means of communication first and foremost, Arabic sociolinguistics misses the opportunity to tap into a layer of meanings and symbolic values that may otherwise be available to the researcher. Second, the interest in quantitatively based analyses in Arabic sociolinguistics (and in sociolinguistics generally; see Cameron 1997) creates a bias, driven by logico-positivist impulses, against studies which do not rely on this mode of investigation. Studies of this kind can therefore be easily dismissed as "unscientific" or "pseudo-scientific". Third, Arabic sociolinguistics in its quantitative mode is handicapped by the invisibility of *national* identity as a prominent factor in the theoretical impulses which historically informed this discipline (Labov 1966, 1972). Arabic sociolinguistics of the 1970s and 1980s in particular created aspects of the Arabic language situation – particularly dialectal and sociolectal variation – in the image of the urban-based, North American model on which it relied for its inspiration (see Walters 2002). This was understandable at the time when the thrust of this research was to test the applicability of the Labovian model outside its original context.

The primary aim of the present research is therefore to fill the above gap, thus contributing to the study of nationalism in the Middle East from a cross-disciplinary perspective. Another aim of this study is to encourage Arabic sociolinguists to delve into other aspects of language and national identity from a qualitative perspective. Finally, it is hoped that this work will highlight the importance of symbolic meaning in the study of nationalism.

2. WHAT IS NATIONAL IDENTITY?

There is nothing novel in saying that identities are complex, variable, elastic and subject to manipulation (cf. Maalouf 2000). This is the position in all the disciplines which deal with identity, whether as a collective or personal unit of analysis. This multi-dimensional nature of identity, and its mutations across disciplinary boundaries and theoretical paradigms, makes it difficult to account for its meaning. It is therefore not my intention to contrive a concept of identity which can be applied uniformly throughout the present study. This is not possible; and, at any rate, such a task is beyond my competence. It may therefore be useful to repeat here what I said in a previous study on the Arabic language and national identity (Suleiman 1997: 127):

> Being so wide-ranging in scope, it is not surprising that the concept of identity defies precise description. This fact should not however deter us from delving into those questions of collective affiliation which constitute the scope of identity, not least because of the persistence of this notion as an operative factor in all aspects of human life. In a sense it would be impossible to understand man as a social being without invoking a category of thought similar to what we describe by the notion of identity. A degree of conceptual vagueness is therefore inevitable, but not so cripplingly as to deny us the possibility of an informed treatment of identity-related subjects.

Broadly speaking, collective identities are anchored in relation to such variables as genealogy, age, gender, sexuality, class, occupation, locality (be it regional, district, village and so on), tribe, clan, religion, confession or sect, ethnicity, nationality or state citizenship. The fact that these and other variables normally appear as discrete members of a list does not mean that collective identities are neatly segmented along similar lines. Furthermore, the fact that we talk about collective identities as categories of social definition should not mask the principle that these identities are experienced at the personal level, and that it is the individual who experiences these identities and gives them meaning in his or her social and cultural setting (see Cohen 1994). It is by virtue of this principle that we can say that collective identities weave in and out of each other in different ways at different times depending on the salient features of the situation in which a person finds him- or herself. However, this principle of mutation does not mean that collective identities are unstable, albeit that some are amenable to change more quickly than others. For example, occupational, class, local and state identities may undergo change more easily than religious or national identities, but this does not make the former set of identities unstable or chameleon-like. Even when identities seem to have undergone significant change, residual impulses continue to emanate from them, thus making them able to serve as the basis of individual or collective action.

As I have mentioned, the aim of this book is to consider conceptualizations of national identity in the Arab Middle East as these coalesce around Arabic. This limitation of scope demands some explanation of how national identity is deployed here. Smith identifies what he calls the five "fundamental features" of national identity (1991: 14): "1. an historic territory, or homeland; 2. common myths and historical memories; 3. a common, mass public culture; 4. common legal rights and duties for all members; 5. a common economy with territorial mobility for members". Smith states that this concept of national identity is based on a "peculiarly Western concept of the nation", justifying this by the fact that the "Western experience has exerted a powerful, indeed the leading, influence on our conception of the unit we call the 'nation'" (ibid.: 9). Although the first three "fundamental features" above allow for the definition of national identity without reference to political community or state, the last two features imply a denial of this possibility. This denial is problematic for the study of national identity in the Arab Middle East. National identity in this part of the world may straddle state borders, and more than one ethnicity (politicized cultural identity) may coexist within the same state. This denial is also problematic because it is not possible to say that there exist throughout the Arab Middle East "common legal rights and duties" or a "common economy with territorial mobility" for all the people of the area. Such rights, duties and economic mobilities as do exist in the Arab Middle East are invariably related to the multiplicity of states as independent legal entities. If accepted, the above specification of national identity would rule as unwarranted the positing of supra-state and sub-state national identities. In particular, it would declare as unwarranted all talk about an Arab national identity. The whole concept of an Arab national identity would be in doubt, questioning with it the validity of more than a century of embryonic and fully fledged nationalist thinking. At best, the Arab nationalist discourse would be one not about an Arab identity *per se*, but about an Arab national consciousness as a precursor to this identity. At worst, the above concept of national identity would declare Arab nationalist thinking misguided and bogus.

Accepting the above specification may also be taken to imply that national identities can be quickly induced if states are created over territories whose populations share the first three fundamental features. The fact that a state can endow people with "common legal rights and duties" and that it can extend to them the right to "territorial mobility" and participation in a "common economy" must, logically speaking, imply that national identities can be fabricated in a very short time. There should therefore be little difficulty in producing an Egyptian, Lebanese or Syrian national identity that is exclusive of other national identities. The fact that this is not entirely the case testifies to the inadequacy of the above specification of national identity.

To avoid the above problems, the concept of national identity must be formulated in different ways to suit the imperatives of different sociopolitical contexts. For the Arab Middle East, this would require the division of the above set of fundamental features into two components. Features 1 to 3 in Smith's list are necessary for the establishment of a *cultural* concept of national identity. However, for such an identity – sometimes called ethnicity – to exist, there should also obtain a political consciousness that is capable of making these features available for deployment in the political arena, including the establishment of a common state. The existence of the state, embodied in features 4 to 5 in Smith's list, is necessary for the creation of national identity in the *political* sense. As we shall see later, both types of national identity are presumed to exist in the Arab Middle East.

To help frame the discussion of national identity which will follow, I will highlight a number of principles which inform the present study. First, I believe that Grew (1986: 35) is fundamentally right when he asserts that national identity is not "simply a natural growth" among the people who exhibit it. National identity is a construct, in both the intellectual and the historical senses. It is fashioned out of history, or, more correctly, interpretations of history. The involvement of the elite in fashioning it is absolutely fundamental to formulating its intellectual foundations and, also, to popularizing it as the basis of mass political action. These observations will be borne out in this study (see Chapter 3).

Second, in recent discourse on the construction of national identity, such terms as "imagined", "invented" and "myth" have come into vogue to describe different aspects of the nation. While the empirical and theoretical utility of these terms cannot be denied, I agree with Schöpflin (1997: 26) that "there are clear and unavoidable limits to invention and imagination" in constructing national identity. Schöpflin specifies "resonance" as the criterion which sets this limit. Imagination, invention and mythologizing work only to the extent that they can successfully exploit authentic and highly significant aspects of the culture of those for whom a particular national identity is being constructed. Resonance applies within these limits, which are invariably rooted in the past. Smith (1997: 56) comes to more or less the same conclusion, although he pushes the literal meanings of "invention" and "imagining" too far when he declares that the "golden age" which a particular nationalism manipulates "is not a form of invented tradition, nor is it made up of 'shreds and patches', nor again is it merely an imagined community".[1] Using Smith's findings (ibid.: 58), we may unpack the content of Schöpflin's concept of "resonance" by saying that it relates to those aspects of the culture in a nationalist discourse that are characterized by "authenticity, rootedness, continuity, dignity and destiny".

Third, as used in the present work, the concept of national identity emerges from the ideological articulations of nationalism (cf. Miller 1995: 17–47). Hence my concern with the range of ideas which intellectuals, educators and people of letters have put forward to describe the role of Arabic in forming, promoting and maintaining various conceptualizations of national identity in the Arab Middle East. While answering to a predescriptive or "objective" reality, these ideologies aim at elaborating and redefining national identity for particular political purposes. Using functionalist models of description and explanation in the social sciences, we may say that nationalism as ideology aims at the externalization and objectification of national identity as a prerequisite for its internalization by members of the putative nation in its newly refashioned form. The fact that advocacy is central to ideology in this sense is inevitable. In addition, treating ideology as discourse, we may say that concepts of national identity are subject to varying interpretations by members of the (putative) nation. It is ultimately they who can act upon it and convert it into reality. Whether they do act on it or not, and if they do whether their effort will be met with success or not, is epistemologically immaterial here.

Reiterating the point made above, in this study I am more concerned with nationalism as ideology than as a mass movement or mode of political action, although the categorial distinction between the two is normally more honoured in the breach than in the observance. It is important that we bear this restriction in mind to avoid the fallacy of category-hopping. This fallacy may take the form of arguing that if the Arab nation is indeed defined by its language, and since Arabic is common to all Arabs, then why is it that the Arabs are politically divided? The response to this is a simple one: the ideological assertion of *x* does not necessarily mean that *x* will be acted upon to achieve a given political objective. By choosing to concentrate on nationalism as ideology, rather than as movement, the present study takes a neutral stand as to whether the Arabic language is capable of bringing about the political unity much desired by the more politically active among the cultural nationalists in the Arabic-speaking world.

Fourth, the ideological conceptualization of national identity in the Arab Middle East is constructed in two ways. On the one hand, it exploits the power of contrast by invoking a significant Other. This contingent view of identity is based on the premise that difference is essential for the maintenance of boundaries between nations. Termed "playing the vis-à-vis" by Boon (1982, cited in Cohen 1994: 11) in anthropology, this mode of conceptualization of national identity is most evident in the early articulations of Arab nationalism which tended to be visualized in relation to Turkish nationalism within the Ottoman Empire (see Chapter 4). This is also the case in some statements of Egyptian and Lebanese nationalism (see Chapter 6) which posit Arab nationalism as the significant Other. On the other hand, national identity in the Arab Middle East is sometimes articulated without direct reference to a significant Other. Comparisons with other nationalisms are intended not to emphasize difference and contrast but to add further substantiation to a pertinent feature of national identity. This positive approach to the ideological articulation of national identity is best exhibited in the more mature versions of Arab nationalism (see Chapter 5). In practice, the two modes of conceptualization of national identity tend to be mixed.

Fifth, although the interaction between language and national identity is a feature of many nationalisms, this is by no means a universally accepted premise (see Chapter 2). Furthermore, it is not always clear what the nature of this interaction is. Some scholars treat language as an *ingredient* in a mixture of factors that make up the national self. Others treat it as a *component* in a set of features that define this self. There are also those who talk of language as a *marker* or *attribute* of national identity, rather than as an ingredient or component of it. Scholars of this persuasion sometimes employ the alternative terms "badge" or "emblem" to signify this relationship.[2] This multiplicity of terms indicates a lack of clarity in the study of nationalism. Rather than making tenuous distinctions between these terms, the present work will utilize them with little distinction.

Sixth, in conducting this study I am aware that, for some, "national identity [is] hardly an attractive subject of study in a world that had so cruelly experienced it as nationalism, imperialism, militarism, and racism" (Grew 1986: 33). This sense of "awkwardness" (ibid.: 39) about national identity – which is sometimes mixed up with national stereotypes or views about the existence of a national character or mind – should not, however, mask the great achievements of nationalism, not least the creation of many monuments of high culture in many societies (see Chapter 2). It is also the case that national identities will not disappear off the face of the earth if they are made the target of an academic boycott. It is therefore not feasible or desirable to replace the scholarly scrutiny of national identity by burying our academic heads in the sand. It is in this spirit that the present study is conducted and offered. And, in offering it, I am aware that any national identity is far more complex than the inevitably reductive descriptions one finds in the literature.

3. THEORETICAL AND EMPIRICAL SCOPE

The scope of the present study is restricted in two ways. First, it deals mainly with standard Arabic, the language of writing and formal oral expression. Reference to colloquial Arabic, the language of everyday speech, is made whenever this is invoked by the nationalist ideology under consideration. This is, for example, the case in some articulations of Egyptian and Lebanese nationalism. Reference to colloquial Arabic takes several forms. Some supporters of standard Arabic tend to dismiss the colloquial as a corrupt and base form of the language which is unworthy of marking the Arab national identity. The argument goes that a people with a proud heritage and high aspirations for the future cannot possibly accept such a variety as an ingredient of their national identity. Standard Arabic only can serve in this capacity. This is typically the case in Arab nationalism. However, some Arab nationalists believe that colloquial

Arabic can serve as a source of neologisms and other terminologies which the standard language lacks. They therefore argue that colloquial Arabic should be exploited for this purpose. Territorial nationalists divide between those who support the colloquial and those who favour the standard form of the language, although the upper hand in the debate between them tends to be for the latter. Witness the fact that standard Arabic continues to be the official language in all Arab countries, in spite of the efforts of the colloquialists to promote their favoured varieties. Being aware that the gap between the two forms of the language is a source of pedagogic concern in Arabic-speaking countries, supporters of the standard call for reforms to simplify the way Arabic grammar is taught in schools. They also call for using standard Arabic in teaching at all levels of the school curriculum and in higher education as well. The fact that these suggestions have been mostly ignored – and that those who support the standard rarely use it in everyday speech – does not undermine the symbolic status of the language for most Arabic-speakers.

The dominance of the standard in nationalist discourse is understandable. In spite of its overtures to folk culture, nationalism tends to favour high culture. Some would actually say that the sociopolitical status of high culture in modern societies is part and parcel of the growth of nationalism. If, as Benedict Anderson claims in *Imagined Communities* (1991), the growth of nationalism is intimately interwoven with the workings of print capitalism, it follows that, as the medium of writing, standard Arabic has a head start over the colloquial (see Holt 1996).

But this is not the only reason for the dominance of standard Arabic in the nationalist discourse in the Arab Middle East. Although nationalism is associated with modernity and modernization, it always seeks to establish its credentials as an ideology and movement by locking into a past heritage, a "golden age", of which it can be very proud. Relying on standard Arabic, nationalism in the Arab Middle East can define for itself a usable past, a source of tradition and authenticity which can enable it to stand its ground in relation to other nationalisms inside and outside its immediate geographical context. Being stigmatized in the Arabic intellectual tradition, and having very few literary or other texts to its name, colloquial Arabic cannot provide the nationalists with a usable past which they can interpret and manipulate to their advantage. No wonder, therefore, that the cause of the colloquial was espoused only by a few modernizers in territorial nationalism who wished to separate their own concept of nationalism from the Arab past. But, since it is not possible to achieve this separation without causing a rupture with Islam, the basis of the religious identity of the majority of Arabic-speakers, any attempt to replace the standard by the colloquial as the marker of a particular territorial nationalism is inevitably met with religious opposition.

In geographical terms, the scope of the present study is restricted to the Middle East, effectively the Levant and Egypt. The fact that most ideological articulations of nationalism in the Arabic-speaking world originated in this area explains this restriction. Arab nationalism developed in the Levant first while under Ottoman rule, and only later found its way to other parts of the Arabic-speaking world. Egyptian and Lebanese nationalisms are the result of their own special environment. This is not the place to delve into the conditions which instigated these nationalisms. The following statement by Gershoni and Jankowski (1986: 81) sums up very well the kind of areas where such an instigation may be sited:

> Profound structural crises, severe political and social upheavals, fundamental social changes, the resultant loss of stability and self-confidence, a collective sense of the collapse of an old order and the impending advent of a new era – these are the elements that characterise those transitional periods of history during which human beings, particularly intellectuals, feel impelled to try to establish a new collective image for their society.

These conditions obtained in North Africa in the first half of the twentieth century, at the time when both the Arab Middle East and North Africa were engaged in a struggle against the ruling colonial powers, mainly Britain and France. The language issue was involved in both struggles, but more so in North Africa owing to the colonial policy of promoting French over Arabic in education and the institutions of the state. Here, the fight *for* Arabic was endowed with the symbolism of noble resistance. It was also considered an integral part of mass political action against the colonial power. The immediate aim of this fight was trying to eliminate the Otherness of Arabic, the indigenous language, against the hegemony of French, the colonial tongue. But, rather than disappearing after independence, the Otherness of Arabic continued in a somewhat muted way under the banner of *taʿrīb* (Arabization/Arabicization), with some of the promoters of French in this period being the very elite who, before independence, had fought against its hegemony. The situation in the Middle East was different. Although it came under attack from Turkish, French and to a lesser extent English, standard Arabic never lost its commanding position among those to whom it was a common language.

The challenge for Arabic in North Africa was further complicated by the existence of another indigenous language, Berber. The Berber-speaking populations in Algeria and Morocco supported Arabic against French during the nationalist struggle for independence in the first half of the twentieth century. But the situation changed after independence. Berber-speakers started to assert their own identity through an increased emphasis on their language, thus curtailing the resort to Arabic as a marker of an interethnic national identity in these countries (see Tilmatin and Suleiman 1996). The fact that no other significant indigenous language existed in the Arab Middle East to challenge the commanding position of Arabic – with the exception of Kurdish in Iraq (see Blau and Suleiman 1996) – meant that the emphasis placed on the language in the construction of national identity could proceed in Egypt and the Levant unfettered by interethnic rivalries in this area.

Another factor characterizes the difference between the Middle East and North Africa. In the Arab Middle East, the emphasis on Arabic in the construction of national identity allows the nationalists to create a distinction between their brand of nationalism and Islamic nationalism. This was particularly the case in Arab nationalism, which sought to allocate faith to the domain of private religiosity. It is also true of Egyptian nationalism and some articulations of Lebanese nationalism. This appeal to language in the Arab Middle East is intended to enable the non-Muslims, namely the Christians, to participate in the life of the nation as full members rather than as the members of a marginalized religious community. In North Africa, particularly Algeria and Morocco, the situation is different. Language divides, but religion unites (see al-Jabiri 1995) – I am of course not including the small Jewish community in Morocco in this characterization. It is therefore strategically more prudent to emphasize the ties of faith in articulations of national identity in North Africa, although Tunisia may be different in this domain. This appeal to religion is signalled most strongly in Morocco, where the monarch carries the title of *amir al-mu'minin* (Commander of the Faithful).

The above differences between the Middle East and North Africa constitute part of the rationale for concentrating on the Arab Middle East alone in the present work. The fact that this part of the Arabic-speaking world was also the cradle of the most dominant and best-articulated pronouncements of national identity in the modern world constitutes another reason, as the present study will bear out.

4. ORGANIZATION OF THIS BOOK

Building on the above discussion of national identity, the aims and the theoretical and empirical scope of the present study, this book is divided into five substantive chapters and a conclusion. Chapter 2 provides an elaboration of some of the points raised here in Chapter 1, the introduction. It delves into some aspects of nationalism for the purpose of delimiting the scope of the study further, and to isolate a set of concepts which will be utilized in the ensuing chapters. The first part of the chapter is aimed at students of language, particularly Arabic, who may not be familiar with the discourse on nationalism in the social sciences. The second part of the chapter explains for the benefit of non-linguists the difference between the functional and symbolic dimensions of language and how these may be exploited in articulating a particular nationalism.

Chapter 3 deals with aspects of the past which satisfy the condition of resonance in dealing with the issue of Arabic and national identity in the modern world. Statements in praise of Arabic as a unique language in the doctrinal sense, and as a language with unsurpassed qualities in comparison with other languages, are highlighted. The chapter shows how these statements formed the foundations of a view of the Arabs which declares them as the wisest of all nations. This attitude was a factor in inducing an anti-Arab feeling, with linguistic overtones, among the non-Arab Muslims in medieval times. This in turn motivated a defence of the Arabs in which the language as a marker of group identity played an important part.

Chapter 4 moves the discussion to the modern period. It looks at the development of the Arab national identity and how this relates to language within the Ottoman Empire. In historical terms, the focus is mainly on the second half of the nineteenth century and the first two decades of the twentieth century. The discussion shows how the development of Arab nationalism responded to the development of Turkish nationalism, and how the emphasis on Arabic in the former was the counterpart of the emphasis on Turkish in the latter. "Playing the vis-à-vis" is, however, not the only mode of defining the Arab national identity during this period. This is shown through an examination of the work of Ibrahim al-Yaziji, whose interest in Arabic and its nationalist connotations derives from the set of values the language can autonomously sustain.

Chapter 5 deals with two major statements of Arab nationalism in its cultural mode. These are provided by Satiʿ al-Husri and Zaki al-Arsuzi. In these and other statements of Arab nationalism, language is constantly invoked as a paradigmatic, if not the most paradigmatic, factor in defining Arab national identity. In spite of this common feature, the emphases of the above statements are different. Thus, while al-Husri tends to invoke history as the second basis of his nationalist ideology, al-Arsuzi invokes a kind of linguistic philosophy which sees in the lexico-semantic resources of the language a vindication of the uniqueness of the Arabs and the innateness of their genius.

Chapter 6 is devoted to a discussion of territorial nationalism in the Arab Middle East and how this relates to the language issue as a factor in the conceptualization of national identity. In particular, emphasis is placed on Antun Saʿada's Syrian Nationalism, Egyptian nationalism and Lebanese nationalism. Language figures in all of these nationalist ideologies, but in different ways. In some cases, it is only one marker among other equally important markers. In other cases, the language is subjugated to more important markers, for example the environment. In yet other cases, the language is denied any definitional function whatsoever.

Chapter 7, the Conclusion to this study, provides a general statement of the main themes raised in earlier chapters. It also points to other dimensions of the interplay between language and national identity in the Arabic-speaking world which would benefit from further studies of the kind presented in this book.

Being about language *and* national identity, rather than how national identity is marked or enacted *in* language, the present work will not investigate the truth claims of the assumptions about Arabic or other languages made by nationalist or prenationalist thinkers. Arabic does not constitute the data for this book, but pronouncements about Arabic as a marker of national identity do. Views to the effect that Arabic is more beautiful, logical, concise or difficult to learn than other languages will not be challenged by demanding supporting evidence or by producing evidence to the contrary. These and similar views will be accepted at face value. The same will also apply even when a statement about Arabic is factually suspect. Linguists may find this methodological stance irritating, but it is one that is consistent with the kind of research to which this study belongs, an example being Joshua Fishman's magisterial monograph *Language and Nationalism* (1972).

In providing a reading of a large number of pronouncements on language and nationalism in the Arab Middle East, I often had to deal with texts that are extremely opaque or hopelessly amorphous. Most of these texts have hitherto not been subjected to analysis of the kind presented here. Deciphering the meanings of these texts has been one of the major research objectives of this work. Generating a coherently organized body of data which can be subjected to further scrutiny and analysis by interested scholars is another objective of this research. Thus, what the reader may perceive as clear and coherent sets of ideas in the following pages are often the result of a great deal of textual spadework at the levels of analysis, synthesis and systematization. The discussions of al-Arsuzi (Chapter 5, section 4) and al-Hajj (Chapter 6, section 5.2) provide examples of where analysis and synthesis proved particularly challenging.

The present work does not seek to defend a particular nationalist ideology against its rivals. In this respect, a neutral stance is adopted. It was, however, judged to be important to convey to the reader the *affective* force involved in the enunciation of the various nationalist ideologies dealt with in this work. This decision reflects the fact that task-orientation and motivation is a major feature of all nationalisms. At times, some of the ideas expressed may be judged to be based on prejudice or bias; but this should not be taken as an expression of the views of the present writer. Students of nationalism often have to deal with prejudice and bias in their data. However, those who are coming to this work from a different angle may be disconcerted by my reluctance to rebut or denounce what are seen to be prejudiced views. Little can be done about this beyond what has just been said.

I have assumed in this work that the reader is familiar with the basic facts of the Arabic language situation. It may, however, be useful to reiterate some of these here for the benefit of readers whose expertise lies outside Arabic and Middle Eastern studies. Arabic is the common language of well over 300,000,000 speakers in the world. Most of these speakers live in the Arabic-speaking countries of the Middle East and North Africa. The status of Arabic as a world language is connected with its being the language of the Qur'an and the Islamic sciences which support its interpretation as a text and source of legal pronouncements for Muslims. Broadly speaking, the Arabic language situation is characterized by diglossia: the existence of a formal or "high" variety, and the vast array of dialects which constitute the informal or less formal or "low" variety. The bulk of this work is directed at the "high" variety, to which I have referred as standard Arabic to distinguish it from the colloquial or "low" variety whenever the contrast between the two is invoked. In contexts where this is not the case, the term "Arabic" is used without any qualification to designate the standard or "high" variety. At times, the term "Arabic" is used to refer to the totality of the Arabic varieties, without distinguishing between standard and colloquial. The context will make this clear.

Finally, a few features of the present work are in need of explanation. First, the endnotes in some chapters are intended to provide background material for the different constituencies of readers at whom this book is aimed. Second, in certain places I have included Arabic material in the body of the book or in endnotes. I have done this for three reasons: (1) to help the reader establish the full meaning of terms with approximate translations in English, (2) to support what may be regarded as improbable assertions when rendered in English, and (3) to convey to the reader the flavour of some of the texts under analysis. Third, I have used full transliteration in the Bibliography, but declined to do so in rendering names in the text for reasons of accessibility to those readers who are not specialists in Arabic. Technical terms, however, are rendered with full transliteration as also are titles and quotations in Arabic. Finally, the dates in parentheses next to the names of people mentioned in the text indicate the year of death of the person concerned. The Muslim year precedes the Common Era date.

2

Setting the Scene

I. DEFINITION: THE ACHILLES HEEL

The concepts of "nation", "nationalism" and "nationality" – as well as their composite correlatives "national character, national consciousness, national will and national self-determination" (Snyder 1954: 7) – have been the subject of debate by political scientists, sociologists, anthropologists, historians, lawyers, educators and social psychologists. Scholars from these backgrounds approach these notions from different perspectives dictated by varying methodological viewpoints and discipline-orientated theoretical considerations as to the kinds of data which constitute their particular scope. It is therefore not surprising that definition is the Achilles heel of nationalism studies, as emphasized by Anderson (1991), Hobsbawm (1983), Smith (1991) and Snyder (1954), to mention but a few of the leading scholars on the subject. The only epistemological consolation here is that this situation is typical of other branches of the humanities and social sciences where equally complex, varied and, thus, malleable phenomena constitute the topic of investigation. I will therefore eschew the problem of definition in this chapter by providing a framework of analysis to guide the reader in discerning the meanings of terms rather than to define these in an essentialist manner.

I am of course aware that such an approach may be seen as a flight from rigour. My reply is a simple one: the pursuit of definitional rigour as an ultimate criterion in nationalism studies would lead to the dissipation of intellectual energy and, more seriously, to the collapse of meaning, imperfect though this is, for little or no gain at all.[1] Declining to discuss the role of Arabic in the formation of national identity because of the absence of watertight definitions of the concept of nation and its derivatives would be tantamount to denying the historical and political meanings of a host of culturally seminal discussions of the topic in modern Arab(ic) discourse. The aim of this study is indeed to establish the meanings of these discussions, while acknowledging that the basic concepts in terms of which these meanings will be explicated are not clearly defined. As Edwards (1988: 1) points out, "Questions of language and identity are extremely complex. The essence of the terms themselves is open to discussion and, consequently, consideration of their relationship is fraught with difficulties."

Before launching this explication, it may be useful to outline some of the factors which render nationalism such a difficult concept to define in a rigorous manner. One factor is the difficulty of defining the term "nation" itself, owing to (1) the novelty or modernity of nations as sociopolitical constructs in historical terms, which, nevertheless, seems to contradict the "subjective antiquity" of the nation "in the eye of nationalists" (Anderson 1991: 5); (2) the different types of nation that have come into existence during the past two centuries; (3) the specific social and political environments associated with the emergence of different nations which have given rise to historically contingent factors in nation-formation, such that factors relevant in one period in history may not be so relevant in another, even when these factors appear to be similar or labelled by the same terminology; and (4) the inevitable variety of approaches that have been developed to study this phenomenon which, according to Liah Greenfeld (1992: 7), is "the source of the conceptually evasive, protean nature of nationalism and the cause of the perennial frustration of its students".

In this connection, Hobsbawm (1990: 6) is right when he points out that the attempt to fit nations as "historically novel, emerging, changing, and ... far from universal entities into a framework of permanence and universality" (i.e. that of objective nationalism) has led to essentialist criteria for defining the nation that are "fuzzy, shifting ... ambiguous, and as useless for the purposes of the traveller's orientation as cloud-shapes are compared to landmarks". In addition to the inevitable changes in the meaning of nationalism in the course of history, this term has been subjected to what Snyder (1954: 9) aptly describes as a "process of naturalization and nationalization" across linguistic and political boundaries. This has led to its extension to sociocultural terrains that are sometimes vastly different from each other, or from the one that has acted as their initial referential anchor.[2] This feature of nationalism has led Smith (1991: 79) to describe it as "chameleon-like" and as being able to lend itself to "endless manipulation", depending on the specific nature of the context in which it is applied. The combination of these factors makes the process of linguistic and cultural translation, and, therefore, conceptual generalization in the study of nationalism a very precarious one indeed. Furthermore, these factors highlight the vagueness of the various understandings of the nation and its technical derivatives in the literature. Anderson (1991: 5) characterizes this situation in terms of what he calls the paradox of the "formal universality of nationality as a socio-cultural concept [versus] the irremediable particularity of its concrete manifestations".

Definitions of nationalism are also complicated by the complexity of the relationship between nationality and ethnicity[3] on the one hand, and the nation and the state on the other. Thus, it is not always easy to tell when ethnicity ends and nationality begins, or whether or not the existence of the sovereign state is a necessary criterion for the existence of the nation as a recognizable or even legal entity (see Chapter 1). To this may be added the important theoretical difference between nationalism as an ideological construct, or an elite-generated set of organizing doctrines, and the same term in its capacity as a designation for the emergence of national consciousness as a movement or mass phenomenon. This distinction between ideology and movement is particularly important since, as Hobsbawm (1990: 11) points out, "official ideologies of states and movements are not guides to what is in the minds of even the most loyal citizens", a view shared by Breuilly (1993: 63), who states that "nationalist ideology is neither an expression of national identity ... nor the arbitrary invention of nationalists for political purposes". The fact that nation-formation is a process which takes place over a long period of time rather than being an event with a defined beginning and end adds to the intractability of defining the nation.

It is therefore invariably difficult to specify the "point in the process at which a sufficient portion of a people has internalised the national identity in order to cause nationalism to become an effective force for mobilising the masses" (Connor 1990: 100). These difficulties amply justify Gellner's (1983: 2) cautionary note that definitions of "nationalism, nation, nationality and state must be applied with common sense". The force of this cautionary note is particularly pertinent in the Arab context, where the existence of pan-Arab nationalism as a supra-form of national self-definition among Arabic-speaking peoples adds to the weight of the terminological discrimination which scholars of nationalism have to apply. The need for this discrimination is highlighted in the following statement on the subject (Sharara 1962: 227):

> There are four words which people confuse whenever they talk of nationalities. These are: nation (*umma*), fatherland (*watan*), people (*sha'b*), and state (*dawla*). They frequently use the word "state" when they mean "nation", and talk of "fatherland" to signify "people" or else speak of "people" when they intend the "nation", without distinction between the meaning of these vocables, or precise realization of what they denote, or a firm grounding in the differences between the respective concepts.

But if nation and its terminological derivatives are not amenable to precise definition, will the notion of "identity", which occurs as a qualified substantive in the title of this book, fare any better? The answer to this is a definite "No!" (Chapter 1, section 2). To begin with, social identities, of which national identity is only one, are varied and complex. They additionally include "familial, territorial, class, religious, ethnic and gender" identities (Smith 1991: 4), which are as difficult to define as national identity is. In addition to the fact that these identities are not fixed in time or social space, they often overlap with each other in ways which defy systematization. Thus, regional identities may overlap with class-based ones which, together or separately, may override gendered self-definition or vice versa. In some cases, religious and ethnic identities are closely allied to each other, although these identities may not coincide with single territorial associations. The Druze in the Middle East who are territorially spread over three states – Israel, Lebanon and Syria – exemplify this point. The prominence of identities as modes of self-identification may also vary from situation to situation, depending on the saliency of those features of the situation which the individual judges to be relevant. This makes identities negotiable, to use a common term in the literature. In addition, it is important not to think of identity in terms of sameness, or as an essentialist and, therefore, reductive concept which projects national self-definition as a grid of boxed associations. But it is also important not to let the methodological commitment to "context[s] of opposition and relativities" (Tonkin et al. 1989: 17) deny the efficacy of characterizing aspects of identity in ways which invoke objective properties relevant to it. Appropriating Gellner's (1983: 2) cautionary note above, we may say that definitions of identity, especially national identity, "must be applied with common sense". A good example of this attitude in the context of Arab identity is provided by Hudson, who, having identified Arabism and Islam as the two main components of this identity, proceeds to qualify his conclusions as follows (1977: 54):

> There is, in short, such variety of expression of Arabism and Islam, and such tolerance of diversity and multiple identifications within each ... that few generalizations about the behavioural consequences of these identities are valid. Nor is it right to conclude that the existence of such pluralism negates the communal solidarity implicit in the ethnolinguistic and religious bonds which the Arabs share. The valid conclusion is simply that Arabs feel strongly that such feelings do not preclude a variety of other identifications, practices, and ideologies, nor are they precluded by them.

Yet, in spite of these definitional difficulties, nationalism or national identity is an important force in modern-day society, as it has been over the past two centuries. To understand the saliency of national identity and its function in the modern world, Smith (1991: 163) provides the following explanation which, being of a general nature, will be assumed as one of the background premises of this study:

> Transcending oblivion through posterity, the restoration of collective dignity through an appeal to a golden age; the realisation of fraternity through symbols, rites and ceremonies, which bind the living to the dead and fallen of the community: these are the underlying functions of national identity and nationalism in the modern world, and the basic reasons why the latter have proved so durable, protean and resilient through all vicissitudes.

2. TWO MODES OF DEFINING THE NATION

In spite of the above difficulties in specifying the technical meaning of nation, nationality and nationalism, two principal modes of defining the nation exist in the literature. The first mode is generally referred to as the *objective* definition of the nation. The second mode is designated as the *subjective* definition. Although the choice of the terms "objective" and "subjective" is an unfortunate one, owing to their being technically loaded, the following discussion will set out the sense in which these two types of definition are deployed in the literature. Other modes of defining the nation exist, including the boundary and the ethno-symbolic approaches which will be dealt with below.

Objective definitions of the nation revolve around the specification of a set of criteria in terms of which individual nations can be characterized.[4] These criteria usually include territory, state, language, common culture and history. Religion is sometimes added to these criteria, usually as a corollary, although the situation may vary from case to case. In its strong form, the objective definition of the nation stipulates that if, and only if, the full set of designated criteria apply to a given group of people, the group concerned can be treated as a nation proper. This may be exemplified by Joseph Stalin's (1994: 20) definition of the nation as a "*historically constituted, stable community of people, formed of a common language, territory, economic life, and psychological make-up manifested in a common culture*" (original emphasis). Stalin (ibid.: 21) categorically states that it is "*only when all these characteristics are present together that we have a nation*" (original emphasis); hence the assignation of this definition to the strong variety type. The weak form of the objective definition obtains when no stipulation is offered to the effect that the full set of designated criteria must apply to a group before the group in question is established as a nation. This means that the set of designated criteria may apply in its entirety or only in part to a particular group; and yet, in the latter case, this is considered to be sufficient to confer on the group concerned the status of nation. In most situations of this type, an element of national consciousness as a constitutive ingredient in the formation of national identity is an absolute requirement. An example of this type of objective definition, in which national consciousness is explicitly invoked, is offered by Krejcí and Velímsky (1981: 44–5):

> There are ... five objective factors which can contribute to the identification of a group as a nation: territory, state (or similar political status), language, culture and history. When positive answers to all of these criteria coincide there can be little doubt that the respective community or population is a nation; then usually the sixth, subjective criterion, national consciousness, is also present. But there are situations where some, or even most of the objective criteria are missing and yet the community feels itself to be a nation ... The subjective factor of consciousness is the ultimate factor which eventually decides the issue of national identity.

Objective definitions of the nation fail to recognize the complexity of group identity as an act of shifting and overlapping self-ascription, depending on the contextually determined factors of setting and interlocutor(s). In this connection, Hobsbawm (1990: 8) gives the example of a person living in Slough (near Heathrow airport in England) who, "depending on circumstances", may think of him- or herself as "a British citizen, or (faced with other citizens of a different colour) as an Indian, or (faced with other Indians) as a Gujarati, or (faced with Hindus and Muslims) as a Jain, or as a member of a particular caste, or kinship connection, or as one who, at home, speaks Hindi rather than Gujarati, or doubtless in other ways". Continuing with the same line of argument, Hobsbawm (ibid.) points out how people can "identify themselves as Jews even though they share neither religion, language, culture, tradition, historical background, blood-group patterns nor an attitude to the Jewish state". This seems to have been the position adopted by Sigmund Freud, who, as Connor (1994: 203) tells us, "made clear that his [Freud's] own sense of Jewishness had nothing to do with either religion or national pride ... [but was bonded to] ... many obscure and emotional forces, *which were the more powerful the less they could be expressed in words*" (original emphasis). A similar view is held by Ibrahim (1981/2), who states that some people identify themselves as Muslims in spite of the fact that they deviate from the fundamental teachings of Islam. Liah Greenfeld generalizes this criticism by saying that there are "important exceptions to every relationship in terms of which nationalism has ever been interpreted – whether with common territory or common language, statehood or shared traditions, history or race" (1992: 7).

The appeal to national consciousness as a deciding factor in the formation of nations is equally problematic. On the one hand, it reduces national identification as an act of self-ascription to the option of belonging to a single nation or nationality, when, as was observed earlier, identity is both compositionally complex and historically variable. On the other hand, by presupposing the nation, national consciousness emerges as an after-the-event type of criterion, rather than one with real predictive power. Likewise, the objective definition of the nation diverts attention from the nation itself as a problematic construct; in the words of Reynolds (1984: 252), "since the nation exists, belief in it is seen not as a political theory but as a mere recognition of fact". I am also inclined to agree with Karl Deutsch (1966: 97), who emphasizes the role of communicative efficiency – within a context of complementary social communication – over the mere fact of the existence of objective criteria as an important factor in nation formation:

> The usual descriptions of a people in terms of a community of languages, or characters, or memories, or past histories, are open to exception. For what counts is not the presence or absence of any single factor, but merely the presence of sufficient communication facilities with enough complementarity to produce the overall result.

The subjective mode of defining the nation – sometimes referred to as the voluntaristic approach, to contrast it with the involuntaristic nature of objective definitions – emphasizes the role played by *will* in nation-formation. To use Renan's much-celebrated formula, the nation under this approach is "an everyday plebiscite". For example, in recent discussions of the status of Scotland as a nation in its own right within the United Kingdom, the writer Andrew Marr (quoted in *Scotland on Sunday*, 29 November 1998, p. 8) states that "fundamentally, Scotland is a nation because it believes itself to be one", thus adding to the concept of "will" the element of "belief" in a group's nationhood as a supporting factor. Gellner (1983: 53) criticizes the subjective definition because of its elasticity: "If we define nations as groups which *will* themselves to persist as communities, the definition-net we have cast into the sea will bring forth too rich a catch". The subjective definition may also be criticized because the existence of will among members of a group cannot be unequivocally established before the emergence of the nation itself, whether in political or even cultural terms (see Chapter 5, section 3 for a similar view by al-Husri). *Will* therefore emerges as an *a posteriori* rationalization in the study of nationalism rather than as one of its predictive concepts. In addition, subjective definitions are in principle based on the theoretical downgrading of the role played by objective factors in nation-formation, in spite of the fact that this role can be shown to be empirically relevant in some cases.

These difficulties have led some scholars to conclude that "no scientific definition of the nation can be devised" (Edwards 1988: 14), whether in subjective or objective terms. In response to this theoretical dilemma, some scholars, for example Barth (1969) and Armstrong (1982), have shifted the emphasis from criteria that characterize the constitution of the group internally to the role of boundaries and boundary-maintenance in keeping groups apart in the ethnic and national spheres – what has been referred to as "playing the vis-à-vis" in Chapter 1 (section 2). In general terms, these scholars have tended to focus on exclusion rather than inclusion in group-definition, by highlighting boundary-enhancing factors and mechanisms. The adoption of this position is said to allow the student of nationalism to account for vertical change in the constitution of a particular national identity through time, as well as for horizontal variations in that identity across geographical space, so long as the boundary between a particular group and other groups remains substantially uninfringed. Furthermore, the fact that boundaries are socially constructed under this approach enables the student of nationalism to give prominence to the nation as a cultural unit, without having to link it to a politically sovereign territory or state. Finally, the boundary approach has the virtue of widening the scope of factors – sometimes called border guards – which can be deployed in group-definition, including symbolic ones of which language is a prime ingredient. As Hutchinson and Smith (1996: 10) point out, "myths and symbols play a vital role in unifying populations and ensuring their continuity over many generations". In fact, "symbols, customs and ceremonies" are so important that Smith (1991: 77) treats them as "the most potent and durable aspects of nationalism". He (ibid.) further explains their role in articulating nationalist ideology as one of embodying the "basic concepts [of nationalism], making them visible and distinct for every member, [and] communicating the tenets of an abstract ideology in palpable, concrete terms that evoke instant emotional responses from all strata of the community".

Interest in the role of symbols and myths in nation-formation and group boundary-maintenance is one of the main contributions of the ethno-symbolic approach to the study of national identity. A basic tenet of this approach is the interdependence of groups and boundaries, and the importance of boundary mechanisms as "cultural markers of difference" which, "like all things at boundaries, ... must be visible to members of the group and to non-members" (Nash 1989: 10) to be effective barriers of inclusion and exclusion. Symbols as boundary pointers may include dress, language, architecture, food, music, ritual calendars, *rites de passage*, taboos, ceremonials, holidays, national anthems, flags, cenotaphs and tombs of unknown soldiers, among many others. In addition to their function as badges of difference and as devices which permit the "purposeful confusion of meaning" (Horowitz 1985: 218), socially constructed symbols of this type play an important role in maintaining the internal cohesion of the group and in guarding its identity. The fact that most of these symbols are ambiguous or even fictive (in the sense of being socially constructed or fabricated), at least at the level of selection and canonization, is not the issue here, since it is precisely this ambiguous and fictive nature of the symbols which makes them versatile and effective for deployment in nationalist ideology (cf. Balibar and Wallerstein 1991).

3. TWO TYPES OF NATION, TWO TYPES OF NATIONALISM

Broadly speaking, two types of nation are recognized in the literature: the civic or political nation and the cultural or ethnic nation. The former type is often associated with Western nations, paradigm examples of which are France and the Netherlands. The latter type is associated with nations in Eastern Europe and Asia, although the German nation is the best-known example of this model in the literature. The difference between the political (or "old nation") and the cultural nation (or "newer nation") is said by Seton-Watson (1981: 4) to reside in the fact that while, in the former, "the state came first, then national consciousness, and then the nation", for the latter national consciousness came first, "then the nation and the nationalist consciousness, and last the state". The fact that these two types of nation are analytically distinct does not preclude their occurrence as components of the same nationalism, although the way in which the civic and the ethnic are mixed will vary from case to case (see Chapter 4, sections 2 and 3).[5] This constant typological mixing and remixing is one of the reasons why the "nation proved an invention on which it was impossible to secure a patent" (Anderson 1991: 67).

Smith (1991: 9) characterizes the civic or political nation in terms of its possession of "compact [and] well-defined territories". These are often projected, in literary and other forms of communication and exhortation, as the repositories of collective (interpersonal as well as intergenerational) memories, the sites of heroic achievements and the arena of proud aspirations in a seamless progression of history which unites the past with the future through an active and nationally self-aware present (see Chapter 3, section 1). A civic or political nation is further characterized as a "community of laws and institutions with a single political will" (ibid.: 10) in which all members enjoy the same rights and obligations as equal citizens before the law. Finally, the effective application of this legal and political equality of members must depend on a "common civic culture and ideology" (ibid.: 11) which includes, among other things, shared symbols and myths and the existence of a system of education whose task is to enhance socialization and communication across class, regional, religious and gendered boundaries as well as encouraging political participation within what Deutsch (1966: 96) calls a community of "complementary habits and facilities of communication". The importance of print-languages and literacy as factors in the formation of the civic nation is organically connected to this system of mass education.

The ethnic or cultural nation starts from the premise of presumed common descent, which makes the nation a kind of super-fictive family to which all its members irrevocably belong (see Chapter 5, section 2 for references to common descent in the context of Arab nationalism). Under this concept of the nation, once an Arab or German, always an Arab or German, regardless of whether one lives in the native lands of the nation or in diaspora. This concept of the nation is further underpinned by a presumed common culture and a set of traditional values which provide the basis for group-mobilization in the political sphere. Mobilization of this kind is an elite-led activity in which lexicography, philology, archaeology, material culture, folklore, architecture and "political museumising" (Anderson 1991: 183),[6] among other things, encapsulate the data which may undergo a process of mythologization, symbolization and metaphorization in the name of the nation. And although the existence of the state as a politico-legal unit in the nation's homeland is the ideal form of national self-realization, cultural nationalists subscribe to the view that the state and the nation are *categorially* different (though not categorically distinct from each other). As Hutchinson (1987: 13) points out, "the cultural nationalist perceives the state as accidental, for the essence of the nation is its distinctive civilisation, which is the product of its unique history, culture and geographical profile". This view is shared by another student of nationalism, Carlton Hayes (1960: 5), who states that "cultural nationalism may exist with or without political nationalism" as a force for political unity and independence.

The distinction between political and cultural nationalism in the European context is generally exemplified by reference to the French and German conceptions of the nation. Thus, while the French understanding of the nation is said to be "state-centred and assimilationist", the German view of it is projected as "*Volk*-centred and differentialist" (Brubaker 1992: 1). While the French consider their nationhood as the "creation of their state", the Germans treat it as the "basis of their state" (ibid.: 184). In both forms of nationalism, the cultural and the political are important, although they move in different directions on their respective historical axes: from the cultural to the political in German nationalism and from the political to the cultural in French nationalism. In most Arab countries, the pull of cultural (pan-Arab) nationalism counterbalances in varying degrees the imperatives of the political nationalism of the sovereign state, and vice versa (see Chapter 6, sections 5.1 and 5.2). Or, as Tütsch (1965: 31) puts it, "Pan-Arab nationalism, local nationalism inside the partly artificial borders of the ... Arab states [state nationalism], and regional nationalism [for example, Syrian Socialist National Party ideology] grow side by side in competition to [*sic*] each other".

There are different interpretations of cultural nationalism in the literature. For Kohn (1945) and Gellner (1983), cultural nationalism is a reactive movement, or defensive response, on the part of the educated elites, against externally generated challenges to the existing order of the community and its traditional belief systems. Cultural nationalism is said by Kohn to arise in the non-Western world in conditions of "backward ... political and social development" (1945: 329), mirroring in this respect German nationalism which "substituted for the legal and rational concept of citizenship [in the Western, civic concept of the nation] the infinitely vaguer concept of 'folk'" (ibid.: 331). While accepting the above interpretation of cultural nationalism as a "*defensive* response ... to exogenous modernization", Hutchinson (1987: 32) treats it as a movement for "the moral regeneration of the historic community" within an overall framework of authentic, tradition-cognizant modernization (ibid.: 16). This explains the fact that advocates of cultural nationalism tend to be educators and scholars, people of letters and artists who form cultural societies and publish newspapers, journals and magazines to mobilize the community – publicly or illicitly through pamphlet propaganda – both culturally and politically (see Chapter 3, sections 2–4 for Turkish and Arab nationalism). To achieve this aim, cultural nationalists must perform the paradoxical task of reading modernity into tradition at the same time as treating tradition as an expression of modernity. They do this through a double move of particularizing the modern as a manifestation of the native spirit, and generalizing the traditional as an expression of the universal impulses of that spirit (see Chapter 6, section 4 and associated sub-sections for this tendency in Egyptian nationalism). This double move involves universalizing tradition and nativizing modernity in a way which enables the moral and sociopolitical regeneration of the nation to take place.

As do its interpretations, attitudes towards nationalism also vary. While most scholars are content to study nationalism as a multiplex phenomenon of history, politics, law, anthropology, sociology and psychology, some scholars approach it from the perspective of the effects it has on communities, whether these effects are intended or not. Elie Kedourie (1966) provides one of the most scathing attacks on nationalism from this perspective, although he does not consistently separate the movement from the ideology in his critique. Kedourie attacks nationalism as an ideology because it makes the nation as a historically, politically and sociologically "obscure and contrived" construct seem "simple and transparent" (ibid.: 9). Nationalism is also criticized for the belief it engenders in its followers that nations are unique blocks of humanity; for transforming language from an instrument of communication into a "political issue for which men are ready to kill and exterminate each other" (ibid.: 70); for making "extremely difficult the orderly functioning of a society of states" (ibid.); for mixing language with race (linguism) as emblems of a politically impregnated identity; for being the invention of "literary men who had never exercised power, and appreciated little the necessities and obligations incidental to intercourse between states" (ibid.: 70–1);[7] for operating in a "hazy region, midway between fable and reality" (ibid.: 71); for making "use of the past in order to subvert the present" (ibid.: 75); for looking "inwardly, away from and beyond the imperfect world" in a manner which "ultimately becomes a rejection of life" (ibid.: 87); for fomenting "civil strife between the generations" (ibid.: 101);[8] and for disrupting "whatever equilibrium had been reached between the different groups [in the community], [by] reopen[ing] settled questions and … renew[ing] strife" (ibid.: 115). Kedourie concludes his attack on nationalism by saying that "The attempt to refashion so much of the world on national lines has not led to greater peace and stability. On the contrary, it has created new conflicts, exacerbated tension, and brought catastrophe to numberless people innocent of all politics" (ibid.: 138).

Although Gellner (1983: 125) rejects Kedourie's attack on nationalism for being anti-historical, for believing that nationalism is a "contingent, avoidable aberration, accidentally spawned by European thinkers", rather than seeing it as a phenomenon that is "inherent in a certain set of social conditions [which], it so happens, are the conditions of our time", he nevertheless agrees with Kedourie that "nationalism has often not been so sweetly reasonable" (ibid.: 2) and that, in a "nationalist age, societies worship themselves brazenly and openly" (ibid.: 56) and, one may add, chauvinistically. Gellner, however, provides his own critique of nationalism as an ideology, rather than a movement or phenomenon, on the grounds that it "suffers from pervasive false consciousness" (ibid.: 124). First, "it claims to defend folk culture while in fact [seeking to forge] a high culture" (ibid.). Second, "it claims to protect an old folk society while in fact helping to build up an anonymous mass society" (ibid.). Third, it "preaches and defends continuity, but owes everything to a decisive and unutterably profound break in human history" (ibid.: 125). And, fourth, "it preaches and defends cultural diversity, when in fact it imposes homogeneity both inside and, to a lesser degree, between political units" (ibid.). This is why, Gellner tells us, the "self-image" of nationalist ideology and "its true nature are inversely related" (ibid.).

Anderson (1991: 141) considers attacks on nationalism of the kind launched by Kedourie's to be one-sided. He points out how the emphasis on "fear and hatred of the Other" as ugly projections of nationalism ignore the fact that "nations inspire love" which, when associated with self-sacrifice for the community, extends into various forms of literary expression, including poetry, prose, music, dance and the arts. Anderson is also indirectly critical of Gellner's inability to appreciate fully the role of myths and symbols in nation-formation, believing them to be deviations from the historical truth rather than motifs whose aim is to mould reality. By concentrating on "*what is* [rather than] *what people believe is*" (Connor 1978: 380, original emphasis), Gellner denies himself the opportunity of accessing discourse from a critical perspective to derive what may be called rhetorical meanings in which historical and sociological truth is not a prime consideration. Hobsbawm (1990: 12) recognizes this point when he states that "nationalism requires too much belief in what is potentially not so". Renan makes a similar point when he says: "getting its history wrong is part of being a nation" (quoted in Hobsbawm, ibid.). Finally, from the perspective of this work, Kedourie's attack on nationalism suffers from a deficient understanding of the function of language in society. He tends to emphasize its communicative role and to downgrade its symbolic yield, although the latter is central in a number of domains, including those of personal and group identity.

4. LANGUAGE AND NATIONAL IDENTITY

Whether objectively or subjectively defined, and whether or not one characterizes it in boundary or ethno-symbolic terms, the nation is often associated with language as a marker of its identity. Students of nationalism who emphasize the language–national identity link, in the German Romantic tradition advocated by Herder and Fichte, point to the fact that language is the most important instrument of socialization, of making humankind human. In particular, they point to the fact that language-acquisition takes place in a speech community, that language and thought are inseparable and that languages are different from each other, and that these facts stamp the individual and the community with an imprint that is uniquely their own. The primordiality of language as a "given" of national identity in some ideological constructions is rooted in origins that are untraceable in the depth of time: "No one can give the date for the birth of any language" (Anderson 1991: 144). The durability of living languages as markers of national identity derives from their imagined immutability, in spite of the fact that they are constantly changing in the lexical, grammatical and phonological spheres. In the Middle Ages, the rationale behind the belief in the primordiality of language was rooted in religious belief: the biblical idea of a common origin for humankind and of the existence of a pre-Babel common tongue were instrumental in giving currency to the belief that the "post-Babel differentiation of language [was] the first step in the formation of races and peoples" (Bartlett 1994: 198). This kind of emphasis on the role of language in defining group identity has led some scholars, notably Kedourie (1966: 71), to charge that "there is no definite clear-cut distinction between linguistic and racial nationalism", and that it was "no accident that racial classifications were, at the same time, linguistic ones" (ibid.: 72). The persistence of this charge shows the hold which ideas about language and nationality in the German Romantic tradition still have in the study of nationalism. This is despite the fact that a scholar as great as Max Müller rejected as unscientific all attempts to infer race, a genetic concept, from language, which is not inherited.

For scholars in the German Romantic tradition, language mirrors the soul of the nation and, as such, is the most effective way of apprehending the spirit of the community (see Chapter 5, section 2 for similar views by al-ʿAlayli and al-Bitar).[9] Interest in language as an attribute of identity within and outside this tradition was to a great extent responsible for the preoccupation with lexicography, philology and comparative and historical linguistics in Europe, particularly Germany, in the nineteenth century. Anderson (1991: 71) believes that work in these areas was "central to the shaping of nineteenth-century European nationalism". He is also of the view that bilingual dictionaries, by virtue of the visible equality they created between the vernaculars on the one hand, and between these and the languages of antiquity on the other, created an "egalitarianism among languages" (ibid.: 71), as well as the "conviction that languages were, so to speak, the personal property of quite specific groups … and … that these groups, imagined as communities, were entitled to their autonomous place in a fraternity of equals" (ibid.: 84).

Within this framework of close association between language and national identity, the defence of one's language emerges as a defence of the set of values it encapsulates and transmits from one generation to another. This is why Fichte calls for cleansing the German language from the impurities represented by borrowed words which would contaminate its inner fabric and, inevitably, infect the soul of the glorious German nation (see Chapter 4, section 2 for similar views in Turkish nationalism). Fichte argues that "to take abstract, lifeless Latin terms into German would have a deadening effect [on German, and] would lead Germans to ascribe some of the alien values associated with [these Latin terms] to their German 'equivalents'" (Breuilly 1993: 60). Hobsbawm (1990: 56) calls the interest in language-purification "philological nationalism" which, he claims, "obliged German scientists to translate 'oxygen' into 'Sauerstoff', and today is inspiring a desperate French rearguard action against the ravages of *franglais*". To explain the strength of this primordial association between language and nation, Hobsbawm refers to the two paradigmatic cases of Germany and Italy, which he describes in the following way (ibid.: 102–3):

> For Germans and Italians, their national language was not merely an administrative convenience or a means of unifying state-wide communication ... or even a revolutionary device for bringing the truths of liberty, science and progress at all ... It was more even than the vehicle of a distinguished literature and universal intellectual expression. It was the *only* thing that made them Germans and Italians, and consequently carried a far heavier charge of national identity than, say, English did for those who wrote or read that language.

Language interlocks with national identity in other subtle ways. As the primary means of socialization, language enables the individual, through the mere fact of early childhood acquisition and lifelong formal and informal education, to participate in the life and culture of the community across the horizontal axis of social space – by creating communities of intercommunicating individuals in present time – and the vertical axis of social and intergenerational time (cf. Hayes 1960). Language carries out this role in what Fishman (1980: 87) describes as a "peculiarly sensitive web of intimacy and mutuality". In particular, language acts as the medium for connecting the past to the present and the future, thus bestowing on the past by virtue of its durability or pastness a "weight of authority, legitimacy and rightness" (Nash 1989: 14) which, in turn, accrues to language itself through the power of close association and intellectual transmission. Language also plays a part with other communication facilities – including "learned habits, ... symbols, memories, patterns of land holding and social stratification, events in history, and personal association" in enabling nationality as a "complementarity of social communication" to come into being (Deutsch 1966: 97). Identification with a language and loyalty to it are aims of nationalism; it seeks to inculcate them in its members through literacy and education.

In delivering these functions, language is the medium which makes the nation as an "imagined community" imaginable. It connects the individual in social time and social space to fellow nationals whom he or she will never hear of, meet or know. Furthermore, language confers on the community the property of being "simultaneously open and closed" (ibid.: 146). It is open because "one's 'mother' tongue is not necessarily the language of one's 'real' mother" (Balibar 1991: 99), which leaves the door open for others to join the nation, particularly in its political interpretation, through the act of language-learning in adult life. As Hobsbawm (1990: 21) explains in the context of French civic nationalism, "in theory it was not the native use of the language that made a person French ... but the willingness to acquire this". A similar situation seems to have obtained for "the hispanophone founder of the Basque National Party (PNV) ... [who] had to learn [Basque] as an adult" (ibid.: 119). The same was the case for Sati' al-Husri, the greatest ideologist of pan-Arab nationalism in the twentieth century, who switched from Turkish to Arabic only as an adult (see Chapter 5, section 3). This seems to hold true for Ziya Gökalp, the most important ideologue of modern Turkish nationalism, who is said by some to be of Kurdish origin (see Chapter 4, section 2). Ibrahim (1981/2: 70–1) cites an example from Egypt during the 1967 war, when the police instituted tough "stop and search" measures in Cairo and other major Egyptian cities to prevent Israeli spying activities. Ibrahim tells the story of an Egyptian behaving suspiciously who had to rely on confirmation of his identity by members of his neighbourhood to escape arrest by the Egyptian police, in spite of the fact that he had a valid Egyptian identity card on him. In contrast, a Frenchman was able to escape arrest because he addressed the police in Arabic, broken though this was.

Paradoxical as it may seem, the nation as an imagined community is conceptualized as a closed construct partly by virtue of language itself. As Anderson (1991: 148) explains, acquisition *per se* is not the issue in examples of this kind; what matters is the fact that acquisition needs to take place in time: "What limits one's access to other languages is not their imperviousness but one's own mortality. *Hence a certain privacy to all languages*" (emphasis added).

The close connection between language and national identity is sometimes cast within a framework which emphasizes the non-uniqueness of the former in characterizing the latter. This non-uniqueness receives a variety of interpretations in the literature. It may be taken to mean that language and nation do not mutually imply one another. Max Weber (1948: 172–3) spells out this principle by emphasizing three facets of the language–national identity link: (1) "a 'nation' is not identical with a community speaking the same language"; (2) "a common language does not seem to be absolutely necessary to a 'nation'"; and (3) "some language groups do not think of themselves as a separate 'nation'". It also means that language is but one marker of national identity among a set of markers which may include such attributes as territory, common culture and descent, shared memories and so on. In multilingual societies, people may be competent in more than one language, to which they may be attached in competing or complementary ways. There are also situations, especially among illiterate persons in remote areas of the world, where people are not even aware of the proper name of their language. Brass (1991: 26) tells us that, in such areas, people "may very well go on speaking their language and cultivating their fields without becoming concerned that their language is being neglected and without developing any sense of solidarity". Brass (ibid.: 70) also reminds us that "many people, if not most people, never think about their language at all and never attach any emotional significance to it". Hobsbawm (1990: 57) expresses this point more memorably when he says that "where there are no other languages within earshot, one's own idiom is not so much a group criterion as something that all people have, like legs". This same point is reiterated by Edwards (1988: 47), who states that: "it is with group contact that linguistic identity issues become most pressing". We also know that people do change their languages voluntarily. Such a change is not as catastrophic for the individual as some national romantics would like us to believe. While accepting that language plays an important role in national identity formation, Karl Deutsch (1966) nevertheless believes that it does so most effectively when allied to other factors which together help create complementary channels of social communication. In some cases, complementary channels of communication may exist in spite of language, not because of it. Deutsch illustrates this by citing the example of a German-Swiss newspaper editor who stated in his autobiography that he had more in common with French-Swiss people than with Austrian Germans (presumably owing to the existence of extralinguistic complementary channels of communication in Switzerland): "The French-Swiss and I were using different words for the same concepts, but we understood each other. The man from Vienna and I were using the same words for different concepts, and thus we did not understand each other in the least" (ibid.: 97).

There are also examples from the history of nationalist movements which show that unity of language cannot prevent secession, as happened in relation to English and Spanish in North and Latin America respectively. In other cases, the injection of language as a criterion of national identity is a late addition in some nationalist movements. In Ireland, Irish became an issue in the nationalist movement only after the establishment of the Gaelic League in 1893. In Finland, language did not become an issue in the nationalist movement until around 1860. The linguistic element in the Catalan nationalist movement came to the fore only around the middle of the nineteenth century. Hobsbawm (ibid.: 62) tells us that "the influx of Francophone foreigners into the rural communes of Flanders [in the nineteenth century] was resented more for their refusal to attend mass on Sundays than on linguistic grounds". In some cases, religious conversion can be a decisive factor in shaping different identities for communities who share the same language, as happened with the Croats and the Serbs as a result of their allegiance to Roman Catholicism and Orthodoxy respectively.

The non-uniqueness of language does not, however, challenge the fact that language can serve as a most effective marker of identity, of boundary between groups. Language has been used in this capacity since ancient times. The Greeks used it to distinguish themselves from the "barbarians", those who could not speak Greek and therefore were unintelligible. In the conflict between Gilead and Ephraim (Judges 12:4–6), friend was told from foe by the correct articulation of the word *shibboleth*. The use of medical Arabic terms by Jewish doctors in Poland instead of Latin ones, used by Christian doctors, may have been deployed as a border guard, or marker of ethnic identity (Armstrong 1982). Similarly, the use of the Hebrew script by Jews to record aspects of their theology in Arabic in Spain and elsewhere in the Arab-controlled areas in North Africa and Asia may be viewed as an attempt at ethnic differentiation. However, it is only in the age of nationalism that language starts to assume the function of a marker of national identity.

To be fully effective, the role of language as a boundary marker or guard requires a distinction between two functions of language: the communicative or instrumental and the symbolic which, although interrelated in ordinary language use, are nevertheless analytically distinct (cf. Chapters 3 and 4); this is clear from the continued salience of the latter function even in the absence of the former. Edwards (1988: 18) stresses this distinction, pointing out that ignorance of it "can lead to lack of clarity and, indeed, misdirection of effort among linguistic nationalists". The role of language as a marker of group boundary is therefore associated more with its symbolic than its communicative function. Some students of nationalism believe that interest in the functional allocation of languages to particular communicative domains (what is called status-planning in sociolinguistics) and language reform (what is called corpus-planning in sociolinguistics) acquire greater significance in a speech community in proportion to the dominance of the symbolic over the communicative function in the community in question. Anderson (1991: 13) expresses this figuratively in a different context by the apparently paradoxical formula "the deader the language, the better" (see Chapter 4, section 4). The symbolic significance of language explains the demand by the majority group in a multilingual community to accord its language official primacy over other co-territorial languages (see Chapter 4, sections 2 and 3). In situations of this kind, language becomes a symbol of power and domination. It is this symbolic function of language which underlies the revival of Hebrew in Palestine at the beginning of the twentieth century, since at the time Hebrew was communicatively restricted to a small set of domains and was by no means the language either of the Jewish inhabitants of that country or of those Jews who came to live in it during that period. It is also the significance of this symbolic function which made the Irish national movement after 1900 launch its "doomed campaign to reconvert the Irish to a language most of them no longer understood, and which those who set about teaching it to their fellow countrymen had only themselves begun to learn very incompletely" (Hobsbawm 1990: 110). The importance of the symbolic function as a category in its own right is also evident in the attitudes of the children of emigrants to the language of their ancestry, which Gellner (1964: 163) regards as an expression of the Three Generations Law whereby the "grandson tries to remember what the son tried to forget". Edwards (1988: 48) exemplifies this by Italian-Americans who "may still feel themselves different from others in the larger society, even though Italian may be only a symbolic cultural entity". The importance of the symbolic function of language is further exemplified by the 1975 findings of the Committee on Irish Language Attitudes Research which revealed that "strong sentimental attachments to Irish were not accompanied by language *use*, nor by desire to actively promote it, nor yet by optimism concerning its future, among the population at large" (ibid.: 51). To deal with this function of language, Eastman and Reese (1981: 113–14) suggest the term "associated language" in the context of ethnicity, which they define as follows: "An associated language may comprise a set of shared lexical terms, involve the use or knowledge of just the name of the language which the group's ancestors may have spoken, or it may be a particular language used by all members of the group in all situations".

Finally, the symbolic function of language is not restricted to its verbal dimension alone; it also extends to its written manifestation. This is particularly true of Arabic, whose script plays an important role as a boundary marker, particularly vis-à-vis the Latin and Cyrillic scripts which have gained at its expense by the "defection" to these scripts of Turkish, Malay and a host of other languages in Central Asia and sub-Saharan Africa – including Somalia which, ironically, is a member of the Arab league. Yet, in spite of these defections, the Arabic script still functions like Chinese characters to create a community out of signs not sounds, not just with respect to the Islamic culture at whose centre the Qur'an stands, but also in the context of the civic and cultural conceptualizations of the nation in the Arabic-speaking countries.

5. CONCLUSION

The aim of the above discussion was to provide a general overview of some of the main issues in the study of nationalism, as a prelude to outlining a framework for setting up the major parameters which will guide the discussion of the role of Arabic in articulating national identity in this work. This I will do in the present section, albeit briefly.

To begin with, the term "nation" will be used in this study to cover both the civic-political or territorial nation within the boundary of the sovereign state, for example the Egyptian or Lebanese nation (see Chapter 6), and the cultural-ethnic nation as associated with pan-Arab nationalism, the foremost proponent of which in the Arab context is Sati' al-Husri (see Chapter 5, section 3). Antun Sa'ada's concept of the Syrian nation partakes of the political and the cultural currency of nationalist ideology (see Chapter 6, section 2), although, by insisting that the state is a factor in nation-formation, Syrian Nationalism leans more towards the political than the cultural conception of the nation.

The importance of observing the above distinction between the cultural and the territorial forms of nationalism is particularly significant here owing to the precariousness of the sociocultural translation that is inevitably involved in transferring an intellectual discourse, the discourse on national identity in the Arab Middle East, into a foreign language, English. The ill-formedness of the basic notions of nationalism in European and Arabic discourses on the subject adds a further element of indeterminacy in the present project. Using as an analogy Victor Hugo's notion of translation – in the technical sense – as an act of violence against the recipient nation and its language (Lefevere 1992), we may say that the transfer of the Arabic discourse on nationalism into English will inevitably involve conceptual and linguistic violence against both the source and target cultures and their languages. It is therefore important to minimize this violence as much as possible to avoid falling into the Procrustean trap of judging the Arabic concepts of nation (*umma* and *sha'b*) and nationalism (*qawmiyya* and, sometimes, *jinsiyya*) as though they were exact equivalents in all instances of their European, particularly English, counterparts (see Khalafalla 1981).

It is also important to avoid reading nationalist ideologies in the Arab Middle East as though they were echoes of their European counterparts. To illustrate this point, I will consider the emphasis on folk culture and the vernacular in the latter. In connection with folk culture, Gellner (1983: 57) mentions how nationalism "usually conquers in the name of a putative folk culture. Its symbolism is drawn from the healthy, pristine, vigorous life of the peasant, of the *Volk*." Unlike many other scholars, however, Gellner is careful to point out that this image of nationalism represents an inversion of reality, since nationalism in fact aims at forging a high culture instead of defending the folk culture it avows to promote. In the Arab nationalist context, whether one actually talks about political or cultural nationalism, the emphasis is mainly on high culture, not folk culture; this is organically linked to an attitude which favours the standard over the dialectal forms of the language as the vehicle for publicly sanctioned cultural expression in the diglossic language situation so paradigmatically characteristic of Arabic. This bias towards high culture is confirmed by the comparatively low status which oral, folk literature has within the Arab literary canon. It is also reflected in the less-than-flattering attitude towards the peasant (*fallāḥ*) in classical and modern Arabic literature. In his book *Modern Arabic Literature and the West* (1985: 27), Badawi points out how in the "classical Arabic tradition the villager, the tiller of the soil, was more often than not an object of contempt ... Agriculture, *al-filāḥa*, was definitely considered one of the lowest occupations, suitable only for the meanest of human beings." He adds that "it was the beauty of nature, and not the beauty of the life of the *fallāḥ* who lived in close proximity with nature, that was the object of the poet's praise. Likewise, it was the garden, not the gardener, which elicited a positive response from the numerous poets who composed countless poems about gardens in Islamic poetry" (ibid.: 28). Not even the intervention of the Romantic movement at the beginning of the twentieth century could alter this well-entrenched attitude, which derives its currency from a set of sociocultural beliefs of great antiquity and authority. With the weight of tradition fully and aggressively ranged against it, folk culture in the Arabic-speaking countries stands little chance of being considered a worthy fount for the propagation and maintenance of nationalist ideology, especially of the cultural type, although state nationalism seems more amenable to exploiting this culture to its advantage. The fact that rural varieties are stigmatized in Arabic-speaking countries, for example Jordan and Palestine (Suleiman 1993, 1999b), is another piece of evidence that supports the thesis under consideration here (cf. Chapter 3, section 3).

The role of the vernacular (for example, French, German and so on) as a formative force in the rise of European nationalisms is historically different from articulations of national identity in the Arab Middle East. First, whereas the rise of the vernaculars in Europe was connected to the religious upheavals of the sixteenth century and to the attendant translation of the Bible from Latin into these vernaculars, the emphasis on the standard in nationalist ideology among Arabic-speaking peoples was the result of a radically different set of sociopolitical circumstances. These included exogenous challenges of various kinds and intensities, the drive for modernization and the struggle for political independence in which the language was seen as a boundary marker between the in- and out-groups. The fact that the Qur'an, Islam's primary sacral text, was in Arabic acted as a centripetal force of internal cohesion on the linguistic front, unlike in Europe where the Latin Bible was the source of centrifugal vernacularization. Furthermore, whereas the Latin Bible, in spite of its antiquity and textual authority, was essentially a translation, the Qur'an is not. The fact that the Qur'an is seen as the word of God verbatim meant that it was considered untranslatable (cf. al-Bundaq 1980 and Shumali 1996). As Anderson (1991: 14) points out, there is no concession in this context "of a world separated from language that all languages are equidistant (and thus interchangeable) signs for it". This set of doctrinal principles meant that there were no calls for rendering the Qur'an into the dialects, which, had they materialized and been implemented, could have led to the emergence of an Arab(ic) vernacularizing trend in the European mould. To this we may add the fact that whereas the gap between classical and medieval Latin in the post-Renaissance period was widening as a result of the purifying interventions of the humanists, the gap between the standard and the spoken varieties in the Arabic-speaking countries was, if anything, slowly shrinking in the nationalist era (in the nineteenth and twentieth centuries) owing to the spread of literacy and the ongoing simplification of the language grammatically and stylistically. In other words, while the widening gap between the two forms of Latin in the post-Renaissance period created a space which the vernaculars could communicatively fill, the shrinking gap between the standard and the local varieties, at least at the level of reception, made this less of a possibility for Arabic.

Second, whereas print technology under Anderson's analysis (1991) was instrumental in turning the vernaculars into national languages on the European scene, the same cannot be said of Arabic in its sociopolitical milieu. Thus, while it is true that print technology brought to Arabic a much wider field of "exchange and communication" than it previously had, it is nevertheless not true that it "created" this field, as happened with the vernaculars in the European context (ibid.: 44). While the textualization of Arabic into visible marks preceded the introduction of print technology, textualization of the European vernaculars was in an important sense the outcome of this technology. Print technology gave these vernaculars their "new fixity", which in the fullness of time helped confer on them an "image of antiquity" (ibid.). The situation in Arabic was almost the reverse. Print technology did not confer on Arabic an "image of antiquity". On the contrary, it challenged this image by injecting a feeling of modernity into its written manifestations. However, by making Arabic available to a territorially extended readership, print technology did foster a feeling of a community in the present among those who had access to the fruits of its loom.

Definitions of the nation in the Arab Middle East follow a variety of approaches. In some cases, they subscribe to the *objective* mode of defining the nation. This is the case in al-Husri's brand of Arab nationalism, whereby language and history are treated as the two ingredients which define Arab national identity (see Chapter 5, section 3). As we shall see later (Chapter 5, section 2), al-ʿAlayli and al-Bitar follow a watered-down version of this approach, but they veer towards a *subjective* mode of defining the nation. This is clear from the hesitation these two scholars express as to whether all the criteria they list for defining Arab national identity are necessary in such a definition. In some cases, a boundary or contingent mode of defining the nation is invoked. This is particularly evident in defining the Arab national identity in the Ottoman Empire (see Chapter 4, section 3). In this context, Arab national identity is generally defined in relation to Turkish national identity, with Arabic and Turkish acting as the primary sources of national identification respectively. This mode of defining the nation is also invoked in some articulations of Egyptian nationalism where the significant Other is Arab nationalism (see Chapter 6). In this respect, Egyptian nationalism seems to build on an anti-Arab tradition designated as *shuʿūbiyya* in medieval Islamic society (see Chapter 3, section 5).

Finally, in discussing the role of Arabic in the formation of national identity in the Arab Middle East, reference will be made to both the symbolic and the functional roles of the language. In spite of their being categorially distinct, these two roles of the language normally occur together in nationalist discourse. In some cases, the symbolic role is given visibility over the functional. This was particularly the practice in pronouncements on Arab national identity during the Ottoman period. In other cases, the functional role is promoted over its symbolic counterpart. This is particularly characteristic of Arab nationalism as set out by al-Husri (see Chapter 5, section 3). In yet other cases, for example in al-Arsuzi, the functional is delivered through the symbolic powers of signification which the language possesses. These and other issues in the present and the preceding chapter will guide much of the following discussion.

3

The Past Lives On

I. INTRODUCTION

The presentness of the past is a defining feature of the discourse of all nationalisms, as is the presumed pastness of their present. In this discourse, the past and the present enact the drama of continuity and change as they characterize the emergence of the modern nation, its development, successes, trials and tribulations (cf. al-Husri, *Ārā' wa-aḥādīth fi al-waṭaniyya wa-l-qawmiyya*, 1984a: 37, 67–73). The past plays an authenticating and legitimizing role; it signals continuity, cohesion and, therefore, a feeling of intimacy and belonging between members of the nation. It confers on the nation the appearance of vertical unity in diachronic time, thus enabling it to counterbalance the horizontal diversity of cultural and physical spaces in synchronic time. In a way, the past is part of that essential mortar which keeps the building blocks of the modern nation anchored to each other and attached to some imagined or real roots. As Joshua Fishman puts it (1972: 70), the "long ago is a desirable point of departure" in nationalist discourse because it is "relatable to religious and temporal glories", "uncontaminated by the currently stigmatized [foreign or] anti-models", and "for the man in the street, any claims made for it are less confirmable, [thus making it] infinitely more manipulable" than other models which the present on its own may commend. It is this flexibility of the past which makes it suitable for the culling of group-identity symbols with the power to evoke and motivate. It is also this flexibility which enables nationalists to avoid the paralysing fixity of, and the excessive reverence for, the past.

For the nationalists, the past is the storehouse of old glories, common suffering, dim memories and other distant and authenticating voices which are imagined to have left their imprint on a variety of cultural products – including language – whose significance in the present varies from nation to nation, and, in the history of the same nation, from time to time (for the role of the past in Arab nationalism, see al-ʿAli 1986, al-ʿAysami 1994, Farah 1994, Freitag 1994, al-Nuss 1994, al-Qaysi 1986, Tarabishi 1993, Zurayq 1959). The past provides the nation with an authenticating image of its present self which makes it feel secure within its own definitional frames of reference. Nationalists therefore use the past as the basis of an energizing dynamism which enables the community they address to mobilize for the purpose of defending itself against externally generated challenges, while, at the same time, embracing change and projecting it as part of the inner fabric of this past in an almost seamless progression of history into the present and beyond. This attitude towards the past is displayed to full effect in the "manifesto" of the First Arab Students' Congress, held in Brussels in December 1938 (in Haim 1962: 101):[1]

> It is the new Arab renaissance which pervades the Arab nation. Its motive force is her glorious past, her remarkable vitality and the awareness of her present and future interests. This movement strives continuously and in an organized manner toward well-defined aims. These aims are to liberate and unite the Arab homeland, to found political, economic, and social organizations more sound than the existing ones, and to attempt afterward to work for the good of the human collectivity and its progress.

Coupled with the emphasis on modernization, which directed change in modern nationalist discourse often represents, the past provides the nation with motivational impulses of a formational kind whose aim is to achieve task-orientated goals of an integrationist and sociopolitical nature (cf. al-Husri's *Ārā' wa-aḥādīth fi al-tārīkh wa-l-ijtima*, 1985e: 9–19). This function of the past is echoed by Joshua Fishman when he says that, in nationalist discourse, the past is "mined, ideologised, and symbolically elaborated in order to provide determination ... with respect to current and future challenges" (1972: 9). This interest in the past to cast and recast modern nationalisms explains the constant inventing and reinventing of traditions in nationalist discourses,[2] in which the museum plays an important *re*-presentational part, giving rise to what Benedict Anderson aptly describes as "political museumising" in the new and even not-so-new nations (1991: 183). The role of tradition in nationalist discourse is also recognized by Nash (1989: 14), who states that it "bestows upon the past a weight of authority, legitimacy and rightness" which, in turn, bestow "upon the most humble member of the group a pedigree, allowing him to identify with heroic times, great deeds, and a genealogy to the beginning of things human, cultural and spiritual" (see Chapter 2, section 1).

Paradoxical though it may seem, the mining of the past in nationalist discourse makes nationalism Janus-like, in that it is as much forward-looking as it is backward-orientated. This point is forcefully recognized in Arab nationalist discourse, an example of which is the following statement by Nuseibeh (1956: 62–3): "In periods of transition and transformation, a nation's vision of itself is beclouded and confused. Then most of all it needs men who by profound insight into the soul of the past heritage, by comprehension of the problems of the present, and by vision of the future can synthesize an amorphous mass of ideas and aspirations in the task of reconstruction." Fishman (1972: 9) expresses the same point when he states that nationalism "seeks to derive unifying and energizing power from widely held images of the past in order to overcome a quite modern kind of fragmentation and loss of identity". It is this back-projection of the present into a mythic or real past which infuses the socio-cultural and politico-operational aims of nationalism with authenticity and motivational force within the modernization project. We may express this differently by saying that the forward-projection of the past into the present endows modernization with an authenticity which can transcend the appeal to the material benefits of this modernization as the main legitimating force within nationalism. The success of a nationalist movement or ideology will therefore depend, in part, on reining in the conflicting forces of authenticity and modernization in the community in a manner which enables change to take place without appearing to jettison the legitimizing element of tradition.

The role of the past in constructing nations and nationalisms has been recognized by major scholars in the field. One such reference will suffice here. Anderson (1991: 11) states that the nations to which the nation-states "give political expression always loom out of an immortal past". The primordiality of language, the fact that "No one can give the date for the birth of any language" (ibid.: 144), makes it the most suitable and, perhaps, most authenticating cultural product for expressing the link of a nation with the past in what Fishman (1980: 87) calls "a peculiarly sensitive web of intimacy and mutuality". It is, however, necessary in relating the present to the past in the study of nationalism to be aware of the lure of what Hobsbawm (1990: 74) calls "retrospective nationalism", the unwarranted reading into the past of modern nationalist trends, symbols and currents. Breuilly (1993: 61) also warns against this tendency in nationalist discourse: "The notion of a return to the spirit of the past was often accompanied by a historical perspective which read the appropriate trends into events. Figures in the past became instruments of the national destiny or obstacles in its path." An example of this retrospective nationalism in Arab nationalist discourse is provided by the Egyptian linguist Ibrahim Anis in his pioneering work *al-Lugha bayn al-qawmiyya wa-l-ʿālamiyya* (1970).[3] Basing himself on specious evidence to construct the past in the image of an ideologized present, Anis concludes that "Arab nationalism emerged before Islam on the basis of language alone" (ibid.: 176), and that the Arab nationalist credentials of the Christian poet al-Akhtal (90/708) assured him of the enviable position of "state poet" (ibid.: 178) at the court of the (Muslim) Umayyad caliph ʿAbd al-Malik Ibn Marwan (86/705). This spurious evidence consists of recounting how the Muslim caliph did not object to al-Akhtal appearing in his court drunk and wearing a cross round his neck, and of the latter's disparaging remarks to his wife about her bishop being as ritually unclean as his (the bishop's) donkey's tail. This so-called evidence also extends to a line of poetry which al-Akhtal directed at one of his enemies, lampooning him for the fact that his mother was not of pure

Arab stock.[4] This retrospective nationalism on the part of Ibrahim Anis culminates in his statement that "the boundaries of Arab nationalism [in the early Islamic period] were defined by the spread of the Arabic language" (ibid.: 190), and that "wherever the language took root, Arab nationalism did the same" (ibid.).

A term that is often used to describe the group symbols which nationalists cull from the past to construct modern nationalisms is *myth* (cf. Chapter 1, section 2). Hugh Seton-Watson (1981: 5) refers to this use of the past as "historical mythology", which he characterizes as a "mixture of truth and fantasy, a simplified version of a nation's historical past". Gellner (1983: 56) expresses a similar view: "The cultural shreds and patches used by nationalism are often arbitrary historical inventions. Any old shreds and patches would have served as well" (cf. Chapter 1, section 2 and n. 1). He adds (ibid.): "The cultures [nationalism] claims to defend and revive are often its own inventions, or are modified out of all recognition". Although it cannot be denied that invention and arbitrariness are characteristic of the attempt to relate the present to the past in nationalist discourse, it is nevertheless the case that a blanket statement of the kind offered by Gellner fails to describe the complexity of the situation which falls within its scope. The most telling criticism of this statement is its failure to recognize fully that what matters in assessing these "shreds and patches" from the past is – strictly speaking – not their empirical truth or falsity, but their *efficacy* as transformed and elaborated instruments or symbols of ethno-cultural and political mobilization in pursuit of national objectives. In addition, the fact that certain symbols may or may not have universal currency as factors which promote national identification leaves unexplained their predominance as ingredients which can and do promote such identification in many nationalisms. As Overing (1997: 1) points out, "the use of the term 'myth' is more a judgmental than a definitional or propositional procedure: its attribution requires a judgment having to do with standards of knowledge or its organization". Finally, the fact that there are cases in nationalist discourse where the reference to the past is rooted in a reality which, though mediated and constructed, is not entirely fictional or mythical further challenges Gellner's position. References to the role of Arabic in nationalist discourse constitute a prime example of this fact. Therefore, to avoid the connotations of the term *myth* in the literature on nationalism, it may be more appropriate sometimes to refer to certain elements of the past as *imagined* or *constructed*, but only if being imagined or constructed is not in this context categorially opposed to being *real*.

The aim of this chapter is to examine the Arabic intellectual tradition in premodern times (before Napoleon's invasion of Egypt in 1798) with a view to isolating those aspects of this tradition which are directly related and relatable to the theme of language and group identity in Arab nationalist discourses in the modern period. My interest here is that of the cultural historian who is more concerned with trends in time rather than in chronology *per se*, although the two cannot be separated from each other: trends do take place in time. In carrying out this task, vigilance against retrospective nationalism – the reading of the modern nationalist trends into the articulations of the role of the language in defining an Arab identity in premodern times – will be exercised. But this vigilance should not lead to over-vigilance or paranoia, thus diluting the force of some of those aspects of the Arabic intellectual tradition which appear to embody ingredients of group identity that are akin to pronouncements of a *similar* nature in nationalist discourses. Although similarity is different from sameness, the following discussion will show that the past does not always have to be invented to support the claims made in a particular nationalism. As Gershoni and Jankowski (1997: xxv) state, "nationalism is simultaneously real and imagined, authentic and invented, concrete and discursive"; and yet the "differentiation between imagination and reality in the study of nationalist thought is specious [owing to the fact that] nationalist imaginings become part and parcel of nationalist reality, and attempts to separate them only obscure an understanding of the phenomenon" (ibid.: xxv–xxvi). The discussion of various modes of nationalist discourse later in this study will serve as ample proof of the premise which the title of this chapter signifies: the past is often alive and kicking. It is this which enables elements in the past to be endowed with "resonance" of the kind described in Chapter 1 (see section 2).

2. IN PRAISE OF ARABIC

Praise of a group's language is a well-known phenomenon in pre/proto-nationalist, nationalist and postnationalist discourse, although the rhetorical purpose of this praise may vary from one period to another. In prenationalist discourse, such praise often has a religious, ethnic or even local dimension. In nationalist discourse, praising a group's language often aims at internal cohesion and/or external differentiation for sociopolitical purposes of integration and task-orientation. In postnationalist discourse, the same phenomenon may aim at political consolidation or the expansion of socioeconomic benefits for the in-group at the expense of out-groups within or outside the state. The aim of this section is to outline a set of themes which are often adduced in the literature as evidence of the special status of Arabic in relation to other languages in its premodern (pre-nineteenth-century) cultural milieu, particularly insofar as these relate to the discourse on nationalism in the Arab context.[5]

It is a well-known fact that the prestige of Arabic in the world derives from the role of the language as the medium of the Qur'an and that of the vast intellectual tradition to which Islam has given rise since its appearance on the world stage in the seventh century. The Qur'an reflects on this in often laudatory terms. Thus, in Qur'an 12:2 the point is made that Muhammad's revelation was in Arabic: "*innā anzalnāhu qur'ānan 'arabiyyan*" ("We have sent it down as an Arabic Qur'an"). This is made in the form of an emphatic statement (indicated by *innā* preceding the verb *anzalnāhu*) which sets out God's will and His desire in a way that favours the language in cosmic terms. This fact is underlined in Qur'an 26:195, where the language of the revelation is described as "perspicuous" Arabic (*mubīn*), thus signalling its quality to those who wish to consider the veracity of God's message to humankind. In Qur'an 14:4, God states as a general principle the fact that every messenger was made to address his people in his and their own language, which fact confers on Arabic and its native speakers a special place in Islamic cosmology. This principle explains why the revelation was sent to Muhammad in Arabic, and not in another language (Qur'an 41:44): "*wa-law ja'alnāhu qur'ānan 'ajamiyyan la-qālū lawlā fuṣṣilat āyātuhu 'a'a'jamiyyun wa-'arabiyy*" ("Had We sent this as a Qur'an [in a language] other than Arabic, they would have said: 'Why are its verses not explained in detail? What! A foreign (tongue) and an Arab Messenger?'"). The opposition between Arabic and foreign languages (*'arabiyy* versus *a'jamiyy*) in the context of the revelation is further accentuated in Qur'an 16:103, where the language of those who accuse the Prophet of fabrication is said to be of the latter kind. By drawing this contrast, the Qur'an puts Arabic in a favoured position as the communicative medium for expressing God's universal truths; it further establishes the task of expressing falsehood vis-à-vis the Qur'an as the communicative function of other languages. This is why the language of the Qur'an (39:28) is said to be devoid of any crookedness.

Considered together, these portions of the Qur'an provide a clear picture of the elevated status Arabic has in Islam. This status is amplified further in the Prophetic *ḥadīth* (traditions) literature. In one such *ḥadīth*, the Prophet is reported to have related to his cousin and the fourth rightly guided caliph, 'Ali, that the angel Gabriel descended from heaven and said to him: "O Muhammad! All things have a master: Adam is master of men, you are the master of Adam's descendants, the master of the Rum [Byzantines/Greeks] is Suhayb [Ibn Sinan, one of the Prophet's companions of that origin], the master of the Persians is Salman [al-Farisi, a companion of the Prophet of Persian origin], the master of the Ethiopians is Bilal [Ibn Rabah, a companion of the Prophet of that origin], the master of the trees is the lotus (*sidr*), the master of birds is the eagle, the chief of months is Ramadan, the chief of weekdays is Friday and Arabic is the master of speech" (cited in Goldziher, 1966, vol. 1: 195). In another *ḥadīth*, the Prophet is reported to have established a clear link between three elements of his mission: the fact that he is an Arab, that the Qur'an is in Arabic and that the language of Heaven (*janna*) is Arabic. The combination of these elements constitutes the basis for enjoining all Muslims to love the Arabs: "*aḥibbū al-ʿaraba li-thalāth: li-annī ʿarabiyy, wa-l-qur'ān ʿarabiyy wa-kalām ahl al-janna ʿarabiyy*" ("Love the Arabs for three reasons: because I am an Arab, the Qur'an is [revealed in] Arabic and the speech of the people of Heaven is Arabic": al-Tufi 1997: 246). It is therefore not surprising that the Prophet exhorts his community to learn Arabic and to aim at stylistic excellence in their Arabic speech. It further explains why knowledge of Arabic grammar is regarded by the consensus of the *ulema* as a collective obligation (*farḍ kifāya*) on the Muslim community, and as personal obligation (*farḍ ʿayn*) on those who wish to specialize in the legal sciences.[6] The emphasis on Arabic in the Qur'an further reflects the privileged position of the language among the Arabs of pre-Islamic Arabia as the medium of their most highly prized cultural product, poetry – for it is primarily in response to the status of poetry that the principle of the inimitability of the Qur'an (*Iʿjāz al-qur'ān*) is formulated.[7] The fact that the Qur'an was revealed in Arabic is treated in the literature as proof to the Arabs of its divine origin, in addition to its being an argument against their attempts to deny that Muhammad was God's true Messenger.[8]

This linkage between Islam, the Arabs and the Arabic language is given full expression by the linguist Abu Mansur al-Thaʿalibi (430/1038–9) in the short introduction to his book *Fiqh al-lugha wa-sirr al-ʿarabiyya* (1938).[9] Al-Thaʿalibi reiterates this linkage in a series of related premises and conclusions. First, he states that since whoever loves God will also love His [Arab] Prophet, and whoever loves the Arab Prophet will also love the Arabs, it follows that whoever loves the Arabs will love the Arabic language, in which the best Book (Qur'an) was revealed and communicated to the best people among the Arabs and non-Arabs (*ʿajam*). Second, al-Thaʿalibi states that whoever God guides to Islam will believe that Muhammad is the best of all Messengers, Islam the best of all religions, the Arabs the best of all nations (*umam*) and the Arabic language the best of all languages and tongues. Third, because God has honoured Arabic by making it the language of His revelation to the best of His creation (Prophet Muhammad) – to which may be added the fact that it is the language of Muhammad's best followers in this world and the hereafter – it is inevitable that God will preserve this language until the end of time. This is done by a group of scholars – among whom al-Thaʿalibi implicitly includes himself – who renounce the pleasures of this world and devote themselves selflessly to the pursuit of this aim.

This triad of religion (Islam), the people (Arabs) and the language (Arabic) is reiterated by the Andalusian rhetorician Ibn Sinan al-Khafaji (460/1067–8) in his book *Sirr al-faṣāḥa* (1982).[10] An interesting feature of al-Khafaji's treatment of this triad is the emphasis he places on the relationship between the people and the language over that of the relationship of religion to either of its partners. In this context, al-Khafaji posits an organic relationship between the language and the people (*qawm*), whereby the high prestige of the language reflects the unsurpassable qualities of the people. Al-Khafaji's views on this topic may be expressed by the following gist translation of a passage from his book (1982: 52):

> The superiority of the Arabic language over other languages is part and parcel of the superiority of its Arab speakers as a nation (*umma*) unsurpassed by other nations in quality of character. It is therefore not unreasonable to assume that if the Arabic language is indeed the creation of the Arabs by convention it is bound to reflect the quality of their character. In claiming this, I am not driven by blind allegiance to either the language or its speakers.

Al-Khafaji isolates a number of features which he believes justify assigning to Arabic a communicative status higher than that attributed to other languages.[11] First, Arabic is said to have a vast and rich lexicon – in comparison with other languages such as Greek (*rumiyya*) – partly due to its proclivity for synonymy. As Goldziher (1966, vol. 1: 195) writes: "When seeking to demonstrate conclusively the richness of Arabic, the Arabs had always boasted [*sic*] of the unequalled variety of synonyms in their language". Second, Arabic is characterized by communicative economy, in the sense that it deploys minimal linguistic resources to convey meanings with high informational content; this idea, as an application of Occam's razor principle, may be expressed differently by saying that, in comparison with other languages, Arabic can do more with less. This is said to be most evident in translation into and out of the language, whereby (1) an Arabic target text tends to be shorter than its corresponding source text, and (2) a foreign target text tends to be longer than its Arabic source text. Third, Arabic has extremely well-developed rhetorical resources which, when combined with the preceding two features, make it possible to improve the meanings of texts that are translated into it. The converse of this is also true: Arabic texts translated into other languages are said to suffer from serious translation loss, owing to the fact that these languages are rhetorically impoverished in comparison with Arabic. In supporting this claim, al-Khafaji relies on the evidence of a bishop called Abu Dawud, who is said to be equally proficient in both Arabic and Syriac. According to this bishop, when a Syriac text is translated into Arabic its stylistic quality tends to improve, but when an Arabic text is translated into Syriac it tends to lose much of its stylistic quality because of the – comparatively speaking – impoverished resources of the language. Fourth, Arabic is characterized by a phonological structure which does not encourage the occurrence of successive consonants that belong to the same place of articulation. This property of the language endows it with articulatory ease, which the principle of lightness (*khiffa*) in the Arabic grammatical tradition expresses.[12]

Whether the above claims about Arabic are factually true is not the issue here. What matters for our purposes is that these "properties" of the language are treated as an expression of the "superior qualities" of the Arabs in comparison with other peoples. One of these qualities is generosity, which sets the Arabs apart from the Indians, Ethiopians, Turks and, especially, the Persians and Byzantines, who see little shame in being stingy. Another quality of the Arabs is sound intuition and penetrating judgment, which enable them to surpass even the Greeks in wisdom. The Arabs are a proud and honourable people, whose endurance, patience and courage make them supremely equipped to deal with the hardships of the desert and to triumph over the testing conditions which characterize its physical and social milieu. The Arabs – men and women, young and old – are further characterized by loyalty and the ready willingness to give succour to whoever seeks their help and protection.

This (untestable) interaction between language and group characteristics is extended to grammar and the use of pure Arabic. It is to this ingredient in the Arabic intellectual tradition that I will turn next, but not before adducing some evidence which shows that the correct application of grammatical rules in speech is regarded as a highly prized attribute. Thus, it is reported that the second caliph 'Umar urged the Muslim community to learn the correct forms of speech because they enhance a person's wisdom, mental powers and honour.[13] The jurist 'Amr Ibn Dinar (126/743–4) – who, significantly, is of Persian origin – reiterates the same theme when he says that the acquisition and application of the correct forms of Arabic is an honour which brings a person public recognition.[14] The historian Abu al-Hasan al-Mada'ini (225/839–40) subscribes to the same view when he says that the ability to deploy Arabic correctly can compensate for the absence of other desirable attributes in men.[15] This is exactly what the judge al-Awqas (169/785) nurtured, for although he was unbearably ugly he was, we are told, still able to rise to the position of judge in Mecca owing, among other things, to his ability to use pure and correct Arabic. The sources report how, on one occasion, this judge was more concerned about a drunken man's ungrammatical use of the language than his breaking the Islamic prohibition on the consumption of alcohol.[16] Thus, instead of reminding him of the serious nature of the latter offence and punishing him for it, he proceeded to correct his ungrammatical language.

The above views reflect the importance of the link between language, religion and people in the Arabic intellectual tradition. Although many of the views put forward by al-Khafaji are scientifically unwarranted, thus deserving the appellation "myth", what is important here is not their factual truth or falsity but their *rhetorical* or symbolic value as assertions of ethnic distinctiveness and superiority. The role of language in underpinning these assertions indicates its capacity to be used as an attribute of national identity in the modern period.

3. *ḤIKMAT AL-ʿARAB*: WISDOM OF THE ARABS

The principle of *ḥikmat al-ʿarab* (wisdom of the Arabs) lies at the heart of grammatical analysis in the Arabic intellectual tradition. It creates an important link between "the language" and "the people", who are originally taken to mean the Arabic-speakers of Central Arabia (Najd and the immediately surrounding areas) up to (approximately) the middle of the ninth century. In particular, this principle is related to the explanatory part of the grammatical enterprise – as opposed to its descriptive portion – which is dubbed *taʿlīl* (roughly "causation") in the sources, although, strictly speaking, causation does cover descriptive aspects of the language as well (Suleiman 1999c). Broadly speaking, causation aims at providing explanations, rationalizations or justifications that set out why certain significant features of the language are the way they are. This is generally done by offering various types of *ʿilla* (cause) which specify that "*x* is the case because of *y*". Some of these causes are more plausible/testable than others in empirical terms, but this should not detain us here. Suffice it to say that the study of causation concerns the methodological foundations of Arabic grammatical theory. The fact that the "wisdom of the Arabs" principle is anchored to this level in Arabic grammatical thinking indicates the centrality of the link between people and language in the Arabic intellectual tradition.

As the starting point for dealing with this association between language and people in the context of causation, I will consider aspects of the seminal study by Ibn al-Sarraj (316/928) of the grammatical structure of the Arabic language, *al-Uṣūl fī al-naḥw* (1985). Ibn al-Sarraj begins this study by pointing out that Arabic grammar is inductively derived by the (earlier) grammarians from the speech of the Arabs, as these were originally defined (see preceding paragraph). In so doing, the grammarians identified the conventions and purposes/aims which the earliest speakers of the language had initiated. Grammar establishes these conventions and purposes by using two types of cause. The first type corresponds to what is called grammatical rule in common parlance or traditional grammar. The second type of cause – called *ʿillat al-ʿilla*, the cause of the cause, or meta-cause – seeks to provide explanations for causes of the first type. Thus, whereas a first cause may take the form of a statement to the effect that "the subject occurs in the nominative, and the object in the accusative", the second type of cause seeks to explain why this is actually the case in the language. The ultimate aim of causes of the second type is said to be twofold: (1) to infer the wisdom of the Arabs as this is embodied in the first causes, and (2) to explain the divinely sanctioned superiority of Arabic over other languages.

This view of causation is shared by Abu al-Qasim Zajjaji (337/948) in his book *al-Īḍāḥ fī ʿilal al-naḥw* (1959). Al-Zajjaji divides the causes into three types: pedagogic, analogical and argumentational-theoretical, allocating to them the two tasks of description and explanation in grammar (see Suleiman 1999c, Versteegh 1995). Although al-Zajjaji does not explicitly anchor his discussion of these causes to the "wisdom of the Arabs" principle, it is nevertheless clear that his study serves the two aims established by Ibn al-Sarraj. The gist of al-Zajjaji's position is that Arabic grammar (in the postdescriptive sense) uncovers the inherent structural correlations, patterns and symmetries that exist in the language (Suleiman 1990), and that it is these structural correlations, patterns and symmetries which signal the intrinsically refined qualities of both the language and its speakers.

The idea that the task of grammar is to capture the inherent properties and patterns of the language, and that the postdescriptive articulation of these properties and patterns in grammatical treatises corresponds to their predescriptive counterparts, is reiterated by Ibn Jinni (392/1002) in *al-Khaṣā'iṣ* (n.d.) as part of the overarching theme of the "wisdom of the Arabs" principle in grammatical theory. Like the famous grammarian al-Khalil, Ibn Jinni believes that the Arabs display a sound intuitive knowledge of the inner patterns of their language which, on occasion, they can articulate explicitly, though often without deploying the technical terminology of the grammarians. This shows that the Arabs are in tune with the inner pulse of their language, and that they have a well-developed intuitive knowledge of its inherent properties. An example of this type in the literature concerns al-Mu'arrij (195/811) of the Bedouin tribe of Sadus who is reported to have said: "I came from the desert and knew nothing of the rules of the Arabic language, my knowledge was purely instinctive and I first learnt the rules in the lectures of Abu Ziyad al-Ansari al-Basri" (cited in Goldziher 1966, vol. 1: 108).

Viewing this type of evidence from the perspective of the association of language with people, I agree with the observation made by Bohas et al. (1990) that "in Ibn Jinni's opinion speakers are grammarians without knowing it, and capable, thanks to their inherent wisdom, of making the very generalizations which the professionals of grammar try to formulate" (ibid.: 29). Although modern linguistic theory would rule that the Arabs are not unique in this respect, what really matters here is the fact that an association is established between the speakers' intuitive knowledge of the structure of their language and the wisdom principle mentioned above. Also, what matters here is not the factual truth or falsity of the evidence given in support of this association, but the fact that this association is asserted and used as a guiding criterion in the conduct of linguistic inquiry, regardless of whether this inquiry is pursued in an autonomous or a non-autonomous fashion.

Ibn Jinni is a firm believer in the superiority of Arabic over other languages. To support this view, he adduces a number of linguistic arguments of a fairly complex nature, which I will leave out of consideration here.[17] But he also resorts to reporting the evidence of grammarians whose acceptance of the superiority of Arabic involves a comparative dimension based on their competence in other languages and their knowledge, directly or indirectly, of the grammars of these languages. One such report is provided by Ibn Jinni's famous teacher, the grammarian Abu 'Ali al-Farisi (377/987) who, as his name indicates, is of Persian origin. Ibn Jinni states that this grammarian considered Arabic to be a finer language than Persian, and that he was supported in this by other grammarians, including al-Sijistani (255/869), who was the teacher of the famous linguist al-Mubarrad (285/898). By tracing his views to al-Mubarrad, Ibn Jinni confers on them a legitimacy which the longevity of tradition and the weight of authority make very compelling in their cultural milieu.

Clearly, the view from causation in establishing the link between language and people is an extremely interesting one. This link is underpinned by the "wisdom of the Arabs" principle in two very important ways. On the one hand, it is this principle which is thought to give the language its internal equilibrium and symmetry (see Suleiman 1991), and its balance and harmony, as structural imprints of the genius of the people who, in the mists of time, were its progenitors. On the other hand, through the acts of description and explanation, causation recaptures the ingredients which make up this wisdom. Under this interpretation, causation becomes a process of discovery and confirmation of what is already there – the wisdom of the Arabs. By starting from the wisdom of the Arabs as a foundational premise, and then returning to it as a reconstructed fact through the twin instruments of description and explanation, Arabic grammar assumes a set of values, cultural and methodological, which make it the mediating link between the language and the people in identity terms. This is an important finding of this research because it anchors this link at a level of intellectual abstraction which radiates beyond grammar into a host of neighbouring disciplines whose data are linguistic in nature. I will return to this point in section 5 below.

4. *LAḤN*: SOLECISM[18]

The association of language, religion and people is further articulated through the vast body of literature on *laḥn* in the Arabic intellectual tradition,[19] although the relationship of *laḥn* – henceforth, solecism for ease of reference – to the components of this triad tends to vary from time to time, with prominence being given to language and religion at times and to language and people at others. Broadly speaking, solecism designates deviations from the correct norms of the language, whether these deviations are systematic or unsystematic in nature. What is interesting about solecism, however, is that it draws attention to the role of the anti-norm – for this is what solecism represents in systemic terms – as an important reminder of the linguistic and, more significantly from our perspective here, the extralinguistic connotations of the norm as an emblem of group identity. Seen as a kind of "malfunction" on the linguistic and sociolinguistic levels, solecism acts as a reminder of the correct and corrective functions of linguistic norms as descriptive and pedagogic tools which protect the language from corruption and ensure its vitality as a symbol of a groupness rooted in a pristine past. We may refer to this orientation as "linguistic fundamentalism" here, but only if the term "fundamentalism" is used in a neutral sense rather than with its negatively loaded connotations in the Western discourses on Islam in the modern world. Solecism therefore has two dimensions: the dimension of the present, in which the anti-norm is located; and the dimension of the past, from which the norm emanates. It is there, in that pristine past, that the wisdom of the Arabs as a predescriptive canon first applied. And it is only by returning to that past that the purity of Arabic and the wisdom of its people can be excavated and reconstructed as a first step in moulding the present in the image of the past.

Let us explain how these broad-brush statements apply to the discussion of solecism in the literature. In the beginning, during the early Islamic period, solecism was seen in a predominantly religious context, in which it was considered as a deviation from the true path. This is explicitly stated in the *ḥadīth* literature. Overhearing the corrupt speech of one of his followers, the Prophet is reported to have asked members of the community to correct him because his utterance represented a deviation (*ḍalāl*) from the correct path. It is also reported in the literature that the second caliph ʿUmar punished his son for the occurrence of solecism in his speech, and that he ordered Abu Musa al-Ashʿari, his governor in Yemen, to punish one of his clerks for having committed a solecism in a letter he composed for the caliph (Anis 1960: 18). Some scholars, we are told (cf. al-Anbari n.d.: 46), took these stories to indicate that the caliph regarded deviation from the correct norms of the language as a punishable offence. In a similar vein, the famous jurist al-Hasan al-Basri (110/628) is reported to have considered the occurrence of solecism in reciting the Qur'an to be an act of fabrication – albeit unintended – against God, as did al-Sikhtyani (131/748–9), who used to ask God's forgiveness every time he committed an act of solecism (cf. al-Tufi 1997: 251). Al-Hasan al-Basri is also reported to have considered solecism in the speech of an *imām* to be a valid reason for removing him from office (Ibn ʿAbd Rabbih 1928, vol. 2: 18). This explains the many references in the literature which highlight the need to apply correct *iʿrab* (short-vowel case endings) in reciting the Qur'an. It is reported in this connection that the Prophet had enjoined the Muslim community to do so, as did the caliph Abu Bakr and the Prophet's companion Ibn Masʿud.

The repugnance of solecism to early Muslim society is summed up by the famous linguist Abu al-Aswad al-Du'ali (69/668), who says that it has the same foul smell as rotting flesh or meat. Abu al-Aswad further expresses his horror and dismay that some of the street vendors and merchants of Basra could run successful businesses in spite of the occurrence of solecism in their speech. This censuring attitude is also displayed by the caliph 'Umar, who admonishes a group of men for the occurrence of solecism in their speech more than he does their bad arrow-shooting skills, although learning this skill, together with swimming and horsemanship, is strongly commanded by the Prophet to his community. This censuring attitude towards solecism receives its ultimate expression in the Arabic intellectual tradition in the refusal to treat the body of *ḥadīth* literature as a valid source of data for linguistic analysis, in spite of the fact that this literature constitutes the second source, after the Qur'an, for the derivation of legal rulings. The occurrence of solecism in this literature owing, in part, to the involvement of non-Arab Muslims in the transmission of the corpus of *ḥadīth* is given as the reason behind this attitude.

It is in this context of censuring solecism and promoting correctness in speech, particularly in relation to the recitation of the Qur'an, that Arabic grammar had its early beginnings at the hands of Abu al-Aswad al-Du'ali. Although the circumstances of this event vary from one report to another in the literature, one thing is certain: the development of grammar was intended as a corrective measure to arrest the spread of corruption in the language; it further represented an attempt at recapturing the linguistic essence of that highly prized pristine past before it was too late to do so, hence the designation "linguistic fundamentalism" earlier. At a different level, grammar may be seen as a fulfilment of God's will in the Qur'an, of His promise to preserve the Qur'an, which can be securely achieved only by preserving the language in which it was revealed. However, two of the reports which set out the conditions that occasioned the formal beginning of grammatical activity in early Islam are particularly significant because of their confluence on one matter. The first of these has the caliph 'Ali attributing the occurrence of solecism in Arabic to the linguistic contact between the Arabs and Muslims of non-Arab origin (*a'ājim*, sing. *'ajam*). The second report makes the same point, but is attributed to Ziyad Ibn Abih (53/673), the Umayyad governor of Basra in southern Iraq who was renowned for the purity of his speech or eloquence (*faṣāḥa*). What is significant about these reports is that they locate – in a boundary-setting manner (cf. Chapter 1, section 2) – the source of solecism outside the community of original Arabic-speakers, attributing it to the linguistic contact which the military successes in early Islam brought about.[20] This theme of linguistic contact endured well beyond this period, as is evident from the oft-quoted statement – reiterated by the famous philosopher al-Farabi (339/950) – which describes the limits the grammarians set as a guiding principle for eliciting linguistic data for grammatical analysis.

Because of the importance of this statement, it is given in full below (see Suleiman 1999c: 22–3):

> Linguistic data were not accepted from the tribes of Lakhm or Judhama because they neighboured the Egyptians and the Copts; nor from Quda'a, Ghassan or Iyad because they neighboured the people of Syria who were predominantly Christian and used languages other than Arabic in their ritual prayers; nor from Taghlib and Namir because they neighboured the Byzantines who spoke Greek; nor from Bakr because they neighboured the Nabat and the Persians; nor from 'Abd al-Qays because they lived in Bahrain, thus mixing with the Indians and Persians; nor from Azd of 'Uman because they mixed with the Indians and Persians; nor from the people of Yemen because they mixed with the peoples of India and Ethiopia and because Ethiopians were born amongst them; nor from Banu Hanifa, the inhabitants of Yamama or Thaqif or those of Ta'if because they mixed with the foreign merchants who resided in their countries; nor from the townships of Hijaz (*ḥāḍirat al-Ḥijāz*) because the language transmitters noticed that their language was corrupted by mixing with members of foreign nations (*ghayrihim min al-'umam*).

The importance of the principle of linguistic contact as a solecism-inducing factor is well established in the Arabic grammatical tradition. In the eighth and ninth centuries, and even earlier, this principle received two expressions vis-à-vis data-elicitation and collection. On the one hand, in pursuance of the principle of purity of speech (*fasaha*), some linguists used to travel deep into the desert to reside among Bedouin tribes who were thought to have avoided contact with non-Muslim Arabs or Arabs who had mixed with them, especially in the newly established centres of Basra and Kufa. On the other hand, the grammarians collected data from some Bedouins who attended the markets that sprang up around Basra, especially al-Mirbad, provided that the informants in question were thought to have shunned contact with city-dwellers. The sources report that shepherds, hunters and raiders were particularly favoured, although the financial rewards, such as they were, offered to these informants sometimes led to professional abuse and data-fabrication.[21] These practices are indicative of the importance attached to the pure form of the language in the Arabic intellectual tradition, both as a repository of the wisdom of the Arabs in bygone times and as a boundary-setting device between the various groups, social and ethnic, which made up Muslim society of the day. This purity of language had an additional sociopolitical dimension, which is publicly expressed in the custom of sending the sons of caliphs in the Umayyad period to live in the desert to learn to speak Arabic correctly in preparation for assuming office later in life. However, this did not happen all the time. In this connection, the sources tell us that the caliph al-Walid Ibn 'Abd al-Malik (96/715) committed many errors in his speech, and that his father ascribed this to the fact that he did not send him to the desert to learn the pure speech of the Bedouins.

In addition, the above practices shed light on an important feature of Arab nationalist discourse in the modern period (see Chapter 1, section 5): the almost complete absence in most of this discourse of a return to, or the eulogization of, the speech of the peasant ("or of some other but equally sheltered population") who, in the literature on nationalism, is/are regarded as "noble and uncontaminated" and, therefore, as having "kept his/their language pure and intact" (Fishman 1972: 69; see also Chapter 2, section 5). The Arab nationalist discourse is not entirely unique in this respect; witness the return to Sanskrit rather than the language of the peasant in Indian nationalism. It is, however, interesting to note that the emphasis placed on the language of the sheltered Bedouin in the first centuries of Islam – in what may be regarded as one of the earliest examples of status language-planning in the sociolinguistic literature[22] – does represent a kind of return in earlier times to a formal or symbolic analogue of the peasant in modern nationalist discourse. It is as though, by having had the return to the past performed at an earlier stage in the Arabic intellectual tradition, Arab nationalist discourse could not recreate this same return again. More importantly, the emergence of a more glorious, heroic and recent past in the period following the rise of Islam provided the modern nationalist elite with an even more unifying and evocative point of reference than the one afforded to the Arab linguists in the eighth and ninth centuries. The past is a relative concept: this is particularly true here. Modern Arab nationalism returns to a past in which a codified, elaborated and cultivated form of the language had been achieved through the work of the grammarians centuries earlier. At this point of contact, the symbolic peasant had already disappeared as an embodiment of the "noble and uncontaminated" folk so much beloved by nationalists. For the grammarians, the past was much earlier, prior to their finishing the task of codification, elaboration and cultivation. In this past, the Bedouin did exist as a "noble and uncontaminated" construct, but this was no nationalist age.

The point was made earlier in this section that the Umayyad period (661–750) brought about a change in the attitude towards solecism. Whereas the association between language and religion was paramount in the early Islamic period, greater weight started to be given to the association of language and people in the Umayyad period. It is, however, important not to think of these two kinds of association as mutually exclusive within the triad of language, religion and people established above. This is why, in the first sentence in this paragraph, I have talked about a change *in*, not *of*, the attitude towards solecism.

This change in attitude towards solecism seems to have had a sociopolitical dimension. The sources are full of anecdotes which show how solecism was seen as a defect which can undermine the public standing of a person in whose speech it occurred. This applied as much to caliphs as to other members of the bureaucracy. Thus, the sources tell us how the Umayyad caliph ʿAbd al-Malik Ibn Marwan likened solecism to a face ravaged with smallpox, and how the stress of having to avoid solecism in his Friday sermons turned his hair white prematurely. 'Abd al-Malik is also reported to have said that whereas correct language enhances the status of a commoner, solecism detracts from the status of a nobleman,[23] so much that he himself used to avoid using solecisms in speech even when the context demanded it, as in joke-telling where authenticity required replication and imitation of corrupt speech. By contrast, 'Abd al-Malik's son al-Walid, who became caliph after his father's death, was a notorious *laḥḥāna* (a person who habitually committed solecisms in his speech), a fact which made him the butt of jokes even in his own court. In one such well-known case, al-Walid is reported to have asked a Bedouin who his father-in-law was, saying: "*man khatanaka?*" ("Who circumcised you?") instead of the correct form "*man khatanuka?*" ("Who is your father-in-law?"). When the Bedouin answered that he was circumcised by a Jew, al-Walid started to laugh. The Bedouin did not take the caliph's implied insult lying down. He told the caliph that what he (the caliph) actually meant to say was not *khatanaka*, but *khatanuka*, and then proceeded to tell him who his father-in-law was.[24] In another story, we are told how the caliph 'Umar Ibn 'Abd al-'Aziz (101/720) corrected al-Walid's Arabic in public when the latter attempted to correct one of his own servants. So repugnant was solecism to 'Umar Ibn 'Abd al-'Aziz that he used to refuse to help beggars if they committed solecism when asking for help or charity. It may be interesting to note here that a similar attitude towards beggars existed among some Arab nationalists in modern times (see Chapter 4, section 3).

So important were the sociopolitical implications of solecism that the famous al-Hajjaj (95/714), governor of Iraq, sent the grammarian Yahya Ibn Ya'mar into exile because the latter, at the insistence of the former, dared to point to instances of solecism in the governor's recitation of the Qur'an.[25] Knowing how repugnant solecism was to al-Hajjaj, one of his officials, a certain Kathir Ibn Kathir, committed a gross grammatical error in his presence on purpose. The sources tell us that this was a ruse by the crafty official to force al-Hajjaj to fire him to avoid being forced to accept a posting which he did not fancy.[26] To avoid the ignominy of committing solecisms in public, a non-Arab court poet would sometimes secure the services of a professional reciter, who would read his poetry for him in public without error. Fear of committing solecism also led to an exaggerated pronunciation of some Arabic phonemes by non-Arabs, especially /ḥ/, /'/ and the emphatic sounds /ṭ/, /ḍ/ and /ẓ/. Finally, the censuring attitude towards solecism meant that it was tolerated, or was thought to be appropriate, only in the language of slave girls and young and coquettish women. And, in the society of the day, no man worthy of the name would dare stoop so low!

The above discussion highlights aspects of the Arabic intellectual tradition which show the strong association of language, religion and people. In particular, it shows the value accorded to correct language use in this triad, and how the emphasis on this permeated linguistic, sociolinguistic and legal facets of this tradition. Worthy of note in this context is the strong assumption in the Arabic intellectual tradition that the ability to speak Arabic without solecism was an important consideration in public, especially political, life. The discussion also highlights how language was seen as a boundary-setting device at the social and ethnic levels. By ascribing the onset of solecism to the linguistic contact between the Arabs and non-Arab Muslims, the Arabic intellectual tradition endows language with functions of ethno-cultural groupness which it later assumed more forcefully (see Chapters 4 and 5). It is to this aspect of the association of language, religion and people that I will turn next.

5. *'AJAM* AND *'ARAB*[27]

Contrastive group self-identification by means of ethnic labels is an ancient phenomenon. The Greek term *ethnos*, from which the word "ethnicity" and its derivatives originate, is the paradigmatic ethnic label par excellence. Tonkin et al. (1989) provide an interesting analysis of the development of the meaning of this term. Roughly speaking, the term was initially used to signify groups of animals, but was later extended to refer to groups of warriors, the Furies, the Persians and foreign or barbarian peoples. In the New Testament, the term is used to refer to non-Christians and non-Jews, as an equivalent of the term *goyim*. At a later stage, the meaning of the term *ethnos* was rendered by the word *gentile* to signify group otherness, particularly in the religious sphere. But, in a strange twist of semantic development, the term later (fifteenth century onwards) started to mean Greek Orthodox, as it now signified the otherness of this group as a religious *millet* in the predominantly Muslim Ottoman Empire. Similar contrastive self-identification is practised by other groups whose claim to fame may not have the same pedigree as that of the ancient Greeks. Gypsies, as Rom, contrast their own world to that of the *gaje*. As Hechter (1986: 276) points out, "Gypsy survival is due to strongly held Gypsy beliefs that the *gaje* world is polluted, and only the Rom are clean". The term *baljikiyyin* (Belgians) used in Jordan to refer to Jordanian citizens of Palestinian origin belongs to this category of ethnic labels (see Suleiman 1999b).

Returning to *ethnos*, Tonkin et al. (1989) tell us that the full meaning of this term as an ethnic label of contrastive self-identification emerges from its place in a lexical network of related terms, including the Latin *genus*, *populus*, *tribus*, *natio*, *barbarus* and *civis* whose legacy in "modern Romance languages, and in English, is a complex and rich moral vocabulary, laid out along dimensions of inclusion and exclusion, dignity and disdain, familiarity and strangeness" (p. 13). Of particular interest for our purposes here is the use of the derived adjective *ethnikos*, in early Christian times, as a close synonym of *barbaros* which signified "those who spoke unintelligible languages" (ibid.), thus making language the ethnic symbol and boundary-setting device par excellence. An awareness of this function of language and its ethical and moral implications is found in the Arabic intellectual tradition, hence the rejection by Ibn Hazm (456/1064) of Galen's belief in the superiority of Greek and in the inferiority of other languages which are likened to the barking of dogs or the croaking of frogs.[28] Armstrong (1982: 5) emphasizes this function of language and its moral and ethical connotations when he states that terms like "*goyim*, *barbaroi* and *nemtsi* all imply [a] perception of the human incompleteness of persons who could not communicate with the in-group, which constituted the only "real men". Usually, in their original application such terms singled out one or two alien neighbours, and by reference to such aliens, large ethnic groupings came to recognize their own relatively close relationship." Within this framework of usually boastful inclusion and deprecating exclusion, the failure of the out-group to come to grips with the language of the in-group is seen as a fault in the former, rather than as a result of any impenetrability which this language may have. As a rule, linguistic impenetrability is usually ascribed to the language of the out-group, which is often considered an obstacle to the progress of civilization as an avowed aim of the in-group and its civilizational mission in history. The attitude towards Japanese by some Europeans provides an interesting example here: the Basque Jesuit missionary Francis Xavier (1506–52) is said to have described this language, on account of its difficulty, as an "invention of the devil" whose aim was to impede the progress of Christianity. Similarly, some Arabists expressed the view that the grammar of numerals in Arabic was an invention of the devil to torture those who wished to learn the language.

The above contrastive self-identification between the Arabs and the non-Arabs (*ʿajam*), as constructed by the former, may be illustrated by the following incident from the early period of Islamic history. It is reported in the sources (see Arslan 1994) that the Banu Taghlib, a Christian Arab tribe from the Arabian Peninsula, refused to pay the poll-tax to the second caliph ʿUmar on the grounds that they were Arabs who could not be treated like non-Arabs (*ʿajam*) (ibid.: 292). In the end, they agreed to pay double the going poll-tax rate on condition that their payment was treated as a form of charitable contribution and not as poll-tax which, the Banu Taghlib argued, the infidels among the non-Arabs (*aʿlāj*, singular *ʿilj*) had to pay (ibid.: 292). What is interesting about this report is the contrastive ethnic self-definition of Arab versus non-Arab which the Banu Taghlib invoked, in place of the religion-based one of Muslim versus non-Muslim, to justify the non-payment of the poll-tax. In the process, the Banu Taghlib constructed a matrix of group self-definition which was more complex than the binary one operated by the caliph. Whereas the caliph operated in terms of a binary distinction between Muslims and non-Muslims, the

Banu Taghlib operated in terms of a four-way distinction between Muslim Arab, Muslim non-Arab, Arab non-Muslim and non-Arab non-Muslim, and that they did not regard themselves to be on the same par as this last group. On the contrary, the fact that they used the term *'ajam* in an unqualified manner in their interaction with the caliph indicates that they regarded themselves to be on a par with Muslim Arabs. Also, the fact that the caliph was willing to tolerate the above classification and its implications for the principles which governed his tax policy, even if his reasons for this were administrative and political, indicates the residual power which the bonds of Arabness in its tribal context held in the early Islamic period.

In the Arabic intellectual tradition, the term *'ajam* and its derivatives are best understood in the context of the network of semantic relations outlined in the preceding two paragraphs.[29] In particular, this term serves the ethno-cultural function of group exclusion conveyed by the two ethnic labels *ethnos* (in its premodern meaning) and *barbaros*, although not always with the same negative connotations.[30] The term *'ajam* is used in pre-Islamic discourse to refer to non-Arabs (cf. Nuseibeh 1956: 12), and this sense is preserved in the Qur'an where the term occurs four times (16:103, 26:198 and 41:44 (twice)) to designate a binary group classification between Arabs and non-Arabs on the basis of language. In adopting this mode of classification, the Qur'an must have followed established usage. The juxtaposition of *a'jamī* (relative adjective of *'ajam*) to *'arabī* in this usage constitutes a kind of sign in semiotic terms, in which the one term recalls the other in a relation of mutual implication. In addition, it is clear from the sequential ordering of the terms in this sign, and their pragmatic loading in their texts, that the term *a'jamī* is the *marked* category, in the sense that it signifies what is – in terms of the Qur'an as revelation – a deviation from the standard or norm, *'arabī*, in the same way as the feminine gender is generally treated as the marked category in relation to the unmarked masculine gender in grammatical analysis. This markedness of *a'jamī* is signalled by the fact that the Qur'an is manifestly in Arabic. It is also signalled by the fact that *'arabī* is the referentially specific term, whereas *a'jamī* is the non-specific one. In other words, while we know that *'arabī* signifies a relationship with the Arabic language, we do not know for certain the language or languages signified by *a'jamī*, although Persian may be the primary language in this category. If so, *'arabī* must be treated as a term of positive and specific inclusion, while, in contrast, *a'jamī* must be viewed as a term of exclusion, residual inclusion or inclusion by default. Looked at from a different angle, *'arabī* is a term of in-groupness, while *'ajamī* is a term of out-groupness. The fact that language is treated as the classificatory principle which makes possible the above distinctions shows powerfully the importance attached to language in the Arabic intellectual tradition as a symbol of ethno-cultural identity and as a boundary-setting device. Hourani (1983:

260) describes this situation in the following terms: "as far back in history as we can see them, the Arabs have always been exceptionally conscious of their language and proud of it, and in pre-Islamic Arabia ... there was a unity which joined together all those who spoke Arabic and could claim descent from the tribes of Arabia". Playing the vis-à-vis constitutes the very substance of the distinction between *ʿarab* and *ʿajam* in the literature.

The conversion of many non-Arabs to Islam in the wake of the Islamic conquests generated contradictory implications for this linguistically based group identification. The prestige of Arabic as the language of the Qur'an was now significantly enhanced by its deployment in new communicative domains, notably those of the new sciences, the administration and the military. This made Arabic an even more potent symbol of group identity for its speakers and, self-contrastively, for those of the newly conquered populations, especially the elite. For the former, Arabic became an empowering symbol of prestige, inclusion and in-groupness. For the latter, Arabic became a symbol of exclusion and (their) out-groupness, a function it never served before. This new situation represents a subtle, but important, modulation in what may be called, following Bourdieu (1992), the dynamics of the ethno-linguistic market at the time. Whereas in pre-Islamic and early Islamic Arabia the populations in the territories the Arabs acquired later did not identify themselves as non-Arabs or non-Arabic speakers, this picture started to change after the conquests in that the identity of the populations in these territories began to be formulated in such terms. Whereas before the conquest the populations of the conquered territories defined themselves principally by what they were – or by what they were not, but without reference to the Arabs – after the conquest they started to define themselves, albeit not exclusively, by what they were *not* by reference to a new and commanding classificatory principle represented by the Arabs and their language.

But it is normal in situations of this kind for the linguistically dispossessed, especially the elite, to start acquiring and cultivating the new resource, as happened with Ismaʿil Ibn Bulbul – a Persian vizier to the Abbasid caliph al-Muʿtamid (279/892) – who, in speech and writing, "indulged in the most choice linguistic finesses in order to pass more easily as a full Arab" (Goldziher, 1966, vol. 1: 133). In a situation of this kind, a new dynamic begins to develop, leading to a reworking of the basis upon which in-groupness and out-groupness, inclusion and exclusion, are constructed. That this in fact happened in Muslim society is evidenced by the subtle changes in meaning which the word *ʿajam* seems to have acquired. Whereas *ʿajam* earlier meant being non-Arabic-speaking, particularly of Persian origin, later the term started to signal speaking the language with difficulty, or speaking it with characteristic interferences from the mother-tongue. Although this mutation in meaning may be thought to represent a reduction in the *efficacy* of language as a group symbol of contrastive self-identification, it however does not challenge the definitional role of language as a boundary-setting device – hence the existence of attempts in the literature to outline stereotypical mother-tongue interferences into Arabic as a means of maintaining group-identity boundaries.[31] It is, I believe, in this context (fourth/tenth century) that the reference to Arabic as *lughat al-ḍād*, the language of the phoneme /ḍ/, assumes its maximal definitional function or significance, although as a term it may have been in existence at the time of the Prophet.[32] This definitional function of /ḍ/ is reflected in a poem by the famous poet al-Mutanabbi (354/965), who considers himself the most honourable person among his own people, who, in turn, are said to be the pride of all those who spoke the *ḍād*.[33] The definitional potential of /ḍ/ is also commented on by Ibn Jinni in his famous book *Sirr ṣinā'at al-i'rāb* (1993, vol. 1: 214–15), in which he says: "let it be known that /ḍ/ belongs to the Arabs alone; it is rarely [if ever] found in the speech of the *'ajam*". This presumed distinctiveness of a group's language is often found among other nations, although it may not always be signalled by a special term of the kind under consideration here. Witness the claim made by the French nationalist writer, Charles Murras (1886–1952), to the effect that no Jew or Semite could achieve complete mastery of the French language to the extent that he could appreciate the full beauty of Racine's line in *Bérénice*: "*Dans l'orient désert quel devint mon ennui*" (cited in Kedourie 1966: 72).

Calling Arabic *lughat al-ḍād* is not just a matter of signalling the distinctiveness of the language by claiming that /ḍ/ is unique to it (al-Jahiz, quoted by 'Uways 1977: 245 and al-Khafaji 1982: 56). It is, more significantly, a way of renaming the language, of giving it a new label that is derived not from the name of the people who originally spoke it or the area where it was originally spoken, but from the articulatory difficulty which the phoneme in question is said to present to hapless foreigners striving for mastery of the language.[34] Under this reading, the phoneme /ḍ/ becomes an authenticating emblem, a border guard and a defining symbol of group identity, signalling, as Anis (1970: 201) indicates, who does or does not belong to the in-group. This explains, Goldziher tells us (1966, vol. 1: 115), why "mistakes in language by [Muslims of non-Arab origin] were derided in the most offensive manner and people appeared outraged when a foreigner presumed to criticize an Arab in matter of Arab language and poetry",[35] in spite of the fact that "the most eminent grammarians and the most eager researchers into the treasures" of the Arabic language were of non-Arab lineage. This also explains the existence of statements in the literature which set out stereotypical renditions of /ḍ/ that characteristically signal membership in a particular ethnic group.[36] Here again, language provided a criterion for contrastive group definition which, as shall be explained in the next chapter, survived well into the modern period. Witness the use of the term *lughat al-ḍād* and *al-mutakallimūn bi-l-ḍād* in the nineteenth and early twentieth centuries to refer respectively to Arabic and Arabic-speakers as a group that is distinct from Turkish and Turkish-speakers (see Chapter 4, sections 3–4). Witness also the survival of this term in modern Arab culture as a boastful name for Arabic, and its use as a name for at least one journal devoted to research on the language, *al-Ḍād*, published in Baghdad in the second half of the twentieth century.

Much of this contrastive self-identification by means of language took place in a sociocultural context dominated by *shu'ūbiyya* (cf. al-Duri 1981) and its anti-Arab polemic in which Persians, Nabat (Nabataeans), Copts and Berbers participated.[37] Roughly speaking, *shu'ūbiyya* designates "a movement within the early Muslim society which denied any privileged position of the Arabs" (Enderwitz 1996: 513–16).[38] *Shu'ūbiyya* attacks on the Arabs covered rhetoric, oratory, weapons, military skills, genealogy and – most important from the perspective of this research – language, which has caused Anis (1970: 192) to describe *shu'ūbiyya* as a linguistic conflict (*ṣirā' lughawī*). The attacks on Arabic, which Goldziher (1966, vol. 1: 192) similarly dubbed "linguistic *shu'ūbiyya*", aimed at various aspects of the language, but they were all intended to challenge the claims of superiority attached to it by the Arabs and non-Arab grammarians alike (cf. section 3 above). One such attack took the form of an apocryphal *ḥadīth* in which the Prophet is claimed to have said: "If God intends a matter which demands tenderness he reveals it to the ministering angels in … Persian, but if He wishes for something demanding strictness He uses Arabic" (Goldziher 1966, vol. 1: 157). In another version of this tradition, tenderness and strictness are replaced by pleasure and anger respectively (ibid.).[39] The difficulty, however, in assessing the full extent of the *shu'ūbiyya* attacks on the Arabic language is that very little of the literature on this topic has come down to us. And, since most of what we know can only be reconstructed from the rebuttals offered by the opponents of *shu'ūbiyya* – whether of Arab or non-Arab lineage – who rose in defence of the Arabic language, I will concentrate on these works, particularly those of Ibn Durayd (321/933), al-Anbari (327/938), Ibn Faris (395/1004) and al-Zamakhshari (538/1143) because of their immediate relevance.[40] It should be noted, however, that many of the references to the superiority of Arabic over other languages made in sections 2 and 3 above belong to this anti-*shu'ūbiyya* discourse.

Ibn Durayd's rebuttal of the *shu'ūbiyya* claims in his book *al-Ishtiqāq* provides a suitable starting point for this discussion because of its twin preoccupation with genealogy and language (in particular, etymology), which, as Goldziher (1966, vol. 1) rightly observes, constitute the main targets of *shu'ūbi* polemic. The main thesis in *al-Ishtiqāq* is that Arabic proper names are embedded in an etymology which defines what may be called linguistic genealogies by means of derivational networks (*ishtiqāq*) whose roots lie in the lexical stock of the language.[41] Thus, the extensive etymologies which make up the bulk of *al-*

Ishtiqāq are offered not as an exercise in lexicography but as a way of refuting the claim that Arabic names are derivationally rootless and, therefore, arbitrary. This refutation is further taken to represent a denial of the claim that the famous grammarian al-Khalil had said that Arabic names are etymologically arbitrary, which claim is used by the *shu'ūbiyya* as a basis for their attacks on Arabic. Although the point is not explicitly made in *al-Ishtiqāq*, for Arabic names not to be derived from a native lexical stock would be unthinkable because it would amount to a denial of the principle of the wisdom of the Arabs, and it is this principle which Ibn Durayd is ultimately defending. This is clear from the attempts made by Ibn Durayd to show that the social context often plays an important role in the choice of a name – for example, calling a newly born baby boy Ramadan because he was born during this month – a fact which makes names of this kind sociolinguistically significant and culturally motivated. The statement that "the Arabs have systems of naming their male off-spring" (Ibn Durayd 1958: 5) sums up this point well. This interest in names in modern nationalist discourse is evident in Turkish (see Chapter 4, section 2) and Arab nationalism (see Chapter 5, section 2), albeit in a mode of engagement different from that of Ibn Durayd.

This principle of the wisdom of the Arabs is also invoked in al-Anbari's defence of the occurrence of *aḍdād*, words with the same phonological form but opposite meanings,[42] in his book of the same name (1987). The charge here – which al-Anbari attributes to a party peddling heresy, falsehood and contempt for the Arabs – is that words of this type can lead to communicative difficulties and even failure. This, the charge goes, shows the deficient wisdom of the Arabs and their meagre rhetorical abilities. It also shows a lack of regard for the need to maintain a relationship of exclusive mutual implication between the signifier and the signified in words as signs.

Al-Anbari provides an interesting defence of Arabic, based on the principle of the wisdom of the Arabs, which shows the deficient reasoning of the proponents of *shu'ūbiyya*. First, he points out that this party shows little appreciation of the role which linguistic co-textuality and situational contextuality play in the processing of speech and the recovery of meaning. This failure in understanding how language works reduces it to a notational system devoid of all creativity. Second – and this is only implicitly given by al-Anbari – by combining homonymy and synonymy into one category called *aḍdād*, the Arabic lexicon acquires expressive resources, limited though these may be, which other languages lack. Third, some *aḍdāds* express a close semantic relationship between the sets of words they involve, thus signalling a core meaning in both; this may be exemplified by the word *muḥtall* in contemporary Arabic, which refers both to the occupier (Israel) and the occupied (Palestinians) as in historical Palestine. Fourth, some *aḍdāds* are the result of dialect-mixing; for example, the word *jawn* came to mean both "white" and "black" as a result of such mixing. The fact that in some cases it is not possible to establish the cause(s), *'illa*(s), which is/are responsible for the occurrence of a given *aḍdād* item in the language does not refute the principle that the Arabs are a wise people (ibid.: 7–8, gist translation): "If someone asks about the cause behind calling a man *rajul*, and a woman *imra'a* ... you should answer as follows: this is because of causes that are known to the Arabs, but which we have failed to discover, completely or in part. The Arabs cannot be said to have ceased to be knowledgeable because we [the grammarians] are unable to state with clarity the causes behind their speech." It is interesting to note in this connection that this conclusion was rejected by al-Arsuzi in his attempt to anchor Arab nationalism in relation to Arabic (see Chapter 6, section 4).

Ibn Faris' response to the *shu'ūbiyya* attacks on Arabic are embodied in his treatise *al-Ṣāḥibī fī fiqh al-lugha* (1993). Some of the themes he dealt with were discussed earlier (see section 2), namely in the defence of synonymy in Arabic. Reference was also made above to the role of this synonymy in enriching the Arabic lexicon and the effect this has on translating into and out of the language – views which the Andalusian linguist Ibn Sinan al-Khafaji shared with Ibn Faris in what may have been, for the former, a similar *shu'ūbiyya* milieu in Muslim Spain in the fifth/eleventh century. The use of *i'rab* (short-vowel case endings), which endows the language with syntactic flexibility through free word order, is regarded by Ibn Faris as a distinguishing feature of Arabic, as is the capacity of the language to deploy a host of rhetorical devices. Although all languages do serve the communicative functions to which they are put, none, so Ibn Faris believes, does so more economically and elegantly than Arabic.

Al-Zamakhshari's rebuttal of *shu'ūbiyya* is given in the beautifully crafted introduction to his famous book *al-Mufaṣṣal fī al-naḥw* (1840).[43] The fact that al-Zamakhshari felt impelled to write about this topic, well after the sociopolitical embers of this movement had subsided in the sixth/twelfth century, shows – as Goldziher (1966, vol. 1: 191) rightly observes – the enduring nature of linguistic *shu'ūbiyya*. However, this time the nature of the encounter between the proponents and opponents of Arabic across the *shu'ūbiyya* lines takes a fairly new direction. First, there is a clear and open identification of *shu'ūbiyya* by name in *al-Mufaṣṣal*, whereas, in the works I have discussed earlier, references to this movement were effected by allusion. Second, there is a strong identification between Arabism and Islam. This identification is extremely important in view of the attention given to this issue in Arab nationalist discourse in the twentieth century (see Chapter 5, section 5).[44] Third, the bankruptcy of *shu'ūbiyya* is signalled by the absence of any attacks it made against Arabic in any language other than Arabic itself, which – al-Zamakhshari argues – shows the unassailable position of the language. As Norris (1990: 47) wittily points out, "even the most fanatical *shu'ūbī* expressed his sentiments in the tongue first spoken by the Arabian lizard-eaters he so despised". A similar charge is levelled in the twentieth century against the proponents of the vernacular (*'āmiyya*) in its various dialectal forms (see Chapter 6), who hardly ever use it to expound and popularize their views (cf. Shakir 1972). Fourth, and this is the most significant point, al-Zamakhshari's defence is not a defence of Arabic *per se* but of Arabic grammar, especially as it pertains to *i'rab* (short-vowel case endings). The gist of al-Zamakhshari's defence in this connection is that knowledge of Arabic grammar is a prerequisite to the study of the Islamic sciences, particularly the law. Al-Zamakhshari emphasizes this because of claims made by the proponents of *shu'ūbiyya* in which they belittle the value of grammar, or even reject it.

It is of course true that, by defending Arabic grammar, al-Zamakhshari defends the Arabic language and, indirectly, reaffirms the validity of the "wisdom of the Arabs" principle which stands as a bulwark against the attacks of *shu'ūbiyya*. But there is more to this defence than that. This defence shows the increasing abstractness of the debate over Arabic, and the increasing finesse with which it is now articulated. In a sense, al-Zamakhshari's ultimate defence of the language does not reside in what the introduction to *al-Mufaṣṣal* actually says, but in the very act of inscribing/producing *al-Mufaṣṣal* itself, a book in which the nuts and bolts of grammar are set out. It is as though, by shifting the defence of the battle line from an immediate concern with the language to a concern with the grammar of the language, one shifts the symbolism of ethnocultural groupness from language as a fully living system of communication to grammar as a representational device. In diachronic terms, this reflects a passage in the symbolism from productivity to increasing fossilization, which accurately reflects the changing status of Arabic over the centuries as a medium of communication. Although the idea in nationalist discourse that *the deader a language the greater its symbolic power in constructing group identity* does not apply here – because Arabic was never a dead language, contrary to what Shivtiel states (1999: 131) – the fact remains that, by endowing grammar with symbolism of this kind in the Arabic intellectual tradition, the passage from a premodern and a prenationalist age to a modern and nationalist one in the nineteenth century is made much easier. This is why Arab authors in the second half of the twentieth century were still engaged in fighting battles against what was called modern *shu'ūbiyya* with almost total disregard for historical discontinuities (Bayhum 1957 and 1962, al-Bazzaz 1962, al-Fikayki 1968).[45] This was especially true of the 1980s in Iraq during the Iran–Iraq war (cf. al-Khatib 1983, al-Shahhadh 1990, 'Abd al-Tawwab 1990, Muhammad 1990, 'Abd al-Mu'min 1990, Dhihni 1990). Symbols strike a deep chord in a people's psyche. This is the source of their durability, and this is why the past in nationalist discourse lives on and can loudly resonate.

6. THE ARABS AS A NATION (*UMMA*): FURTHER EVIDENCE

It is clear from the above discussion that the role of Arabic as a symbol of ethnic identity in premodern times is culturally and historically sanctioned. Evidence for this role is derived from a variety of sources, including the religious and the linguistic sciences. References to this role are available in the Qur'an and *ḥadīth* literature. In the latter, Imam Malik reports that the Prophet considered competence in Arabic to be the basis for identifying a person as an Arab: "O people! God is one, and your father is one. No one inherits Arabic from his father or mother. Arabic is a habit of the tongue. He who speaks Arabic is an Arab" (cited in Anis 1970: 180). It is remarkable that the definition of Arabism in the last sentence has been included, almost verbatim (see Chapter 5, section 2), as part of the definition of the Arab nationalist ideology of the Baʿth party and the Arab nationalist movement (cf. Arab Baʿth Party Constitution in Haim 1962, and al-Husri 1968). This highlights the strong association which exists between language and people in the conceptualization of group identity in Arab culture, although the historical roots of this association are usually framed in an Islamic context. This is made clear by the famous jurist Imam Shafiʿi (204/820) in his *Risāla*, in which he points out that a Muslim ceases to be an Arab if he has no competence in the language, and that he becomes an Arab if he acquires the language. Al-Shafiʿi is clearly arguing against descent or lineage as a defining criterion of Arabness, but this is not the only view on this matter in the Arabic intellectual tradition. In the eighth/fourteenth century, the jurist al-Shatibi (789/1388) put forward the opposite view in his book *al-Iʿtiṣām*, arguing that linguistic competence in Arabic does not make a person ethnically/racially Arab, owing to the abiding importance of lineage among the Arabs as an authenticating criterion of identity.[46]

The strength of the language-and-people association is further reflected in various ingredients in the Arabic linguistic tradition. Some linguists establish an organic link between the collective character of the Arabs and the qualities of their language, insisting on the superiority of the latter over other languages (section 2). The patterned regularities of Arabic are seen as a reflection of the wisdom of the Arabs (section 3). The discussion of solecism and how it was induced by linguistic contact between Arabs and non-Arabs in the wake of the Islamic conquests highlights the role of Arabic in defining ethnic and social identities (section 4). The *shuʿūbiyya* attacks on Arabic and its grammar reflect the role of the language as an emblem of identity, and the desire to challenge that role to undermine the cultural and ethnic hegemony of the Arabs. Considering this range of associations between language and people – and their historical and cultural depths – it is no accident that Arab nationalists in the modern period (following Napoleon's invasion of Egypt in 1798) turned to language as the primary criterion in defining the cultural and sociopolitical identities of the Arabic-speaking peoples. I will deal with this topic in the next two chapters, but not before showing here that this attempt at collective self-definition by reference to language is not without precedent in historical and sociopolitical discourse in the Arabic intellectual tradition.

One of the best treatments of this topic is offered by the historian al-Masʿudi (345/956) in his books *al-Tanbīh wa-l-ishrāf* and *Murūj al-dhahab wa-maʿādin al-jawhar*. Al-Masʿudi approaches the topic of the definition of the nation (*umma*)[47] with due historical care, arguing that different criteria of nationhood assumed different degrees of definitional prominence at different periods in history. Thus, while the existence of a unified or unitary political power over a defined territory was a criterion of nationhood in ancient times, this was less so in later periods. For al-Masʿudi, the three defining properties of a nation are its natural disposition or character (*shiyam ṭabīʿiyya*), sociocultural constitution (*khuluq ṭabīʿiyya*) and language (*alsinatuhum*). Although it is not possible to specify the meanings of these terms precisely – for example, al-Masʿudi designates language (sometimes variably) as *lisān* or *lugha* – and although the term "nation" here cannot be regarded as a synonym of the same term in the modern sense,[48] there is no doubt that language for him constitutes the most important criterion in defining nationhood. Both Khalidi (1975) and Nassar (1992) emphasize this point. Khalidi sums this up as follows (1975: 89–90):

> The concept of a nation for [al-Masʿudi] is largely linguistic. Language is the most important constituent of a nation. Land is a minor factor since certain nations, the Turks for instance, split and migrated but still retained their nationhood. A unitary kingdom is also of minor importance since some nations, e.g. the Persians, were living in politically fragmented kingdoms but were still described as Persians. Physical and other characteristics played an important role in the earliest times but we hear less of this in later periods. In other words, while certain factors like land and a unitary kingdom were important in the early period of world history, they ceased to have much importance thereafter, *while language remained the most important single constituent of nationhood.* (emphasis added)

This objective definition of nationhood is adopted by the philosopher al-Farabi (339/950), using more or less the same terms as al-Masʿudi: similarity in social make-up or constitution, natural character or disposition and a shared language and speech.[49] However, there are two subtle differences between al-Masʿudi and al-Farabi. First, while the former approaches the definition of the nation from a historical perspective, the latter deals with this unit from the perspective of the political philosopher whose approach may be considered as a-historical or a-chronological, although it cannot be divorced from history. Second, although al-Masʿudi is aware of the contrastive self-definition of nationhood which his criteria generate, he nevertheless does not articulate this fact explicitly. By contrast, al-Farabi explicitly mentions the role of these criteria in inducing internal cohesion within the nation and external differentiation in respect to other nations. Awareness of this differentiational function of the criteria indicates an appreciation in the Arabic intellectual tradition of the role which a boundary approach to the definition of the nation may play in the discourse on the subject (see Chapter 1, section 2).

7. CONCLUSION

It is clear from the discussion in this chapter that the role of Arabic as a symbol of group identity in premodern times is sanctioned in a variety of domains and intellectual enterprises. It is part of the linguistic thinking of the Arabs, the religious sources and Islamic theology. It is also part of the historical and social discourse on what makes up a group and what keeps it apart from other groups, of the internal bond between its members and the external boundary between itself and other groups. It is therefore not surprising that Arab nationalist discourse in the modern period has resorted to language, owing to its "resonance" in Arab culture, as the mainstay of an Arab national identity. It is also not surprising that the modern formulations of this role are sometimes framed in a manner reminiscent of premodern sentiments vis-à-vis the language, as the following quotation from Qunstantin Zurayq's seminal treatise (*al-Wa'y al-qawmī*, 1938) on Arab nationalism illustrates (cited in Nuseibeh 1956: 69–70):

> It is the duty of the nationally conscious [Arab] to ponder his language in order to know its genesis and how it spread and to comprehend its superior qualities over other languages and the special endowments which enabled it to achieve complete mastery over ... vast regions. For every language possesses a unique genius and attributes which distinguish it from other languages. And the Arabic language among all other languages has shown great vitality in its meticulous structure, the extent of its dissemination, and its flexibility, which has fitted it to serve an efficacious instrument for expressing the various arts and sciences. For all these reasons it behoves us to try to discover the secret of this vitality and to lay our hands on the unique powers which our language represents in order to utilize these powers in organizing our present and building our future.

The above references to the "superior qualities [of Arabic] over other languages" and its "special endowments" in matters of communicative "vitality", "meticulous structure" and "flexibility" are modern reformulations of old themes, showing how *the past lives on* and how it interacts with the present in nationalist discourse. The fact that language is seen in these reformulations as the key to unlocking a power and a vitality which can organize the present and build the future indicates the strength of the assessment of its motivational role in Arab nationalist discourse. It is to this theme that I will turn in the next chapter.

This "communion of the past and the present" vis-à-vis the language is regarded by Arab nationalist thinkers as a "source of strength" in their socio-political modernization project (ibid.: 78). Language is thought by most nationalist thinkers to be best suited of all the ingredients of Arab nationalism to create this communion. In comparison with other ingredients, it requires but a modicum of intervention and invention before it can be pressed into active service as a symbol of shared identity. Evidence for this, from a totally different context, may be indirectly derived from Charles Ferguson's (1972) treatment of the attitudes and beliefs which Arabic-speakers display towards the language situation in present-day Arab societies. One of these attitudes, called "myths" by Ferguson,[50] revolves around a host of beliefs which enunciate the superiority of Arabic over other languages in a variety of spheres, including the beauty of its rhythmical cadences, its "grammatical symmetry and 'logical' structure" (ibid.: 377), the "vastness and richness of its lexicon" (ibid.) and its "sacred character" (ibid.: 378). Although this attitude towards the language is little more than an imagined construct (I prefer this to the term "myth"), being similar in this respect to the attitudes which speakers of other languages hold about their own languages, Ferguson recognizes its relative uniformity among Arabic-speakers (ibid.: 375): "Although the Arabic speech community is very large numerically, and spread over a vast *expanse* spatially, the myths about the language are relatively uniform throughout the community". It is this uniformity of the attitudes, rather than their empirical truth or falsity, which matters in Arab nationalist discourse and what, ultimately, makes language the most efficacious symbol of group identity to them.

Contrasting this with the role of historical tradition in the nationalist enterprise, Nuseibeh obliquely argues – following Renan – that "oblivion, even historical error [may be essential factors] in the creation of a nation" (ibid.). Nuseibeh (ibid.: 80) is aware that historical traditions are "in themselves a two-edged weapon: they contribute to solidarity by keeping alive memories of common historical antecedents and to dissipation by resuscitating unsavoury historical episodes in which every history abounds". This is why selection, recasting and even invention are important features of nationalist discourse, although the extent to which intellectual acrobatics of this kind need to be practised varies from one nationalist ingredient to another. Nuseibeh's views on this topic in relation to history in nationality-formation are interesting and still as valid today as they were half a century ago; they also provide us with a fitting end to this chapter, taking us back full circle to where we began (ibid.: 79):

> The truth is that historical tradition is a factor contributing to integration provided it is presented in the right way. That is to say, it is not so much a question of creating the present in the image of the past as it is re-creating the past in the image of the present. The pretence of this mental debauchery claiming to be history rather than

> political propaganda becomes less sinful when we take into account the sincerity of those who preach it and the formidable difficulties inherent in preaching historical truth.

In modern times, the debate over the origins of Arab nationalism has tended to focus on its formative impulses. As pointed out in Chapter 2, many Arab writers on the topic consider language as one of the most important impulses in this nationalism, and they trace its operative roots back to the rise and spread of Islam. The importance of the language in this context is acknowledged by Antonius in his classic treatment of this nationalism, *The Arab Awakening* (1938). However, Antonius places the origins of this national awakening in the Western-inspired linguistic and literary renaissance in the Levant in the nineteenth century. But his analysis is challenged by Zeine (1966), who argues that the term "awakening" is a misnomer. He states that the Arabs' sense of collective identity – rooted as it was in the range of themes discussed in this chapter – was in no need of being woken up in the nineteenth century, for it was fully alive in spite of the four centuries of Ottoman rule of the Arabic-speaking peoples. As evidence of how the past can be made to live on, Zeine's position, which I will quote below in full, is an interesting one, not least because it seeks to eliminate the much-quoted phrase "Arab awakening" from the discourse on Arab nationalism (1966: 146):

> If by Arab awakening be meant the awakening of Arab consciousness and Arab identity, i.e. *al-'urūba*, then the term "awakening" is a misnomer. Throughout the four centuries of Ottoman rule, the Muslim Arabs never ceased to think of themselves as Muslims and as Arabs and they, certainly, did not forget their Arabic language.

By holding this view, Zeine builds on that assessment of Arab national identity which seeks to ascribe its genesis culturally to impulses that predate the modern period. An example of this assessment is provided by Albert Hourani (1983: 260):

> That those who speak Arabic form a "nation", and that this nation should be independent and united, are beliefs which only became articulate and acquired political strength during the [twentieth] century. But as far back in history as we can see them, the Arabs have always been exceptionally conscious of their language and proud of it, and in pre-Islamic Arabia they possessed a kind of "racial" feeling, a sense that, beyond the conflicts of tribes and families, there was a unity which joined together all who spoke Arabic and could claim descent from the tribes of Arabia.

4

The Arabic Language Unites Us

Liṣānu al-ḍādi yajmʿunā[1]

1. INTRODUCTION

One of the aims of Chapter 3 was to show that Arabic has many of the ingredients which make it eminently suitable to play the role of one of the primary markers of national identity in the modern period. In dealing with this theme, the resonance of Arabic (see Chapter 1, section 2), reference was made to the position of the language as the focus of a host of cultural conceptualizations which projected it as the source of pride of its speakers and as the evidence of their positive moral character and value system (cf. Saliba 1993). The point was also made that the belief in the systematic nature of the language was taken to provide an indication of the fine qualities of the mental make-up of its speakers (see Chapter 3, section 2). In addition, Arabic was viewed as a major boundary-setter between the Arabs and the non-Arabs in the increasingly expanding empire in the first few centuries of Islam (see Chapter 3, section 5). This inevitably made it the target of attacks by non-Arab members of the Muslim community, who charged that it was mainly through borrowings from other languages that Arabic was able to overcome its Bedouin past and become the language of a cultural heritage which, though Arabic, was not specifically Arab. The fact that many non-Arabs were involved in the analysis and codification of the language was given as an example of the veracity of this view.

It may, however, be suggested that for these latent group-identity impulses to be triggered and to become endowed with overtly nationalist meanings, a specifically modernizing input, whether political or cultural, would have to come into play. It is generally agreed (see Tibi 1997: 80) that the Napoleonic invasion of Egypt in 1798 heralded the onset of this input on both the political and cultural fronts in Egypt itself and, indirectly, beyond Egypt in the Arabic-speaking lands.[2] As a manifestation of an increasingly hegemonic Europe, this invasion foreshadowed the introduction in the Levant of other modes of European cultural penetration in the form of modern printing presses, the development of journalism, the translation of literary and scientific works, and the production of new translations of the Bible into Arabic (cf. Thompson 1956). These developments were sustained by the increasing spread of literacy, political liberalization in the form of the *Tanzimat* administrative reforms in the Ottoman Empire in the nineteenth century (cf. Davison 1963) – although these progressed in fits and starts – and the increased contact with the West in the commercial and political spheres at the sub-state level in the Levant.

There is common agreement among scholars of Arab nationalism that Greater Syria was the main arena in the development and promotion of this Arab nationalist ideology and movement. It is also generally agreed that Arab nationalism first started as a cultural phenomenon (see Chapter 2, section 3) but later developed into a more overtly political movement at the beginning of the twentieth century (cf. Tibi 1997: 61, 66, 116). The transition from the cultural to the political mode of conceptualization and action in this nationalism occurred as a result of the Turkification policies of the Young Turks,[3] following their ascendance to power in the Ottoman Empire in 1908. This view sees the transition from Ottomanism to political Arabism as a reaction to the transition from Ottomanism to political Turkism among the Turkish elements in the Ottoman Empire.

The aim of this chapter is to examine the implications of the above view in relation to the role of the Arabic language in articulating two major issues in Arab nationalism: those of identity and modernization in the second half of the nineteenth century and the first two decades of the twentieth century. To set the scene for this discussion, I will show how the mirroring phenomenon between Arab and Turkish nationalism on the political front at the beginning of the twentieth century also obtained at the linguistic level in the second half of the nineteenth century. One of the aims of this chapter will therefore be to show that Arab cultural nationalism was to some extent a reaction to Turkish cultural nationalism, as was the case between these two nationalisms on the political front. It should not, however, be concluded from this that I take a sequential cause-and-effect view of the relationship between these different forms of nationalism in the Turkish and Arab contexts – with Turkish nationalism in the cultural and political domains giving rise to their counterparts in the Arab sphere – or that the cultural in these two nationalisms is divorced from and always precedes its political counterpart. Such a sequential cause-and-effect view of the phenomena under consideration here would be too simple an explanation for the multi-faceted complexity of nationalism in any context.

2. FROM OTTOMANISM TO TURKISM: THE TURKIFICATION OF THE OTTOMAN TURKS[4]

The transition from Ottomanism, the view that the Turkish elements of the Ottoman Empire were Ottoman first and Turkish second, to Turkism, the view that they were Turkish first and Ottoman second, was a slow process which spanned the nineteenth century, with points of high intensity occurring at various times in the second part of that century. The core of this transition consisted of various attempts to define group identity in ways which constructed the Turks as a nation – in the cultural sense of this term – standing apart from other groups in the Empire, particularly the Arabs. Language was the main instrument in this enterprise in symbolic and functional terms.

This was not a fortuitous choice. First, it is consistent with the general tendency in the nineteenth century to construct nationality on linguistic grounds, following the German model; this was true of ethnic groups in the Balkans under the Ottoman Empire as it was of other groups outside this sphere of political influence in Central Europe. The choice of language for collective self-definition thus reflects the modernity of the age. It further constitutes a symbolic and material step towards reversing the waning fortunes of the Empire in an increasingly combative and acquisitive context of imperialistic power relations in which Europe was in ascendance. Second, the promotion of language over religion as the marker of group identity enables its advocates to construct a new sociopolitical definition of the collective self which decentres co-religionists in the state, the majority of the Arabs, and centres co-native speakers outside it, mainly the Turks in Central Asia. This in turn helps create a concept of national territory which encompasses groups and communities outside the borders of the Ottoman Empire. Third, the facts that Turkish was full of Arabic and Persian words which often maintained their original grammatical categories, and that Turkish poetry followed the rules of Arabic prosody, provided the advocates of the new identity with a highly productive opportunity to practise their purification tendencies in a publicly visible manner. Fourth, in a period not unaccustomed to sudden changes in the political fortunes of high officials, autocracy, external threats, internal turmoil, intrigue and counter-intrigue, and censorship, language in the Ottoman Empire served as a most useful conduit for setting out what are essentially political views of a discernibly schismatic and irredentist character.

It may be said that a major problem facing the advocates of Turkism in its cultural mode was altering the Turks' view of themselves as Turks. In the nineteenth century, the term "Turk" had negative connotations (see Landau 1981, Lewis 1968). Heyd (1950: 76) tells us that this term was used to designate its referent as a "rude [and] uneducated villager", and that this usage was reflected in a number of proverbs which, according to Gökalp, originated in the big urban centres. Evidence of this attitude is further found in some British writings of the period (see Kushner 1977: 20). These negative views of the Turkish collective self are confirmed by Turkish writers during the second part of the nineteenth century. The famous Turkist Shemseddin Sami wrote in his six-volume encyclopaedic dictionary *Kamus-ül-A'lam* (1890–1900) that "some peoples who are of Turkish origin do not accept this name [Turk] and consider it to be an insult" (quoted in Kushner 1977: 21). During the same period, the writer Ahmed Midhat published a series of articles in the newspaper *Iqdam* in which he deplored the self-contempt with which some Turks regarded themselves and other fellow Turks. He believed that this attitude "prevented the emergence of a national consciousness" and a "sense of pride in one's nation" (ibid.: 30). The issue facing the Turkists was therefore one of changing the image of the Turk in his own eyes, particularly in Istanbul and the other big urban centres. In dealing with this issue, the Turkists hit on language as the linchpin of a host of themes to advance their aims.

A formative but mediated input into this process of instilling Turkishness into the Turks – what I have called "the Turkification of the Ottoman Turks" in the title of this section – derived from the work of the Orientalists. Publications on various aspects of Turkish history and culture started to appear in the nineteenth century, and these had an enthusiastic reception among the elite, particularly the Turkists. One such work is by the Frenchman Joseph de Guignes, *Histoire générale des Huns, des Turcs, des Mongoles, et autres Tartares occidentaux* (Paris, 1756–8). Another is by a Polish convert to Islam, Mustafa Celaleddin Pasha, *Les Turcs anciens et modernes*, published in Istanbul in 1869. However, by far the most influential work in this category was Arthur Lumley Davids' *A Grammar of the Turkish Language* (London, 1832), which provided the first systematic treatment of the spoken varieties of Turkish inside and outside the Ottoman Empire, in addition to information about the history and culture of the Turks, all cast in a discourse full of admiration and respect for them. Works by other Orientalists claiming linguistic and ethnic relations between the Turks and other peoples (for example, the Finns, Hungarians and Estonians) who were said to form a Turanian group enjoyed great currency among the Turkists. Kushner summarizes the net effect of these works in the following words (1977: 10): "The scholarly works of Orientalists acquainted Ottoman Turks with their language and ancient history, and with the contemporary Turkic-speaking peoples living outside the boundaries of the Empire in Central Asia, the Volga Region, the Caucasus and Iran."

The Orientalist input into the formation of Turkish identity, indirect though this was, triggered an interest in two types of constructed continuity: (1) a historical continuity with a past linking the Ottoman Turks with their presumed ancestors in pre-Islamic times, and (2) a synchronic cultural-cum-linguistic continuity with other Turkish-speaking peoples outside the borders of the Ottoman Empire. These two constructed continuities in turn generated a concept of national territory, the ancestral homeland, which encompassed areas outside the control of the Ottomans in Central Asia. Linguistic work on the language varieties spoken in this imagined territory, which came from authors inside and outside the Ottoman Empire, became a deliberate act of "nationalist philology" in the cultural sense of this phrase (see Chapter 1). Travellers, traders, immigrants and even dervishes – who used in their devotional prayers a more rustic form of Turkish than the hybrid Ottoman Turkish variety – unwittingly played an indigenizing role in this nationalist philology. Interest in Turkish folk literature in the nineteenth century, under the influence of the German Romantics, provided another domain through which this nationalist philology began to be advanced. This multi-source interest in the language found expression in the Turkish-language press and other forms of printed material published in the second half of the nineteenth century.

The interest in this identity-orientated form of nationalist philology, coupled with the drive towards modernization in the nineteenth century, was responsible for suggestions and practices whose aim was to modernize the language by (1) simplifying it and (2) equipping it with the necessary lexical resources to enable it to cope with the demands of an age of fast-moving technological developments. The introduction of a new educational system and the institution of administrative reforms in the first half of the nineteenth century, aided by the development and popularity of the press, motivated simplifications in style in Ottoman Turkish; they also led to the publication of new grammars, lexica and textbooks. Ordinances and edicts were promulgated in this period to make mandatory the shift from an old, highly formal and ornate style of official communication to a more simple and functional style. Interest in the simplification of the language also covered what was perceived to be the chaotic orthography of Ottoman Turkish owing to the inadequacy of the Arabic script for rendering the phonemic, particularly vowel, distinctions peculiar to that language. This immediately brought to the fore the question of the linguistic hegemony which Arabic exercised over Turkish, a hegemony that is particularly reflected in the lexical domain in the guise of many borrowings which Turkish had incorporated from Arabic. For some Turkists, effective modernization in the form of orthographic simplification and lexical enrichment could be achieved only by turning to the sources of modernity in the West and, for reasons of authenticity and national self-assertion, to the indigenous culture of the Turkish speakers themselves. This double move began to marginalize Arabic and to cast it aside as an Other's language in the two areas that mattered: modernization and identity-formation.

Let us consider how this distancing strategy was brought about, and how it turned into a form of action against which the Arabists in the Ottoman Empire felt impelled to produce a counter-reaction. This distancing strategy manifested itself in an intricate web of causes and effects that ultimately led to the parting of the ways, first culturally and then politically, between the Arabs and the Turks in the Ottoman Empire. This is why the following discussion will not be chronologically organized, since the main interest here is in the general trends that obtained in this period rather than in the onset and dissolution of any particular suggestion, measure or event. In this context, it is important to remind ourselves of one of the points made earlier in this section, namely that debates about language in the Ottoman Empire had as much to do with non-linguistic agendas as they had with linguistic ones, if not actually more at times.

One of the points raised by the Turkists concerned the name of the language, whether it was Ottoman or Turkish. Needless to say, the Turkists championed the latter designation on the grounds that their language is structurally related to other Turkish varieties outside the Ottoman Empire, notwithstanding the fact that it is orthographically and lexically indebted to Arabic and Persian. The Turkists also argued that Ottoman was the name of the state, and that this should not be confused with the name of the language. To give effect to this chain of reasoning, they published textbooks, grammars and dictionaries which referred to the language as Turkish; they also published many articles in the press which traced the connections between Turkish and other Turkic languages or varieties outside the Ottoman Empire, both synchronically and diachronically.

The debate over the name of the language was essentially a debate over identity, in particular which of the three aspects of the identity of the Turks came first: the Ottoman, the Islamic or the Turkish. This debate took as its point of reference the idea that language is the marker of identity par excellence and that, therefore, it is the ultimate boundary-setter between the different socio-political groups in the state. Defending one's language against other languages thus emerged as a defence of one's identity, which increasingly came to be designated in national terms. If Turkish is the marker of Turkish identity, it must therefore serve as the foundation of a Turkish national culture; and if this means purging the language from external influences, even those that are derived from the languages of co-religionists, then so be it. Shemseddin Sami expresses this view in the magazine *Sabah* (8 August 1898, quoted in Kushner 1977: 62):

> The first symbol of a nation and a race, its foundation, and its common property, shared equally by all its members, is the language in which it speaks. People speaking one language constitute one nation and one race. Each people and nation must therefore first of all bring order into its language.

The last sentence in the above quotation is tantamount to declaring that the injection of order into Turkish, which in social-value terms is the non-linguistic equivalent of linguistic systematicity, must include purging it of excess Arabic borrowings at the lexical and grammatical levels. Since the domination of Turkish by Arabic turned the former into a composite or hybrid language which, lexically and grammatically, is neither the one nor the other, then this demands an interventionist policy to restore order to the language. In doing this, the Turkists sometimes marked words in dictionaries as Arabic, Persian or Turkish to signal the foreignness of the former two. In forming new words, they suggested the use of lexical items derived from Arabic and Persian roots, provided that the words concerned were not in active use in these two languages, or have meanings that are different from their meanings in the donor language. And when Necib Asım in 1900 proposed a list of fifteen sources for the lexical expansion of the language, Arabic occurred as number thirteen, just before Persian and European languages.[5] The sentiment exhibited in this rank ordering of possible donor languages or sources for Turkish lexical expansion was expressed by one Turkist journalist and writer, Said Bey, as follows (ibid.: 63; al-Husri ascribes the same view to Diya Pasha in *Muḥāḍarāt fī nushū' al-fikra al-qawmiyya*, 1985: 98): "Let the one who seeks Arabic go to the Arabs, those who seek Persian, to the Persians, and the 'Frenks' to 'Frengistan'; but we are Turks and we need Turkish".

This attitude towards Arabic did not go unchecked. A group of Ottoman Turks, the most notable among them being a famous teacher of Arabic called Haci Ibrahim Efendi, took it upon themselves to challenge the Turkists. Haci Ibrahim pointed out that since the state is Ottoman, not Turkish, the language therefore is Ottoman, not Turkish, thus at a stroke denying the validity of the argument that the name of the state and the language need not be congruent. The Ottomanists also argued that the historical depth of the contact between Turkish and Arabic gives the lexical items borrowed by the former from the latter an authenticity that far exceeds the nebulous connections between the Turkic languages (of Turkey and Central Asia) which are constructed on the basis of a dim and distant past. In addition, Arabic borrowings are borrowings from a rich and beautiful language, being different on this level of sociolinguistic values from the "crude and deficient" (Kushner 1977: 65) lexical items which the Turkists wished to borrow from other Turkic languages. Removal of Arabic words and rules of grammar from the language is therefore bound to reduce the sociolinguistic prestige of Turkish and its functional efficacy as a means of communication: "If we do this we shall have to speak without a language", declares Haci Ibrahim (ibid.).

The Ottomanists further argued that Arabic is the universal language of Islam as well as the tongue of the Arabs, who are a numerically important group in the Ottoman Empire. As Muslims, the Turks needed Arabic for religious and spiritual purposes. Arabic was also important for sociopolitical reasons, since its rejection as a source for Turkish would be seen by the Arabs as a symbolic "slap in the face" and as an attempt to undermine the bonds of Ottomanism that brought the two groups (the Turks and the Arabs) together.

The Turkists responded by insisting on the separation of language and religion. They pointed out that the Bosnians and Albanians maintained their religion (Islam), but without sanctioning the same linguistic input from Arabic into their languages as exists in Turkish, and without insisting on knowledge of Arabic as some of the Turkish Ottomanists did. Haci Ibrahim also argued that knowledge of Arabic cannot be regarded as a "criterion for good faith" (ibid.: 69), since Christian Arabs know and use Arabic but are not Muslims.

Many of the ideas of the Turkists found expression in the works of Ziya Gökalp (1875–1914), the main theoretician of Turkish nationalism, although Gökalp did not espouse some of the extremist positions on lexical purification and orthographic reform advocated by members of this group. Gökalp held the view that language was the marker of national identity, and that, therefore, the "Turkish nation [is] the totality of Turkish-speaking Muslims" (Heyd 1950: 100). Gökalp further believed that the revival of the Turks socially and culturally as a nation was dependent on the revival of their language. In practical terms, this implied an extension in the functional domains allocated to the language to all aspects of the life of the nation, including literature and religious practice. In the latter sphere, Gökalp advocated the replacement of Arabic by Turkish in all aspects of the ritual prayer, except those that demand direct reference to the Qur'an itself, a position which he felt was consistent with the teachings of the Imam Abu Hanifa (150/767), whose legal school was dominant in Turkey. Such an extension was consistent with the nationalist doctrine in its German Romantic mode in terms of which "religious worship should be conducted in the language of the people" (ibid.: 102). Writers must therefore write in simple language. For this to happen, the language must undergo a controlled lexical cull to rid it of some of the foreign words (mainly Arabic and Persian) that have entered it, especially when these demand adjustments to the morphological and syntactic rules of the language. This call for simplification was motivated by a non-linguistic objective which looks at language as the "touchstone of nationality" and which "regards independence in the sphere of language as a necessary condition to political independence" (ibid.: 115).

By the beginning of the twentieth century, the debate between the Ottomanists and the Turkists was effectively won in favour of the latter. Turkish became the subject of national pride, and writers started to extol its virtues as a pleasant, harmonious and precise language with fixed word order and few exceptions. The enhanced status of Turkish during the last quarter of the nineteenth century was reflected in its adoption as the official language of the state in the short-lived 1876 constitution, which additionally stipulated that knowledge of Turkish was a condition for election to Parliament and for employment in government administration. Turkish was also declared an obligatory subject in all schools in the Empire, including all the foreign schools which for a long time enjoyed special privileges granted to them under the Capitulations. The declared intention behind the imposition of these measures may be expressed as follows:

linguistic diversity in the state can lead to sociopolitical fragmentation and uneven development. It is therefore essential to spread knowledge of the official language as a bond of affiliation between all Ottomans and as the medium of communication between the state and its citizens. Knowledge of Turkish was seen as an instrument of identity-formation, political consolidation and modernization. At another level, however, this emphasis reflected fear of political disintegration and the "awareness that the Turks were the only real support of the state" (Kushner 1977: 96). Some Turkists were aware of the need to tread lightly in dealing with Arabic-speakers. Thus, one writer wrote in the magazine *Iqdam* in 1899: "There is no doubt how greatly important it would be in these times ... to attempt at least to teach Turkish to all people of the Ottoman Empire, so that no one but the Arabs would know a language other than Turkish" (ibid.: 95). The Turkification policy which the Young Turks imposed on the Arab provinces on coming to power in 1909 may therefore be viewed as an intensified continuation of a trend whose beginnings had started much earlier in the nineteenth century. Rather than representing a break with the past, the Young Turks articulated some of the dominant Turkist themes in the Hamidian period (1876–1908) to their logical conclusions. It may therefore be possible to say that the overt attempts to Turkify non-Turks in the post-1909 period were not an aberration but the realization of a dominant sociopolitical trend in the Ottoman Empire in the preceding half-century.

Let us now consider the implications of what has been said above for the development of Arab nationalism from its cultural beginnings in the nineteenth century to its transformation to an avowedly political movement in the first two decades of the twentieth century. To begin with, the debate over the status of Turkish in the Empire was part and parcel of a larger debate about non-linguistic matters, which included the status of the Ottoman Turks vis-à-vis other groups in their sociopolitical sphere. As the largest non-Turkish group in the Empire, and as the group whose language was the target of lexical culls in spite of its being the medium of religiosity and spirituality for the Turks, the Arabs were implicated in a debate not of their own making. It can therefore be legitimately assumed that many of the issues raised in this debate heightened the Arabs' perception of their own – first cultural and then political – identity in a reactive and boundary-setting mode of ethnic/national interaction. I believe this must have been the case because of the interethnic elite contact which existed in the various centres in the Empire. In particular, the fact that many Arabic-speaking Ottomans lived in Istanbul and knew Turkish made it possible to (1) monitor the debates which filled the Turkish-medium newspapers at the time, and (2) pass on the content and aims of these debates to their compatriots in the Arabic-speaking provinces (cf. al-ʿUraysi 1981). As Khalidi (1991: 60) points out,

> In pre-1914 Istanbul, at any one time there were normally several thousand Arab government officials, military officers, students, businessmen, journalists, and visitors. Most were drawn from the élite of the Arab provinces ... and they were arguably as influential a group of Arabs as any in the Middle East, albeit lacking the direct contact with the rest of their own society and its local politics, which their counterparts at home retained. An Arabic-language paper [*al-Ḥaḍāra*, Civilization], published in Istanbul by Shaykh 'Abd al-Hamid al-Zahrawi, was influential in all Arabic-speaking regions, with its articles reprinted in the Cairo, Beirut, and Damascus press.

Taking the Turkists' argument first, their insistence on treating the Turkish language as a marker of a specifically Turkish identity had its counterpart in the insistence by Arabists that Arabic delivered the same function in its cultural-cum-political domain. It may even be argued that, because of the religious significance of Arabic for Islam, its long and distinguished history and its penetration of Turkish both lexically and grammatically, Arabic was felt by Ottoman Arabists to be better placed than Turkish to play the role of identity-marker (cf. al-'Uraysi 1981). Furthermore, the Turkists' argument that language comes before religion as a factor in identity-formation may be seen to have played into the hands of those who promoted Arabic as that ingredient which unites all the Arabic-speaking peoples regardless of their religious affiliation. This is exactly the position taken by Christian Arabists, although the position of the Muslim Arabists may not have always been as clear-cut. In addition, the Turkists' view of a national territory that is geographically coextensive with the spread of the language found its counterpart among Arabists, who started to adopt a definition of the national territory that completely or partially overlapped with the limits of the language, with Egypt in particular forming the target of many of these inclusive or exclusive attempts at limiting the national territory (cf. Tauber 1993: 264–7). Finally, the incessant calls by the Turkists to wrest Turkish from the lexical and grammatical clutches of Arabic, and the antagonistic tone of those calls sometimes, must have infused the debate over language policy in the Empire with the emotional charge that is often necessary to trigger the appropriate counter-response, as we shall see later.

It may also be argued that the position of the Turkish Ottomanists contributed to this cumulation of mirror-image effects. By highlighting the special status of Arabic both as a lexical resource for Turkish and as the language of Islam, the Ottomanists underlined its prestige in the eyes of its speakers. Some even argued that, while the Turks had the upper hand over the Arabs in military and administrative terms, the Arabs had commanding cultural and literary superiority (cf. al-Husri's *Muḥāḍarāt fī nushū' al-fikra al-qawmiyya*, 1985b: 111). As Zeine (1966: 10–11) points out, the "Arabs were proud that the Arabic language – their most cherished and precious heritage, after Islam – remained the spiritual language of the Turks". Furthermore, by pointing out that the anti-Arab(ic) feeling peddled by the Turkists was bound to drive a sociopolitical wedge between the Arabs and the Turks,[6] the Ottomanists highlighted what the Arabists may have privately thought. Seen as concessions by the Ottomanists, the above arguments may have functioned on the Arabist side not as attempts at reconciliation only, but also as an admission of differentiation. If this is the case, their role must be seen as delaying, but not stopping, the inevitable on the national front. The Turkification policies of the Young Turks provided the final spur.

3. FROM OTTOMANISM TO ARABISM: PRELIMINARY REMARKS

The debate over the Turkish language culminated in the Turkification policy of the Young Turks after their effective takeover of power in 1909, following their Revolution in July 1908. Although the application of this policy was wide-ranging, in this work I am only interested in the language-planning implications of this policy for the shift from covert to overt political nationalism in the Arabic-speaking provinces of the Empire. This policy aimed at the maintenance of the Empire by making power the preserve of the new Turkish elite and by countering all secessionist tendencies among non-Turks, particularly the Arabs. But instead of producing the intended result, this policy succeeded in alienating the Arabs (who originally enthusiastically welcomed the Young Turk Revolution)[7] and in providing the spur which transformed the hitherto largely cultural nature of their nationalist movement into an increasingly overtly political one. The success of this transformation derived from the existence in the nineteenth century in (Greater) Syria of facilitating conditions – what Deutsch (1966: 96) has called rudimentary "complementary facilities of communication"– brought about by the spread of education and the emergence of a literary renaissance (*nahḍa*) rooted in the indigenous past. Coupled with these two factors, the rise of journalism, the improvement in postal services and other means of communication, the expansion in the number of printing presses and the betterment in the quality of their output all conspired to create a print culture in Syria which sought to harness the modernizing impulse in the emerging national milieu to its authenticating roots.

According to George Antonius (1938) – and in this he is not alone – the seeds of the Arab nationalist idea were first politically cultivated, though with no immediate yield, by Ibrahim Pasha (son of Muhammad Ali, governor of Egypt) during his occupation of Syria between 1832 and 1840.[8] In pursuing his political and dynastic ambitions, Muhammad Ali, through his son Ibrahim, tried to make his territorial claims coextensive with the spread of the Arabic language in its Middle Eastern context (excluding North Africa). This *de facto* recognition of the role of language as a boundary-setter in nation-state-building by Muhammad

Ali is implicitly recognized by Palmerston in a letter dated 21 March 1833, to the British Minister at Naples, in which he wrote: "[Muhammad Ali's] real design is to establish an Arabian kingdom including *all the countries in which Arabic is the language*" (quoted in Antonius 1938: 31, emphasis added). More or less the same point was made a year earlier by the British Consul at Alexandria who, in January 1832, reported that "[Muhammad Ali's] immediate object is to establish his authority firmly in the Pashaliks of Acre and Damascus; after which to extend his dominion to Aleppo and Baghdad, throughout the provinces, *where Arabic is the language of the people*, which he calls the Arabian part of the Empire" (ibid.: 25, emphasis added). It is therefore not surprising that Ibrahim Pasha, who unlike his father spoke Arabic, once said about himself: "I am not a Turk. I came to Egypt when I was a child, and since that time, the sun of Egypt changed my blood and made it all Arab" (quoted in Hourani 1983: 261). Although one needs to be careful not to interpret such statements as a recognition of the existence of the Arab nationalist idea in Syria in the first half of the nineteenth century, or of the seriousness in identity terms of Ibrahim Pasha's self-declared Arabness, the fact still remains that these statements constitute a recognition of the latent power of the language in promoting the idea of Arabness and the political benefits that may accrue from harnessing its power for real tasks. Ibrahim Pasha's attempt to appeal to the Arabs' Arabness failed because, among other things, it was an idea that came ahead of its time in a region where other forms of group identity were dominant. However, the anticipatory force of this attempt as a projection of things to come cannot be ignored, especially when coupled with the increasing flow at the time in Egyptian printed materials coming into Syria[9] and the support given to education in this province by Ibrahim Pasha, limited though this was.[10]

Recognizing the importance of print culture and education long before these ideas were given currency in the study of nationalism by Benedict Anderson in his classic study *Imagined Communities* (first published in 1983), George Antonius (1938: 40) wrote: "Without school or book, the making of a nation is in modern times inconceivable" (see Cleveland 1997 for a discussion of this point). In the context of Arab nationalism, the expansion of the educational system in Syria in the second half of the nineteenth century – whether through the implementation of the provisions of the education law of 1869 (cf. Tibawi 1969: 168), the increase in and the revitalization of community schools along religious lines or the introduction of missionary schools[11] – led to a linguistic and literary revival which created its own momentum. The use of Arabic as the medium of instruction in parts of this system gave the language an added boost. Dictionaries and encyclopaedias,[12] classical Arabic literary texts, textbooks for schools and translations of foreign works started to appear in editions whose quality (especially those produced by the Jesuit Press) and affordability appealed to an expanding and more discerning reading public. Two new translations of the Bible into Arabic appeared – an American-sponsored Protestant translation and a French-sponsored Jesuit translation – each with its own distinctive style, but both aiming at casting the source text in a form of Arabic that was both accessible and dignified to suit its status as a Sacred Book (see Chapter 6, section 4.2 for Taha Husayn's suggestion in relation to the Arabic version of the Bible used by the Coptic Church in Egypt). Aided by the popularity of journalism, a new Arabic style started to develop which, while rooted in the sources of its own grammatical tradition, aimed at lexical simplicity and reduced stylistic ornateness. This new feature of the language was seen as part of the modernizing impulse of an educated elite who, after the 1860 civil strife in Lebanon, sought to stress the common interests between Christians and Muslims by promoting the bonds between them created by, among other things, that very same language.

Special mention must be made here of the adoption of Arabic as the medium of instruction for all subjects in the American missionary schools in Lebanon, the success of which led to the introduction of Arabic in the French mission schools whose pupils were mostly drawn from the Maronite community (see Tibi 1997: 100).[13] In particular, reference must be made to the Syrian Protestant College – now the American University of Beirut – which used Arabic in this capacity from its inception in 1866 until 1882, when it began to be replaced by English.[14] The use of Arabic in this college was promoted not for any nationalist reasons *per se* by its American masters, but for reasons that are germane to the Protestant philosophy of encouraging the use of the vernacular in all aspects of the missionary enterprise,[15] and – only indirectly – for the effect which any nascent nationalist consciousness may have had on promoting the work of the mission, particularly among Muslims whose bonds of common faith with Ottoman Turks had to be modulated and redirected.[16] It is no accident, therefore, that one of the big debates – initiated by the weekly *al-Nashra al-usbūʿiyya* in 1881 – about whether to use Arabic or a foreign language as the medium of instruction more or less coincided with the shift from Arabic to English in the educational process at the Protestant College. It is also no accident that one of the reasons given in this debate for the use of Arabic as a medium of education related to the need to train individuals who could serve the missionary cause. In an interesting article in this debate, the Lebanese ʿAbdallah Jabbur (1991: 18–19) put forward the view that training the native missionaries and others in Arabic was necessary to enhance their ability to "bring the good news/good tidings" to "all the Arabs", since if the Bible was not delivered to them they would remain ignorant and bereft of "civilization proper". It is interesting to note here that a secularist form of this argument is present in most articulations of Lebanese nationalism in the twentieth century (see Chapter 6, sections 5.1–2). Jabbur further stressed that the adoption of foreign languages as the medium of instruction in schools would lead to fragmentation in the body of a nation whose group identity was premised on the unity of its language.

The fact that Arabic was used as the language of instruction for the modern sciences, including medicine, in the Protestant College meant that American missionaries had to learn the language and to use it in teaching and in the production of textbooks, whether newly written or in translated form.[17] This expansion in the functional domains of the language was significant in two important ways. First, it led to a lexical revitalization of the language, although it also raised questions about its efficacy in pedagogic terms. Second, the use of the language in teaching the modern sciences by Western teachers bestowed on it a stamp of modernity by a constituency which, for Ottoman subjects, emblematically represented the sources of that modernity in its original environment. It is therefore not surprising that the above period was dubbed the "golden age" in the history of the language in institutional terms (see Dumat 1991: 97–103). It is also not surprising that the change from Arabic to English as the language of instruction was the subject of criticism in the press at the time, and may actually have been partly responsible – although I cannot prove this point – for the publicized delay in the implementation of this policy in the teaching of medicine in 1881 (see Khuri 1991: 28). Opposition to this change was not restricted to native Arabic-speakers only, but extended to some American faculty members at the College, leading to the resignation of Cornelius van Dyck (1818–95) when his compatriot George Post (1838–1908) won the battle for the change.[18] The following quotation from Tibi (1997: 101) provides a balanced assessment of the contribution of the American mission schools, intended or not:

> The American missionaries only modernized Arabic to have a more suitable means at hand for their religious activities. It was an entirely unintended consequence of their work that the revival of the national language inaugurated a literary renaissance, but this naturally suited the missions in that the movement gradually undermined the loyalty of the Arabs towards the Ottoman Empire.

3.1 The Placards

Considering the increasing awareness of the role of language as a marker of group identity and as the medium which can replace religious affiliation as the common bond par excellence between Muslims and Christians in Syria, and considering the literary revival which this interest spawned in the second half of the nineteenth century, it is not surprising that the adoption of Arabic as an official language in the Ottoman Empire was one of the main demands pursued by the elite at the time, long before the active promotion of Turkification by the Young Turks in 1909 and after. The best and, in a sense, the most dramatic expression of this demand occurred in the third of a series of placards which clandestinely appeared in Damascus, Beirut, Tripoli and Sidon in the second half of 1880 and the first half of 1881 (see Zeine 1966: 171–3 for the texts of three of these placards).[19] In a clear reference to the attacks on Arabic by the Turkists, and in rousing language full of references to past Arab glories, the third placard (dated 14 January 1881) considers the plight of Arabic under the Turks to be second only to their attacks on the *sharī'a* (sacred law); the opening part of this placard reads as follows (for a full translation of the placard, see Tibawi 1969: 165):

> O people of the fatherland! You are aware of the injustice and oppression of the Turks. With a small number of themselves they have ruled over you and enslaved you. They have abolished your sacred law (*sharī'a*) and despised the sanctity of your revered books ... They have passed regulations to destroy your noble language.

The authors of the placard went on to urge the Arabs to correct these injustices by the sword, referring to their Turkish oppressors as *'ulūj al-turk*, which Tibawi translates as "uncouth Turks" (ibid.). This translation fails to capture the additional ideas in the word *'ulūj* of the "bully", the "unbeliever" and the "person who does not speak Arabic or speaks it but with a foreign accent". What is interesting for us here is the last of these meanings, because it allows us to associate the word *'ulūj* with the foreignness of a person as displayed in his or her speech. This meaning of the word *'ulūj* (singular of *'ilj*) signals strong collocational associations with the word *'ajam* (see Chapter 3, section 5).[20] A well-known example of this in the literature is the reference to Ziyad al-A'jam (d. 718/19), court poet to the Khurasani leader al-Muhallab Ibn Abi Sufra (82/701), as *'ilj a'jam* by virtue of his non-Arab (Persian) extraction and his heavy Persian accent (see Fück 1980: 42–3). Another example occurs in the report about the refusal of the Christian Arab tribe of Banu Taghlib to pay the poll-tax (see Chapter 3, section 5).

This placard is also important because it lists the recognition of Arabic as an official language in Syria as the second – after autonomy – of the three demands which its authors call on the Turks to grant the Arabs, or (and this is another interpretation of the placard) for the Arabs to wrest from the Turks by the use of force: "Secondly, recognition of the Arabic language as official in the country [Syria] and of the right of those who speak it to complete freedom in publishing their thoughts, books and newspapers, in accordance with the demands of humanity, progress and civilisation" (see Tibawi 1969: 165–6). The wording of this demand is extremely interesting. On the one hand, it links denying the language an official status to the imposition of censorship, and the reversing of the former to the lifting of the latter, as though to signal that it is only through the native tongue that a person can achieve true and meaningful freedom of thought. On the other hand, the wording suggests that a person's status as a full human being, as well as the attainment of progress and modernization in a society, are dependent on recognizing the linguistic and freedom-of-expression rights of a group. As such, this demand shows a level of sophistication in framing the philosophico-linguistic roots of Arab nationalism that has hitherto gone unrecognized in the literature. The fact that such a level is achieved in the case under consideration here is all the more remarkable because of the textual demands of brevity and directness required in the placard as a linguistic genre.

Two linguistic features of the placards are worthy of comment. First, the style of these placards was varied to put the authorities off the scent of their authors. Grammatical errors were also deliberately committed for the same reason (see Tauber 1993: 16). Second, in reporting on these placards to the British chargé d'affaires in Istanbul, the Acting Consul-General John Dickson in Beirut wrote (see Zeine 1966: 64): "The language ... in which some of these placards are couched would show that they are the composition of educated persons. Competent judges of Arabic declare the style to be of the purest kind, such as only those acquainted with the Koran and Arab poetry would use ...". The reference to poetry is significant because of the utilization of six lines from Ibrahim al-Yaziji's famous ode (see section 4 below) as a closing coda in the third placard, notwithstanding the fact that Dickson's report, despatched on 3 July 1880, predates this placard. The identification of a Qur'anic influence in the placards is even more significant because it seems to have led the British and French consuls in Beirut to conclude that the placards were the work of Muslims, not Christians (Tibawi 1969: 167). We now know of course that this is wrong, because one of the placards was written by Faris Nimr (c. 1854–1951),[21] a Christian from Lebanon. What is particularly significant, however, is the "sectarian views" on language-production held by the two consuls. The implicit assumption by the two consuls that the Qur'anic flavour of the style of the placards indicates Muslim authorship is contradicted by the adoption of the same style by Christian Arabs (see section 4).

Students of Arab nationalism treat the placards as one of the first overtly political expressions in the history of the movement, although these placards had little popular support at the time. In addition to autonomy and the recognition of Arabic as an official language in Syria, the placards demanded that Arab soldiers serve in their local areas in the Arabic-speaking provinces, preferably under Arab officers. These demands remained at the very heart of the Arabs' conditions for a political settlement with the Turks in the Ottoman Empire. They were adopted by the many secret and public organizations – cultural and political – which sprang up in various parts of the Empire to defend the Arabs' rights to full equality with the Turks, especially after the rise of the Young Turks to power in 1909 and their vigorous imposition of the policy of Turkification in the Arabic-speaking provinces. What concerns us below is the language issue in the programmes of the Arab organizations; but this will be preceded by a short outline of the Turkification policies of the Young Turks as they relate to language (see also the discussion in section 2 above).

3.2 Resisting Linguistic Turkification

Extreme elements among the Young Turks sought to save the Empire by assimilating non-Turkish groups – using coercion if necessary – into Turkish culture and language, hence the term "Turkification". Being the largest and one of the most politically suspect groups, the Arabs were the primary target of this policy. Turkish was imposed as the language of instruction in all state schools. Turkish teachers were appointed to teach Arabic grammar through Turkish, a practice to which the Arab teachers had to conform. One of the pupils at the lower secondary school in Damascus at the turn of the twentieth century reported how his Turkish teachers spoke Arabic with a Turkish accent, and how the Turkish teachers were unable to distinguish between the masculine and the feminine in their teaching (see al-Afghani 1971: 23). At the secondary school in Damascus (*Maktab 'Anbar*), a famous Arabic-language scholar and man of letters – Shaykh Tahir al-Jaza'iri (1852–1920)[22] – was replaced by a Turkish teacher (ibid.: 24).[23] The Arabic grammar curriculum was the same as that taught in the Turkish-speaking schools in the Turkish part of the Empire. This meant that Arabic was taught to Arab pupils not as a native language, but as a foreign one. This was particularly the case in the state schools which were predominantly attended by pupils of Muslim background; non-Muslim pupils fared better because they attended their denominational schools which, under Ottoman law, enjoyed a measure of freedom in educational policy denied to state schools. The use of Arabic was outlawed both inside and outside the classrooms at all times. A pupil caught using the language was publicly shamed and subjected to corporal punishment. Arabic was also outlawed in the courts and in all correspondence with the government administration. All members of Parliament had to be proficient in Turkish. Inflammatory articles appeared in the Turkish-medium press attacking the Arabs and their language, and threatening them with enforced linguistic Turkification. The editor of the Turkish newspaper *Ṭanīn* wrote (see Tauber 1997: 56–7): "The Arabs do not stop prattling in their language and they are total ignoramuses in Turkish, as if they were not under Turkish rule. The government is obligated in such a case to force them to forget their language and to learn the language of the nation that is ruling them." Another Turkish writer declared (ibid.: 57): "The government is obligated to force the Syrians to leave their homes and to turn the Arab countries, especially the Yemen and the Hijaz, into Turkish settlements in order to spread the Turkish language, which must become the language of religion".

This attitude towards Arabic and the Arabs is further reflected in an article written in *Ṭanīn* by one of the (government) hand-picked Turkish members of Parliament representing Baghdad, in which he expressed his surprise that none of the (Arab) native inhabitants of Diwaniyya (outside Baghdad) could talk to him in Turkish. An Arab newspaper took him to task over this, saying that what was more strange was that the member of Parliament could not speak the language of the people he represented (see al-Afghani 1971: 32). Arab students in Istanbul had to endure racial taunts by their Turkish teachers. One of the Turkish officers at the military academy in Istanbul is reported to have said to an Arab cadet in his class: "Be certain that Turkish is better for us than Islam and that racial zealotry is one of the best things in society" (see Tauber 1993: 58). These and similar attacks on the Arabic language represented an intensification of the views (see section 2 above) that were in circulation during the Hamidian period (1876–1909). They further reflected the derision with which the Arabs were regarded by some Turkists, as the following terms of abuse or "ethnic slurs" (see Allen 1983, Muhawi 1996 for this notion) in their discourse testify: "scrounging Arabs" (to refer to the Arabs of Hijaz), "filthy Arab", "dumb Arab" (to refer to a stupid person), "an Arab wog" (to refer to a black animal, especially a dog, or to a slave), and "getting the hell out of Damascus" (to refer to a place whose people one cannot stand).[24] Resisting these views and discursive practices was one of the imperatives of the Arab national movement.

One mode of resisting Turkification was overtly political in nature, in the sense that it was embodied in the programmes of the many societies – secret and not so secret – and cultural and literary clubs which the Arabs established inside and outside the Ottoman Empire in the three or so decades before the outbreak of the First World War (see Mahafza 1980 and Ra'uf 1986). Broadly speaking, this mode of action consisted in calling for making Arabic, alongside Turkish, an official language of the state in the Arabic-speaking countries. This demand is articulated in the programme of the Decentralization Party (established in 1912/13). Article 14 of this programme states: "Every province will have two official languages, Turkish and the local language" (Tauber 1993: 124). Article 15 continues: "Education in each province will be provided in the language of its residents" (ibid.). Article 14 in the programme of the Reform Society of Beirut states: "The Arabic language will be recognized as an official language within the province [Syria]. It will be recognized as an official language, in conjunction with the Turkish language, in the Parliament and the Senate [Upper House]" (ibid.: 139). The Reform Society of Basra advocated the implementation of similar policies. Article 19 in the constitution of this society states: "The local Arabic shall be the official language in all affairs of the [province of Basra] and among its inhabitants. The same shall apply to every courthouse, and all announcements shall be written in Arabic" (ibid.: 167). Article 24 states: "Officers knowing Arabic shall be employed in their own country …", and

Article 25 states that "All sciences and arts shall be taught in our schools in Arabic ..." (ibid.). The status of Arabic as an official language was also the subject of one of the resolutions of the 1913 Paris Congress,[25] in which Arab elites met to press their demands on the Young Turks government in Istanbul. Paragraph 5 in the resolutions of this congress states: "The Arabic language must be recognized in the Ottoman Parliament and the Parliament must decide that it will be an official language in the Arab [provinces]" (ibid.: 193), although this formulation later underwent a subtle change in the form in which it was transmitted to the European powers: "The Arabic language must be recognized in the Ottoman Parliament and considered official in the Syrian and Arab countries" (ibid.: 194). In the same year, the Decentralization Party issued a four-point manifesto outlining its demands. Points 2 and 4 in this manifesto deal with the language issue. The former reads as follows (ibid.: 206): "Freedom in educational issues. Most important is that all education should be in the Arabic language and that its administration should be the responsibility of the local councils." The latter states: "The Arabic language will be recognized as official in all the Arab [provinces], and the government activities in these provinces will be conducted in Arabic. No official will be employed in the Arab provinces unless he is one of their residents and can speak Arabic well ..." (ibid.: 206). The Young Turks understood the non-linguistic ends behind these linguistic demands, and they sought to frustrate their implementation. Thus, in a meeting of some of the Young Turk leaders in January 1914, it was decided to "implement the policy of Turkification of all non-Turkish races in the country by eliminating the nationalist societies that were founded in it ..." (ibid.: 225).

This measure was judged to be necessary to stave off the increasingly assertive proclamations put out by some of the Arab societies. In one such proclamation (1913),[26] the Arab Revolutionary Society (*al-Jamʿiyya al-Thawriyya al-ʿArabiyya*) – an offshoot of the *Qaḥṭāniyya* society founded in 1909 – called for "complete Arab independence" from the Ottoman Empire (for the full text of the proclamation, see Zeine 1966: 176–7), instead of the decentralization solution which the majority of the Arab societies were calling for at the time. The proclamation attacks the Turks and praises the Arabs in language that is both evocative and rousing, thus emphasizing the instrumental role of language in task-orientated terms in the nationalist enterprise. It lists many of the grievances of the Arabs and calls on them to get rid of the Turks, whom it describes as *ʿulūj* with all the connotations that accrue from such a term (see section 3.1 above).[27] What is important about this proclamation from our perspective, however, is the view of the Arabic language it presents and the direct manner in which it responds to the Turkification policy in its linguistic domain.

First, the proclamation refers to the Arabic language as one of the ingredients – in addition to common territory and interests – which make the Arabs a nation in their own right. In pursuing this theme, the proclamation treats Muslims, Christians and Jews as a unity, declaring that "religion belongs to God alone". It further reminds members of these faith communities that at least they can communicate with each other in a language that is their own, but they cannot do so with the Turks. Second, the proclamation treats the enmity of the Turks to Arabic – the language of God's *Arabic* Qur'an and that of God's true *Arab* Prophet – as a nullification of the bond of faith between the Arabs and the Turks. Referring to the suggestions made by the Turkists to use Turkish in the call to prayer and in performing the ritual prayers (see section 2 above), the proclamation treats this as an attempt to undermine the position of Arabic as the primary language of Islam. The proclamation then declares that Turkish is unfit to act in this capacity: it is a fabricated, counterfeit or hybrid language, and the best parts of it are actually stolen from the sacred Arabic tongue and the sweet Persian tongue. Third, the proclamation makes clear that the Arabs cannot progress without independence and without using their language in education, business and all legal provisions.

The second mode of resisting Turkification was through the active promotion of Arabic culture and the Arabic language. One of the best representatives of this trend was the Arab Revival Society (established in Istanbul in 1907), which later had to change its name to the Syrian Revival Society to comply with government orders to remove the word "Arab" from its title after the imposition of Turkification. The aim of this society, which had a branch in Damascus, was to spread Arabic culture. It did so by organizing meetings at which members studied the Arabic language, Arabic literature and history. On Thursday nights, we are told (see al-Afghani 1971: 37), members of the society would meet to read and discuss a poem from Abu Tammam's famous classical collection *Dīwān al-Ḥamāsa*. Discussions were conducted in standard Arabic, no matter how difficult this was for some members. In their enthusiasm for standard Arabic, members agreed to remove all Turkish borrowings from it in response, it would seem, to the attempts by the Turkists to purge Turkish of Arabic words.[28] Members also agreed to use this high form of Arabic at Istanbul cafes, and to replace the Persian numerals traditionally used in backgammon by their Arabic equivalents, although this does not seem to have had a long-lasting communicative effect (witness the currency of the Persian numerals these days). Thus, instead of using *shesh-pesh*, for example, they would use *arbaʿa-khamsa* (four-five). Some members went so far as to refuse to offer beggars any charity until they had asked for it in standard Arabic, the formulae for which members of the society would teach them (cf. Chapter 3, section 4 for a similar practice by the Umayyad caliph ʿUmar Ibn ʿAbd al-ʿAziz).

This enthusiasm for standard Arabic was also exhibited in the establishment of the little-known Society of Eloquence (*Jamʿiyyat al-Ifṣāḥ*) in Beirut, whose main aim was to encourage the use of the standard language. Some Arabists went even further. Al-Afghani (ibid.: 166) tells us of an attempt by the Lebanese Amin Nasir al-Din in 1901 to cast all the news in his newspaper in poetry. One issue contains three short poems describing a snowstorm in Jizzin (in Lebanon) and the destruction it caused, a visit of a foreign frigate to Beirut and a meeting of the Austrian Parliament in Vienna in which the Speaker delivered an obituary of Queen Victoria that drew the ire of the opposition, who, in return, expressed their support for the Boer against the English.

A third mode of resisting Turkification before and after the rise of the Young Turks was the resort to poetry to rebut the attacks mounted by the Turkists against the Arabs and Arabic. An example of this is a poem by the blind Palestinian poet, Sulayman al-Taji al-Faruqi, which he addressed to Sultan Muhammad Rashad, successor of Abdul Hamid after the 1909 Young Turk revolution; in it, he reminds the Sultan of the Arabs' past glories and their innately excellent character, before he tells him that the neglect of Arabic and the ban on using it in the schools had led to its decline (ibid.: 44). Amin Nasir al-Din considers the attacks of the Turkists against the Arabs in whose language the Qur'an was revealed as no more than an expression of inferiority on the part of the Turks (ibid.: 49). Another poet, Fu'ad al-Khatib (ibid.), attacks the Turks for maligning the language of the Qur'an, and he rejects their claims that the Arabs' attempts to modernize their culture through their language are a form of dissension or civil strife in the Empire. The Lebanese poet ʿAbd al-Hamid al-Rafiʿi (ibid.: 45) describes the Turks as a bunch of hypocrites who feign love of Islam, treating their attacks against Arabic as the best evidence of this hypocrisy.

3.3 The Intellectuals Speak

Let us now consider the contribution of some members of the intellectual elite whose ideas on language are important for an understanding of the sociopolitical situation in the Ottoman Empire between 1876, the beginning of Abdul Hamid's reign, and the end of the First World War. Lest the reader think that the language issue was always cast in a nationalist framework, I will begin by considering the contribution of two Islamist reformers, Jamal al-Din al-Afghani (1839–97) and ʿAbd al-Rahman al-Kawakibi (1854–1902). Both of them believe that the Muslims constitute one nation. However, al-Kawakibi differs from al-Afghani in assigning political primacy in this nation to the Arabs by virtue of their close association with Islam, including the fact that Arabic is the language of the Qur'an. Of the twenty-six points he lists to outline the "excellent qualities of the Arabs", three relate to their language (see Haim 1962: 79–80; the second number indicates the original number in the list as given by Haim): (1/19) "Their [the Arabs'] language, of all the languages of the Muslims, takes greatest care of knowledge; it is preserved from extinction by the noble Qur'an";

(2/20) "The language of the Arabs is the language common to all the Muslims, who number 300 million souls"; and (3/21) "The language of the Arabs is the native language of 100 million people, Muslim and non-Muslim". It is interesting to note here that the last point shows an awareness on al-Kawakibi's part of the role of language in creating non-religious bonds of identity, although the main thrust of his argument remains religious in character. As Zeine (1966: 70–1) rightly says, al-Kawakibi's "bitter attacks against the Turks do not make him an Arab nationalist".

Likewise, al-Afghani's recognition of the role of language in creating group bonds which are perhaps as strong as, if not actually stronger and more lasting than, those created by adherence to the same faith does not make him a nationalist thinker in the traditional sense:

> There are two kinds of bond between people: the bond of language and the bond of faith. The bond of language is the basis of nationality (*jinsiyya*). Language is more stable and more permanent than faith [in this regard]. Witness the fact that some nations had changed their religion twice or even three times during a thousand years without this affecting their linguistic or national unity. We can therefore conclude that the bonds of language are more lasting than the bonds of faith in human life. (quoted in al-Bazzaz 1993: 543)

Nor does the fact that al-Afghani advised Sultan Abdul Hamid to make Arabic the official language of the Ottoman Empire to strengthen the Islamic character of the state make him an advocate of Arab nationalism. However, this interest in language on the part of al-Kawakibi and al-Afghani serves to show the extent to which non-nationalist elites were aware of the affiliative role of language and of the need to harness its power for political purposes. We may illustrate this point by reference to al-Afghani. Hourani (1983: 118) states that al-Afghani's reasoning in this connection was motivated by the following conviction: "if only the Ottomans had adopted the Arabic language as that of the whole empire, its people would have had two links [religion and language] instead of one, and it would have been united and strong".

The language issue was also dealt with by Muhammad Rashid Rida (1865–1935), an Islamist thinker whose views on the nature of the Islamic revival and the political means of achieving it changed with the changes in the political scene during his adult life. However, it would be true to say that his views on the role of language in identity-formation remained more or less the same throughout his long and active career as the editor of the famous newspaper *al-Manār* (1898–1935). In his excellent study of this period in Rida's life, Muhammad Salih al-Marrakishi (1985: 456–69) identifies four areas in the linguistic debates at the time to which this thinker contributed: (1) the relationship between Arabic and Islam; (2) the Turks and Arabic; (3) the struggle between standard Arabic and the colloquials; and (4) the establishment of a language academy to oversee the protection and modernization of the language. Since only the first two points relate to the scope of this study and fall within the interests of the period under consideration here (1876–1918), I will restrict myself to them only.

Rida established a relationship of mutual dependency between Arabic and Islam. He believed that Islam depended on Arabic and Arabic depended on Islam in an organic and indissoluble manner.[29] This led him to the view later in his career that knowledge of Arabic was a necessary condition for being a full Muslim. In putting forward this view, Rida invoked the authority of the famous jurist Imam Shafiʿi (150/767–204/820), although he exaggerated his views on this topic. So organic was the relationship between Arabic and Islam that Rida considered any attack on the former to be an attack on the latter in a modern form of *shuʿūbiyya*. He therefore attacked the Ottoman Turkists and the Young Turks for seeking to undermine the language. In an article he published in *al-Manār* in 1913, he castigated the Young Turks for failing to spread Arabic as the most important language of the Empire. Arabic, he believed, was more worthy of sponsorship and promotion than Turkish in the Empire for five reasons (ibid.: 461): (1) Arabic is the language of the Qur'an, and the Qur'an is the primary source of Islam, which is the official religion of the Empire; (2) Arabic is the language of the Islamic *sharīʿa*, which is the basis of legality in matters of personal and civil law in the Empire; (3) Arabic is the language of the majority of Ottoman subjects; and, since the majority of the Arabs do not know Turkish, it is incumbent on the Turks to learn Arabic for the efficient running of the state; (4) Arabic is needed by most Ottoman subjects for reasons of faith and the performance of religious duties; and (5) Arabic is the most important source of Turkish, so knowledge of Arabic is necessary for a full knowledge of the Turks' – by implication, derivative – language.

Towards the end of the First World War, Rida's hitherto Arab Ottomanist views started to change in the direction of a more assertive Arab Islamist outlook. Whereas before he had campaigned for an Ottoman state in which the rights of the Arabs were respected, and the position of Arabic was recognized and operationalized in the terms set out above, now he started to advocate a more Arabist position in which, implicitly, the role of the language had to be slightly modified. He outlined his views on this matter in terms in which a relationship of equivalence between Arabism and Islam was established (quoted in Hourani 1983: 301): "I am an Arab Muslim and a Muslim Arab ... My Islam is the same in date as my being Arab ... I say, I am an Arab Muslim, and I am brother in religion to thousands upon thousands of Muslims, Arabs and non-Arabs, and brother in race to thousands upon thousands of Arabs, Muslims and non-Muslims." In this respect, Rida shifts to a position similar to al-Kawakibi's. On the one hand, he considers the Arabs – the majority of whom are Muslims – to be the core component in a revived Islam. On the other hand, he believes that the ties of language and culture create bonds of unity between Muslim and non-Muslim, mainly Christian, Arabs.

A different kind of contribution to the debate about language and identity, in the context of Turkification, was offered by ʿAbd al-Ghani al-ʿUraysi (1891–1916) and Amin Abu Khatir. Both of these writers were Arabist Ottomanists in their declared intentions, although this may not have been more than an attempt on their part to hedge their bets until such a time as the fortune of the Empire was finally decided. ʿAbd al-Ghani al-ʿUraysi's contribution to the burgeoning scholarship on Arab nationalism has been little studied, perhaps because his life was cut short by his Turkish executioners in 1916 in Beirut, along with other suspected leaders of the increasingly politicized Arab national movement. His main contribution to the debate over Arab nationalism was through his articles in the newspaper *al-Mufīd*, which he partly owned and published under the titles *Lisān al-ʿArab* and *Fatā al-ʿArab* whenever the authorities ordered it to be shut down (see Khalidi 1981).[30] The first of these surrogate titles, which may be translated as *The Voice of the Arabs*, is interesting because of the lexical associations it makes with language through the meaning of the word *lisān* as "tongue" (as in speech), and the identity of the name itself with the title of the best-known Arab dictionary, Ibn Manzur's *Lisān al-ʿArab*. It is important to note here that al-ʿUraysi's views on the language issue in the debate over Arab national identity are explicitly framed in the context of resisting the Turkification policies of the Young Turks in all spheres of application. In carrying out this task, al-ʿUraysi (1981) tells the Turks that the Arabs are the lifeline of the Empire and, in a play on words, that *al-Mufīd* is an Arabist newspaper, *fa-l-mufīd ʿarabī*, which semantically doubles up as "what is beneficial for the Empire is Arab/of Arab nature". He also reminds the Turks that their anti-Arab Turkification policies render them Islamic renegades (*al-atrāk al-ẓālimīn al-kafara*, ibid.: 162), supporting his view in this connection – though not in the particular context of this quotation – by quoting eleven of the Prophet's *ḥadīths* (traditions) which equate full belief in Islam with the love of the Arabs (ibid.: 65). It is significant that the last two of these *ḥadīths* deal with the sanctity of Arabic and its special place in Islam (ibid.): "God has not sent a revelation to any of the Prophets except in Arabic", and "He who among you can speak Arabic should not speak Persian".

Perhaps al-ʿUraysi's best-known views on language and national identity occur in his Paris Congress speech (20 June 1913), in which he raised the question of whether the Arabs had the right to form a [national] group (*hal li-l-ʿarab ḥaqq jamāʿa*) (ibid.: 107):

> According to political science, groups do not deserve to have this right unless, following the German model, they have linguistic and racial unity; or, following the Italian model, they have historical unity and unity in customs and traditions; or,

> following the French model, they have a common political will. If we consider the case of the Arabs from all these perspectives, we will find that they [the Arabs] have unity of language, race, history, traditions, customs and political ambitions. It is therefore an inalienable right of the Arabs, supported by the full weight of political science, to form a group, a people (*sha'b*) and a nation (*umma*).

It is interesting that al-'Uraysi does not list religion as one of the ingredients in the formation of a group at any of the above (ill-defined) levels, in spite of the fact that he considers religion as a factor that unites the Arabs and the Turks in Ottoman citizenship (*waṭaniyya*)[31] but not nationality (*jinsiyya*). It is also interesting to note in this connection that al-'Uraysi declares on a few occasions that full citizenship in the Ottoman Empire is meaningless without the recognition of nationality. This explains al-'Uraysi's appeal to all Christian, Jewish and Muslim Arabs to work together in pursuit of their legitimate national rights as first and foremost an Arab group. It is also interesting that al-'Uraysi is fully aware of the important voluntarist element in nationality-formation – what Renan called the "daily plebiscite" in his conception of the nation (see Chapter 2, section 2). It is this awareness which enables us to treat *al-Mufīd* as an instrument for moulding the ingredients of Arab nationalism as the basis of a task-orientated programme of action, wherein the purposeful willing of the nation to come into existence will lead to its concrete existence at some future point. In addition, it is interesting to note that al-'Uraysi treats the unity of language as the most important ingredient in constituting the Arab nation. Considering this, it is incumbent on the Arabs to resist the Turkification policies of the Young Turks.

This resistance may be pursued through a variety of means. Foremost among these is pressing the Ottoman authorities to recognize Arabic as the primary official language, before Turkish, in the Arabic-speaking provinces in the schools, the courts, the army and the public administration. In articles in *al-Mufīd* on this topic, al-'Uraysi demands that this recognition be enshrined in the constitution of the Empire, rather than having it promulgated in ministerial edicts or bye-laws which can be changed at the whim of whoever is in power, at any time (ibid.: 21).

Second, al-'Uraysi calls on the Arabs to force the foreign schools in the Arabic-speaking provinces, particularly the French-sponsored ones, to give Arabic the status it must have as the national language of the people whose children study at these schools (ibid.: 230 and 215–17). Al-'Uraysi argues that since language is the primary means of acculturation in the schools, it is important that Arab children should be taught through their language, rather than the languages of others, if they are to emerge as full members of their community. Recognizing the importance of language as a factor in nation-formation and modernization, al-'Uraysi calls for the promotion of three languages in all schools in Syria, in the following order: Arabic (the national language), Turkish (the official language) and a foreign language which could be either French or English.

Third, al-'Uraysi calls on the Arabs to show loyalty towards their language. He therefore calls on them to shun the use of foreign languages in their personal and public lives, including the pretentious use of French in business cards, a practice so prevalent that even those who do not know French have started to follow it (ibid.: 206). He also launches a bitter attack against the postal services in Beirut which use Turkish and French, but not Arabic, in their public notices and note-headed telegraph papers. In an article in *al-Mufid* (ibid.: 204–6) called *Tafarnus al-'arab (The Francophonization of the Arabs)/Tafarnas al-'arab (The Arabs have become Francophonized)* – thought to have been penned by al-'Uraysi – the use of French is ridiculed, and contrasted with the care and respect which the French and the English bestow on their languages in communicating with others. To drive this point home, al-'Uraysi tells his readers that he witnessed this pride in one's national language on several occasions. On one such occasion (ibid.: 206), an English visitor to Beirut is said to have refused to use French with a Lebanese hotel-owner, insisting that the owner look for an interpreter to mediate between them. But he also tells them, with great pride and enthusiastic approval, how an Arab official refused to talk to his Turkish superior in Turkish outside office hours, insisting that once outside the municipality building where he worked he would use Arabic only.

Fourth, al-'Uraysi calls on the Arabs to shun the use of ornate language and pompous personal titles in their writing, which he regards as an abhorrent importation from the Turks whose wont it is. In an article entitled "Glorification [of the Other] is a Sign of Humbleness and Submissiveness", al-'Uraysi calls on the Arabs to reject the linguistic practices of the Turks, where the elevation of the addressee and self-deprecation on the part of the addresser is the norm between people of different social standing.[32] Al-'Uraysi regards this antiquated practice as a deviation from the more egalitarian norms of expression which the Arabs applied in addressing their caliphs and, even, Prophet Muhammad himself. Lest this be regarded as an idle call on the part of al-'Uraysi, he makes the point that, since the persistence of external appearances can change the essential qualities of an object, the frequent use of pretentious language and pompous titles can change the moral character of those who indulge in it. Hence the title of the article above. It is interesting to note here that the Turkists were aware of this fact and that they sought to simplify the highly formal style in their language in official documents (see section 2).

Let us now turn to Amin Abu Khatir, for whom the Islamic identity of the state was not strongly engaged as a central agent in its political constitution. In an interesting article in the Egyptian magazine *al-Muqtaṭaf* (October 1913), Amin Abu Khatir (1854–1922)[33] offered a very perceptive analysis of the relationship between language and national, as opposed to civic, identity and applied this to the situation in the Ottoman Empire. Abu Khatir takes as his starting point the inadequacy of defining national identity in racial terms. He also regards as inadequate all attempts to define national identity in terms of common interests, a shared past history, shared customs or a common citizenship. Language, argues Abu Khatir, is the criterion of national identity par excellence, so much so that the status of a language in the world may be considered as a shorthand for the status of the nation that speaks it (see Khuri 1991: 139). In a thinly veiled reference to the Turkification policy of the Young Turks, Abu Khatir points out that a self-respecting nation would fight to the bitter end to defend its language against all aggressors who seek to undermine it by outlawing its use in education, in the courts and in dealings with all organs of the state. Abu Khatir expresses this in a metaphoric way, stating that "since it is not possible to convince a person of sound judgment that he should have his head cut off, by the same token it is not possible for any set of laws to convince [metaphorically, force] a nation to abandon its language" (ibid.: 140).

Abu Khatir argues that some politicians consider decentralization as the best solution to the problems facing nationally composite states, of which the Ottoman Empire is one. Under such a solution, the languages of the different nationalities would be recognized as equal partners, and each would have its own sphere of operation based on demographic and geographic factors. Abu Khatir argues that although this solution may work in the short term, it will not do so in the long term. He points out that since the efficient running of state affairs will perforce demand the use of one language, there is no eschewing the fact that one of the languages in such a composite state would emerge as the official language, and that the speakers of that language will inevitably emerge as the favoured nation. Abu Khatir argues that this situation would create a two-tier citizenship: a first-class citizenship for those whose language is chosen or emerges as the official language, and a second-class citizenship for the rest. Compromise over linguistic issues in status-planning terms (see section 4 below) cannot therefore be effected in ways which can achieve equality of prestige and privileges between nations. In this scheme of things, linguistic survival is equivalent to biological survival, with the clear implication that only the fittest in both cases will survive or win. In another thinly veiled reference to the post-Paris Congress discussions about the recognition of Arabic as an official language in the Arabic-speaking provinces in the Ottoman Empire, Abu Khatir urges the Arab representatives who were sent to negotiate with the Young Turks in Istanbul not to compromise over the legitimate and nationally life-sustaining demands of their people. He suggests that it is the Arabs' right, under any system of natural justice, to defend their language against the Turkification policies. He also points out that the Young Turks should heed this and grant the Arabs their linguistic and other rights, on the basis of a principle of equality, if they wish the Empire to survive. Should this not happen, then the Young Turks must be prepared either to use force to Turkify the Arabs, or accept that the Arabs will use force to achieve their independence. That the latter was considered the more likely result, and that such a conclusion could occur soon, was in no doubt in Abu Khatir's mind.

It is clear from what has been said in this and the preceding section that the Ottoman Empire was in a no-win situation similar to that which the Austro-Hungarian Empire faced in the second half of the nineteenth century (see Anderson 1991: 84–5). As with German vis-à-vis Hungarian in the latter sphere, Turkish acquired the double status of a "universal-imperial" and a "particular-national" language in relation to Arabic and other languages in the Ottoman Empire. This presented the authorities with an insoluble dilemma. The more they sided with Turkish and supported it, the greater the resistance of Arabic and other speakers against the language and the Empire. Similarly, the more concessions the authorities made to Arabic and other languages, the greater the dismay and enmity which the Turkish-speakers felt towards these languages and their speakers, and the greater the demands made by the speakers of these languages for further concessions. Against this background, the analysis given by Abu Khatir above seems to characterize well the dilemma facing the Ottoman Empire.

4. IBRAHIM AL-YAZIJI: FROM IMMEDIATE AIMS TO UNDERLYING MOTIVES[34]

The title page of George Antonius' classic study *The Arab Awakening: The History of the Arab National Movement*, published in London in 1938, carries as an epigraph in beautiful Arabic calligraphy the first hemistich of the first line of the ode composed by Ibrahim al-Yaziji (1847–1906): *tanabbahū wa-stafiqū ayyuhā al-ʿarabu* ("Arise, ye Arabs and Awake!").[35] This was not fortuitous. It was meant to signal some of the main themes in Antonius' assessment of the emergence of the Arab nationalist idea in the second half of the nineteenth century. In particular, Antonius intended it to highlight the cultural nature of this nationalism in its initial stages, although he was aware that culture and politics cannot always be separated from each other, even if it was intellectually possible to posit the view that a cultural awakening is a prerequisite of nationalism in its political mode. More specifically, the choice of this hemistich draws attention to the role of literature as a means of communicating the nationalist idea which, Antonius (1938: 60) points out, was "borne slowly towards its destiny on the wings of a renascent literature". It further underlies the linguistic component in this nationalism; for, if Ibrahim al-Yaziji is remembered for anything at the beginning of the third millennium, he is certainly remembered for his call for and contributions to the revival of the Arabic language towards the end of the nineteenth century and the beginning of the twentieth. As William Cleveland says about Antonius, he believed that language was the "most decisive feature of the Arab nation, and his analysis of the twin concepts of language and culture serves as the foundation of his claim that an Arab nation exists" (1997: 69).

Antonius' views on the emergence of Arab nationalism have been subjected to critical inquiry in recent years (see Cleveland 1997, Haim 1953, Hourani 1981, Kirk 1962 and Lukitz 1984). One criticism of his work concerns his views on agency and periodization, in particular his attribution of the formal beginnings of this nationalism to the work of the enlightened elites of the Syrian Scientific Society which was established in Beirut in 1857 and whose membership was drawn from Christians, Druze and Muslims.[36] Another criticism concerns the significance he attached to the work of the missionary schools in the Levant in the nineteenth century (see section 2), and to the role of the Christians of Lebanon in propagating this nationalism. One argument states that "while education has been a potent factor in the awakening of the Arab Near East, the role of *missionary education* in the *national-political* enlightenment of the Arab youth in the second half of the nineteenth century has been greatly exaggerated" (Zeine 1966: 46–7, original emphasis). Another argument states that nationalism "did not exist in the minds of the masses of the people of the Near East at that time" (Zeine 1966: 59–60), and that the Christians of Lebanon were "first and foremost" interested in emancipating "the *Lebanon* [original emphasis] from the Turkish yoke" (ibid.: 60). Some scholars, notably Ernest Dawn (1991), have gone even further. Dawn (ibid.: 11) considers the prevailing ideology of Arab nationalism to be a twentieth-century creation, and that this ideology was a "development from Islamic modernism", although some Christian Arabs participated in it. These are interesting issues to pursue, but their investigation and assessment lies beyond the scope of the present study. Instead, I will concentrate in this section on the ideas put forward by Ibrahim al-Yaziji for the revival of the Arabic language,[37] using them as a test case for showing that Antonius' views on the cultural nature of Arab nationalism in the second half of the nineteenth century and the role of the language as the major ingredient in this nationalism are not wide of the mark. By discussing the work of Ibrahim al-Yaziji below, I also hope to show the extent to which the cultural roots of Arab nationalism had developed during the second half of the nineteenth century, and the contribution made by this important Christian thinker in propagating this nationalism. In addition, this discussion will demonstrate that high style and Qur'anic references are not the preserve of Muslim writers, thus contradicting what the British chargé d'affaires in Istanbul intimated in his commentary on one of the Beirut placards (see section 3.1).

In pursuing this task, I will use as an organizing framework some of the insights of language-planning, which were indirectly applied above. On the one hand, these insights enable us to treat Ibrahim al-Yaziji's work on the revival of the Arabic language as an example of *corpus-planning* which, in his case, applies mainly to lexical elaboration and the simplification of pedagogic grammars as the twin channels of linguistic modernization.[38] His defence of standard Arabic against the dialects may be interpreted as a matter of *status-planning*,[39] but only in the weak sense of this concept owing to the futility in practical policy terms of the calls to replace the standard by a dialect or dialects in the Arab context (see Chapter 6). On the other hand, this framework allows us to relate issues of corpus-planning to the non-linguistic ends they are often intended to serve. As Robert Cooper (1989: 35) reminds us in his excellent study of language-planning in its social context,

> Language planning is typically carried out for the attainment of nonlinguistic ends such as consumer protection, scientific exchange, national integration, political control, economic development, the creation of new élites or the maintenance of old ones, the pacification or cooption of minority groups, and mass mobilization of national or political movements ... *Definitions of language planning as the solution of language problems are not wrong, but they are misleading.* They deflect attention from the underlying motivation of language planning. Inasmuch as language planning is directed ultimately toward the attainment of nonlinguistic ends, it is preferable ... to define language planning not as efforts to solve language problems but rather as efforts to influence language behaviour. (emphasis added)

In corpus-planning terms, most of al-Yaziji's interest in the revival of the Arabic language concerns the imperative of enhancing its communicative potential in a fast-moving world of new ideas and inventions emanating from an increasingly hegemonic West. Al-Yaziji believed that although the Arabic of his day was characterized by lexical deficiency, this deficiency was due not to any lack of lexical resources on the part of the language *per se* but to the state of its speakers who, over centuries of misrule and neglect, had led impoverished lives materially and otherwise. He expresses this diagnosis in a variety of ways, all revolving around the theme that the vitality of a language derives from the vitality of its people. This analysis premises a true revival in the fortunes of the Arabic language on a genuine revival in the state of its people without, however, denying that attempts by the elite to revive the language can be a factor in the general revival of its people. In the latter mode of this revival, language becomes an important instrument of social change. It is this interactive and reiterative nature of the relationship between language and people which underpins al-Yaziji's firm belief in the necessity of his and similar proposals for enriching the lexicon of the Arabic language by exploiting its morphological resources to coin new terms, appropriating disused words to designate new concepts, extending the meanings of some words to encompass related meanings and Arabising/Arabicising foreign words.

In the field of grammar, al-Yaziji's corpus-planning suggestions mainly pertained to the need to produce new streamlined and simplified pedagogic grammars which can help language-users deploy it correctly, whether in speech or in writing. This interest in the communicative functionality of grammars is also evident in his end-of-session address to the 1890 graduates of the Patriarchate School in Beirut. He called on them to tailor their interest in grammar to their communicative needs, lest the excessive preoccupation with the former deflect them from the active use of the language as an instrument of scientific and cultural modernization. Al-Yaziji further devoted his attention to correcting mistakes made by writers in the press media in a series of articles he published in his magazine *al-Ḍiyā'* in 1905 and elsewhere. He justified this activity by pointing to the long reach of the press media as a diffuser of new usages and as the surrogate legitimizer of grammatical errors.

Let us now turn to the non-linguistic ends behind these corpus-planning activities, to what I have called in the title of this section the *underlying motives* that lie behind the immediate or declared aims of language-planning proposals. The two overarching themes here are, first, the role of language as the marker par excellence of the identity of its Arabic-speakers as a nation in their own right, and, second, the importance of placing the efforts to revive the language within a modernization framework in which the promotion of a rational attitude and a scientific outlook in Arab life have pride of place. Interest in these two ingredients in the modernization framework is evident from the attempt in *al-Muqtaṭaf* (a popular Egyptian journal) in 1881 to define some of the operative concepts in the art of rational debate for the benefit of its readers (see Khuri 1991: 27). These included *mujādala* (argument), *mukābara* (refusal to admit one's untenable or erroneous position), *mu'ānada* (argumentation out of ignorance), *mughālaṭa* (sophistry), *munāqaḍa* (contradiction), *mu'āraḍa* (fallacy of asserting the consequent) and *ghaṣb* (rejecting the opponent's premises before they are validated). It is as though by defining these terms the editors of *al-Muqtaṭaf*, Ya'qub Sarruf (1852–1927)[40] and Faris Nimr (c. 1854–1951), were trying to provide some of the standards for producing and assessing the debates their and other newspapers initiated at the time, an example of which is an article in *al-Muqtaṭaf* in 1882 (ibid.: 54–7). The fact that these terms had currency in various branches of the Arabic intellectual tradition bestows the desired authenticity on their modern applicability.

The key point in the first theme (language and identity) is the repeated assertion by al-Yaziji that language and nation are two sides of the same coin. In a series of articles published in *al-Bayān* in 1897–8, al-Yaziji posits an equivalence relation between language and nation (*al-lugha hiya al-umma bi-'aynihā*,

Khuri 1993a: 62). He spells this out by pointing to the role of language as the carrier of a nation's cultural and scientific heritage and as the boundary-setter between itself and other nations (*hiya al-faṣl al-fāriq bayna umma wa-umma*, ibid.). The Arabic language is therefore projected by him as the only effective bond between the members of the nation (*fa-hiya 'illat al-ḍamm al-ḥaqīqiyya*, ibid.), a bond whose integrative power far exceeds that of the disintegrative influences of race, religion and customs, as well as transcending the conditions of political, economic and social division which characterize the community of Arabic-speakers (ibid.). This view of the connection between language and nation underlies al-Yaziji's belief – expressed in *al-Ḍiyā'* in a series of articles published between 1899 and 1900 – that the very existence and vitality of a nation depends on the existence and vitality of its language. Al-Yaziji returns to this theme in his discussion in *al-Ḍiyā'* (1901–2) of the relationship between the standard and the dialectal forms of Arabic, where he declares that the former is the *sine qua non* of the Arab nation (*fa-lā baqā' li-umma bi-dūn lughatihā*, ibid.: 232).

Al-Yaziji's view of the role which language plays in defining national identity, exaggerated though this may be in some of its formulations,[41] is consistent with the claims made by Antonius about the relationship between these two constructs in Arab nationalist thinking. It is this identification between nation and language which causes al-Yaziji to decry the use by some Arabic-speakers of foreign greetings terms, such as *bonjour* and *bonsoir*, in place of the rich array of greetings terms in Arabic (see al-'Uraysi's views on this matter in section 3.3 above; see also Chapter 5, section 2 for similar views by al-'Alayli). Al-Yaziji believes that those who use the foreign terms need to be educated in the love of the homeland and in the importance of developing a positive self-image in relation to other nations which, in the full sweep of history, are less culturally endowed than their Arab nation. In a different place in *al-Bayān* (1897–8), al-Yaziji points to the danger posed by foreign schools which, by promoting their own national languages among Arabic-speaking pupils, create bonds of affiliation between these pupils and the nations whose languages they learn at the expense of their native tongue and the bonds of nationhood it generates.[42] This phenomenon was commented on in the same vein by Muhammad Kurd 'Ali, President of the Arab Academy in Damascus and author of *Khiṭaṭ al-Shām* (1926, vol. 4), who wrote (quoted in Tibawi 1969: 178): "We have met [in our travels in Greater Syria] men and women educated at foreign schools who became neither Arabs nor Europeans: they speak at home a language other than their own, and exhibit sentiments other than those of the Syrian, nay, they hate their own tradition and history and their country is black in their eyes".[43]

In setting out these views, al-Yaziji constantly refers to the Arabs as an *umma* (nation), albeit a stateless one. This term occurs in his writings hundreds of times, sometimes correlated with the word *al-lugha* (the language) and at others with the word *lughatunā* (*our* language) as its defining ingredient. Al-Yaziji is aware of the political division of the Arabic-speaking peoples into different entities and spheres of imperial or colonial influence, but this does not stop him from identifying these people as one *umma* in the cultural sense of this term. Evidence for this can be derived from two directions. On the one hand, al-Yaziji believes that the dangers facing Arabic in the lands directly controlled by the Ottomans, as a result of their increasingly Turkifying tendencies, are comparable in national-identity terms to those facing the language in the French-occupied countries of North Africa. There is no doubt that, for al-Yaziji, the countries of North Africa and the Arab Middle East form the constituents of this nation. A reference to this occurs in his reflections on the phenomenon of stress (*nabr*) in Arabic phonology, where he provides evidence for his views on this linguistic phenomenon from the dialects of the Levant, Egypt, North Africa and the Arabian peninsula.

On the other hand, al-Yaziji is of the opinion that Egypt is an important part of the "Arab nation" (*al-umma al-ʿarabiyya*, Khuri 1991: 53) – or just the nation (*al-umma*), as he generally calls it – although in one or two places he designates the people of Egypt as the Egyptian nation. Thus he points out that, of all the Arabic-speaking lands, Egypt is best qualified to lead the language-revival movement in the modern period (ibid.: 62). This explains the various calls he made to the Egyptian elites and the Egyptian government to set up a language academy to lead the effort to revive the language lexically and grammatically and to protect it against the corrupting influences of foreign languages and the colloquials. The fact that al-Yaziji was aware of the many obstacles facing such a project, including the reluctance of the Egyptian elite and official bodies to place Egypt in a sphere of Arab national identity, is significant: it shows the extent to which he believed Egypt to be an integral part of the Arab nation.

This belief was reflected in the comments he made on a language conference held in Cairo towards the end of the nineteenth century to deal with issues of lexical revival facing Arabic at the time as a result of the influx of foreign terminologies. While welcoming this initiative as one which dealt with a "grave matter" facing the nation, al-Yaziji was critical of the conference organizers, who restricted participation in it to the Egyptians only. Al-Yaziji argued that since the issue concerned all Arabic-speakers, not just the Egyptians, participation in the conference should have been made open to all those who were competent to contribute to the debate, regardless of their citizenship. He believed that this would have enhanced the work of the conference, since Egypt on its own did not possess the necessary expertise in foreign languages to be able to discuss issues of language contact and lexical revival single-handedly. Al-Yaziji went even further, deploring the restrictive policy of the organizers as a form of "autocracy" (*istibdād*, ibid.: 59) which undermined the "bonds of unity" (*'urwat al-wi'ām*, ibid.) between the Egyptians and other groups of Arabic native speakers. It was also a policy which went against the grain of Arab history during the golden age of Arabic translation when the Abbasid Caliph al-Ma'mun (218/833) used non-Arabs to transfer into Arabic the lore of other nations. In short, al-Yaziji believed that although the aim of the conference was a legitimate and laudable one, the restriction of participation in it to the Egyptians only went against (1) the spirit of national affiliation generated by the language, (2) the general thrust of Arab culture at that moment in its history when it embodied the very ideals the modern Arab renaissance wished to excavate, revive and recreate, and (3) the principles of cooperation and democratic participation which a rejuvenated Arab nation had to espouse and vigorously promote if it was to advance forward on a sure footing.

Let us now consider the second theme in the non-linguistic ends of al-Yaziji's work on the revival of the Arabic language: the promotion of a rational and scientific outlook in Arab life. Point (2) in the preceding paragraph provides a suitable entry into this topic. It signals that any revival of the language as a central component in the modernization of the Arab nation must be rooted in a proper appreciation of the role of the past as a motivating factor, linguistic guide and source of authenticity. Consideration of the past glories of the language and its speakers is sufficient to fill the modern Arab with pride and to confirm him in the conviction that his language has the necessary resources to partake in the modern Arab renaissance fully and constitutively (cf. Chapter 3, section 1). For this to happen, a determined attempt must be made to excavate Arabic lexica and related works to discover the dormant resources of the language for task-orientated ends in the linguistic and, indirectly, non-linguistic spheres of modernization. Al-Yaziji is nevertheless aware that such an attempt must not degenerate into an "imitation" which slavishly reveres the past without tapping into its empowering potential.

This reference to the past is sometimes used not just to authenticate a modern solution to a perceived problem, but also as a strategy of protecting the language against interferences from foreign proper names. In his discussion of Arabicization, al-Yaziji states that all borrowed materials must either be made to conform to the phonological and morphological patterns of the language, in which case they melt into it and lose much of their foreign identity, or they are deliberately made to signal their foreign origin. The latter strategy, which may be called foreignization or exoticization, is proposed for proper names, although this necessitates the introduction of new symbols in the Arabic script (see Chapter 5, section 2 for al-Bazzaz's opposition to the use of foreign names in public notices). Al-Yaziji justifies this expansion in the script by invoking a similar solution which Ibn Khaldun proposed in his *Muqaddima* to transcribe words borrowed by Arabic from Berber, Turkish and European languages. By making this reference, al-Yaziji legitimizes the present in terms of innovative and authoritative aspects of the past, thus bestowing on his own proposal the seal of innovation in a double move of authenticity and modernization. Re-creation of innovative aspects of the past in the present is considered by al-Yaziji no more than a reinvigoration of the latent capacities of the nation which, when harnessed properly, can lead to its revival as a leading member in the community of modern nations.

A major aspect of modernization for al-Yaziji is the promotion of science, the method and its results, as a regenerative force in the life of the nation. Thus, his writings are full of references to the importance of science for the advancement of civil and political life (see Chapter 6, section 4.1 for a somewhat similar attitude by Salama Musa in the context of Egyptian nationalism). In particular, science is seen by him as a source of power for any nation in promoting its own interests and in resisting the pressure from other nations. Al-Yaziji, however, is mainly interested in science as a mode of reasoning and investigation, as method; and this enables him to treat science as one indivisible element which applies to the humanities and non-humanities alike. He sets out his views on this matter in the first issue of the magazine *al-Ṭabīb* (*The Physician/Doctor*), relaunched in 1884 following the suggestion of its first editor, Dr George Post (see section 3), after a period of withdrawal from circulation. Al-Yaziji takes this opportunity to proclaim an expansion in the readership of the magazine to include merchants and shopkeepers, farmers, pharmacists, doctors, poets and prose-writers, civil servants and those engaged in formal oral delivery (ibid.: 20). There is no doubt that al-Yaziji sought to expand the original readership (physicians/doctors) of the magazine for reasons of commercial viability, but his main motivation was one of promoting an attitudinal, if not actually a behavioural, change in his intended elite readership – and, through them, other members of the nation – in which science as a method rules supreme. This is clear from his editorial policy in *al-Bayan*, launched in Egypt in 1897, where a wide readership was aimed at to ensure that this attitudinal vision reached as wide a section of the national elite as possible.

The point that interests us most in all of this is the place of language in this new vision. By making the Arabic language the topic of many of his essays in his various magazines with their expanded readership, al-Yaziji aims to save it from routinization, from the normal conception of it as a decentred medium of communication to a centred view of it as an object of modernization, and as the medium through which the promotion of science as method is effected. In this scheme of things, language starts to assume a heightened symbolic visibility in addition to its communicative functionality, as was the case in Turkish nationalism, where Gökalp "sought to make the national revival of the Turkish language … a stepping-stone to a similar renaissance in other fields of culture and social life" (Heyd 1950: 110). Thus, if the Arab nation is to emerge as a nation on a par with other modern nations, it must attend to science as method and to its national language as a subject or domain to which this method can be applied, and through which the results of this method can be communicated. To press the claim that Arabic can be the object of scientific study, al-Yaziji stresses in several of his articles the systematic nature of the language and the fact that, in spite of its diachronic mutability and synchronic variability, it is rule-governed. And, to show that this indeed is the case, he sets out his observations on the systematicity of Arabic in the first issue of the relaunched *al-Ṭabīb*, published in 1884, although the title of this magazine may at first suggest that language is one of the least likely candidates as a topic for promulgating the principle of the indivisibility of science as a method. And, since most of al-Yaziji's views on the systematicity of Arabic are no more than reiterations of the Arab grammarians' descriptions of the language, the application of the scientific method here receives the authentication of tradition which, as I have explained earlier, is a defining feature of modernization as conceived by this proponent of modernity.

It may, however, be argued that al-Yaziji chose language as the topic of his discourse on science as method because of his own personal expertise on this subject, and that, consequently, one should not read too much into this choice. While it is undeniable that al-Yaziji was first and foremost a linguist, it is widely acknowledged that he had considerable expertise in astronomy, about which he wrote and which, we assume, he could have chosen as the topic for promulgating his conviction that science as method is the most highly prized possession of any developed nation. The fact that al-Yaziji chose not do so indicates that his selection of language as a test case for promulgating his views on science and nation-building is deliberate, not accidental.

Al-Yaziji's commitment to the scientific method as an important attitudinal ingredient in the modernization of the Arab nation is organically linked with the espousal of a rational attitude which considers the validity of a thesis or point of view before it considers the motives behind it. Here again, al-Yaziji chooses a linguistic controversy to highlight his views on the matter. The controversy in question revolved around the call in Egypt towards the end of the nineteenth century, mainly by British civil servants (see Chapter 6, section 4.1), to (1) use the colloquial in place of the standard as the medium of formal education, and (2) replace the Arabic alphabet by a Roman one. Proponents of these two proposals argued that the adoption of these two measures would enable the Egyptians to deal with the problem of illiteracy and, therefore, modernization in an effective way. Unlike other critics of these proposals, al-Yaziji refused to reject them *a priori* for being motivated by non-linguistic ends rather than purely linguistic ones. Instead, he tried to establish whatever merits they had on linguistic grounds, and then proceeded to refute them. For example, al-Yaziji concedes that the adoption of the colloquial may indeed be conducive to an accelerated promotion of science in Egypt, but he argues that a revived standard form of the language can do the same while, additionally, preserving the Arabs' link with their cultural heritage as a component in the definition of national identity.

The attempt to highlight this rational mode of argumentation is a deliberate one on the part of al-Yaziji. He refers to it in several places in his essays. One such reference occurs in his review in *al-Ṭabīb* (1884) of Dozy's *Supplément aux Dictionnaires arabes*. Before proceeding to criticize this dictionary, al-Yaziji reminds his readers of the great service which Dozy had rendered to all Arabic-speakers by compiling this work, then adds that his own espousal of the scientific attitude imposes on him the obligation of evaluating this work in a balanced but critical manner (Khuri 1993a: 39). This critical attitude as a mode of thinking extends to the Arab cultural products of the past as it does to those of the present, even when in the present they are penned by the author himself or by his father. Thus, some of al-Yaziji's articles in *al-Ḍiyā'* for the years 1905–6 deal with the linguistic errors that he and his father had made in their poetry. Al-Yaziji specifies these errors, outlines their sources, then proceeds to correct them, aiming all the time to show that the adoption of science as method means constant vigilance which, when aided by a rational attitude, leads to accepting legitimate refutation even when the object of this refutation is one's own ideas.

Al-Yaziji regarded imparting the scientific and rational approach as the primary objective of modern education in the Arabic-speaking lands. But he also believed that this approach can be effective only when coupled with an outlook on language which places it at the centre of all intellectual endeavours. To illustrate these themes, I will refer to the end-of-session address to the graduates of the Patriarchate School in Beirut, which al-Yaziji was invited to deliver in July 1890 (see Jeha 1992: 85–105).

The main theme in this address is the importance of espousing the scientific approach as a mode of inquiry and as a form of scholarly behaviour. As a mode of inquiry, the scientific approach characterizes learning as a lifelong activity with commitment to accepted standards of proof and counter-argumentation, as well as to standards of enunciation in which obfuscation and doubtful evidence are rejected. As a mode of scholarly behaviour, the scientific approach imposes on its practitioners the need to avoid personal criticism. But it also requires them to be open to criticism, which they should never deflect whenever it is justified. However, for all of these values to be realized, the practitioners of the scientific approach must always strive to express themselves in clear and precise language which, inevitably, demands that they familiarize themselves with as much as they need of the linguistic sciences. Language, the Arabic language, is therefore central to the success of the scientific approach as a medium of modernization. This is why al-Yaziji declares that in every nation competence in one's language is given priority over all other sciences, and that this should be the norm among the educated elite in the Arab nation (see Chapter 6, section 5.2 for a similar view by Kamal al-Hajj in the context of Lebanese nationalism). The fact that al-Yaziji received many linguistic questions from his readers about correct usage must have been seen by him as an indication of the importance attached by these readers to competence in the language and as a vindication of his above views. Al-Yaziji must also have considered the fact that the questions he received at *al-Bayān* and *al-Ḍiyā'* came from inside and outside the Arabic-speaking countries (Egypt, Lebanon, Palestine, Syria, Iraq, Hijaz, the Argentine, Brazil, the Dominican Republic, Italy and the Philippines) as a confirmation of his view that the Arabs formed a nation in the cultural sense, regardless of their citizenship status or geographical distribution. In addition, the fact that many of the questioners from outside Egypt were, judging by their names, Christian served to show that the defining function of Arabic in national terms cut across religious affiliations.

Let us now consider some of the strategies which al-Yaziji deployed in setting out his views on language and national identity, and in propelling Arabic-speakers on the road to modernity. As far as the issue of language and identity is concerned, al-Yaziji deliberately employs the term *a'ājim* and its derivatives (see Chapter 3, section 5) to designate non-Arabic-speakers and their languages. Often, the context makes it clear that the term *a'ājim* includes all non-speakers of Arabic regardless of their religious affiliation. This has the effect of creating an equality in *'ujma* (foreignness) between the Turks, whom al-Yaziji wished to distinguish from the Arabs in national-identity terms, and others, including the speakers of English and French in whose colonial or imperial spheres of influence the Arabs lived. To underline the identity difference between the Arabs and the speakers of other languages, al-Yaziji additionally uses the term *lughat al-ḍād* (the language of *ḍ*) to designate the Arabic language and all the linguistically based connotations that accrue from this expression (see Chapter 3, section 5).

By using the above two terms, al-Yaziji invokes their historical and cultural legacy of differential self-identification in a way which telescopes the present into the past and uses the latter to inform parallel situations in the former. Furthermore, he uses these two terms to frame his description of the occurrence of linguistic corruption in the Arabic of his day as *laḥn* (solecism), thus creating another platform from which to invoke the resonant potential of the past. In one of its implications, the term *laḥn* implies the existence of a foreign agency behind the linguistic corruption (see Chapter 3, section 4). It also implies the need to put in place counter-measures to protect the Arabic language against marauding linguistic influences, hence the references by al-Yaziji in this context to Abu al-Aswad al-Du'ali (see Chapter 3, section 4), who was entrusted with the first major corpus-planning project in the early Islamic period. The use of the term *laḥn* additionally places al-Yaziji's effort to revive the language in a rich historical context, endowing it with a strong motivational force by virtue of its indirect connection with the preservation of the language of the Qur'an. Al-Yaziji warns his readers that failure to protect their language from the effects of solecism may turn it into a laughable, hybrid dialect on a par with Maltese, whose linguistic identity is not certain.

The above link with the language of the Qur'an is not accidental in al-Yaziji's work. A survey of his essays in the various magazines he published shows that one of his favourite strategies in motivational terms consisted of quoting the Qur'an directly or of creating intertextual links with it for the effect these will have on his readers. First, these references are intended to create bridges of unity between al-Yaziji, a Christian, and his intended audience, the majority of whom are most probably Muslim. By creating intertextual links with the Qur'an, al-Yaziji intends to turn its text into a national linguistic-cum-cultural asset that belongs to all Arabic-speakers regardless of their religious affiliation. This has the effect of communicating to al-Yaziji's Muslim readers the idea that, although the Qur'an unites them with the Turks doctrinally, it does not do so linguistically or culturally, and that it is in these two arenas, through the text of the Qur'an, that the Muslim and Christian Arabs come together as one nation in the face of the Turks. To show how extensive these intertextual links are, I will list some of the numerous statements made by al-Yaziji together with the Qur'anic material they recall (the translations below, especially those of the Qur'anic material, are approximate):

1. *hal atā 'alā al-sharqi ḥīnun mina al-dahri lam yarji' li-l-'ilmi fīhi ṣadā* (Khuri 1993a: 19)
   Has not the East/Orient (*sharq*) passed through a period of time when science had no mention (lit. echo) in it?

1a. *hal atā 'alā al-insāni ḥīnun mina al-dahri lam yakun shay'an madhkūrā* (Qur'an 76:1)
   Has not man passed through a period of time when he had not been mentioned?

2. *wa-yaṣilūna fī khidmatihi ānā'a al-layli bi-aṭrāfi al-nahār* (ibid.: 52)
   And they (those who serve the cause of science) work day and night in its service.

2a. *wa-min ānā'i al-layli fa-sabbiḥ wa-aṭrāfi al-nahār* (Qur'an 20:13)
   And glorify thy Lord night and day.

3. *yawma lā yanfa'u mālun wa-lā banūna illā man atā Allāha bi-qalbin salīm* (ibid.: 53).
   The day when wealth and sons will not avail, but he alone will prosper who brings with him to God a sound heart.

3a. *yawma lā yanfa'u mālun wa-lā banūna, illā man atā Allāha bi-qalbin salīm* (Qur'an 26:88–9)

The day when wealth and sons will not avail, but he alone will prosper who brings with him to God a sound heart.

4. *li-yaqḍiya Allāhu amran kāna maf'ūlā* (ibid.: 82)
God may accomplish that which had been decreed.
4a. *wa-lākin li-yaqḍiya Allāhu amran kāna maf'ūlā* (Qur'an 8:42)
But God may accomplish that which had been decreed.

5. *wa-l-salāmu 'alā man ittaba'a al-hudā* (ibid.: 123)
Peace be to him who follows the guidance.
5a. *qad ji'nāka bi-āyatin min rabbika, wa-l-salāmu 'alā man ittaba'a al-hudā* (Qur'an 20:47)
We have come with a Sign from your Lord. Peace be upon him who follows the guidance.

The above discussion shows that language for al-Yaziji is the leitmotif around which a range of interrelated themes coalesce. It is the ingredient which makes a community a nation. In so doing, language cuts across racial and religious modes of self-definition among Arabic-speakers. Language is also the subject in terms of which the twin themes of modernization – science as method and rationality – are promoted in symbolic and communicative terms. Language thus emerges as the means of bringing about an attitudinal change in the modern Arab nation, and acts in its revived form as a symbol for that modernity. Considering all of these features, it is not surprising that Antonius suggested language as the linchpin of establishing the Arabs as a nation in the cultural sense. The fact that al-Yaziji sought to canonize Arab nationhood in poetry – the Arabs' primary mode of literary expression – in his famous ode alluded to at the beginning of this section adds to his role as one of the founders of Arab nationalism.

To understand the depth of al-Yaziji's commitment to his views on language, identity and modernization, I shall consider them briefly in relation to two major debates in the intellectual circles towards the end of the nineteenth century and the beginning of the twentieth century. One debate, initiated by the weekly *al-Nashra al-usbū'iyya* in 1881, deals with the use of foreign languages for learning non-language-based subjects in the schools. A similar debate took place at the time, and it dealt with the replacement of Arabic by English as the language of instruction at the American Protestant College in Beirut in 1882 (see section 3). Opinions on the issue of using foreign languages were divided between those favouring their use and those who rejected it, with each group adducing arguments in favour of their position based on the role of language in identity-formation and modernization. The second debate revolved around Arabic diglossia, and which of the two varieties, the standard or colloquial, should be promoted in status-planning terms in Arabic-speaking countries. Again, this debate was framed by reference to the two categories of identity and modernization. These two debates, and the host of self-definition issues with which they interlocked, show the sociopolitical importance of the language in the period under consideration. Al-Yaziji's views must be seen as part and parcel of this general atmosphere among the elites, one of whose strands was to consider the ways and means by which their people could develop and catch up with the West. However, on a different level, these debates show that al-Yaziji held to his views in spite of the currency of alternative orientations on the linguistic modernization front which he could have, if he so wished, adopted. What is remarkable about al-Yaziji's position, therefore, is the consistency and dogged determination with which he expressed it. Equivocation is not his trait. He believed that Arabic was the marker par excellence of the national identity of its speakers, as well as the means of delivering the coveted results of modernization in all spheres in a thoroughly modernized and modern idiom. The fact that al-Yaziji pursued the first of these themes from a base in Egypt, at a time when the country was more absorbed in its own territorial identity (see Chapter 6), further underlines his Arabic-based nationalist credentials.

Considering the extensive nature of the evidence that has been marshalled above, it is not surprising that George Antonius regards Ibrahim al-Yaziji as one of the earliest proponents of Arab nationalism in its cultural mode, a view reiterated more recently by Mikha'il 'Awn (1983). The fact that Antonius failed to consider al-Yaziji's contribution to this nationalism beyond the references he made to his famous ode may have contributed to this linguist's relative invisibility in the burgeoning scholarship on Arab nationalism in the West. It is for reasons of wanting to rectify this lacuna in the study of Arab nationalism that I have devoted a large portion of this chapter to considering aspects of al-Yaziji's thinking. This discussion has also shown the following: (1) the sophisticated nature of Arab nationalism in its cultural mode during the last two decades of the nineteenth century, (2) the organic interactions between language, nationalism and modernization, (3) the role of the past in underpinning this triadic interaction, and (4) the attempt to invoke the linguistic medium of the Qur'an as a national bond that overrides the differences in religion among the Arabs.

5. CONCLUSION

In this chapter, I have tried to show that, for the study of Arab nationalism to proceed properly, it must consider the development of this phenomenon, on both the cultural and political levels, in the wider context of the emergence of Turkish and, to a lesser extent, other (Balkan) nationalisms in the Ottoman Empire in the last quarter of the nineteenth and early decades of the twentieth century. In particular, I have tried to suggest that the double trajectory of the

Turkifying trend in the Ottoman Empire – which was first aimed at the Turks before culminating as a policy objective that was coercively targeted at the Arabs – played a crucial role in the shift from the cultural to the political in the development of Arab nationalism. The above discussion has also tried to show that the analysis of this shift cannot be complete without considering the role of language in it both materially and emblematically. Language in this context emerged as the object of modernization in material terms and as the vehicle through which the fruits of modernization in other spheres can be expressed and promoted in the Empire. But language was also used emblematically as the marker of group identity which increasingly expressed itself in national terms. In debates about this, language served as the site of contestation in relation to which issues of group inclusion and exclusion could be articulated without incurring the full wrath of the censor. The use of language in this manner was considered as a manifestation of the language-planning principle which says that most of the so-called linguistic debates about language reform in the world, whether of the status or the corpus type, are ultimately aimed at non-linguistic ends. This is certainly true of the call for Arabic and Turkish reforms which were used as a blatant camouflage for putting forward views of a covertly political nature.

The increasing politicization of the language issue in Arab nationalism depended on the successful excavation of the Arab heritage. The connections between Arabic and Islam were projected in a nationalist guise that had the full support of the Prophet's traditions. Reference to the foreignness of the Turks was articulated intertextually by invoking the boundary-setting meaning of carefully chosen and strategically sited expressions from that heritage, including the terms *ʿajam*, *ʿilj* and *lughat al-ḍād*. Poetry, the Arabs' primary art form, was pressed into service to express a cultural identity that is nationally *sui generis*. But poetry was also used for motivational effect. Complaints about the neglect of Arabic in education and the state apparatus were expressed in poetry to criticize the Turks and to shame the Arabs into action. This occurred in poems specifically composed for this purpose, as well as in placards and proclamations which sometimes began by quoting a line of poetry and ended by quoting a few more. None of this would have happened without the emergence of a literary renaissance which was sustained by an expanding school system consisting of a state sector, an indigenous private sector and a foreign or missionary sector. The increasing popularity of journalism and the introduction of modern printing presses with greater and better output fed into this renaissance and derived support from it. In this increasingly complex web of cultural innovations and nascent political developments of a nationalist kind, Arabic emerged as that ingredient which unites Arab Muslims and Christians into a new identity that separates them from the Turks. This process was accelerated after the rise of the

Young Turks to a position of seemingly uncontested power in 1909. Secret societies and cultural clubs championed the cause of the language for the symbolic significance it has in Arab life and heritage, and for its efficacy as a conduit for expressing overtly nationalist demands. In expressing these demands, some nationalist thinkers showed themselves familiar with the various modes of defining national identity in Western political thought. This does not mean that Arab nationalism was an importation from the West. A careful assessment of the roots of this nationalism is bound to show that it is more home-grown than transplanted from the outside, although "home" here must be understood as the Ottoman Empire in all its diachronic and synchronic complexities. Western ideas were important as the framework in terms of which the emerging conception of an Arab nation could be formulated and presented to the outside world for the purpose of achieving specifically political aims.

On a different level, the above discussion is intended to serve as a critique of the study of Arab nationalism which, thus far, has suffered from the lack of an integrative theoretical perspective and, more cripplingly, the reluctance to adopt a view of the phenomenon which expands the types of data which can shed light on it beyond their current historical and political limits (cf. Hutchinson and Aberbach 1999). In particular, although language has often been acknowledged as the primary feature of Arab nationalism, and as the surrogate channel through which suppressed political ideologies can make themselves visible, little work has been done on its role in this phenomenon. This has, in my view, led to an impoverished understanding of Arab nationalism – and other territorial nationalisms in the Arabic-speaking countries, for that matter – although the studies by Armbrust (1996), Baron (1997) and Suleiman (1993, 1994, 1996b, 1997, 1999a, 1999b) have offered a way forward which this work is intended to pursue.

Finally, the move from the cultural to the political in the development of Arab nationalism in the period under consideration in this chapter may be interpreted as a move from the covertly and indirectly political to the overtly and directly political in nation-formation. Or, looked at as a back-projection from the present to the past, this development may be visualized as a move from what is overtly and directly political to what is overtly and directly cultural. The idea that cultural nationalism can be "purely cultural", in the sense of being devoid of any political impulses, is therefore not possible without denying the open-endedness of cultural signification. Furthermore, it is not possible to insist that the "cultural" in cultural nationalism is purely cultural without denying the fact that what the sender sends, and what the receiver receives and reconstructs, may not always be identical. It may therefore be more helpful in the study of nationalism to say that the cultural can never be ascertained to be devoid of political meanings, in the anthropological sense of the term "political", and that the political can never be ascertained to be devoid of cultural signification, in the anthropological sense of the term "cultural". What matters therefore in the study of nationalism is the assessment of the mix of these two dimensions at any one stage in the development of a given nationalism, rather than ascertaining the existence of their logically impossible mutual exclusion.

5

Arabic, First and Foremost

fa-lisānunā al-ʿarabiyyu khayru muwaḥḥidi[1]

1. INTRODUCTION

The status of Arabic as a marker or ingredient of an Arab national identity which distinguishes speakers of the language from the Turks within the Ottoman Empire was set out in Chapter 4. Initially, language delivered this function in a predominantly cultural mode of collective self-definition which, nevertheless, was not devoid of sociopolitical overtones. The imposition of Turkification as a policy objective in the last years of the Ottoman Empire helped transform this nascent Arab nationalism into a more overtly political one. Arab cultural clubs and societies were established to pursue a variety of overtly or covertly nationalist aims within the Empire, building in this effort on the achievements of a cultural and literary revival which gave the Arabs a sense of pride in their past heritage (see Chapter 3). Poets, lexicographers, linguists, essayists, teachers and students participated in this revival, benefiting in this process from the increased contact with the West at a rate – and at a level and of a quality – unprecedented in the past. Language was central in this newly emerging enterprise of contrastive self-definition. It was the ingredient which separated the Arabs from the Turks. And, by virtue of its seemingly non-political nature, it served as the conduit for setting out ideas which could escape the ever-alert eye of the censor, who was not reluctant to exercise his authority, as happened several times to al-ʿUraysi's newspaper *al-Mufid* (see Chapter 4, section 3). However, the separation of the Asian part of the Arabic-speaking world from the Ottoman Empire at the end of the First World War marked a subtle change in the role of language in self-definitional terms. Whereas before the break-up of the Empire the language was pressed into service primarily as a criterion which externally *bounded* the Arabs, it was now increasingly projected as an ingredient which *bonded* them internally. Using the words of the celebrated Egyptian poet Ahmad Shawqi (1868–1932), which he uttered in a different context, Arabic started to be promoted as a metaphorical "fatherland" or "homeland" (*wa-mā al-ʿarabiyyatu illā waṭan*), as the soil in which a group's national identity is rooted and to which it gives sustenance and life.

The idea that language is a marker of national identity was not restricted to men of letters only in the last few decades of the Ottoman Empire. It was articulated in studies of a more schematic nature long before the collapse of the Empire after the First World War. As early as 1870, Francis al-Marrash (1836–73) distinguished between the two concepts of *waṭan* (the place to which a person belongs, the fatherland) and *umma* (the group of which a person is a member, the nation), without insisting on the necessity of the fatherland and the nation being united under the jurisdiction of a single, unitary state (see Nassar 1994: 212–14). In discussing the application of the latter concept in the context of Greater Syria, al-Marrash points to the role played by language – in addition to customs and the belief in common interests that override faith boundaries and sectarian differences – in defining national identity. The importance of the language ingredient in this concept of the nation, although limited by the other two factors, is evidenced by the attacks al-Marrash mounted against those who code-switched to foreign languages in their speech or those who favoured these languages in attitudinal terms (see Chapter 4, sections 3–4 for similar views). It is also signalled by the fact that he deplores the dialectal differences between the Syrians which, we must assume, he considers a danger to the linguistic bond that unites them.

The distinction between fatherland and nation is also made by the Egyptian Azhari educator Hasan al-Marsafi (1815–90) in his short treatise *Risālat al-kalim al-thamān* (*A Treatise in Explanation of Eight Terms*), first published in Cairo in 1881. The eight terms dealt with in this treatise are: *umma* (nation), *waṭan* (common territory), *ḥukūma* (government), *'adl* (justice), *ẓulm* (tyranny), *siyāsa* (politics), *ḥuriyya* (freedom) and *tarbiya* (education). Of these terms, "nation", "fatherland" and "education" – particularly the first and the last – receive most attention. The other terms are dealt with sparingly, especially "politics", which is dealt with in passing only. Since the main interest in the present work lies in issues of language and national identity, I will restrict myself here to al-Marsafi's definition of the nation insofar as it relates to language as its major ingredient. It may be helpful before launching this discussion to point out that al-Marsafi's *Risāla* was most probably intended as a reflection on the emerging national culture in Egypt. Al-Marsafi's *Risāla* is therefore a confirmation of the currency of the above concepts in Egypt in the second half of the nineteenth century rather than an attempt to inject them into Egyptian political life during that period. It is, however, not always easy to understand what al-Marsafi actually means by a particular term. This reflects (1) the inherent indeterminacy of these terms conceptually, (2) their recency in Arabic sociopolitical discourse, (3) the loose formulations in which the author sometimes casts his explanations, owing to the dictation method he used in composing his *Risāla* because of his blindness, and (4) the poor quality of the first printed copy of this treatise. It further reflects the desire by al-Marsafi to fit these terms into a mould which suited Egypt's sociopolitical realities in the last two decades of the nineteenth century. In particular, it signals the desire to establish Egypt as a modernizing nation-state on a par with other developed states, without regard to the bonds of religion which may unite it with the Ottoman Empire.

Al-Marsafi defines the nation as a "group of people with a common bond which, induction tells us, may be language, territory, or faith" (1984: 63). Al-Marsafi then tells us that nations united by a common language have a greater claim to nationhood than those united by territory and faith. He explains this by invoking the innate nature of language in human life on the individual level and its character as an inalienable property of its speech community on the social. As the major instrument of socialization, a common language creates affiliative bonds between its speakers and sets them apart from the speakers of other languages (see Chapter 2, section 4). So important is the role of language as a barrier and facilitator of inter-nation communication that al-Marsafi compares different linguistically defined nations to non-communicating animals (*al-ḥāyawānāt al-ʿujm*) until they learn each other's language. Although a major criterion of nationhood, the existence of a common language does not necessarily correlate with the existence of a single state with political jurisdiction over those who speak the language concerned in the territory they inhabit.

It is however not clear whether, according to al-Marsafi, all those who speak Arabic constitute one nation, in spite of the fact that the kind of Arabic this author reveres and wishes to promote through education is standard Arabic, the language of the Qur'an, rather than the "corrupt" dialects which are infected by solecism (see Chapter 3, section 4). Al-Marsafi's commitment to this form of the language is evidenced by (1) the emphasis he places on simplifying the way it is taught to learners to enable them to use it more correctly in public life, and (2) the blistering attack he launches against the imams of mosques whose Friday sermons are replete with grammatical errors. There is, however, no mention in the *Risāla* that the Arabs constitute one nation by virtue of the fact that they share a common language. The term *al-umma al-ʿarabiyya* (the Arab nation) occurs once only in this work (p. 162), but not to specify the nationhood of this nation by reference to the linguistic criterion. Moreover, although the term *al-ʿarab* (the Arabs) occurs a few times in the *Risāla*, it is nevertheless used to refer to the Bedouin inhabitants of Egypt – reflecting the usage of the time in Egypt and the influence of Ibn Khaldun's terminology on the author – rather than "the Arabs" in Arab nationalist discourse. But if al-Marsafi does not explicitly recognize the existence of an Arab nation, he equally does not rule it out. If anything, it is more likely that al-Marsafi would be more willing to entertain the existence of an Arabic-speaking nation – considering his views on the lack of unity among Muslims historically – than one based on Islam. The fact that the term *al-umma al-miṣriyya* (the Egyptian nation) is used by this author a few times does not contradict this conclusion, owing to the fact that this term is often anchored in relation to the criterion of territory. And since, he tells us, this criterion is not as effective as its linguistic counterpart in the formation of nations, the above conclusion concerning the role of language as a basis of an Arab nation, albeit a latent one, remains intact.

The view that language is an ingredient in nation-formation, and that Arabic plays this role for its speakers, was promoted by other writers before the collapse of the Ottoman Empire. One such writer was ʿUmar Fakhuri (1895–1946)[2] in his book *Kayfa yanhaḍ al-ʿarab?* (*How Can the Arabs Rise?*) – first published in Beirut in 1913 and reissued in 1981 – in which he puts forward the view that language is one of the "highest manifestations of nationalism" (1981: 141), in combination with common origin and common history. Another writer whose views on the topic are worthy of mention is Salah al-Din al-Qasimi (1887–1916),[3] who worked tirelessly to promote the teaching and learning of Arabic as a means of resisting the Turkification policies of the Young Turks (see Chapter 4, section 3). His interest in this field was motivated by the conviction that language is a component of nationalism, that the Arabs constitute a nation, and that since the "surest way of bringing about the demise of a nation is eliminating its language" it was incumbent on the Arabs to defend their language against the Turkifying policies of the Young Turks (1959: 45).

But these and other attempts at linking nation with language in the Arab context remain vague when it comes to deciding whether or not all those to whom Arabic is a common language belong to the same nation. One of the first and perhaps clearest pronouncements on this issue was made by Najib ʿAzury (1873?–1916) in his book *Le Réveil de la nation arabe dans l'asie turque* (published in Paris in 1905), in which he set out his ideas on Arab independence from Turkish domination (see Wild 1981). ʿAzury believed that the Arabs in the area east of Suez constituted one nation, regardless of their religious and sectarian differences, and that this nation should form an independent kingdom under the leadership of a member of the Khedival dynasty in Egypt. But he specifically excluded from the scope of this nation the Arabic-speaking peoples of North Africa and Egypt, in spite of the fact that they shared with the Arabs in Asia the same language which, in this context, he regarded as a factor in nation-formation. The exclusion of the countries of North Africa may be explained by the fact that they were under French domination at the time, and that any attempt to include them in his project would have earned him the enmity of the French, whose support he needed in the struggle against the Ottoman Empire. His exclusion of Egypt, which was under British control at the time, may also have been motivated by considerations of a similar nature as well as by his dislike for the Egyptian leader Mustafa Kamil, whose pro-Islamic and pro-Ottoman policies ʿAzury regarded as false. But he also argued that the Egyptians do not qualify for inclusion in this Arab nation owing to their different racial origins (he says they are descended from an African Berber family), the well-defined geographical borders of Egypt, and the fact that before the incorporation of Egypt into Islam the Egyptians did not speak Arabic. The last of these arguments is a curious one, since the same may be said of other communities in the projected Arab nation in Greater Syria and Iraq. This view, however, is fully understandable in its own political context as set out in the preceding few lines. However, the fact that he called for his proposed Arab kingdom to be headed by a member of the Khedival dynasty in Egypt indicates his willingness to leave the door open for Egypt to be part of this kingdom.

The main aim of this chapter is to investigate a set of contributions which goes beyond 'Azury by seeking to incorporate into one nation all those to whom Arabic is a common language in the Middle East and North Africa. Advocates of this ideology, which is referred to in the literature as pan-Arab nationalism – or Arab nationalism for short – treat language as one of the major ingredients in nation-formation. For some, Arabic is in fact the major ingredient which binds the Arabs to each other internally and which sets them apart from other nations. The two nationalist thinkers whose views will constitute the bulk of this chapter are Sati' al-Husri and Zaki al-Arsuzi. However, before dealing with these two thinkers, I will discuss the contributions of a few important, though less seminal, modern writers to show the depth of the trend in modern Arab thought which associates national identity with language.

2. UNDER THE BANNER OF ARABIC

The first writer I will deal with is the Lebanese linguist and jurist al-Shaykh 'Abdalla al-'Alayli (see Ba'albaki 1984, Dimashqiyya 1984, Khuri 1984, Mruwwa 1984, Sa'd 1984 and Tarhini 1985), whose modernizing work on various aspects of the Arabic language is part and parcel of his belief in its role as a factor in Arab nationalism (see Chapter 4, section 4). Al-'Alayli's (b. 1914) major work in this field is *Dustur al-'arab al-qawmi* (*The Arabs' National Constitution*), first published in 1941 and twice reprinted since, the last time in 1996 (all references below are to this edition). This is an interesting work because of the range of views on Arab nationalism that it contains. It is also interesting because the author sought through its elevated style and its unusually fully vowelled script to signal aesthetically and grammatically the type of Arabic he wished to promote in the national enterprise: a standard language that was grammatically correct and, hence, capable of invoking the linguistic sensibilities of the Arabs in all the Arabic-speaking countries. This rich symbolism of the book reflects the author's view of this work as the national "constitution", *of* and *for* the Arabs.

Although al-ʿAlayli does not spell out how his book functions as a "constitution", the following may offer some explanations. It is the national constitution *of* the Arabs by virtue of the fact that it recognizes the status of Arab nationalism as an intuitively felt component of Arab subjectivity. In this sense, Arab nationalism predates, historically and logically, all the studies which seek to explain it or, more correctly, uncover it. As such, Arab nationalism can be said to exist independently of the theoretical and descriptive accounts which deal with it. Furthermore, his book is the national constitution *for* the Arabs because it sets out to objectify this intuitive nationalism by reference to nationalism in the West, but without imposing the special properties of the latter on the former.

In spite of the emphasis this work lays on careful and correct (linguistic) enunciation, there are at least two major problems in dealing with it. These concern, first, the vagueness with which some of its major concepts are articulated, and, second, the lack of consistency it exhibits in dealing with the role of some of the factors at work in nation-building. An example of the first problem is the definition of Arab nationalism al-ʿAlayli gives (1996: 101):

> Arab nationalism is the feeling by the Arabs of becoming aware of their full social existence in an intuitive (or subjective) way rather than in an objective manner, so much so that [1] their imagining of the Arab community as a psychological and life-sustaining (or biological) construct is always intensely present in their lives emotionally, and [2] every Arab instinctively and compulsorily experiences the strong and wide-spread bonds [in this community] in a way which helps him psychologically internalise the visible existence of the community concerned.

Al-ʿAlayli points out that this is not a definition in the logical sense of the term, but an attempt to capture those aspects of Arab nationalism which predate it epistemologically, that is, independently of all the attempts to explain it in the literature. This definition further reflects al-ʿAlayli's essentialist belief that Arab life is characterized by a "mystical quality" which informs Arab nationality in a formative manner; hence the references in the above definition to the instinctiveness and intuitiveness of Arab nationalism and the almost mystical quality which imbues the definition concerned. Al-ʿAlayli further believes that the Arabs differ in this respect from the West which "sold its soul to the devil of uncompromising rationality", leading to what he calls confusion (*balbala*) and restlessness (*qalqala*) in Western thought. This extends to the literature on nationalism, which has failed to provide watertight definitions of the nation, nationality and nationalism for universal or even for particular application.

Under this view, it may be argued that the above vagueness in the definition of Arab nationalism does no more than reflect the inherent vagueness of the phenomenon designated by this concept in its generic form and particular context (see Chapter 2, section 2 for similar views). Rather than exhibiting any methodological failure on the part of al-'Alayli, the vagueness of his definition of Arab nationalism is projected as unavoidable. This position on the part of al-'Alayli is worthy of highlighting because it serves as an example of similar views in the discourse on Arab nationalism. Thus, in an article first published in 1940, Michel 'Aflaq (1993a) – the founder and one of the leading ideologues of the Arab Ba'th Party – deplores as reductive and intellectually subversive the attempts in Arab nationalist discourse to define Arab nationalism by using categories imported from the West and applied to this nationalism in a way which does violence to it. In a memorable statement of his views, Aflaq (1993a: 80) declares that "the Arabs do not need to learn anything new to become nationalists. On the contrary, they need to forget most of what they have learned [about nationalism] to regain that direct link they once had with their pure and authentic [nationalist] disposition. Nationalism is not a science, but a matter of memory, a living memory." In two further articles published in 1940, Aflaq refers to Arab nationalism as an "act of love before everything else" (1993b: 74) and as a "sweet fate" (1993c: 76) in an attempt to signal his view that (1993a: 79) "the biggest danger to Arab nationalism is the extreme preoccupation with abstract thought [about what it means]".[4]

Let us now turn to the lack of consistency in al-'Alayli's *Constitution* before discussing his views on the role of language in nation-formation. In some cases, the inconsistency takes the form of outright contradiction. This is characteristic of his views on the relationship between the nation and the state, which he regards as categorially distinct from each other in the sense that the former is a "natural" phenomenon while the latter is an artificial construct. Thus, whereas he says that "a nation cannot exist without a state" (1996: 96), he later tells us that a nation can lose its independent state without losing its status as a nation in its own right (ibid.). In other cases, the lack of consistency takes the form of assessing the contribution of a particular nation-building factor in different ways. Thus, while he says that the existence of natural geographical borders is a factor, but not a primary one, in nation-formation, he later treats this same factor as the most important element in nation-building, perhaps under the influence of the ideology of the Syrian National Party of Antun Sa'ada (see Chapter 6, section 2). This lack of consistency extends to the role of language itself in nation-formation. Thus, whereas he says that language is more important than geography in nation-formation (ibid.: 90), he later tells us that it ranks third after geography and common interests in this enterprise (ibid.: 110). There is, however, no doubt that, overall, al-'Alayli treats language as one of the most important ingredients in the formation of Arab nationalism, as I will explain below.

Al-'Alayli's interest in the role of Arabic in nation-building pertains mainly to its communicative function, with some consideration for its symbolic significance. This lack of concern with the symbolic dimension of the language is consistent with al-'Alayli's views on Arab nationalism, which exclude religion in the traditional sense from its scope. Thus, *Constitution* lacks the usual references in the Arab nationalist discourse to the symbolic significance of Arabic in its capacity as the language of the Qur'an. The absence of these references is all the more conspicuous owing to the pre-eminence of al-'Alayli as one of the leading Muslim jurists of Lebanon in the twentieth century. But it is the identity of this thinker as an Arab nationalist from Lebanon which holds the key to explaining why he chooses to exclude religion as a factor in Arab nationalism. Being aware of the divisive nature of religion in the Lebanese context, the author excludes it as a factor in Arab nationalism, although he recognizes the need to include its spiritual dimension and moral imperatives as part of the fabric of the Arab nation. He expresses these views by saying that "religion has no place in nationalism" (ibid.: 150), and that "religion is the cause of all the catastrophes between the sons of the same nation, even the same town" (ibid.). In this respect, he is different from the Lebanese nationalist Kamal Yusuf al-Hajj, whose views will be dealt with in Chapter 6 (section 5.2), and more akin to the Arab nationalist thinkers al-Husri and al-Arsuzi, as we shall see below.

Al-'Alayli describes the role of language in nation-formation in four ways: (1) language plays the greatest role in nation-formation (ibid.: 90), and it is the mainstay in any stable national structure (ibid.: 104); (2) language is a national habit (ibid.: 110); (3) language is not a product of race (ibid.: 90), which amounts to a rejection of linguism (see Chapter 2, section 3); and (4) language is a necessary but not sufficient ingredient in nation-formation. The other ingredients of Arab nationalism in the order in which al-'Alayli lists them are (after language): common interests, geography, common origin or race, common history and common customs and traditions. However, al-'Alayli later divides these factors implicitly into two categories: a primary category, incorporating geography, common interests and language in this descending order of importance; and, a secondary category incorporating the rest, whose function is to strengthen the working of the primary factors although they are not essential constituents in defining the nation. This classification of the factors and their ranking within the primary category contradicts the above description of the role of language in nation-formation in two ways. On the one hand, it compromises the position of language as the mainstay of nationalism by placing it after geography and common interests in the primary category, as has been pointed out earlier in this section. On the other hand, the treatment of language as a "national habit" (ibid.) has the effect of removing it from the primary category and assigning it to the less important secondary category or, at least, of casting doubt on the legitimacy of assigning it completely to the primary category of nation-formation ingredients. In spite of these contradictions, there is no doubt that language for al-'Alayli remains one of the most significant affiliative bonds in Arab nationalism.

Al-'Alayli points out that language delivers two important functions in the nationalist enterprise. The first function is that of serving as a medium of communication between those to whom it is a common tongue. By virtue of this function, language creates bonds of affiliation between its users through the exchange of ideas and experiences. And, as the means of recording the nation's history and past glories, in addition to articulating its culture and vision of the future, language underpins these affiliative bonds and envelops them in such a way that it becomes in itself a mirror of the nation's feelings and thinking. In playing this role, language brings its socializing function to bear on the development of members of the nation in a way which no other nation-forming ingredient can match. The second function of language, which is not unrelated to the first, is that of serving as a boundary-setter between its speakers and others (see Chapter 2, section 2). Al-'Alayli expresses this role of language by pointing out how people tend to be drawn to those whose languages they share, and how they may shun or ignore those whose languages they do not know.

Owing to the importance of language in nation-formation, al-'Alayli believes that it is incumbent on the Arabs to nurture their language in at least two ways. First, it is the duty of the specialists among them to simplify the language, to improve the methods for teaching it, and to provide the tools which can protect it against foreign infiltration and internally induced ossification, particularly in the lexical field. It is in fact this realization on the part of al-'Alayli which made him one of the most prolific writers on all aspects of the Arabic language. Thus, in addition to his seminal publications *Muqaddima li-dars lughat al-'arab* (1938, published when he was 24 years old), *al-Mu'jam* (1954) and *al-Marji'* (1963), al-'Alayli published dozens of articles in many newspapers and magazines in Lebanon and elsewhere in the Arabic-speaking world (see a list of these articles in Tarhini 1985). Second, al-'Alayli believes that the Arabs must dedicate themselves completely to their language and they must shun any form of allegiance to other languages. In their ardent zeal for Arabic, the Arabs must treat with "contempt and loathing" (1996: 103) any Arab who uses a foreign language in preference to his own sacred and sublime tongue. In his dedication to Arabic, al-'Alayli believes that in the context of Arab nationalism the Cartesian principle "I think, therefore I am" must be replaced with the maxim "I think in Arabic, therefore I am an Arab" (ibid.: 126–7).

Although this is nowhere explicitly stated in *Constitution*, there is no doubt that al-'Alayli's attack on foreign languages is intended as an attack on those who treat French in Lebanon as a surrogate national language alongside Arabic, their native tongue, or even in preference to it. In this sense, al-'Alayli's views on foreign languages are a culmination, in the intensity with which they are expressed, of earlier views concerning the divisive role that foreign languages played in Greater Syria in the second half of the nineteenth century and the early part of the twentieth century. In this respect, al-ʿAlayli is the true heir of al-ʿUraysi (see Chapter 4, section 3) and Ibrahim al-Yaziji (see Chapter 4, section 4). On a different level, al-ʿAlayli's attack on foreign languages in the Arab context must be interpreted as an attack on those who wish to promote extraterritorial bonds of affiliation with the speakers of the languages concerned, for example the French in the Lebanese context (see Chapter 6, section 5), or those who seek to promote what he regards as outmoded forms of territorial nationalism as an alternative to an all-inclusive Arab nationalism (see Chapter 6).

It should not, however, be understood from this that al-ʿAlayli disapproves of all types of territorial nationalism in the Arab context. He distinguishes between two types of territorial nationalism: (1) Arab territorialism, which he conditionally approves of insofar as it considers itself a step towards overall Arab nationalism and works vigorously to promote it, and (2) what he calls geological-archaeological territorialism. He categorically rejects this form of nationalism because, being schismatic and a fossilized form of self-definition, it seeks to undermine and replace Arab nationalism as a form of group identification; examples of this type of nationalism are Phoenicianism in Lebanon, Pharaonism in Egypt and Assyrianism in Iraq (see Chapter 6). Addressing the proponents of these "reprehensible" territorial nationalisms, al-ʿAlayli invokes the language factor in nation-formation to make the point that, since the languages to which these nationalisms hark back are dead languages, these nationalisms themselves must be declared dead too. Unlike Arabic, which is a living language, the languages to which these ossified nationalisms refer failed to withstand the challenges posed by other languages. In marked contrast to these languages, Arabic expanded its pool of speakers through conquest or through more peaceful exchanges between the Arabic-speakers and other communities. These facts make Arabic more suitable than any of the purportedly alternative languages to be the standard-bearer of Arabism as the only viable form of national identification in the Arabic-speaking lands.

These ideas on language and national identity have found their way into the early work of Nadim al-Bitar (1948–93). This writer describes the community of ideas and feelings created by language using terms that are peculiar to al-ʿAlayli in his *Constitution*, including *ʿadwā* (for the spread of ideas) and *taʿaṣṣub* (for uncompromising dedication to the Arabic language). In some cases, he merely paraphrases what al-ʿAlayli says: "language is the mainstay of any stable national structure" (al-Bitar 1993: 192 and al-ʿAlayli 1996: 104). And: "language is no more than thoughts and feelings masquerading as words" (al-Bitar 1993: 191

and al-ʿAlayli 1996: 34). The fact that an important nationalist thinker like Nadim al-Bitar (1979, 1981, 1982) seems to follow in the footsteps of al-ʿAlayli in explaining the role of language in nation-formation testifies to the importance of the latter's contribution to this area in Arab nationalist thought.

Al-Bitar highlights the two functions of language in nationalism: the communicative and the differential or boundary-setting. By means of the former, a nation comes together as a result of the transfer of ideas and feelings vertically through time and horizontally across space. The existence of a print culture which covers the four corners of the Arabic-speaking world is a testimony to this power of the language. Through the latter function, a nation sets itself apart from other nations. So important is language for differential identity in nationalist thought that what is peculiar to a nation is hardly ever adequately translatable into another language (see also Chapter 6, section 5.2). Although al-Bitar does not pursue this point beyond these limits, it may be argued on the basis of what he says here that the "untranslatability of the Qur'an" thesis – which is widely held in the Arabic intellectual tradition – is but an expression of the peculiarly Arab (national) character of the text of the revelation. In this respect, he follows in the footsteps of al-Yaziji (see Chapter 4, section 4). In addition, al-Bitar believes that language is worthier than a nation's independence for its survival. Thus, a nation which loses its independence may one day regain it. But, if a nation loses its language, it will surely perish and die. This explains the attempts by diasporic communities to preserve their languages, whether functionally for in-group communication or symbolically for marking the self against the other or for linking that self with its ethnic past (see Chapter 2, section 4). The fact that al-Bitar seems to be primarily concerned with the functional (or communicative) role of language in national self-identification, and only tangentially interested in its symbolic potential, further shows the affinities between him and al-ʿAlayli, whose views on this issue were set out above.

This similarity also extends to al-Bitar's position towards territorial nationalism in its two forms above. Thus he rejects the schismatic type of this nationalism, which he believes was aided and abetted by the colonial powers to undermine the affiliative force of Arab nationalism. This, al-Bitar argues, is the reason behind what he calls the *shuʿūbī* (see Chapter 3, section 5) attacks on the Arabic language, which took the form of promoting the colloquials as media of communication and as symbols of national identity at the state level. However, his position concerning the second type of territorial nationalism, which considers itself as a step on the way towards full Arab nationalism and state unity, is a little more equivocal. Being aware that the Arabs in the second half of the twentieth century were divided into several political entities, he had little choice but to recognize that as long as these entities worked towards achieving full Arab unity, then their brand of nation-statism may be tolerated. Al-Bitar was prepared to tolerate this form of territorial nationalism as long as it remained of a transitory character. And, in order to make sure that what is avowedly intended to be transitory does not become permanent, he believes that it is incumbent on entities of this type (1) to promote the *idea* of a single Arab state as a nationalist political objective, and (2) to strengthen the forces of unity between the Arabs, particularly on the language front. To achieve this aim, measures of the kind suggested by al-ʿAlayli above must be put in place and vigorously pursued.

However, al-Bitar is aware that this is a precarious position to take. This is so because, more than any other Arab nationalist thinker I know of, he is fully alive to the role of the state, whether this is intended or not, in creating a sociopolitical dynamic within its own sphere of influence which can alter the course of Arab nationalism. His views on this matter are guided by his reading of history, wherein political unity in the past was regarded as the factor which endowed particular groups of people with common bonds that were later put to use as ingredients in nation-formation in the nineteenth and twentieth centuries. Applied to language in the Arab context, it would be possible to say that its unifying role on the national level in the modern period was the result, rather than the cause, of earlier political unity which projected it as a language of widespread communication in its heyday. The fact that this was the case in the past must surely indicate that it can happen again in the future, but in the opposite, schismatic direction. Al-ʿAlayli was aware of this, but he sought to counter it by taking an essentialist interpretation of Arab subjectivity and Arab nationalism. Under this view, Arab nationalism, once formed, is not subject to change, at least in a radical way. Unlike al-ʿAlayli, al-Bitar is an avowed relativist and, as such, he is aware of the malleability of identity and of the mutations it can undergo in response to the factors at work in its own sociopolitical sphere. This means that none of the ingredients of nationalism he lists in the Arab context (common race, common language, common history, common territory, common literature, common culture, customs and traditions, common interests, and the idea of one state) is immune to change, though some are more resistant to manipulation by the state than others. Of all these ingredients, language is the one which is most resistant to manipulation. It is this fact which makes al-Bitar recognize Arabic as the principal affiliative bond in Arab nationalism.

The view that Arabic is the principal centripetal force of Arab unity capable of countering the centrifugal power of the territorial state is embedded in the discourse of the Baʿth Party, and in that brand of Arab nationalism which the late Egyptian President Nasser adopted in the wake of the dissolution of the union between Egypt and Syria in 1961. Thus, article 9 of the constitution of the Ba'th Party declares that the "official language of the [projected Arab] state, as well as that of all the citizens, is Arabic" (Arab Ba'th Party 1962, "Constitution"). This article further adds that Arabic "alone is recognised in correspondence and in teaching". Article 10 defines an Arab as one "whose language is Arabic, who has lived on Arab soil, or who, after having been assimilated to Arab life, has faith in his belonging to the Arab nation". A similar position is taken by President Nasser in *al-Mīthāq al-waṭanī* (the National Charter), in which he declares that the unity of language, history and aspirations (in this order) between the various Arab peoples reveals the unity of the Arab nation and point to its ability to overcome the political differences between the Arab states (see Nassar 1994: 318–99). This unifying role of the language explains the enormous interest in cultivating it as a medium of communication. Thus, in the canon of Arab nationalism, cultivating the language becomes an article of faith, as Ziyada (1950) states when he calls on Muslim and Christian Arabs to study the Qur'an for its linguistic qualities, although for the former it is additionally the source of their faith (see Chapter 4, section 4). The unifying role of Arabic further explains the calls made by influential proponents of Arab nationalism to protect it against infiltration by linguistic practices imported – directly or indirectly – from outside. An example of this is the call made by the Iraqi scholar and statesman 'Abd al-Rahman al-Bazzaz (1956), who deplored the use of foreign names in shop signs (including cinemas, theatres, hotels and so on) in cities like Cairo, Baghdad and Beirut. Al-Bazzaz also deplored the importation of the Western practice in vogue among some women in Arab society of using their married names in preference to the indigenous Arab practice of keeping their maiden ones. Believing that naming practices are language-cum-culture-bound, and that it is the duty of the Arabs to protect their culture and the naming philosophy (*falsafat al-asmā'*) embedded in it (see Chapter 3, sections 2–3 for related views on names in nationalism), al-Bazzaz further deplored the use of new and fashionable female names, for example *Ahlam*, *Gharam*, *Ibtisam* and *Hiyam* in preference to such names as *al-Khansa'*, *Asma'*, *Khawla*, *Fatima* and *Khadija*, which are culturally and historically sanctioned. The question of names as a linguistic practice which can act on reality to further the political objectives of Arab nationalism is taken up by al-Basir (1993b) in an article concerning the reference to the Gulf as the Persian Gulf. In this article, first published in 1965, al-Basir argues that the weight of historical and geographical evidence supports the alternative name, the Arab or Arabian Gulf, and that this is the name which the Arabs must use and promote to counter the effort by the *a'ājim* (Persians and other foreigners) who use the rival label (Persian Gulf).

The above discussion shows that the early attempts at framing nationalism in relation to language took two forms. Some writers on this topic failed to specify whether or not all those to whom Arabic is a common language constituted a single nation. Francis al-Marrash and Hasan al-Marsafi belong to this category. Other scholars were more specific, for example Najib 'Azury, who explicitly excluded Egypt from the scope of his concept of an Arab nation. It was suggested above that these conceptualizations of the membership of the Arab nation were usually dependent on the nature of the political context in reference to which they were framed. This approach is particularly relevant for al-'Alayli and al-Bitar, who, in formulating their views, were aware of the role played by French and the colloquial in some expressions of Lebanese nationalism. As such, these conceptualizations must be regarded as historically contingent, as – in theory – all other such conceptualizations are. Later attempts at discussing the role of language in nation-formation – for example, those by al-'Alayli and al-Bitar – made the nation coextensive with the community of Arabic-speakers in the countries of the Middle East and North Africa. The most famous attempt at formulating Arab nationalism in these terms was provided by Sati' al-Husri, to whose ideas I will turn next.

3. SATI' AL-HUSRI: ARABIC, FIRST AND FOREMOST

3.1 *Populism: A Question of Style*

Sati' al-Husri (1880–1968) is the most influential exponent of the ideology of Arab nationalism, which – rather than its political manifestations – will be the subject of this section.[5] Al-Husri's sustained advocacy of this ideology in a period extending over four decades was delivered through prose which has the quality of immediacy, of face-to-face interaction. This stylistic feature is consistent with the genesis of many of his writings as public lectures to audiences of mixed professional backgrounds and educational achievements at different kinds of fora in the Arabic-speaking countries, including cultural clubs, schools, teacher-training colleges, universities, institutes of advanced higher education, and radio audiences. This is reflected in the structure of his discourse, often consisting of short sentences and of brief paragraphs, and in the use of lexical cues which highlight this mode of communicative interaction, for example "at any rate" (*Ārā' wa-aḥādīth fi al-waṭaniyya wa-l-qawmiyya*, 1984a: 27), "Gentlemen! Can you believe that …?" (ibid.: 51, 52), "At this very moment, I am looking at the report …" (*Ḥawl al-waḥda al-thaqāfiyya al-'arabiyya*, 1985i: 15), and many others. It is also reflected in his resorting to (1) formulaic and slogan-like repetitions (*al-dawla shay' wa-l-umma shay' ākhar*, 1985d: 30, which may be rendered as "the state and the nation are two different things"), (2) ideational reiterations (*al-'urūba fawq al-jamī'*, 1985d: 49, and *al-'urūba awwalan*, 1985f: 134, which may be rendered as "Arabism first and foremost"), and (3) the clever use of extended analogies and engaging metaphors as heuristic aids to fix an idea in the minds of his audiences, for example the likening of nations to great rivers (ibid.: 19), or the view that the pull of the national language is similar to that of the forces of gravity (1985j: 208). Through these and other stylistic devices like the use of well-sited couplets, the reader enters into an oral-like communion with al-Husri wherein this thinker performs the role of the educator and teacher, in which he excelled in his life before and after the actual dissolution of the Ottoman Empire in the wake of the First World War. This mode of delivery, which often relates the content of the verbal and non-verbal interactions he had with real or imagined interlocutors in face-to-face communication – at times involving his son Khaldun – is consistent with his brand of populist nationalism in whose propagation al-Husri is prepared to use all manners of means, including explanation, persuasion, inculcation, indication, wooing and enthusing, to address both the mind and the heart of his audiences (cf. *Ḥawl al-qawmiyya al-ʿarabiyya*, 1985j: 16). Hence the description of his brand of nationalism as populist.

On a different level, this oral-like quality of al-Husri's discourse exhibits his interest in linguistic performance as a mode of purposeful action (saying is doing), whose aim is to bring about an attitudinal change in the interlocutor for social or political ends. While personally shunning politics in the sense of practice, which he calls "low politics", al-Husri's discourse is still political in the "high" sense: it is intended to motivate people to achieve the political ends lying behind the cultural nationalism which he firmly espouses. In this scheme of things, al-Husri conceived of style as a means to an end, rather than as an end in itself.[6] In adopting this position, al-Husri conforms to his own stipulation that the mission of literature in the formative stage of nation-building is one of education and mobilization rather than one of achieving artistic elegance, beauty and excellence for their own sake. This orientation on al-Husri's part does not spring from the fact that he spoke Arabic with a foreign accent, for there is no doubt that he had a great facility in the language, and that he devoted himself to it completely after he had made the break with Turkish as his chosen medium of intellectual expression in 1919.[7] We also know that, when al-Husri made this linguistic break with his past, there was no going back on his new Arabic-linked identity (see Cleveland 1971: 14).

This shift from Ottoman Turkish to Arabic marked a significant break in al-Husri's thought, but without causing a complete rupture in it. In this context, the break was not just a linguistic one in the sense of exchanging a particular communicative code for another, but a paradigmatic one in which a particular mode of conceptualizing the nation, where language was treated as a secondary factor, was replaced by another in which it was adopted as the primary criterion of nationhood. Thus, whereas al-Husri the Ottomanist could say: "We cannot accept the concept of the Germans [the German definition of the nation by reference to language] because language is the least of the ties which bind the

Ottomans to one another" (translated from Turkish and quoted in Cleveland 1971: 38), al-Husri the Arabist repeatedly declared that the Arabs constitute a nation by virtue of their sharing the same language, in addition to their having a common history. The break in al-Husri's thinking represented a replacement in ideological terms of the French voluntarist idea of the nation, in which the state is a necessary condition of nationhood but language is not, by the German culture-orientated concept of the nation, in which the state is not a defining criterion but language is (see Chapter 2, section 3). Whereas before the end of the First World War al-Husri believed that the preservation of the Ottoman Empire as a nation-state for all the disparate groups it encompassed – regardless of their religious, ethnic or linguistic backgrounds – required the adoption of a French-style concept of the nation, the final defeat of the Empire in that war and the emergence of new states on its territory which resorted to language for self-legitimation led al-Husri to espouse the German model of nationhood. The fact that this German concept of the nation was judged to be the most applicable model in the Arab context – wherein fragmentation had to be replaced by unity as a political objective – gave greater significance to Arabic as an ingredient in this enterprise. With hindsight, al-Husri could now reinterpret his experiences as a state official in the Balkans in a way that publicly recognized the power of language as a bond of nationality, whereas previously he had tended to downgrade his assessment of this role, as has been pointed out above. This shift from the French to the German mode of conceptualizing the nation is summed up in the formula which al-Husri never tires of repeating: "*al-dawla shay' wa-l-umma shay' ākhar*" (1985g: 30), "The state and the nation are two different things". The fact that the two may sometimes coincide is not considered to be definitionally relevant by al-Husri, a view equally forcefully held by al-ʿAlayli and, to a certain extent Nadim al-Bitar, whose ideas were dealt with in the preceding section.

3.2 *Nation, Language and Education*

Nowhere is the continuity in al-Husri's thought before and after the dissolution of the Ottoman Empire more evident than in his belief in the role of education as an instrument of modernization and nation-building. In the person of al-Husri, the role of the nationalist thinker and the educator exist side by side, not as autonomous or independent entities, but as vigorously interacting ones.[8] Education, for al-Husri, can be meaningful only if it is truly nationalist in character, at the level both of content and of practice. This explains why the only official functions al-Husri the Arabist accepted in Syria, Iraq and Egypt were all in the educational field, where he could use his position and influence to promote nationalist education without getting directly involved in politics in the "low" sense of the term. However, this continuity in the transition from

Ottomanism to Arabism in al-Husri's career was marked by a subtle change in his educational thinking. Whereas a voluntarist conception of the nation tends to be liberal and democratic, targeting the individual before the community in the educational enterprise, the cultural approach to the nation inverses this order of priorities by giving more weight to the community over the individual in pedagogic terms. This shift further requires giving more weight to sociology over psychology in the pedagogic field. The fact that al-Husri was able to accomplish this shift in pedagogical outlook in his Arabist phase signals an intellectual reconciliation with Ziya Gökalp, the philosopher of Turkish nationalism (see Chapter 4, section 2), with whom al-Husri debated the relative weight of psychology and sociology in the educational field. Thus, while Gökalp felt that sociology is more in tune with his brand of cultural nationalism, al-Husri felt that psychology was more consistent with his voluntarist conception of the Ottoman nation.[9] This move in outlook on the part of al-Husri made itself felt in his educational policies in Iraq, which, Cleveland tells us (1971: 63), "limited the scope of individual initiative and provided a coherent, controlled national ideology throughout the school system".

When al-Husri made the shift to Arabism as a cause and an ideology, he espoused it completely and in an unwavering manner. This is clear from his interest in a series of educational issues in the language sphere. One such issue is his insistence on Arabizing the curriculum in Syria after the collapse of the Ottoman Empire by making Arabic the sole language of instruction in the schools, and by setting up a committee to find Arabic equivalents for foreign terms, be they Turkish or European in origin. The same Arabizing drive was relentlessly pursued in Iraq, where he sought to restrict the financial and educational autonomy of the foreign-sponsored schools, which, for obvious reasons, pursued their activities in a manner not fully cognizant of Arab nationalism and the role of the Arabic language in it. In a similar fashion, al-Husri decided to remove the teaching of foreign languages from the primary schools in Iraq (see Chapter 6, section 4.2 for a similar position in Egyptian nationalism). In arguing his case against his opponents, al-Husri states that the introduction of foreign languages into the curriculum at this stage is detrimental to national education because it takes time away from the national language without serving the practical or cultural needs of the community in an effective manner. He further points out that, since the difference between Arabic and the major European languages is so great, the introduction of these languages in the primary schools is bound to lead to confusion in learning terms. This is further complicated by the diglossic nature of Arabic, which means that Arab children have to learn the grammar of the *fuṣḥā* form of the language in situations that are less than ideal in acquisition terms (see *Ārā' wa-aḥādīth fī al-'ilm wa-l-akhlāq wa-l-thaqāfa*, 1985c: 68–9). Al-Husri supports these arguments by saying that the teaching of foreign languages at the primary stage in Europe, even in situations where multilingualism obtains, as in Geneva, is delayed at least until the end of the primary phase to avoid any confusion in language-learning terms between the native language and the other co-territorial languages. There is also a sense in which the removal of the foreign languages from the primary schools represents for al-Husri a break with the colonial past, since it was the policy of the colonial powers to promote their languages in the countries they occupied to serve their own self-interests rather than those of the peoples they ruled. An example of this in the Arab context was the French in Algeria, who, al-Husri tells us (see *Aḥādīth fī al-tarbiya wa-l-ijtimāʿ*, 1984b: 87), considered the primary role of education to be the promotion of the French language to encourage feelings of allegiance towards France.

In the same vein, al-Husri also rejected the call by the Egyptian thinker Taha Husayn to introduce Greek and Latin as compulsory subjects in the higher education system in Egypt (see Chapter 6, section 4.2). Using the above arguments concerning the need to devote time to learning the national language – which, by virtue of its diglossic nature and the complexity of its pedagogic grammars, is a demanding task – al-Husri aimed to counter alternative orientations at forging a national identity for Egypt which took it outside its Arab orbit and the challenges of modernization this urgently demanded.[10] In particular, al-Husri considered the call to introduce these two languages into higher education a false attempt to attach Egypt to, or to attach to it, a European and Mediterranean conception of national self which negates, or at least weakens, its Arab identity. In addition, al-Husri believed that the promotion of Greek and Latin would, first, take away from the time available to the teaching of modern European languages and, second, induce a classicism and elitism that looked to the past, rather than to the future where the thrust of modernization in the Arab context ought to lie. Furthermore, by rejecting Taha Husayn's position on Latin and Greek, al-Husri sought to oppose the slavish tendency among Arab educationalists and other elites to formulate their views and policies on grounds that are pertinent to the West rather than to the realities of their own situation in its historical and properly modernizing context. Thus, al-Husri insisted that the arguments advanced by some European educationalists for the validity of Greek and Latin within their education systems cannot be transferred to the Arab context with its own different historical and cultural particularities. Al-Husri wanted to impress on his audience the need to consider as a maxim of modernization that what is good for Europe is not necessarily good for the Arabs. And this extends to the conceptualization of the nation, where it is essential to adopt those views of it which fit the Arab context, although these views may not be completely watertight in theoretical or empirical terms.

3.3 Defining the Arab Nation

Let us now turn to al-Husri's conception of the nation. To begin with, this conception is characterized by two features. First, it is cultural rather than overtly political (see Chapter 2, section 3). Second, it belongs to the objective rather than the subjective variety of definitions of the nation (see Chapter 2, section 2).

The first feature implies that the state is not a necessary or even a sufficient condition for the constitution of the nation. A nation can exist without being associated with a state that is exclusively coterminous with it. Also, the existence of the state does not guarantee that the people who live under its sovereignty constitute a nation in their own right. This is sometimes referred to as "the German mode of defining the nation" in the literature. It is, however, important not to draw the conclusion from this association that al-Husri identifies his conception of the nation with the views of the German Romantics on the topic. Thus, although al-Husri shares with Herder, Fichte and Arndt the view that language is the main ingredient of nationhood, he differs from the last two in his refusal to ascribe to Arabic and the Arabs the status of "original" language and "original" people as these two thinkers did for German and the Germans (see section 4 on this issue). In addition, al-Husri adamantly refuses to turn his interest in language as an ingredient of nationalism into what Kedourie (1966) calls "linguism" (see Chapter 2, section 3), wherein ideas of race and language are said to coincide, or are used to construct a platform from which to launch claims of racial superiority towards other nations and their languages. Finally, al-Husri does not direct his nationalist fervour against an external Other in the same way as some of the German Romantics do in their vehement denunciation of France and the French language. It is with these provisos in mind that I refer to al-Husri's conception of the nation as being in the German mode.

This endogenous versus exogenous orientation in thinking about the nation extends to al-Husri's objective definition of the Arab nation in terms of language and history. In this definitional enterprise, al-Husri is mainly interested in what binds the Arabs internally rather than in what marks them externally from other nations and groups. Within this framework, the external marking of the Arab nation becomes a function of its internally generated self-definition rather than the other way round. This endows the Arab nation with a degree of national self-sufficiency in existential terms which is not definitionally or logically contingent on the existence of a differentiated Other – what is sometimes called "playing the vis-à-vis" (see Chapter 1, section 2). This to some extent underlies al-Husri's refusal to accept the general interpretation in the literature on Arab nationalism and modernism that the Napoleonic invasion of Egypt – as a projection of a different Other – marked a turning point in the cultural history of the Arabic-speaking people; it further explains his refusal to treat this invasion as formatively instrumental in developing the conditions which prepared the ground for the rise of this nationalism later in the nineteenth century. Al-Husri, however, does not deny that Napoleon's invasion acted as a catalyst in this direction; but that is the end of the story (cf. *Ārā' wa-aḥādīth fī al-tārīkh wa-l-ijtimā'*, 1985e: 45–79).

Part of the rationale behind the discussion of the role of Arabic in group-identity formulations in premodern times in this work (Chapter 3) is to lay the grounds for claiming that al-Husri's view on the commanding role of Arabic as an ingredient of the national self in modern times is – in spite of being traditionally associated with the German Romantics – ultimately rooted in its own historical and cultural milieu. Two implications flow from this. The first is that the Arabic intellectual tradition provides al-Husri with a definition of the collective self in relation to language which he could utilize in a subtle, but effective, manner in promoting his own nationalist ideas. Although al-Husri does not explicitly tap into this tradition, giving an impression of almost complete ideological modernity, he must of course have known that a definition of the Arab collective self in relation to language would strike a chord with the elite, and that it would satisfy the criterion of "resonance" by tapping into deep-rooted attitudes towards the language on a more popular level (see Chapter 1, section 2). The second implication makes the German Romantic influence on al-Husri as much one of implying modernity as it is one of substance in theoretical terms. The fact that Germany was the most highly regarded European power at the popular level among the Arabs in the nineteenth century and most of the twentieth century, and that its condition of national fragmentation in its formative stage most resembled that of the Arabs during this period, must have acted as a catalyst in promoting al-Husri's vision of what constitutes the Arab nation.

Let us now consider al-Husri's objective definition of the Arab nation. To begin with, in comparison with most other definitions (for example, al-'Alayli's and al-Bitar's above), al-Husri's definition is compositionally minimalist in that it refers to language and shared history (in that order) as the ingredients of this nationalism. In discussing the relationship between these two ingredients, al-Husri employs the following formula (which he repeats in several places in his writings): "Language constitutes the life of a nation. History constitutes its feeling. A nation which forgets its history loses its feeling and consciousness. A nation which forgets its language loses its life and [very] being" (*Muḥāḍarāt fī nushū' al-fikra al-qawmiyya*, 1985b: 51). Al-Husri further likens language to the key which can enable an imprisoned nation to free itself (cf. *Ārā' wa-aḥādīth fī al-waṭaniyya wa-l-qawmiyya*, 1984a: 68). The importance of language in the definition of Arabness on the individual and collective self levels is clear from the following statement by al-Husri (*Ārā' wa-aḥādīth fī al-qawmiyya al-'arabiyya*, 1985d: 46):

> Every Arabic-speaking people is an Arab people. Every individual belonging to one of these Arabic-speaking peoples is an Arab. And if an Arab does not recognize this, and if he is not proud to be an Arab, we must look for the reasons that make him take this position. His position may be the result of ignorance: in that case we must teach him the truth. It may spring from a false consciousness and deception: in that case we must awaken him and guide him on the right path. It may be the result of excessive egoism: in that case we must try to limit his egoism. But under no circumstances should we say: "He is not an Arab as long as he does not wish to be one, does not accept his Arabness or is disdainful of it". He is an Arab whether he wishes to be one or not in his present condition. He is an Arab: an ignorant, unaware, recalcitrant or disloyal Arab, but an Arab all the same. An Arab who lost his consciousness and feelings, and may have even lost his conscience.

The following statement by al-Husri, which further reveals the role of language in framing his nationalist ideology, amplifies the above specification of who an Arab is (*al-'Urūba awwalan*, 1985f: 14–15):

> Every individual who belongs to the Arab countries and speaks Arabic is an Arab. He is so, regardless of the name of the country whose citizenship he officially holds. He is so, regardless of the religion he professes or the sect he belongs to. He is so, regardless of his ancestry, lineage or the roots of the family to which he belongs. He is an Arab, [full stop].
>
> Arabness is not restricted to those who can trace their origin back to the Arabian Peninsula; nor is it restricted to Muslims alone. It encompasses every individual who belongs to the Arab countries: whether he is Egyptian, Kuwaiti or Moroccan; whether he is Muslim or Christian; whether he is Sunni, Twelver Shi'ite or Druze; and whether he is Catholic, Orthodox or Protestant. [Regardless of what he is,] he is a son of the Arab nation as long as he belongs to the Arab lands and speaks Arabic.

The above is tantamount to saying: "Tell me what your language is, and I will tell you who you are". But al-Husri's interest in language as a nationalist ingredient is far more cognizant of its functionality than of its power of symbolism. Al-Husri is decidedly more interested in the role of language as a means of communication in the nationalist enterprise than in its symbolic connotations, although he is deeply aware of the role of symbols (flags, cenotaphs, border points, national anthems, stamps, coins and so on) in formulating a view of the national self. This is why al-Husri considers the death of a language to be genuinely tantamount to the death of the nation whose tongue it is. Nations for al-Husri are living or natural organisms, in the social sense of the term, and their vitality must therefore be reflected in the vitality of the languages they speak. Similarly, the weakness of a language is indicative of the weakness of the national spirit among its people. Language is therefore not just an ingredient of the nation, but a barometer through which the condition of the nation can be gauged. But what does it mean to say that al-Husri is interested in the functional power of language in defining the nation? How is this functionality ideologized in al-Husri's conception of Arab nationalism?

3.4 *Arab Nationalism and the Ideologization of Language*

The starting point for al-Husri in this matter is the role of language as that factor of differentiation which sets the boundary between man and beast. As a cognitive resource, language is the instrument of thought, which ceases to exist without it. In addition, language is a means of socialization which bonds the individual to a particular culture through child-rearing practices and experiences at an early age. In this social capacity, language further serves as a means of communication between the members of a particular community, thus facilitating the transmission of ideas and feelings between them and creating a feeling of interpersonal intimacy in the process. As such, a language is a bonding agent between those who speak it, bringing them closer to each other while, at the same time, setting them apart from those who speak other languages. And, for the purposes of this study, language is that factor which makes a people a nation by enabling them to imagine themselves as a community that is internally bonded and externally bounded, both synchronically and diachronically.[11] Language is also the carrier of a nation's culture, as this is expressed through its literature and other modes of linguistic production. It is language as the outcome of a common history and as the forger of cultural unity which creates the will in a people to become a nation, thus contradicting Renan on this matter, rather than the other way round. This is a clever move on the part of al-Husri because it enables him to acknowledge the role of "will" in nation-building, while at the same time claiming that this voluntarist mode of defining the nation is but a product of the nation as a cultural construct at whose heart lies the formative power of language. Under this interpretation, language remains primary while will becomes secondary. Furthermore, language is considered as the antecedent from which will flows as a consequent or second-order bonding agent which can enhance the functional role of language as the nation-formation factor par excellence.

This logical, even causal, ordering of factors at play in nation-formation remains rhetorical in nature, in the sense that it is not possible to show in a factually convincing or empirically testable manner that language is indeed the antecedent, and will is the consequent, in nation-building. This challenges the repeated assertions by al-Husri that his theory of a language-based Arab nationalism is historically valid, in the sense that it can transcend the evidential base from which it is derived, at least in its German manifestation. To achieve this, al-Husri deploys three strategies. The first admits that his theory is historically contingent and, therefore, applies within a non-universalist and, to a certain extent, eclectic framework. It is therefore a restricted theory of nationalism, mainly fashioned to suit the Arab context (see Chapter 1, section 1). The second strategy consists of providing evidence from within the realm of the Ottoman Empire, in which the seeds of Arab nationalism were embedded, to show that language is the criterion of nationhood par excellence. The third strategy consists of reinterpreting what is projected as counter-evidence by his opponents, and doing so in a way which turns this evidence into data that corroborate rather than falsify his theory. In the following discussion, I will deal with the last two strategies insofar as they apply to the role of language in nationalism. The first strategy will not be considered here because of its quasi-theoretical nature.

The second strategy is best illustrated by considering examples from within the realm of the Ottoman Empire before its dissolution after the First World War. The primary example in this respect is the Turkification of the Ottoman Turks in matters of language, literature and history which served the cause of Turkish cultural nationalism. It was pointed out in Chapter 4 (section 2) that this cultural nationalism laid down the foundations for a Turkish political nationalism, and that the latter in turn enhanced the later progress of the former under Atatürk. The fact that Turkish was used as a national bond between those to whom it was a common language, inside and outside the Ottoman Empire, is regarded by al-Husri as a confirmation of the efficacy of language as an identity-marker. In addition, the fact that Turkish was made to undermine the bond of religious brotherhood between Ottoman Turks and Ottoman Arabs who professed Islam provides further evidence of this role of language in nation-formation. This same pattern was evident in the Balkans, especially within those Ottoman communities which belonged to the Orthodox Church. It was also evident among the Albanians, who resorted to language in constructing their national identity, thus overriding their division into Muslims and Catholics, on the one hand, and undermining the religious bond which held between the Muslims among them and the Ottoman Turks, on the other.

Within the Balkan context, the Greeks are said to constitute an interesting example of the above trend of relying on language, as an ingredient of culture, in framing their national identity. Al-Husri puts forward the view that the Greek language and the Orthodox faith were both relevant in keeping Greek identity alive in the Ottoman Empire, but that language was more significant in this enterprise than religion. Whereas the Greeks were distinct from the Turks in both language and religion, they were distinct from other Orthodox communities inside the Empire in language alone. This the Greeks never tired of using to their advantage, in all affairs of the Church, at the expense of other Orthodox communities, for example the Bulgarians. In addition, language was the major factor deployed by the Greeks as an organizing principle in resisting the attempts to bring them into the Russian sphere of influence towards the close of the nineteenth century. Al-Husri adds that it was the pull of language and common culture, aided by that of religion, which led to the incremental expansion in the areas brought under Greek sovereignty in the nineteenth and early twentieth centuries. Areas newly liberated from under Ottoman control joined other already independent Greek areas with which they shared a linguistic bond over and above the religious one.

This trend of putting language before religion in constructing national identity in the Balkans is said by al-Husri to have been exhibited very clearly in the Bulgarian context. He explains this by reference to the double dominance over the Bulgarians by (1) the Turks in the political domain, and (2) the Greeks in the cultural sphere. In their struggle for national independence, the Bulgarians first sought to liberate themselves from the cultural hegemony which the Greeks – through the Orthodox Church and its associated institutions and liturgical practices – exercised over them. This effort consisted of attempts which revolved around establishing Bulgarian as the language of education, culture and religion. Al-Husri sketches out the methods used by the Bulgarians to achieve this aim. Schools which taught in Bulgarian, not Greek, started to appear towards the middle of the nineteenth century. This had the effect of turning what had previously been a spoken language into a written one around which a thriving cultural industry of dictionary-making, grammatical scholarship and translation coalesced. Most significant in the last domain was the translation of the Bible from Greek into Bulgarian during this period. Calls to use Bulgarian in the Church liturgy started to appear, but they were met by stiff Greek opposition on the grounds that Greek was a language of the Scriptures and, therefore, the only legitimate one for articulating it in formal church settings. To overcome this opposition, calls were made to establish a Bulgarian Orthodox Church, which would differ from its Greek counterpart in matters of language only. Exploiting the political situation which made them administratively subject to an Ottoman Empire that was keen to weaken the Greeks, the Bulgarians in 1870 obtained a Royal Decree from the Ottoman Sultan permitting them to establish their own Church. The effect of this was to strengthen Bulgarian culture and to underpin the movement for political independence from the Ottoman Empire by exploiting religion as a motivating factor in it. Al-Husri further tells us that this same pattern obtained in Romania, where a Romanian language-based cultural independence from Greek hegemony eventually led to political independence from the Ottoman Empire.

The situation in Yugoslavia provides an interesting case study for testing the limits of al-Husri's theory of nationalism. In dealing with the historically, politically and religiously complex situation in this area, al-Husri is sometimes more cautious about positing a direct and formative link between language and nation-formation – or he is less assertive about the finality of this link. This reflects the awareness on his part that history, in particular, can work in the opposite direction to language in nation-formation. One feels, however, from the tenor of al-Husri's treatment of the subject, which was made public for the first time in 1948, that he is hopeful that the course of future events will confirm the historical adequacy of his theory – or its predictive power, to use a more accurate concept. This is evident from his statement that "the feeling of national unity in Yugoslavia is sufficient to overcome [all the forces of division in this country] and to put an end to all local-territorial tendencies" (*Muḥāḍarāt fi nushū' al-fikra al-qawmiyya*, 1985b: 83). The fact that what al-Husri expected, suspected or strongly hoped would be the case has been shown by the events of recent years to be more in the realm of wishful thinking than in the domain of historical reality may be taken as a refutation of his theory of nationalism, at least insofar as it claims that language is the primary factor in nation-formation.

It is, however, not very difficult to imagine how al-Husri might have responded to this criticism. On the one hand, he might have pointed to the cautious note of his predictions, and to the fact that history, which is the second factor in nation-formation under his theory, has on this occasion assumed greater formative power over language. To make this point, al-Husri would have had to show and explain that historical differences between the constituent members of Yugoslavia (Serbs, Slovenes, Croatians and Bosnians) played a more dominant role than the unifying power of language, or that these differences were far too great to be overcome by the unifying power of language. On the other hand, al-Husri might have pointed to Yugoslavia as a test case which proves the empiricism of his theory in the Popperian sense of the term, that is, its ability to refer to factual situations against which it can be judged. Yugoslavia might have been further projected as yet another example which shows the limits of al-Husri's theory, or its non-universality, a point he himself openly admits in a pre-emptive move to deflect any anticipated criticism. But he might also have deployed counter-strategies of the type he employed to reject the following supposedly recalcitrant cases, which are said by his critics to refute the theoretical and descriptive adequacy of his theory concerning language in nation-formation.

These cases divide into two categories. The first category involves the secession of one territory from another, in spite of the linguistic bond that holds between them. This includes (1) the separation of the United States of America from Great Britain, and (2) the separation of the countries of Latin America from Spain and Portugal, although this will not be dealt with here because it replicates the arguments applicable to (1) above. The second category involves the unity of multilingual states, for example Belgium and Switzerland, against the expectation of fragmentation along linguistic lines as predicted, or projected to happen, under al-Husri's theory. Al-Husri acknowledges the suggestive power of these examples, but he still considers them to be in line with his theory. To explain this, al-Husri resorts to analogy as one of his favourite rhetorical devices to convince his audience that what may seem to be refuting evidence is in fact misdirected and not properly interpreted. Thus he likens the above examples to smoke which rises up in the atmosphere in seeming refutation of the law of gravity, although in fact its behaviour is in total conformity with this law. Let us now consider the above chosen examples in more detail.

Al-Husri's treatment of the USA consists of four elements. The first element is based on the idea that, since the USA seceded from Great Britain before the age of nationalism, it cannot be validly treated as a refuting evidence of his theory. This is one of the major premises of nationalism studies which al-Husri uses to promote his theory in a number of places in his extensive output on the subject, although he does this selectively. The second element considers the independence of the USA as the result of the desire on the part of those who were behind it to rid themselves of the unfair tax-raising policies and other economic restrictions which the British sought to impose on them. They were aided in this by the physical separation of the USA from Great Britain. This is essentially an argument from history which, al-Husri reminds us, is a relevant factor in his theory. However, the fact that physical separation was invoked as an aiding factor in this process is seen by some critics of al-Husri as an admission on his part that geography, contrary to what he repeatedly asserts, is a relevant factor in nation-formation. The third element seeks to challenge the general view that the language of the USA was exclusively English throughout its history. He does this by introducing an implicit distinction between the "official" language and the language of the home in the USA, and another distinction between the majority language and other minority languages in the country. Thus he argues that, although English was the language of the states which formed the original federation, these were later joined by other states in which Spanish or French, not English, was dominant. Although English had the upper hand in this situation, it nevertheless was not the only language. This situation of linguistic diversity continued to exist under the influence of waves of immigrants who introduced their languages into the country and kept them alive through further immigration injections, community schools and associations, and migrant literatures. Al-Husri believes that this situation of linguistic diversity weakens the argument that English was a binding force, of the type he posits in his theory, between the USA and Great Britain.[12] The fourth element shows al-Husri's ingenuity in arguing his case. It consists of a turning of the tables against his critics by pointing out that, if the Americans can still agree to live together in a united state, in spite of their linguistic diversity, then how much more it behoves the Arabs to be more determined to achieve the same kind of unity, in view of their linguistic unity.

Let us now deal with the second category above. Al-Husri considers the unity of Belgium, in spite of the country's bilingual character, to be the result of its history and the distribution of its two languages, French and Flemish. He points out that the intense rivalry between France and Britain in the nineteenth century was instrumental in establishing Belgium as a buffer-state whose territorial integrity was essential for the balance of power between the two competing nations and the cause of peace in Europe. In the linguistic realm, the intricate distribution of the two languages in Belgium, whereby their speakers live cheek by jowl not only in the big urban centres but also in the smallest of villages, has meant that no sensible separation of the two language communities can be achieved without a demographic upheaval on a massive scale. Turning to Switzerland, al-Husri points to its status as a buffer-state that keeps its more powerful neighbours apart as an important factor in its political unity (see also Chapter 6, section 5.2). Furthermore, the fact that the various language communities in Switzerland enjoy full control over their own affairs – except defence and foreign relations – within a vastly devolved system of government has ensured the continuity of the union between them. Al-Husri concludes that the special character of these two examples is too limited in empirical terms to constitute a refutation of his theory. In addition, al-Husri invokes the theoretical premise of the categorial difference between nation and state to claim that Switzerland and Belgium are states, not nations.

Al-Husri (see *Ārā' wa-aḥādīth fī al-waṭaniyya wa-l-qawmiyya*, 1984a: 75–81) reiterates these arguments in his critique of the Egyptian thinker Taha Husayn, who cites the above cases to argue that language cannot form the basis of nation-formation between Egypt and the other Arabic-speaking countries (see Chapter 6, section 4.2). In a similar manner, al-Husri refuses to concede any ground to Lutfi al-Sayyid (see Chapter 6, section 3), Hafni Mahmud Pasha and the writer Ihsan 'Abd al-Quddus, who cite the history of Greece, Turkey and the USA respectively in support of their views that language is not an ingredient in nation-formation in the Arab context. Al-Husri also rejects as bogus all the attempts to construct Egypt's identity in Eastern, African, Mediterranean, Pharaonic or Islamic terms. He declares that Egypt is an Arab country because its language is Arabic, and that being Arab in national terms does not deny Egypt's past and the role this past may play in modulating its identity (see Chapter 6, sections 3, 4, 4.1–2). Al-Husri acknowledges that some Egyptians may feel a bond with their Pharaonic past, but this is a bond with a past that is linguistically dead. And since language is the vehicle and substance of culture, the only bond that the Egyptians can meaningfully have in national-identity terms perforce goes through this language. Egyptian culture, according to al-Husri, must therefore be defined as Arab culture; and, since Egypt shares its language with other Arabic-speaking countries, it must therefore share this culture with them too. This is a significant result for al-Husri, who stresses that "the unity of culture guarantees all forms of unity" (*Ārā' wa-aḥādīth fī al-waṭaniyya wa-l-qawmiyya*, 1984a: 81). Thus, the linguistic unity of Egypt enables the Egyptians to overcome the divisions which religion may induce between them. Furthermore, the unity of Egypt with other Arabic-speaking countries opens the possibility for Egypt to assume a leadership role which it would otherwise be denied. The call "Egypt for the Egyptians" turns out under this analysis to be against Egypt's interests, both internally and externally. Al-Husri concludes his argument by claiming that, as an exercise in self-generation, a territorially conceived national identity for Egypt is short-sighted and misconceived. The fact that such a statement cannot be properly tested is of no concern to al-Husri.

The attempt by al-Husri to downgrade the role of religion as a factor of national identity in Egypt, a point on which he goes far beyond the limits advocated by Taha Husayn, is symptomatic of his secular conception of Arab nationalism. Al-Husri's reading of the history of nationalism in the Balkans is seen as a historical confirmation of this view. Al-Husri believes that this situation, in what is essentially a Christian sphere of religious identification, is applicable in the Islamic context. A paradigm example of this is the fragmentation of the Ottoman Empire into separate entities, in spite of the unity of religious belief between the Turks and the majority of the Arabic-speaking Ottomans under its jurisdiction. Al-Husri sees this as a vindication of his theory, and he therefore approves of the separation between nation-formation and religion which is one of the cornerstones of Turkish nationalism under Atatürk. To the best of my knowledge, this approval of Atatürk is rarely echoed by other Arab nationalists.

3.5 Nation, Language and Religion

Al-Husri's views on the secular character of Arab nationalism hold enormous interest for political scientists and scholars of nationalism. In the present work, however, I will restrict myself to the way in which these views impinge on the interaction between language and religion in al-Husri's thinking. To begin with, al-Husri believes that, in the age of nationalism, religion can be an effective factor in nation-formation when it is of the exclusivist type, for example Judaism, thus allowing for the coincidence of language with religion in nation-formation. This is not applicable to universal religions like Christianity and Islam, owing to the multilingual nature of their faith communities. However, it would be wrong to conclude from this that al-Husri denies that religion can play a role in nation-formation. Any role which religion plays must nevertheless be articulated through its contribution to the language, by spreading and protecting it against fragmentation. Thus, al-Husri claims that the role of Islam in nation-formation is relevant only to the extent that it enhances the position of Arabic as the factor around which conceptualizations of the Arab nation can coalesce. In this context, the fact that Islam turned Arabic into the language of a vibrant culture, and led to the Arabization of many communities, is a relevant factor in Arab nation-formation. But, he adds, this does not make Arabic an Islamic language in national-identity terms, that is, in the sense of serving as a focal point in the calls for Islamic unity as an alternative to Arab unity. Islam is a relevant factor in Arab nationalism insofar as it was involved in drawing, through the spread of Arabic, the boundaries within which the nationalist idea can be activated and promoted in modern times. Islamicized but non-Arabized parts of the realm of Islam fall outside the scope of this idea.

This decoupling of religion, on the one hand, from nation and language, on the other, explains two important features of al-Husri's projection of Arabic as the ingredient of national identity par excellence in the Arab context. The first feature concerns the absence of the usual references to Arabic as the language of the Qur'an in setting out the case of the importance of the language in cultural terms. In addition, this feature is represented in the refusal to exploit for ideological ends the references to the language in the Qur'an itself and the body of the *ḥadīth* literature (see Chapter 3, section 2). These references are conspicuous by their uncompromising absence, unlike the references to the role of literature in forming the national culture.

The second feature consists of breaking what al-Husri implicitly considers as the Muslim monopoly over the language by emphasizing the role it plays in the life of the Christian Arabs. In particular, he highlights the use of the Bible in Arabic by the Christian Arab communities, a trend in which the Protestant missions in Lebanon played a leading role through their epoch-making translation of the Bible and use of the local language in the liturgy (see Chapter 4, section 3). In addition, al-Husri highlights the fact that it was the Christian Arabs of the Levant who, through their formative participation in the literary renaissance of the nineteenth century, have made of Arabic in modern times a language worthy of serving as the marker of an Arab national identity and as the medium of cultural and scientific modernization. By so doing, Christian Arabs provided their Muslim compatriots in the Ottoman Empire with the means through which they could fashion a collective identity for themselves that finally broke the bond of religious identity between them and Ottoman Turks. Thus language, not religion, came to be the highest common denominator between the Arabs in national terms.

Al-Husri's insistence on language rather than religion as a common bond of national identity among the Arabs is clearly designed to override the religious differences existing between them. The fact that religious and denominational identifications were used by the French authorities in Alexandretta (the Hatay region in south-western Turkey) to break up the linguistically based unity of the population in this area, in order to produce a census count in which the Turks were a majority, is seen by al-Husri as an example of the divisive potential of religious and sectarian affiliations. This explains al-Husri's rejection of all forms of religious and sectarian identification in the national body politic, as the last quotation above sets out. However, by ignoring the fact that language may also divide as much as religion does in the Arab world, at least insofar as the existence of other sizeable language communities is concerned (for example, the Berbers and the Kurds), al-Husri fails to offer a comprehensive argument in favour of his view that Arabic is the highest common denominator in the formation of the Arab nation.

3.6 *Between the Standard and the Dialects: The Case for Linguistic Reforms*

The search for the highest common denominator in Arab nation-formation via language is responsible for al-Husri's rejection of all tendencies which promote the dialects at the expense of the standard language. Thus, he rejects the view which calls for the formation of as many Arab nation-states as there are perceptibly overarching Arab dialects. He also rejects the view which correlates the present boundaries of the Arab states with discrete linguistic boundaries of the dialectal kind. Applying the nationalist principle that "language defence is nation defence", al-Husri sets out to show the untenability of the above views, which the Syrian National Socialist Party of Antun Sa'ada (see Chapter 6, section 2) puts forward to counter his language-based Arab nationalism. Al-Husri argues that the so-called nation-state dialects (for example, Iraqi, Syrian, Lebanese or Egyptian Arabic), on which his opponents confer the status of languages, are linguistic labels of little empirical validity beyond their descriptive and geographical domains. Thus, what is traditionally called Iraqi Arabic is no more than an idealized form of a dominant dialect of Baghdad and the areas surrounding it. This dialect is different from the dialect of Mosul, in the same way as the dialect of Aleppo is different from that of Damascus, although the latter is erroneously referred to as Syrian Arabic. What we have, according to al-Husri, is a dialect continuum which does not correlate with the borders of the Arabic-speaking states. Al-Husri further points out that, if the principle of dialect difference as a correlate of state boundaries demarcation is to be applied throughout the Arabic-speaking countries, we would end up with far more states than we presently have. Not only would this lead to more fragmentation than even the supporters of Antun Sa'ada are willing to countenance, but it would also make a mockery of any attempt to construct a theory of Arab national identity in relation to language. And, in the absence of another equally effective principle of nation-formation, the Arab nation would cease to exist. Thus, what the Arabs need is a unified language which can in turn unify them, an instrument of fusion rather than fission. Or, as al-Husri puts it, the Arabs need a "unified and unifying language" ("*lugha muwaḥḥada wa-muwaḥḥida*", in *Fī al-lugha wa-l-adab wa-ʿalāqatihimā bi-l-qawmiyya*, 1985h: 30), rather than a series of dialect-languages which will lead to further fragmentation in the Arab body politic.

In defending this "unified and unifying language", al-Husri rejects the view that the standard language and the dialects will go the way of Latin and its daughter languages. Al-Husri argues that the two situations are vastly different. Standard Arabic, unlike Latin, never lost its dominance in its linguistic heartland. This dominance was maintained through the close association between Arabic and Islam in the capacity of Arabic as the language of the Qur'an. Thus, even when the Arabs came under the control of the Ottomans, whose rule lasted almost half a millennium, standard Arabic never lost its position of dominance in relation to Turkish. This ensured the continuity of the language as the medium of education and culture. Furthermore, in spite of the diglossic nature of the Arabic language situation, the standard language remained intelligible to the elite and, in modern times, gained access to an expanding number of school-educated people. The media, press and electronic, have enhanced this trend. If anything, the trend will be towards convergence, not divergence, in intelligibility between the local varieties and standard Arabic. This, al-Husri believes, will be achieved through a middle form of Arabic in which the standard is cross-fertilized with the dialects (ibid.: 30).

This vehement defence of the standard language contrasts sharply with the lukewarm defence al-Husri provides against the calls to replace the Arabic script by a Roman alphabet. In the literature on the subject, the argument is always made that changing the Arabic script would inevitably lead to a massive rupture with the cultural heritage of the Arabs. The point is also sometimes made that the Turks were able to implement the reform of the script because of an impoverished cultural legacy (whatever that means), a situation which did not pertain to the Arabs. Al-Husri does not mention either of these two arguments, especially the former. Rather, he points out that any such change must take place under conditions of national unity and must be sponsored by a leadership that has the political will, power and resources to implement it. But, since none of these conditions exists in the Arab context, the calls for the reform of the script are bound to lead to friction, division and the dissipation of national energy which is better spent pursuing the goals of unity and modernization.

Clearly, al-Husri objects to the calls to change the script not on grounds of principle, but on the basis of expedience. The impression one gets from what he says is that he would have gone along with this change if the conditions in the Arabic-speaking countries were different. If so, this raises the question as to why al-Husri would espouse such a change. The answer may partly lie in the fact that al-Husri does not believe that the way a language is written is one of its inalienable linguistic properties, the implication being that a change of the script does not mean a change of the language as a system *sui generis*. Although al-Husri does not explicitly make this point, it is not unreasonable to assume that he would accept it. The evidence for this may be derived from his view that the "Arabic language is one thing, and traditional Arabic grammar is another" (see *Aḥādīth fī al-tarbiya wa-l-ijtimāʿ*, 1984b: 53). This is a sophisticated view of the language which goes against the naive-realist, or God's-truth, grain of the Arabic grammatical tradition (see Suleiman 1999c). But such a view of language is not in itself sufficient to make a thinker who regards it as a criterion of the nation accept the abandonment of its script lightly. We must therefore assume that al-Husri's lukewarm opposition referred to above is the result of something deeper. Although we do not have evidence for it, it is possible that al-Husri would have linked such a change to the imperatives of national unity and modernization, to counter the tendency among the Arabs to look back to a past in which religion, rather than the secularized forces of language and history, provided the underpinnings of the future. This, however, will remain in the realm of speculation.

Al-Husri seems to subscribe to the principle that, like charity, modernization in a linguistically defined nation must begin at home by reforming the language itself. Al-Husri considers this principle a part of the strategic edifice of his nationalist theory. In tactical terms, however, the reform of the language is considered by him as the best means of defence against external attack, or as a corrective remedy which can energize the language and make it more suitable to deliver at an enhanced level of nationalist participation. Writing almost half a century ago, al-Husri says that Arabic is going through a "stage of change and transformation after a period of stagnation and inertia" (*Fī al-lugha wa-l-adab wa-ʿalāqatihimā bi-l-qawmiyya*, 1985h: 7), and that this requires the input of all those with an interest in the language, whether linguists or non-linguists. It is for this reason, and because of his interest in Arabic as the mainstay of his nationalist theory, that al-Husri delves into matters of linguistic reform.

Al-Husri's reforms are informed by three principles. The first principle involves the need to reach a rapprochement between the dialects and the standard language; this is important to prevent the diglossic situation of Arabic from turning into a multilingual state of inter-nation differentiation rather than remaining one of intra-nation variation. He thus calls for negotiating the difference between the two forms of the language through active grammatical and lexical intervention, in a two-pronged process of levelling up and levelling down. Language, al-Husri argues, is a living object which must respond to the needs of its users if it is to survive and develop. And, since it is not realistic to expect the standard to replace the dialects in one fell swoop, it is therefore prudent to seek a middle kind of Arabic which can bring this goal into the realm of possibility.

The second principle declares that traditional Arabic grammar, whether in its descriptive or pedagogic form, is different from the grammar of the language in the predescriptive sense. Although this is a methodologically sound principle, al-Husri invokes it not for its empirical value but to pre-empt the charge that his ideas on grammatical reform would distort the structural integrity of the language. His intention, he declares, is the simplification of pedagogic grammar, not the distortion of the language as a self-contained system. This may at times involve a different presentation of the facts of grammar from the one traditionally available in traditional pedagogic grammars. It may sometimes involve offering semantically based definitions of grammatical categories, in place of the traditional definitions which invoke the formal, or inflectional, character of words in constructions. At other times, the required simplification may be achieved by eliminating the various kinds of causes (see Chapter 3, section 3) that make the formal acquisition of grammar such a chore to the learners. In some cases, the simplification of grammar must respond to the clearly perceived needs of the speakers. A good example of this is the need to introduce what al-Husri calls a possessive article into Arabic grammar to encode the idea expressed by *māl* in Iraq, *dhyāl* in Morocco, *bitā'* in Egypt, *ḥagg* in the Arabian Peninsula, and *shét* in Syria (ibid.: 118–19). Al-Husri is, however, aware that none of these proposals for simplification can succeed without challenging "the conservative spirit" (ibid.: 67), and the "paralysis of familiarity" (ibid.), that pervade Arabic grammatical thinking.

The third principle declares that lexical, particularly terminological, development in Arabic is not possible without admitting the following: (1) Arabic has an impoverished terminological stock to designate the never-ending stream of scientific concepts in the modern world; (2) this impoverishment is not one of lexical resources *per se*, but of lexical inertia and a feeling of linguistic smugness which wrongly interprets the static vastness of the Arabic lexicon as a sign of its dynamic richness; and (3) the surest way of plugging the terminological gap in Arabic is to espouse the modern sciences in an active and formative way, rather than in a passive and summative manner. To achieve the goal of lexical innovation, the resources of the language – including derivation, Arabicization and the much-neglected blending – must be pressed into service. In pursuing this task, the linguists can take advantage of the conventionality of terms as labels, to seek equivalents in Arabic which designate their concepts without necessarily translating them faithfully. They can also take advantage of the fact that the lexical currency of a term can eliminate any feeling of "strangeness" or "foreignness" which may be associated with it during the initial stages of its introduction. The cause of lexical reform may be enhanced further by working towards lexical harmonization between the Arabic-speaking countries. As an example, al-Husri gives the names of the calendar months which differ between the various Arab countries. Al-Husri calls for the standardization of these names, giving preference to the indigenous ones over their borrowed counterparts.

Al-Husri's views on the role of language in nation-formation reflect a multiplicity of influences. There is first the influence of the German Romantics. Second, al-Husri's direct experience of life in the Balkans and in the Turkish part of the Ottoman Empire provided him with confirmation of the efficacy of this connection between language and nation. The fact that Arabic was a high-prestige language in the eyes of its speakers meant that its role as the mainstay of his nationalist thinking needed little demonstration or validation. In tapping into these sources of theoretical argumentation and empirical validation, al-Husri was mainly interested in the functional, as distinct from the symbolic, role of the language. He was also able to frame his nationalist views in secular terms, thus marginalizing almost to the point of extinction the connection between Arabic and Islam. Al-Husri was very adept at negotiating his way through competing theoretical positions. Thus he never allowed the legitimizing power of the past to overwhelm his commitment to modernization. Each had its role, but he was more interested in modernization as a twin force of nation-formation than in investing the future with the authenticity of the past. To this end, he projected his treatment of the role of Arabic in nation-formation onto a canvas of European history, which he had to interpret in such a way as to ascribe to his views the legitimacy of modernity and the power of future promise. The path of nation-formation, modernization and secularization is well trodden. Europe has paved the way. The Arabs can follow, but only if they can make the kind of attitudinal adjustments and task-orientation shifts explained above.

4. ZAKI AL-ARSUZI: THE GENIUS OF THE ARAB NATION INHERES IN ITS LANGUAGE

Although he was a contemporary of al-Husri – and also a strong believer in the role of Arabic as the criterion which defines the Arabs as a nation – the Syrian Zaki al-Arsuzi (1900–68) is almost unknown in Western scholarship on Arab nationalism. References to him tend to concentrate on the overtly political and irredentist dimensions of his ideology (cf. Khadduri 1970). References to the central role which language plays in his thinking are almost completely absent in this scholarship (cf. Suleiman 1997: 135–7). The situation in Arab(ic) scholarship on the nation and nationalism is only marginally better (see Ahmad 1981, 'Ala' al-Din 1971, Barakat 1977/8, Nassar 1994 and Nuh 1994), in spite of the fact that al-Arsuzi's ideas started to appear in print in the early 1940s, and that his complete works (six volumes, totalling some 3,000 pages) have been available since the mid-1970s. It is interesting to note in this context that, despite their abiding interest in the language and their common belief that the Arab nation is defined by it, al-Husri and al-Arsuzi do not refer to each other. It is as though a wall of silence exists between them. If one reads al-Husri on his own, one would be excused for thinking that al-Arsuzi does not exist, and vice versa. In this world of disjunctive nationalist theorization, al-Husri emerges as the winner. It is his ideas rather than those of al-Arsuzi which have defined for us the conceptualization of the Arabic language as the nationalist ingredient par excellence.

It would be interesting from the viewpoint of the history of ideas, in any full treatment of Arab nationalism, to try to understand how this situation arose. Here, a few points related to language will suffice. First, although al-Husri and al-Arsuzi are both masters of repetition as a didactic strategy in the dissemination of their ideas, and although both ideologues pepper their discourses with anecdotes for a similar purpose, al-Arsuzi's use of Arabic seems to be self-defeating: it excludes rather than includes. It is a barrier to be overcome on the way to effective communication, rather than an enabler of communication. It is also elitist rather than populist. And it sometimes displays the awkwardness of literal translation, rather than the transparency of a discourse whose ultimate aim is to promote task-orientated ideas and to motivate those at whom these ideas are aimed to act. Second, al-Husri's easy flow of ideas is consistent with the view of the language in the Arab nationalist discourse as the medium of modernization and as the subject of modernization itself. Although al-Arsuzi subscribes to this modernizing view of Arab nationalism, he nevertheless places on it a different interpretation, as we shall see later, which somehow demands a use of the language that harks back to a more traditional stylistic engagement. This sometimes gives al-Arsuzi's discourse an old-fashioned flavour that is suggestive of the past, at a time when the nation was being directed by the elite towards a future based on the insights of Western models of development and progress. Third, while al-Husri is interested first and foremost in the functional role of Arabic in nation-formation, al-Arsuzi is concerned with its symbolic capacities. This difference between them accounts for the transparency of al-Husri's discourse and the obscurantism and opaqueness of al-Arsuzi's. Fourth, although both al-Arsuzi and al-Husri favour an objective definition of the nation, and although they both refer approvingly to Fichte's ideas on the role of language in nation-formation, unlike al-Husri, al-Arsuzi fails to harness the wealth of empirical data which other national and historical contexts seem to provide in support of this thesis. As a result, al-Husri appears more historically well informed in comparison with al-Arsuzi, whose ideas come across as parochial and, at times, nationally self-indulgent, if not actually racist. This disparity reflects the wider difference between them as to the place of the Arab nation and its language in relation to history. Whereas for al-Husri the historicity of Arabic and the Arab nation is a given fact, al-Arsuzi places both almost outside history, as the discussion in this chapter will show.

The central idea in al-Arsuzi's nationalist thinking is that of the revival of the Arab nation in modern times. The implication here is that an Arab nation existed in the past, whose roots al-Arsuzi locates in pre-Islamic and early Islamic times, although on balance the former period seems to carry more weight in nation-formation terms for him. The key to this revival is the rediscovery and re-enactment in modern times of the initial impulses and intuitions embodied in the language lexically, phonologically and grammatically. This revival will further enable the Arabs in the modern period to reconnect with the innate character and genius (*'abqariyya*) which their ancestors in the pre-Islamic and early Islamic times embedded in the language. According to this view, Arabic is the storehouse of an original and specifically Arab view of the world, which must be made manifest if the Arab nation is to regain its vigour and to reposition itself as a leading nation of the world.

Implicit in this view, however, is the belief that the Arab nation lost its direction on the way to modernity from that glorious period of pure engagement with the universe. Al-Arsuzi reflects on this in different parts of his complete works, and he ascribes it to the mixing of races which took place in the wake of the Islamic conquests. In the linguistic sphere, this led to the occurrence of solecism, which is said to have weakened the link between the Arabs and the original impulses inherent in their language. On the meta-linguistic level of grammatical description and explanation, the involvement of the non-Arabs in the codification of the language has meant that they failed to realize fully, owing to linguistic interference from their mother-tongues, the special character of the language as the embodiment of the Arabs' view of life and as the structural articulator of their status as a special nation among nations (see Chapter 3, section 5). In this category of scholars, he mentions by way of exemplification some of the foremost thinkers and men of letters in the Arabic intellectual tradition, including Ibn al-Muqaffa', Avicenna, al-Farabi and al-Ghazali, and he refers to them by a set of "othering" epithets (ibid.: 278): *al-aghyār* (the others or strangers), *al-dukhalā'* (aliens or impostors), and *al-a'ājim* (non-Arabs). But al-Arsuzi fails to demonstrate how this linguistic interference manifested itself in the act of describing and explaining the inner structure of the language. He also fails to square this charge with the view he holds that Arabness is a matter of culture not race. As a result, his ideas on language and nation smack of the "linguism" which Kedourie rightly criticizes in his study of nationalism (see Chapter 2, section 3). Furthermore, none of the thinkers al-Arsuzi mentions can be identified as a professional linguist, although some have delved into matters of language from time to time. And, to cap it all, some of the most fundamental insights in al-Arsuzi's thinking on the Arabic language can be traced back to the work of linguists who are not racially Arab, particularly Ibn Jinni, who was of Greek stock (see Chapter 3, section 3). The following discussion, which is inevitably technical in character, will outline the broad parameters of this link with the past on the linguistic front.

One of the most important of these insights is the assumption of correspondence between the sound (*lafẓ*) and the meaning (*ma'nā*) of the Arabic word as a bi-unity of these two constituents. The implication here is that the relationship between the acoustic and semantic contents of the Arabic word is not arbitrary or conventional, but natural and motivated. Ibn Jinni (*al-Khaṣā'iṣ*, vol. 2: 152) expresses this property of the Arabic lexicon by talking about the contiguity (*imsās*) of sound and meaning in Arabic words. He considers this property as further evidence of the "wisdom of the Arabs" principle, which is central to his thinking and to the entire project of Arabic grammatical theory (see Suleiman 1999c and Chapter 3, section 3). In some cases, the natural connection between sound and meaning is said to be obvious or may require some interpretation and manipulation. In other cases, it is not possible to establish an unequivocal link between these two components of the word. But this does not deter Ibn Jinni from offering the principle of contiguity as an established fact of the Arabic language. Deviations from it are explained by him as examples of the inability of the later generations of Arabic-speakers to fathom the depths of the language, or as the result of the untraceability of the original insights which the Arabic-speakers of old had at the moment of linguistic inception (*al-Khaṣā'iṣ*, vol. 2: 164). This principle has never lost its intuitive appeal down to the present day. Witness the comment by the Lebanese poet Rashid Salim al-Khuri that he can assign meaning to individual letters of the Arabic alphabet, and al-'Aqqad's response that, while this may be true in very many cases, it does not apply across the board.

Let us now consider how the principle of contiguity works by explaining some of the examples given by Ibn Jinni in the second volume of his *Khaṣā'iṣ*. Ibn Jinni begins this discussion by citing the views of al-Khalil (175/791) and Sibawayhi (188/803), the two foremost grammarians in the Arabic linguistic tradition, to establish the intellectual pedigree of his ideas and to give them credibility in the eyes of his readers. The fact that the second of these grammarians is of Persian origin gives the lie to al-Arsuzi's charge that non-Arabs suffered from a congenital inability to understand the inner structure of the language owing to their racial origin.

The principle of contiguity is said to apply at different levels. On the level of word morphology, Ibn Jinni states that some morphological patterns are semantically iconic. For example, the pattern *fa'alān* is said to signify iconically the ideas of disturbance (*īḍṭirāb*) and movement (*ḥaraka*), as in *naqazān* (leaping in the air out of fright) and *ghalayān* (boiling, for water). Another morphological pattern of the same type is *fa'fa'a*, in which the reduplication of *fa'* is said to signify iconically the idea of reiteration or repetition, as in *za'za'a* (to shake violently or to rock) and *jarjara* (to jerk or pull back and forth). A less obvious application of the principle of contiguity is said to apply to the morphological pattern *istafa'ala*, signifying request. Ibn Jinni states that since the verb at inception was used to signify an action that had already taken place – in the sense that the verb as articulatory action follows the action it denotes in the real world – it follows that (1) the request for an action in the real world should precede the action itself, and (2) the request part of the verb should iconically precede the verb itself. We may explain this by reference to the verb *ṭa'ima* (to give food) and its request form *istaṭ'ama* (to ask for food), wherein the prefix *ista-* precedes the verb *ṭa'ima* in its modified form (*ṭ'ama*). Ibn Jinni points out that although the element of iconicity is not immediately apparent in this morphological pattern and in the examples that realize it, owing to the fact that it does apply at a more abstract level than usual, it is nevertheless no less real or valid than its counterparts. What we have here, he argues, is an extension of iconicity by analogy with other more clear-cut examples of the type mentioned above.

The contiguity principle is said to apply at the level of phonological structure too, in the sense that the phonological make-up of the word and/or the arrangement of the consonantal phonemes reflect(s) the meaning of the word concerned iconically. Taking the verb *jarra* (to pull) as an example, Ibn Jinni (vol. 2: 164) says that, as a tense consonant (produced with greater muscular effort and breath force), *j* occurs initially in the word because it mirrors the fact that the initial stage in pulling an object is the hardest and, therefore, the one which requires the greatest expenditure of energy. This is followed by the trill *r*, which is repeated to signify the act of pulling and to recreate iconically the fact that in pulling an object on the ground it often bounces up and down as reflected in the articulation of the *r* itself. Contiguity is said to apply at a more abstract level in the phonological domain. An example of this is the verb *baḥatha* (to look for, to search). Ibn Jinni (ibid.: 163) states that the thick release of occlusive *b* resembles the sound produced by striking the earth with one's palm. The consonant *ḥ*, by virtue of its husky quality, is said to resemble the sound made by the lion or the wolf when it digs the earth with its claws. Finally, the consonant *th* is said to resemble the sound made when the earth is scattered. Ibn Jinni (ibid.) says that this is not a matter of speculation, but a fact which can be discerned by noting the similarity between speech and the extralinguistic reality it recreates.

The principle of contiguity through iconicity is said to apply with greater clarity and frequency in the lexical domain. The main idea here is that of associating distinctions in the semantic imports of pairs of related words to particular consonants in their phonological structure. Thus, the distinction between *khaḍima* (to munch, in respect of soft-textured foods) and *qaḍima* (to gnaw, in respect of hard-textured foods) is correlated with the fact that *kh* is phonetically "lax" (produced with less muscular effort and breath force) and *q* is "tense" (produced with greater muscular effort and breath force). The phonetic feature *lax vs tense* is said to apply in other examples to explain how the meaning of a word correlates iconically with its sound. Thus, the difference between cutting lengthwise, signified by *qadda*, and cutting breadthwise, signified by *qaṭṭa*, is said to correlate with the quality of *d* as tense and *ṭ* as lax, and that this in turn iconically reflects the fact that it takes more effort to cut an object lengthwise than it does breadthwise. Similarly, the difference in meaning between *qasama* (to divide) and *qaṣama* (to pound) is iconically correlated with the fact that *s* is more lax in comparison with *ṣ*.

The principle of contiguity can be extended further to cover, among other things, the correlation between the canonical inflectional endings *u* (*ḍamma*) and *a* (*fatḥa*) and their grammatical functions in marking the agent and patient respectively. Ibn Jinni (vol. 1: 49) states that since *u* is phonetically stronger than *a* (in terms of the muscular effort and breath force required to produce them), and since the agent is the doer of the action whereas the patient only receives the action concerned, it follows that the stronger inflectional ending *u* is assigned to the agent and the weaker ending *a* to the patient (see Suleiman 1999c). Although the iconicity of this correlation operates on the abstract plane, it is argued that it is no less real than the other kinds of iconicity obtaining in the language. In this context, the question of contiguity may be envisaged as a matter of correlation between the grammatical meaning of the inflectional endings under consideration and the amount of energy required to produce them in articulatory terms.

Let us now consider how the principle of contiguity was appropriated and extended by al-Arsuzi, and how he came to regard it as his personal creation. Al-Arsuzi's starting point is his characterization of Arabic as a primary (*bidā'ī*) and original (*badī*) derivational language. Using a terminology that is highly reminiscent of the work of the great Swiss linguist Saussure, he characterizes the Arabic word as a bi-unity of acoustic and mental images which mutually imply each other (*ṣūra ṣawtiyya-mar'iyya*, *al-Mu'allafāt al-kāmila*, vol. 1: 71). However, he differs from Saussure radically in declaring that the relationship between the two sides of the Arabic word is not arbitrary or conventional, but natural. In this respect, Arabic, as the Semitic language par excellence, is said to be different from all other languages, particularly those of the Indo-European family, in that whereas these languages are subject to the laws of historical development, Arabic is not. In setting out this comparison, al-Arsuzi wishes to challenge the

German Romantics' view that German is the original language, without however denying their insight that language is the mirror of a nation's soul. And his frequent unflattering references in this context to French, a language he knew very well, are intended to show that the language of the colonial power in Syria at the time is inferior to the Arabic language. This reflects al-Arsuzi's loathing of, and hostile attitude to, France, which he held responsible for the loss of his native Alexandretta to Turkey in 1939.

The view that the bond between the two sides of the word is natural, not arbitrary, is not new to al-Arsuzi. It existed in different forms in different cultures at different times. However, al-Arsuzi expands this view by extending the range of naturalness beyond its confined and obvious domain of onomatopoeia. In this expanded usage, nature covers three senses which constitute the sources of Arabic words. First, there is the imitation of the sounds of nature, pertaining to a particular object, in the acoustic image of a given set of related words. An example of this is the family of words which, according to al-Arsuzi, derive from the consonantal string *f(a)q* as the acoustic image of the sound of boiling water. The semantic import of this phonological string, al-Arsuzi tells us, is that of compression and explosive release. This impression is encoded in the semantic import of the following words: *faqaʿa* (to open, to gouge out) as in *faqaʿa al-dumla* (he opened the abscess), *faqaḥa* (to open) as in *faqaḥa al-kalbu ʿaynayh* (the puppy opened its eyes for the first time), *faqasa* (to hatch), *faqaʿa* (to explode, to burst), *faqara* (to pierce, perforate) and *faqasha* (to break, to crush, to shell). Other words are assigned to this family; but this will not concern us here. All of these words, we are told, are formed by adding a consonant to the underlying root consisting of *f(a)q*. The same semantic import is said to accrue to a related set of words in which the *q* in *f(a)q* is replaced with *j*. Examples of this are the words *fajja* (to open, to cleave, to gorge), *fajara* (to cleave, to break up), *faja* (to open) and *fajana* (to open).

However, for this analysis to apply, we must entertain two properties of the Arabic language which, according to al-Arsuzi, have not been fully recognized in the history of Arabic grammatical theory. The first is the replacement of the traditional organization of the Arabic lexicon into predominantly triliteral consonantal roots by a new principle of word-formation in terms of which words are derived from more atomic roots mirroring the sounds of nature (wherever applicable). Al-Arsuzi suggests (*al-Muʾallafāt al-kāmila*, vol. 1: 234–5) that this principle of classification never materialized because of the involvement of the non-Arabs in codifying the language, who, owing to linguistic interference from their native tongues, failed to see the extent to which this principle applies (see Chapter 3, section 5). No evidence is produced in support of this charge. The second property is the ability of the Arabic consonants and short vowels to be associated with semantic imports (*qīma bayāniyya*, ibid., vol. 1: 86) of a general nature, as the following example from the consonantal portion of the language is said to show. The consonant *b* in Arabic is said to be associated with the semantic import of becoming clear or visible (ibid.: 88), as in *badara* (be obvious), *badā* (to appear), *baraḥa* (to become generally known), *baraza* (to come into view), *bazagha* (to break forth) and *balaja* (to dawn). The fact that this association does not consistently apply to all words beginning with *b* in the Arabic lexicon does not seem to bother al-Arsuzi in the slightest. Furthermore, the fact that what is at best a vague tendency is raised to the status of a general lexical principle does not seem to impinge on al-Arsuzi's desire to enunciate his brand of linguistic philosophy. Vagueness and over-generalization also apply to al-Arsuzi's characterization of the semantic import of the short vowels, for example *u* (*ḍamma*), which he says expresses "continuous activity" (*al-Mu'allafāt al-kāmila*, vol. 1: 85) by virtue of the strong muscular effort required to produce it in comparison with the other short vowels in the language.

The second source of words in Arabic is the spontaneous, and thus natural (as opposed to contrived), expressions of human feelings and emotions. An example of this is the expression of pain *ākh*, from which is derived the words *akh* (brother), *ukht* (sister) and *ukhuwwa* (brotherhood) as if to suggest the familial bond between members of the family, and the help and succour they give each other when they are in distress (ibid.: 305). Another example is the string *farra* (to fly away, to flee, to gleam), which al-Arsuzi considers to be the root of the word for happiness or joy (*fariḥa*) by virtue of sharing the consonantal string *f(a)r* with it. The semantic import of *fariḥa* is said to conjure up a feeling of freedom and joy similar to that experienced by birds when they hover high in the sky (ibid.: 116). To support this association, al-Arsuzi gives the Arabic idiom *ṭāra min faraḥih* (lit. "He flew as a bird out of joy"), which correlates the experience of joy with the act of flying like a bird. The same consonantal string *f(a)r* is said to be the base for the word *faras* (horse), to signify the speed of the object it signifies. The fact that the associations mentioned above are, at best, speculative or suggestive does not seem to figure in al-Arsuzi's pronouncements on the nature of the Arabic language.

The third source of Arabic words is a set of sounds which are produced in the mouth for no specific communicative function. An example of this is the string *b(a)t*, in which the release of the alveolar occlusive *t* suggests the idea of the cutting off or severing of an object (ibid.: 306). Thus, out of this string, the words *batta* (to cut off, to sever, to decide), *batara* (to cut off), *bataka* (to cut off) and *batala* (to cut off) are derived. Al-Arsuzi gives other examples of other roots and their associated families of derived words to support his analysis, but none of these can turn the speculative and suggestive nature of this analysis into an established fact.

Al-Arsuzi points out that the nature-bound character of Arabic, awareness of which was displayed at its best in the pre-Islamic period, should not however obscure the fact that the language is equally rooted in Heaven. Hence the numerous references to *al-mala' al-'a'lā* (the heavenly host) as the other source of the Arabic language by al-Arsuzi. The linchpin in this part of al-Arsuzi's theory is the story of the creation of Adam from *adīm* (the surface of the earth) as his name indicates, and the reference in the Qur'an that God taught Adam the names of all His creation. The Arabic language, like Adam, straddles the divide between what al-Arsuzi calls *nāsūt* (the world of ordinary human beings) and *lāhūt* (the world of the heavens). Al-Arsuzi supports this interpretation by saying that the Arabs are the source of the Semitic race (*sāmī*); and, since the name of this race is related both to that of heaven (*samā'*) and to the verb *samā* (to ascend), it follows that the Arabs and their language have their source and destiny in the sphere of the heavenly host. In this respect, the Arabs are different from the Aryan race and its Indo-European languages in that the latter are rooted in this world, the *nāsūt*, as opposed to the *lāhūt* of Arabic and the Arabs.

Al-Arsuzi uses the above analyses to launch the idea that the genius of the Arabs inheres in their language (hence the sub-title of this section). This makes Arabic different from all other languages, including its sister Semitic languages, which have lost their connection with the original sources of their inspiration. The true renaissance of the Arabs in the modern period must therefore begin by "reviving" the Arabic language, to enable them to uncover the vision of life internalized in it in all its pristine manifestations. The "idea that the Arabic language can unlock the primordial world of meanings which came into being at the very beginning of time" is said by al-Arsuzi to place the Arab nation in "a unique position unattained by any other nation" (Suleiman 1997: 136). The derivational structure of the Arabic lexicon into overlapping families of words is seen to reflect the organization of the Arabs into a nation of individuals held together by relations of common descent, compassion and common purpose.

Al-Arsuzi constructs this vision of the Arab nation by looking at the connection between the constituent members of the following set of words: *umm* (mother), *raḥm* (womb) and *akh* (brother). The word for "nation" in Arabic is *umma*, which signifies the ideas of motherhood and goal-orientation – by virtue of its root meaning: *umm* (mother) and *amm* (to lead the way) – at one and the same time, as if to capture the views of common historical ancestry and shared aspirations that are associated with the ethnic conceptualizations of the nation. And, since the relationship between brothers, sisters and other members of the extended Arab family is designated by the term *'alāqat al-raḥm*, literally "womb relationship", an additional meaning is added to the signification of *umma* through the root *r-ḥ-m* (to be compassionate; the Compassionate as an attribute of God) to reveal at one and the same time the ideas of compassion and Godliness which the root signifies. In a similar vein, the word which signifies the meaning of solidarity between various members of the nation is *ukhuwwa*, whose stem meaning *akh* (brother) captures this relationship by virtue of its phonetic similarity to the interjection of pain (*ākh*). On the basis of what has been said above, the Arab nation in its ideal form now emerges as a familial, goal-orientated community among whose members relations of compassion and solidarity obtain by virtue of divine intervention and action.

The derivational structure of Arabic and its rootedness in the sounds of nature is said by al-Arsuzi to be the key to shedding light on the relationship between the Arabs and other nations, which in turn can enable scholars to reach a conclusion as to the origins of humanity. Al-Arsuzi exemplifies this by the words for "man" in Arabic, Hindi and Latin: *rajul*, *raja* and *rex* (this is actually the word for "king", not "man", in Latin) respectively. He says that these words can be traced via the stem *rajja* in Arabic (to shake), as in *rajja al-arḍ* (He stamped on the ground and caused it to shake), to the root *r*, which echoes this meaning through its trilling articulation in the mouth. Arabic under this analysis is projected as the storehouse of connections between languages and as the instrument which can unlock some of the most complex and fundamental secrets of humanity. This in turn shows that Arabic is superior to all other languages.

Let us pursue how the revival of Arabic – in the sense of reactivating the vision it lexically and structurally embodies – can lead to the revival of the Arab nation. In addition to explaining this, the following discussion will serve to show the continuities between al-Arsuzi's thinking and aspects of the Arabic grammatical tradition I have outlined above. First, we may mention al-Arsuzi's view that the inflectional ending *u* is stronger than *a*, which Ibn Jinni gave as the reason for assigning the former to the agent and the latter to the patient. Al-Arsuzi introduces a new twist in this line of argument by saying that the association of *a* – as in *katab**a*** – in the canonical form of the verb with the perfect (in Arabic *māḍī*, past), and *u* – as in *yaktub**u*** – with the imperfect (in Arabic *muḍāriʿ*, present), reflects the priority of the present over the past in the division of time. And, since the *muḍāriʿ* form of the verb also signals the future, it follows that the Arabs are more orientated through their language towards the present and the future than they are towards the past (*al-Muʾallafāt al-kāmila*, vol. 1: 185, 331). This in turn shows that the Arabs are by their very nature a progressive people (*taqaddumī*), and not a reactionary nation (*rajʿī*). Second, al-Arsuzi puts forward the view that the structural priority of the verbal sentence (sentence beginning with the verb as the signifier of action) over the nominal sentence (sentence beginning with the noun) in Arabic reflects the importance the Arabs attach to action in life (ibid.: 328). This in turn shows the dominance of the dynamic over the static in Arab life. Al-Arsuzi gives other examples of how the revival of Arabic in the above sense, rather than in its usual meaning of coining new terms, can lead to re-enacting the impulses of a glorious past in the present; but the above examples will suffice to show how this is supposed to work in al-Arsuzi's thinking.

This centrality of language in the modern Arab revival now acquires a new dimension that is consistent with the root meaning of the word *'arab* itself. Al-Arsuzi puts forward the view that the word *'arab* is derived from the root *'arra*, which is used to signify a male ostrich uttering a cry, thus associating the word *'arab* with articulation and enunciation in nature (ibid.: 360). The word *'arab* is formed by adding the sound *b* to this root, albeit in a modified form. And, since *b* is a bilabial sound whose articulation takes place visibly at the external extremity of the vocal tract, the choice of this sound adds the meaning of "clarity" to its underlying root. The meaning of the word *'arab*, according to this analysis, may now be glossed as "to speak clearly"; and it is this meaning which underlies the grammatical signification of the word *i'rab* in the sense of "to use desinential inflections correctly".

Although al-Arsuzi in the analysis given in the preceding paragraph is still operating within the traditional semantic norms of the Arab grammatical tradition vis-à-vis the meaning of the word *'arab* and its derivatives, he nevertheless goes beyond this tradition in claiming that this word is derived from *'arra*. In putting forward this view, al-Arsuzi pays little attention to the fact that the meaning of *'arra* he adopts is one of the most marginal significations of this root. Al-Arsuzi invokes this tradition further, particularly in the interpretation put on it by al-Jahiz when he considers the quality of *bayān* (clarity, purity) in Arabic as the criterion which separates the Arabs from other nations, the *'ajam*. Under this view, the Arabs are said to be different from other nations not by virtue of having Arabic *per se*, but owing to the quality of *bayān* which inheres in the language in a unique and unequalled way (ibid.). This explains al-Arsuzi's insistence on treating the dialects as degenerate forms of Arabic owing to (what he believes to be) their defective character in matters of *bayān*. Al-Arsuzi regards this to be self-evident and, therefore, in no need of proof or demonstration.

The general trend in Arab nationalist thought is to treat Arabic as the marker of the Arab national identity and as the medium of modernization which, in itself, is in need of modernization to enable it to become the communicative instrument of a flourishing and nationally conscious Arab life in the modern period. Although al-Arsuzi has sympathy with this trend, championed by al-Husri and other nationalist thinkers, the thrust of his language-based nationalist ideology is markedly different. Arabic for al-Arsuzi is not just the marker of an Arab national identity in the lands in which it is the dominant language; it is also (and more significantly) the means through which this identity can be revived, enriched and reasserted by invoking the view of life it encapsulates lexically and grammatically. As al-Arsuzi keeps repeating in his publications, the Arabs' genius as explained above resides in their language, and it is only by rediscovering the sources of this genius that the Arabs as a nation can relaunch themselves in the modern period. Reviving the language, for al-Arsuzi, therefore becomes a precondition for reviving the Arabs as a nation. Furthermore, this revival is the guarantee of authenticity which the nationalist spirit must dig out and engage in an age of blind and imitative modernization. True Arab modernization, for al-Arsuzi, cannot be achieved without reinvigorating the future direction of the nation with the formative, language-based impulses of its past. Clearly, what al-Arsuzi is calling for is a radically different engagement with the language than has hitherto been proposed in the Arab nationalist literature. This is what makes him different from all the other thinkers I have dealt with in this chapter. To this may be added the fact that the particular nature of al-Arsuzi's appeal to language, and his attempt to locate the period of unmediated engagement with it, the period of *fiṭra*, mainly in the pre-Islamic period, highlights the thoroughly secular nature of his brand of Arab nationalism. Al-Arsuzi's references to Islam as a system of thought, and to the Prophet Muhammad as a national hero, bolster the secular nature of this ideology. This in turn is intended to override the sectarian differences between the Arabs which the French colonial policy tried to utilize in its administration of and control over Syria.[13]

A full understanding of al-Arsuzi's nationalist thought cannot, however, be achieved without placing it in its historical context. First, by fronting language in the way he did as the criterion of nation-formation in the Arab context, al-Arsuzi aims to challenge the French view of the nation which tends to downgrade the role of language in nation-building. This in turn enables him to put sufficient epistemological distance between his thinking and French thought on the subject, thereby signalling a disjunction in the history of Syria between its pre- and postcolonialist life, on the one hand, and the colonial legacy of France on the other. Hence the many dismissive references in his work to the French language and the role which France played in handing over the Alexandretta region to Turkey. This further explains why, at least in part, he suggests that the Syrian education system replace French by English as the primary foreign language.

Second, al-Arsuzi's nationalist theory is intended to reject the claim made by some German Romantics that German is the "original" language. It is also intended to counter the claim made by the Turkish nationalists, through the "sun-language" theory, that Turkish is the mother of all languages. Al-Arsuzi's attitude towards Turkish is conspicuous by its absence, not only because of his enmity towards Turkey but also because he believes that it is ludicrous that the Turks as *'ajam* would ascribe such a claim to their language. The place of being original (*badī*) and primary (*bidā'ī*) accrues to Arabic, and to Arabic alone, in al-Arsuzi's thinking. Al-Arsuzi is aware of the racial connotations of his views, but he does not consider them to be racist. In this respect, he wishes to distance himself from the racist tendencies of German nationalism in the twentieth century, but without forgoing the claim that under his theory Arabic is, and is capable of being shown to be, the original and primary language in the manner set out earlier in this section.

Al-Arsuzi's impact on Arab nationalist thinking has been negligible, in spite (or because) of the acrobatics of his linguistic theorizing. To begin with, for al-Arsuzi's brand of Arab nationalist thought to be accepted, his radical critique of the Arabic lexical tradition would have to be accepted. This would require a complete overhaul of the principles upon which the Arabic lexicon is based, particularly the dismantling of the dominant triliteral root-orientation of this lexicon. In this respect, al-Arsuzi's ideas require the rejection of a tradition sanctioned by the authority of the entire Arabic grammatical polysystem. Second, al-Arsuzi's alternative system seems to work more through the power of speculation than demonstration. It is only by harnessing the power of suggestion, tenuous semantic overlaps and symbolic representation that we can make al-Arsuzi's ideas begin to work in support of his nationalist ideology. Third, al-Arsuzi's views of Arabic are both reductive and essentializing. The idea that the Arabs have a more or less fixed view of life that is internalized in the lexical, phonological and grammatical structure of their language is tantamount to linguistic fundamentalism. Furthermore, the idea that the most spontaneous expression of this view is located in pre-Islamic and early Islamic times amounts to a kind of historical fundamentalism which may lead to ossification, in spite of the fact that its intention is one of ascribing an authenticity of a secular hue to the nationalist philosophy it seeks to enunciate. Fourth, al-Arsuzi's language-based philosophy runs uncomfortably close to a view of national categories that is not completely devoid of racial overtones, as he himself admits to have been the case in the early years of his thinking. The fact that his views are far-fetched and, in many ways, airy-fairy has contributed to the neglect they have suffered.

5. CONCLUSION

The role of Arabic as the marker and the ingredient of the greatest importance in the formation of the Arab national identity is a major theme in the literature on the topic. Early pronouncements on the subject were either vague as to the membership of the Arab nation, or sought to circumscribe this membership to meet with the political exigencies of the prevailing political situation at the beginning of the twentieth century. An example of the former is the definition of the nation by reference to language by al-Marsafi (section 1). An example of the latter attitude is the attempt to limit membership in the Arab nation to the Arabic-speaking countries in Asia by Najib 'Azury (section 1). These pronouncements gave way to a clear and unequivocal association between language and nation in all the Arabic-speaking countries in Asia and Africa in the work of al-'Alayli (section 2), al-Bitar (section 2), al-Husri (section 3) and al-Arsuzi (section 4). It is in the work of these authors, particularly al-Husri, that the association of language and nation in the Arab(ic) context culminated. This association is invariably linked to an objective mode of defining the nation. If the "will" is important in forming the nation, it is because it represents the prior existence of the nation as a cultural entity, rather than the other way round.

There is general agreement among these nationalist thinkers on the secularist nature of Arab nationalism. The association between language and national identity, in place of the old association between religion/sect and group identity, was promoted to override the faith differences between the Arabic-speaking peoples, a theme well represented in the fairly extensive body of poetry as a meta-nationalist discourse on the Arabic language. In this respect, Arab nationalism develops from its earlier roots in the work of the renaissance (*nahda*) writers in the nineteenth century, for example Ibrahim al-Yaziji (see Chapter 4, section 4). Recourse to the language is further consistent with the position of Arabic as a marker of identity in earlier times. However, one of the main advantages of utilizing language in the conceptualization of Arab subjectivity is the fact that the objective of modernization which the renaissance writers launched could be pursued without encumbrance from the limiting confines of the past. For this modernizing project to succeed, the language must be seen to be functionally able to respond to the terminological, pedagogic and other communicative needs of the Arabs. To achieve this goal, Arabic itself had to undergo modernization both grammatically and lexically. This interest in the functional role of a living and thriving language explains the little explicit interest there is in the work of these scholars in the symbolic significance of Arabic, with the exception of al-Arsuzi. It also explains the interest in reforming the language and invigorating it by the above scholars, particularly al-Husri.

Of the nationalist thinkers dealt with in this chapter, al-Husri stands out as the most influential figure in Arab nationalist thought. Unlike al-'Alayli or al-Arsuzi, his style is characterized by immediacy and communicative efficiency. This is why he is referred to as the populist Arab nationalist thinker par excellence in the literature. Al-Husri shows himself to be aware of the power of language not just to unite but also to communicate. This is why his ideas had such currency in the second half of the twentieth century, and why they generated controversy in the daily and weekly press in Lebanon and Egypt in particular. In comparison, al-'Alayli and al-Arsuzi can be a real chore for the ordinary reader. The use of semi-classical language by the former, and abstract and vague expressions by the latter, meant that their message failed to get through to the intended audience, the Arabs themselves, who at the time did not enjoy the same level of literacy as exists in the Arab world today.

Al-Husri also distinguished himself above the others in adopting a historical, some might say pseudo-historical, approach to dealing with Arab nationalism. In particular, he sought to support his ideas on the nature and direction of this nationalism by evidence he drew eclectically from other contexts, especially European history. This strategy was most effective in the treatment of the relative weight of language and religion in nation-formation. In setting out his observations, al-Husri adopted a descriptive tone, which then served as the basis for prescription in the Arab nationalist context. Furthermore, al-Husri's reflections on the origins and course of European nationalism are used to identify general tendencies which he then uses to argue in favour of his own ideas on Arab nationalism. History is important for al-Husri, not because it can enable the nationalist thinker to resurrect the past, but because it objectifies the nationalist ideology and makes it amenable to empirical investigation. Outright speculation is not a mode of investigation which he uses or of which he approves. In this respect, he is different from al-Arsuzi, whose approach to Arab nationalism may be said to be "philosophical", "metaphysical" and "a-historical" rather than positivist and historical. The interesting thing, however, is that both scholars regard their approaches to the study of Arab nationalism as the only way of building the basis upon which the modernization project of the Arab nation can proceed. For al-Husri, the discovery of historical trends enables the Arabs to step into the future armed with knowledge of what is historically possible and relevant and what is not. For al-Arsuzi, the past – but not just any past, as I have explained above – is the basis for deciphering and calling back into service what may be metaphorically called the "genetic code" of the nation in sociopolitical terms. It is this code alone which can guarantee that the future of the Arab nation will be built on secure grounds. Whereas modernity for al-Husri is located in the future, but with reference to the past, for al-Arsuzi modernity is based on a past without which it cannot take root in the future.

The highly speculative nature of al-Arsuzi's thinking on language and nationalism strains the linguistic parameters within which the Arabic grammatical tradition works. The reduction of triliteral roots to biliteral ones cannot be sustained in descriptive terms. In particular, this alternative view of the Arabic lexicon works through suggestion rather than solid empirical analysis. This view is also motivated by an extralinguistic objective whose aim is to promote a particular type of nationalist enunciation in which language has pride of place in a semi-philosophical mode of thinking. On a different level, al-Arsuzi's ideas are intended to counter the claims made in Turkish nationalism as to the antiquity of Turkish and to its ability to act as the source of all human languages

– what is traditionally known as the "Sun Theory" by Turkish nationalists. The fact that Turkish cannot be shown to articulate a conceptual network of nationalist meanings similar to those culled from Arabic by al-Arsuzi is seen as proof of the falsity of the Turkish claims mentioned in the preceding sentence. In pursuing this line of thinking, al-Arsuzi further aims to settle some political scores in the arena of cultural nationalism insofar as this involves Arabs and Turks. The Arabs appear as a more legitimate nation than the Turks on the stage of human history. This makes the loss of al-Arsuzi's native Iskandarun (Alexandretta) to the Turks all the more unbearable. It may also be a factor behind his views on Arabic and nationalism which, as I have pointed out in the preceding section, border on linguistic racism.

The association of language with nation in Arab nationalism is an example of the phenomenon of cultural nationalism (cf. Hutchinson 1987). In this respect, Arab nationalism is cast in the German mode of defining the nation, without however espousing its racial overtones – the only exception here being al-Arsuzi. This type of nationalism is seen to fit the Arab context best. First, it represents a continuation of the main impulses of this nationalism in the Ottoman period which, not unexpectedly, came to be the dominant impulse in post-Ottoman Turkish nationalism. Second, the lack of insistence on the state as a precondition of nation-formation in cultural nationalism suits the Arab context in which political fragmentation, not political unity, is the norm. Awareness of the role of the state in promoting or depressing cultural nationalism is recognized by some of the scholars dealt with in this chapter, particularly al-Bitar. It is also recognized by al-ʿAlayli, al-Arsuzi and al-Husri, although their views on the subject are offered more in passing acknowledgement of this element – particularly for al-Husri's – than as a serious engagement with this most important topic, as we shall see in the next chapter.

6

The Arabic Language and Territorial Nationalism

1. INTRODUCTION

In Chapter 5, an attempt was made to investigate how language was utilized in promoting a concept of nationalism in the Arabic-speaking countries in which standard Arabic was the primary ingredient. Emphasis in this attempt was placed on the contributions made by Sati' al-Husri (section 3), Zaki al-Arsuzi (section 4) and, to a lesser extent, 'Abdalla al-'Alayli and Nadim al-Bitar (section 2). The role of other ingredients in the definition of Arab nationalism – for example, history, culture, customs and traditions, geography and common interests – is acknowledged by these writers, but none of these ingredients is said to have the primacy of language in this nationalism, with the exception of, possibly, history for Sati' al-Husri. It would therefore be correct to say that Arab nationalism is based on the premise that those who share Arabic as their common language belong to the same nation. Suffice it to say that, by promoting this view of Arab national identity, Arab nationalism succeeded in shaping the ideological terrain in the Arab Middle East in such a way that alternative territorial nationalisms were impelled to deal with this ingredient in setting up their defining principles. They did so by employing a host of strategies whose aim ranges from denying the definitional role of language in nation-formation to relegating it to the level of a support factor that is secondary to other more primary factors, be they geographical or state-orientated in character.

This conceptualization of identity in Arab nationalist thinking is anchored (1) to those elements in the history of the Arabic-speaking peoples which lend support to the language-based mode of definition of national identity, and (2) to the ideas of the German Romantics (see Chapter 3). Viewed from the perspective of these two formative impulses, the Arab nation emerges as a construct that is sanctioned by the past and supported by evidence drawn from the course of nationalism in modern European history. To this must be added the contribution of the struggle between the Arabs and the Turks in the Ottoman Empire in the second half of the nineteenth century and the first two decades of the twentieth century (see Chapter 4). In this context, Arab nationalism in its early stages appears as a response to the rise of Turkish nationalism in the Ottoman

Empire. Being products of more or less the same milieu, both nationalisms follow the same model of nation-formation whereby language plays the defining role.

It was also pointed out in Chapter 5 that one of the main themes in the Arab nationalist discourse is the separation of the nation and the state, in the sense that the latter is not established as a precondition of the former in ideological terms. Time after time, the point is made that, although the state may enhance the cause of Arab nationalism, it nevertheless does not enjoy the same status as language in nation-formation. This valorizing attitude towards the state in the Arab nationalist discourse reflects the situation of political division between the Arabic-speaking countries. It is important to note here, however, that the attempt to fashion a nationalist ideology that is in tune with its own historical and political imperatives is also present in the set of alternative nationalisms which I have dubbed "territorial" in the title of this chapter, as we shall see below. Nevertheless, these nationalisms differ from Arab nationalism in the conviction that the state is an absolute criterion of the nation.

The term "territorial nationalism" in the present work covers a host of nationalist pronouncements which have in common the correlation of a particular ideology with a specific geographical area in the Arabic-speaking world. In some cases, the area in question is more or less identical with the boundaries of a given state, for example Egypt or Lebanon. In other cases, the area in question is regional in character. An example of this type is Antun Saʿada's Syrian Nationalism, whose territorial scope includes the countries of the Fertile Crescent (Iraq, Jordan, Lebanon, Palestine and Syria) and Cyprus (see section 2 below). In some cases, territorial nationalism is expressed through a principle of environmental determinism, as in Egyptian nationalism in the first three decades of the twentieth century (see section 3), Lebanese nationalism as promulgated by Jawad Bulus (1899–1982) in his *Lubnān wa-l-buldān al-mujāwira* (*Lebanon and the Surrounding Countries*, 1973), or (to a somewhat lesser extent) Antun Saʿada's Syrian Nationalism (see section 2). In other cases, territorial nationalism is tied to the state and the structure of political authority it possesses, as in Kamal al-Hajj's brand of Lebanese nationalism, whose aim is to produce an ideological rationalization of the confessional basis of the Lebanese state (see section 6.2 below). In some cases, territorial nationalism constitutes a rejection of Arab nationalism; this is represented by Syrian Nationalism and some articulations of Egyptian and Lebanese nationalism. In other cases, territorial nationalism considers itself an ally of Arab nationalism; this is the position of Jamal Hamdan, whose study *Shakhṣiyyat miṣr* (*The Character of Egypt*) sets out his views on this matter in great detail. Other expressions of territorial nationalism do exist, but they will not concern us here.

Although the present chapter will be (mainly) restricted to articulations of territorial nationalism in Egypt and the Levant in the twentieth century, the impulses of these nationalist ideologies are located in the preceding century. In the Levant, territorial nationalism had as its precursor the ideas of Butrus al-Bustani (1819–83), whose notion *waṭan* (used interchangeably with *bilād* or *iqlīm*, roughly *patrie*) is geographically and socioculturally defined to include Greater Syria. Al-Bustani believes that the environment in which a people lives helps to mould their character and make out of them a broadly cohesive unit with common interests. This sense of social cohesion is strengthened by – but is not dependent on – the existence of a common language and shared customs and traditions which can enable the people concerned to neutralize the forces of division existing between them (see Nassar 1994: 347–60). In putting forward this interpretation of *waṭan* as a self-contained socio-geographical entity, al-Bustani intended to make Greater Syria the focus of loyalty and solidarity of and between the people who lived in it, and to do so in a way which could overcome the divisive influence of the religious and sectarian differences that were responsible for much of the intercommunal strife in Mount Lebanon in his day.

In Egypt, Rifa'a al-Tahtawi (1801–73) paved the way for the emergence of territorial nationalism in the twentieth century. He did so by constructing a vision of an Egyptian nation that is territorially defined and politically anchored to a powerful and modernizing state. The existence of a common language and shared customs and traditions between the Egyptians is said to strengthen this nationalism without, however, uniquely identifying it. Being an ideological rationalization of the status quo in Egypt during al-Tahtawi's lifetime, this concept of Egyptian national identity is made to include religion, thus reflecting the Islamic character of the country and its connections with the Ottoman Empire, of which Egypt was formally a part.

The aim of this chapter is to deal with those articulations of territorial nationalism in the Arabic-speaking countries of the Middle East in which language is invoked in identity-formation. To this end, this chapter will deal with Antun Sa'ada's regional Syrian Nationalism (section 2), Egyptian nationalism (section 3, and section 4 and associated sub-sections) and Lebanese nationalism (section 5 and associated sub-sections). In line with the overall design of this book, the interaction between language and a given territorial nationalism will be placed in its historical and political context.

2. THE ARABIC LANGUAGE AND TERRITORIAL NATIONALISM: ANTUN SA'ADA AND REGIONAL SYRIAN NATIONALISM

In his major work *Nushū' al-umam* (1994), Antun Sa'ada (1904–49) reiterates the point that the nation has been the subject of competing theoretical conceptualizations in different nationalist discourses. The reason behind this, he points out, is the attempt by nationalists to fashion a concept of the nation that suits their own situation and the internal or external challenges facing their people. This may be explained as follows. As a sociological fact, a particular nation partakes in one way or another of the universal or semi-universal characteristics of the generic phenomenon to which it belongs. However, the political state of the nation means that this generic concept is packaged to suit the particularities of the situation to which it is to be applied. As a result, the nation emerges as the outcome of the interplay between the general and the particular, whereby the former is projected as the domain of sociology and the latter is visualized as the realm of politics. Although Saʿada asserts that his book *Nushū' al-umam* (*The Genesis/Rise of Nations*) is a work of "pure sociology" (1994: 17), there is no doubt that the political situation in Lebanon to which it responds had a determining effect on the view of the nation it puts forward.

This situation is characterized by the identitarian duality of Lebanese nationalism and Arab nationalism. The fact that Lebanese nationalism in its early stages was mainly supported by Christians, particularly Maronites, led Saʿada to the view that this nationalism was irretrievably sectarian in character. Similarly, the fact that Arab nationalism was mainly supported by the Muslims led Saʿada to the conclusion that Arab nationalism was a variant of Islamic nationalism. Viewed from these two perspectives, Saʿada's Syrian Nationalism may be seen as an attempt to provide an alternative mode of definition which can overcome the confessional configurations of Lebanese national identity. This explains Saʿada's strong opposition to the above two forms of conceptualization of national identity. It also explains his espousal of a nationalist ideology that is thoroughly secular and thoroughly Syrian in character.[1] Furthermore, it explains why he declares that both Lebanese and Arab nationalism are reactionary (1993) and bankrupt (1976) ideologies which are out of tune with the spirit of the age and the abiding forces which have helped shape the Syrian national character over the centuries.

Saʿada states that he set out "to fight" Arab nationalism because it promotes what he calls a "false sense of Arabness" (1993: 185). Syrian Nationalism, says Saʿada, believes in a "genuine Arabness" (ibid.) in which it is prepared to play a leading role on the basis of cooperation between what are distinct Arab nations in an Arab world that seeks integration, not assimilation, between its constituent members. In a similar fashion, Saʿada declares that the Syrian Nationalists chose "to fight" Christian Lebanese nationalism because it is the creation of the colonialist "will" and the realization of sectarian politics. By promoting the idea that Lebanon is the eastern frontier of the Christian West, Lebanese nationalists adopt an isolationist and false identity for Lebanon (1993: 196) that denies the historical and cultural links between it and the rest of Syria. In addition, Lebanese nationalism denies the environmental basis upon which these links are constructed.

One of the most important principles in Saʿada's concept of the nation concerns the role of the physical environment in shaping the character of a people and in creating different groups among humankind. Broadly speaking, the environment delivers this function through the boundaries it provides between regions, the climatic conditions which obtain in each region, the kind of soil each region has, and, finally, its topography. This view is generally dubbed "environmental determinism" in the literature. As we shall see below (section 4), environmental determinism plays an important role in formulations of Egyptian nationalism.

Saʿada's environmental determinism consists of two components: (1) the earth is made up of different geographical regions and physical environments, and (2) these environments determine the distribution of human beings into distinct groups. He supports these two components by pointing out that "were our earth but one vast plain of equal climatic conditions and without such physical boundaries as deserts, mountains, rivers and seas, it would have been self-evident that mankind would have formed one big society" (1994: 50). Yet Saʿada does not ignore the importance of what he calls the "psychological and individual" factors (ibid.: 55) which a group can bring to bear in moulding the environment to its needs, thus creating its own distinctive history. He expresses this element in his thinking by saying that "there can be no people where there is no land, no group where there is no physical environment, and no history where there is no group" (ibid.). Under this view, history emerges as the creation of a group whose character is shaped by the environment of the territory on which it exists. As a historical phenomenon, the nation therefore partakes of the interaction between the group – as a social entity with common interests and psycho-physical characteristics – and its physical environment, with the emphasis being put on the latter in nation-formation.

But a nation is more than just a social group (*muttaḥad ijtimāʿī*) who share a common life within a well-defined territory. What makes a nation different from other social groups – whether they are defined in terms of village, city or country – is the involvement of political will as a "vital element" in bringing it about (1994: 191). Although Saʿada does not make the distinction, it seems necessary that nation-building as a political enterprise be kept distinct from nation-formation as a sociological phenomenon in his thinking. Whereas nation-formation is largely the outcome of the interaction of a given group with its environment, and the influence which this environment indelibly has on them, nation-building is the outcome of the will of the group concerned to achieve political unity by creating a single state on its territory. Although the state in this sense is not definitional of the nation as a sociological fact, in political terms it constitutes the crown which the nation aims to acquire for itself to protect its own interests. For this to be achieved, a nation must nurture its own nationalism in its capacity as the socio-psychological fusion of the love of the motherland, a keen awareness of the common interests of the group, and the readiness on the part of the group concerned to defend and protect these two.

What is significant from the perspective of the present study is the exclusion of language as a criterion in the definition of the nation in Syrian Nationalism. On the ideological level, this constitutes a rejection of the Arab nationalist idea which considers language as the *sine qua non* of the nation, or as the factor which marks it externally in relation to other nations. Language in Syrian Nationalism is considered as a necessary condition for the existence of human society, in the same way as other species or sub-species in the animal kingdom must have recourse to a means of communication to take care of their needs. Sa'ada expresses this point by saying that language is not the cause of society, but its outcome; it is the result of people coming together to form a group, rather than the reason why the group concerned comes into being in the first place. But he also acknowledges that a common language can aid nation-formation and nation-building by spreading the culture of the nation to its members, and by linking these members to earlier generations of the same nation. A common language can also serve these functions by making it possible for members of the nation to pursue common goals and interests more easily than would otherwise be the case if they did not share the same language. It is often difficult to escape the feeling in dealing with Sa'ada's thinking on the position of language in nation-formation that he is more than prepared "to have his cake and eat it".

Sharing a common language under this analysis may be treated as an attribute (*ṣifa*) of the nation, but not as an ingredient (*'unṣur*) which makes all those who speak the language concerned belong to the same nation. Sa'ada tells us that the disjunction between language and nation at the level of identity is supported by the existence of more than one nation in communities that speak the same language. Thus, not all those who speak Arabic, Spanish or English constitute one nation. By the same token, different national literatures with their own specific flavours do exist through the same language community. Sa'ada also states that the opposite is equally true. A nation may possess more than one language and one literature, which it may share with other nations beyond its borders without this leading to the fragmentation of the nation concerned. That a nation must have access to a common language for general use is understandable; but this is different from saying that this common language makes the nation concerned one with other nations that speak the same language.

Sa'ada believes that the fallacy of defining the nation linguistically was promulgated by the Germans to justify the acquisition of territories where pockets of German-speakers existed outside the borders of Germany. Linguistic nationalism, therefore, was developed by the Germans not through objective study and sound reflection, but as a camouflage for territorial expansion, the implication here being that Arab nationalism can promote a similar attitude among those who espouse it. It is therefore the duty of Syrian Nationalists to refute the claims of Arab nationalism, and to fight it as an ideology which condones territorial expansion. The Syrians, Sa'ada states, have survived many changes of religion and language throughout their long history. Thus, rather than being absorbed into a nation of Arabic-speakers, the Syrians have injected their vigour and vitality into Arabic by translating into the language knowledge they had accumulated through their contact with other peoples and nations. Rather than losing their identity to the Arabs and fusing it into a prefabricated Arabic, the Syrians assimilated Arabic and its original speakers into their national character in a way that is consistent with similar assimilations they had performed in earlier times. Thus, if Arabic is the national language of the Syrians, it is so only in its Syrianized form. Furthermore, consideration of situations elsewhere in the world shows that the pursuit of language as the marker of the national self may lose its intensity after independence has been achieved. Ireland is a case in point. Sa'ada points out how the Irish language went into decline after the creation of the Irish Free State in 1921, thus reversing a long-standing tradition which sought to utilize the language as a marker of Irishness during the long and hard struggle for independence from the British.

By citing this example, Sa'ada wishes to imply that the treatment of language as a marker of the nation is contingent on the factors existing at the time when this association is made, and that this definitional role is weakened considerably when the conditions giving rise to it lose their potency. According to Sa'ada, therefore, language is an accidental property of the nation rather than a definitional criterion of it. Syrian Nationalists believe that this shows the fallacy of the linguistic nationalist principle that language is worthier than territory. In Syrian Nationalism, the opposite is true. Faced with the loss of its language or its territory, a nation will always choose to retain its territory. Without it, the nation concerned will cease to exist. The same is not true of language. The Syrians, we are told, changed their language several times throughout their history, but by sticking to their homeland they have succeeded in preserving their own identity.

Like al-Husri's and al-Arsuzi's, Sa'ada's nationalist thinking is not without problems, chief among which is the mixing of sociology and advocacy. It is therefore not always easy to know where Sa'ada the sociologist speaks and where his nationalist alter ego enunciates. Another problem is the lack of clarity as to where the nation as a sociological fact begins, and where it ends in relation to its political manifestation in the state. On one level, it seems that the will of the nation to achieve political unity is the factor which distinguishes it from sub-national units within its realm. But until this will is realized, it is hard to distinguish between social groups that are nations and those that are not. If so, how can the Syrian nation be defined? The answer to this may be framed in relation to the boundaries which the Constitution of the Syrian National Party sets, although these boundaries were subjected to change by Saʿada at different points in his career. In terms of this position, the Syrian nation may be said to consist of those people who live or have lived within these boundaries. But this begs the question; for, in terms of the environmental determinism which characterizes this nationalism, we must be able to establish how those who live or have lived within these boundaries are all marked by a set of environmentally induced characteristics which, though not necessarily uniform, are still cohesive enough to distinguish them from other nations. Apart from a few remarks, no attempt is made to deal with this issue, perhaps because Saʿada intended to return to it in his book *Nushū' al-umma al-sūriyya*, which has never been published. Saʿada's rejection of language as a marker of the nation may therefore be said to be the outcome of his desire to distance himself from Arab nationalism ideologically, rather than as the logical outcome of the principle of environmental determinism upon which he premises his thinking. On a different level, this rejection reflects Saʿada's awareness of how Arab nationalism plays out on the Lebanese political scene by eliciting an alternative and sectarian mode of national self-definition, namely Christian Lebanese nationalism.

3. THE ARABIC LANGUAGE AND EGYPTIAN NATIONALISM: EARLY BEGINNINGS

Egyptian territorial nationalism operates within the domain of the state. This explains the lack of an intense preoccupation with the state at the ideological level in this nationalism. Instead, the main goal of this nationalism is the formation of a self-conscious nation in the territory ruled by the state. Like other territorial nationalisms in the Arab Middle East, Egyptian nationalism in the period under consideration here projects itself as a form of identification that is more authentic than other competing nationalisms, be they linguistic or religious in orientation. In particular, Egyptian nationalism promotes itself as an alternative to Arab and Islamic nationalism, which are not without their supporters in the Egyptian cultural and political space.

The early beginnings of Egyptian nationalism go back to the start of the nineteenth century, with the French occupation (1798–1803) playing a motivating role in stirring the beginnings of a political consciousness in the country (see Ahmed 1960: 2, Suleiman 1996b: 26). The rise to power of Muhammad Ali in 1805 and his ensuing reforms, especially in the educational field, heralded a period of modernization unparalleled in the modern history of Egypt. One of Muhammad Ali's crowning achievements in this field was the establishment in 1835 of the School of Languages (Dar al-Alsun), whose task was to produce translations from European languages into Arabic (see al-Shayyal 1951). The vigorous translation programme of this school constituted a boost to the functional role of Arabic as an instrument of modernization. This new-found status of the language was further strengthened in symbolic terms by the use of Arabic alongside Turkish in a new functional domain: *al-Waqā'i' al-miṣriyya*, the official *Egyptian Gazette*. Later, Arabic replaced Turkish altogether as the sole language of this important publication, thus reflecting the rising fortunes of the language and its implicit role as the official language of the state. These achievements constituted a vindication of the view expressed at the beginning the nineteenth century by Shaykh Hasan al-'Attar (c. 1766–1835) to the effect that the "power of language" can be used as "an instrument in awakening the mind of Egypt" (Ahmed 1960: 5). This is one of the most abiding themes in Egyptian nationalism.

Muhammad Ali appointed al-Tahtawi to the headship of the School of Languages. From the perspective of the present work, al-Tahtawi's contribution inside and outside this school proved to be of seminal importance in the development of Egyptian nationalism. First, he was responsible for the massive expansion in the functional domains which Arabic was made to serve. He did this through the subject range of the translations he commissioned, which brought the language face to face with new fields of knowledge and lexical expression. To respond to these challenges, al-Tahtawi felt the need to modernize the language to make it more amenable to deliver the extralinguistic modernization programme championed by Muhammad Ali. In practical terms, this meant the introduction of new vocabularies in the form of borrowings from European languages, expanding the semantic domain of words in active use, or activating those words that had lain dormant for a long time by deploying them in new lexical domains. In addition, al-Tahtawi turned his attention to the task of developing new Arabic-language materials for use in the expanding school system in Egypt. In particular, he is generally credited with the pioneering use of tables to summarize points of grammar in the teaching of Arabic language, as evidenced by his *al-Tuḥfa al-maktabiyya fī taqrīb al-lugha al-'arabiyya* (in vol. 5, 1981), which contains around forty-seven such tables.

Second, influenced by French thought on the role of geography in moulding communities and by the need to give legitimacy to Muhammad Ali as the sovereign ruler of Egypt in the face of the rival claim to authority attributed to the Ottoman Sultan, al-Tahtawi called on his countrymen to make a distinction between "brotherhood of country" and "brotherhood of religion", complementary though these two forms of identification were. In pursuing this distinction, al-Tahtawi showed a keen interest in the history of Egypt and displayed a great pride in its Pharaonic past and the potential of this past in motivating the Egyptians to regain their ancient glory, a theme to which I will return later in discussing Egyptian nationalism in the 1920s and early 1930s. As Gershoni and Jankowski (1986: 11) point out, al-Tahtawi "was perhaps the first modern Egyptian writer to view the entire civilized history of Egypt as a continuum and to formulate an embryonic theory of an Egyptian national character that extended from the ancient Egyptians to his contemporaries". Al-Tahtawi believed that it was the role of education to impart these ideas to the Egyptian youth, inculcating them with the idea of *ḥubb al-waṭan* (the love of the fatherland) which, as Hourani (1983: 78–9) points out, "acquires the meaning of territorial patriotism in the modern sense" (see also ʿAbd al-Malik 1983, al-Qirni 1995: 5–32).

The ideas that Egypt is distinct from other entities with which it shares ties of religion or language, and that language is an important element in society – functionally as an instrument of modernization and symbolically as the embodiment of that modernization – constitute the two most important components of al-Tahtawi's legacy to the development of Egyptian nationalism. Witness the impact these ideas had on Muhammad ʿAbdu (1849–1905) and Ahmad Lutfi al-Sayyid (1872–1963). So important was the language issue for Muhammad ʿAbdu that he declared it to be second only to the reform of religious thinking in his scheme of things: "My second purpose has been the reform of the way of writing the Arabic language" (Hourani 1983: 141). This interest in the language found greater expression in the nationalist thinking of Lutfi al-Sayyid, to whose ideas I will turn next.

Lutfi al-Sayyid believed that Egypt was a distinct nation whose people are linked not by religion or language, but by the conditions of their continuous history, their existence in a well-defined territory and the common interests that hold between them. Lutfi al-Sayyid was not opposed to the idea of a community based on Islam or Arabic, but he thought that any such community should be premised on the existence of distinct nations that cooperate with each other without fear of assimilation. For Lutfi al-Sayyid, the Egyptian nation "was something concrete and definite" (Ahmed 1960: 107), as concrete and definite as the land on which it exists. This feature of Lutfi al-Sayyid's thinking has led Hourani to observe with characteristic insight that "what is original in Lutfi's writing is his physical consciousness of Egypt and its countryside" (1983: 177). Hourani continues: Lutfi al-Sayyid "evokes the sights and sounds of the cotton fields, paints in bright colours the virtues and happiness of the good peasant, and exhorts the younger generation to respond to the beauty of nature". The purpose of this mode of writing was to form the political consciousness of the Egyptians and to mould their character in favour of an ideology which promoted the nation as the basis of group loyalty and solidarity. Education through the national language was considered the means to achieving this aim.

This view of education puts language at the heart of Lutfi al-Sayyid's nationalist thinking. As the editor of the newspaper *al-Jarīda* between c. 1908 and 1914, he used his position to advance a range of views on the reform of the Arabic language. Commenting on this aspect of Lutfi al-Sayyid's work, Ahmed (1960: 105) believes that "his contribution to the enrichment of the language will probably be his chief legacy as a sociological writer". Lutfi al-Sayyid believes that Arabic belongs to the Egyptian nation, and that a nation which neglects its language and does not seek to develop it lexically and stylistically lacks an awareness of itself and respect for it. This fact behoves the Egyptian nation to preserve its language and to develop it to meet its own modernization needs. Preservation does not however mean ossification, nor does modernization mean the wholesale importation of lexical resources from other languages. What is required is a strategy which allows the Egyptian nation to strike a happy medium between, first, the traditionalists and the modernizers, and, second, the colloquial and the standard. The ultimate aim of this will be to reform Arabic and to make it the language of science, which does not belong to any one nation to the exclusion of others. To do this, Arabic must be endowed with an ever-expanding stock of scientific terms to enable it to address the needs of its users.

The battle between the linguistic traditionalists, as Lutfi al-Sayyid defines them, and the modernizers is one of attitude towards the past and how it relates to the present and the future. The traditionalists insist that the lexical purity of the language must be preserved by coining native technical terms to designate new inventions and concepts.[2] Failure to follow this principle will lead to a flood of foreign terms, which will compromise the cultural and structural integrity of the language. By holding this position, the traditionalists clearly display a keen awareness of the role of symbolism in conceptualizing issues of linguistic change as emblematic manifestations of larger change in society. What is ultimately at stake here is the attempt to fashion a concept of language and nation that is rooted in the past and that will remain true to it. Foreign lexical imports are believed to undermine this position; that is why they must be resisted.

The modernizers, on the other hand, believe that borrowing terms from other tongues is consistent with the history of the Arabic language. Lutfi al-Sayyid, who considers himself to be among the modernizers, points out that the Qur'an itself contained borrowed terms, and that during the age of translation in the medieval period the Arabs borrowed many terms from Greek, Persian and Sanskrit even when at times they had native equivalents to these terms. Borrowing is therefore not a sign of weakness or corruption, but of strength and the desire to advance forward, hence the use of such phrases as *Ilā al-amām* ("Forward, March!") and *Raqqū lughatakum* ("Develop Your Language!") as titles for some of Lutfi al-Sayyid's articles in *al-Jarīda* in 1913 (1945, vol. 1: 126, 134). Furthermore, borrowings from European languages will represent a case of lexical restitution whereby the Egyptians will reclaim new terminologies in lieu of the terms which the Europeans borrowed from Arabic in the past. Borrowing from European languages thus becomes a case of *quid pro quo*, and not a sign of linguistic weakness as the traditionalists may think.

Borrowings may be done directly from the donor languages, or indirectly via the colloquial which often incorporates the names of new objects well before these names are subjected to scrutiny by linguistic authority. The involvement of the colloquial in this process of lexically replenishing the standard requires some adjustment in the attitude towards the former in society. Lutfi al-Sayyid therefore insists that a new mode of thinking must be developed whereby the colloquial as the site of linguistic corruption is nevertheless considered as a reservoir of lexical and grammatical resources which may be used to enrich and reform the standard. To this end, Lutfi al-Sayyid established it as an aim of the nation to effect a rapprochement between the colloquial as the language of speech and the standard as the language of writing. This will lead to creating a middle language between these two forms of Arabic in a double trajectory of lexically enriching the standard and grammatically correcting the colloquial. In national terms, the new language will represent an important, perhaps the most important, factor in the advancement of the Egyptian nation. It will do so by harnessing the living power of the colloquial to the sanctioned authority of the standard as the language of research and scientific exchange.

Some critics have dubbed Lutfi al-Sayyid's call to create a middle language to bridge the difference between the colloquial and the standard *tamṣīr al-lugha*, the Egyptianization of Arabic (al-Rafi'i 1974: 54–66). They have been helped in this by Lutfi al-Sayyid's use of the term *al-lugha al-miṣriyya* (the Egyptian language) to refer to the spoken Arabic of Egypt (1945, vol. 1: 247), and by his calls to Egyptianize education and Western civilization. The fact that Lutfi al-Sayyid did not seem to have challenged this term (*tamṣīr al-lugha*) may have been the reason behind its currency as a feature of his thinking to this day. This acquiescence on his part – if it is correct – may reflect a belief that a distinct Egypt in national terms would be better served by having a language that is more or less its own, at least in its lexical flavour. There is, however, no way of establishing whether Lutfi al-Sayyid did in fact hold such a belief. What is certain is that Lutfi al-Sayyid was not a supporter of the colloquial, which he held in some contempt as a corrupt form of Arabic. This attitude on his part may be exemplified by his reaction to the use of the colloquial on the stage (1945, vol. 2: 143, translation in Wendell 1972: 280):

> I saw this on the stage of the 'Abbas Theatre when the Abyad troupe presented four plays which had been translated into poetry in the colloquial tongue by the late … 'Uthman Bey Jalal. I saw the great crush of people, the enthusiastic applause, and the tremendous acclaim which greeted these popular plays. I saw everyone [so transported] except for myself and a few of my friends who were of the same mind; who felt

> depressed by the spectacle of [this sick language gaining in strength], jostling the literary language, and forcing it out of the stage; and who were oppressed by having to listen to solecisms [affecting the ends of words].

We may gauge the strength of this interest in the language as a factor in the formation of the Egyptian national consciousness by considering the response in Egypt to the decision by the British to make English or French the medium of instruction in the Egyptian schools. At the secondary level, this resulted in reducing the number of hours devoted to instruction in or through Arabic between 1893 and 1907 (see 'Ali 1995: 97–8). The journalist 'Abdalla al-Nadim (1844–96) published an article in the journal *al-Tankīt wa-l-tabkīt*, entitled *Iḍā'at al-lugha taslīm al-dhāt* ("Language Loss is Surrendering the Self"), in which he called upon the Egyptians to hold on to Arabic instead of surrendering themselves to foreign languages (ibid.: 114–15). The same cause in its wider ramifications was taken up by other journalists and newspapers of the day, including Mustafa Kamil (1874–1908), whose *al-Liwā'* was the scourge of those who promoted foreign languages over Arabic, be they of British or Egyptian origin.

The above discussion shows that, although language was regarded as an important element in Egyptian nationalism in the early stages of its development, it is nevertheless not raised to the status of a characteristic principle of this nationalism in definitional terms. This excludes the possibility of positing a common nationalism that ties the Egyptians to other Arabic-speaking peoples outside Egypt, as pan-Arab nationalism later demanded. However, language is accorded a pivotal role by Egyptian nationalists as an instrument of modernization and as the object of modernization itself (see Suleiman 1996b). This view of the language invokes both its functionality and its power of symbolism. The above discussion also shows the deep desire among the Egyptian nationalists to reform the language by bringing it closer to the colloquial, the spoken language of the people. And all of this is framed within a concept of the nation that is territorially based, conscious of its past history and determined not to let religion be one of its defining ingredients (cf. Gershoni and Jankowski 1986: 13). This set of associations will constitute the main thrust of the next section.

4. THE ARABIC LANGUAGE AND EGYPTIAN NATIONALISM: FULL ELABORATION

The idea that Egypt is a distinct nation that is historically unique and rooted in its geography was the product of a long period of gestation in the nineteenth and early twentieth centuries. Commitment to this concept of Egypt operated even when the tie of religion was invoked as an instrument of ridding the country of British occupation. This was the case with Mustafa Kamil, who never wavered in his belief in the uniqueness of Egypt, even when he turned to Islam as a means of promoting extraterritorial links with the Ottomans to oppose the British (see 'Amara 1976, Nasr 1984). However, the idea that the Egyptian national character was determined by the environment and the social setting to which this gave rise came to the fore as a site of full intellectual elaboration later, mainly in the 1920s and early 1930s. The contribution of Muhammad Husayn Haykal (1888–1956)[3] to the development of this aspect of Egyptian nationalism was of paramount importance in giving it wide currency, principally through the newspaper *al-Siyāsa al-usbū'iyya*, which started to appear in 1926. Other intellectuals participated in this enterprise, as we shall see in the next two sections.

My aim in this section is a limited one: it is to outline the main themes which dominated the articulations of Egyptian nationalism in its territorial form in the period mentioned above. In carrying out this task, I will concentrate on the way language was dealt with in these articulations, painting as much of the socio-cultural context as necessary. It must be noted, however, that the advocates of Egyptian nationalism did not all speak with one voice. Variations existed among them, but they were all agreed that the Egyptian national character was culturally distinct, historically unique and environmentally determined, and that only by accepting this characterization of their collective personality could the Egyptians determine a course of action which, if followed, would lead to the realization of their aspirations of comprehensive and sustainable modernization. Clearly, the task of these advocates was twofold. First, they sought to chisel out of the data available to them a blueprint of the Egyptian national character which responded to the cultural politics of the day, as represented in the 1919 popular revolution, the creation of parliamentary democracy in 1922–3 and the enormous pride which the Egyptians felt in their past (Pharaonic) history as a result of the discovery of the tomb of Tut-Ankh-Amon in 1922.[4] The ending of the Caliphate by the Turkish leader Mustafa Kemal Atatürk in 1923, and the strong advocacy of a Turkish territorial nationalism, aided the cause of the Egyptian nationalists (1) directly by ringing the death knell of the idea of an Islamic nation, and (2) indirectly by giving credence to the ideology of Egyptian nationalism in its territorial mode. Second, the advocates of Egyptian nationalism sought to popularize their brand of national identity as the basis of task-orientation among Egyptians. Their aim here was to convert the ideological into a motivating task-orientated force in the service of the nation and that of state-building.

The principle of environmental determinism is a central premise in Egyptian nationalism. Broadly speaking, the main thesis in this principle revolves around the idea that the physical and climatic conditions of the Nile Valley have endowed the Egyptians with group characteristics which made them distinct from those who surround them. In Egyptian nationalism, this principle was employed as an instrument to underpin the following claims: (1) a direct psychological and racial link exits between modern-day Egyptians and their ancestors, whose civilization came into pre-eminence under the Pharaohs six millennia ago; (2) the Egyptians are different from the Arabs, with whom they share a common language, Arabic; (3) the Egyptians are different from their co-religionists, mainly Muslims; (4) Egypt's great powers of assimilation have enabled it to absorb waves of immigrants and to stamp their mental make-up with the indelible imprint of its character. The popularization of this image of Egypt was channelled through the press. It was also channelled through the school system, particularly in civics books.

The point of interest for us in all of this is the way in which the above constellation of ideas was applied to the role of Arabic in the conceptualization of Egyptian nationalism. The first and most fundamental strategy was to argue that language is not a valid marker of national identity, by citing examples where this is presumed not to be the case. In this context, Muhammad Amin Hassuna pointed out that Arabic is not the language of one Arab nation/people (*sha'b*) but of different Arab nations (see Husayn 1983, vol. 2: 151). Muhammad 'Abdalla 'Anan expressed the view that Arabic came to Egypt with the invading Arabs and that, as such, it does not make Egypt an Arab country (ibid.: 152–4). Arabic in this context was sometimes thought to be similar to Latin, which gave birth to the Romance languages, the implication being that the different Arabic dialects could develop fully in the same direction if they were allowed into writing. This point is reflected in an item by Tawfiq 'Awwan in *Siyāsa al-usbū'iyya* in 1929 (cited in Gershoni and Jankowski 1986: 220):

> Egypt has an Egyptian language; Lebanon has a Lebanese language; the Hijaz has an Hijazi language; and so forth – and all of these languages are by no means Arabic languages. Each of our countries has a language which is its own possession: so why do we not write it as we converse in it? For the language in which the people speak is the language in which they also write.

The point behind this is a simple one: even if language could be admitted as a marker of the nation in abstract terms, Arabic could not play this role because it is not a single language but a set of related languages which ought to be inscribed in writing. Furthermore, owing to the fact that Egypt has its own environmentally determined national character, and since language is an attribute and instrument of this character, it logically follows that the Arabic of Egypt must perforce be different from the Arabics of other environmentally determined nations in the Arabic-speaking world. That 'Awwan does not recognize the distinction between language and dialect above is not the issue here, for what is important in what he says is the fact of his asserting the claim he puts forward, not its factual truth. This mode of argumentation by formal logic, of claiming that something is true by definition, is the second strategy of dissociating language from nation in discussions of self-identity in Egyptian nationalism.

A third strategy in this field consists of adducing empirical evidence, or interpretations of such evidence, which purport(s) to show that the special character of Arabic in Egypt is the result of the interference made by the linguistic substratum in the language (see 'Umar 1970, 1998).[5] This substratum is made up of Coptic, which is said to represent a demotic form of the language of the Pharaohs, ancient Egyptian. The argument runs that Egypt's powers of assimilation ensured that the spoken Arabic of Egypt was impregnated with structural (phonological and grammatical) and lexical properties that reflect this substratum, and that it is these properties which explain the difference between the Arabic of Egypt and that of other Arabic-speaking regions which, by the same token, reflect their own linguistic substrata. It is not difficult to see in this a reflection of the claim made by some Coptic Egyptian nationalists, for example Murqus Samika, that all Egyptians are Copts, but some happen to be Muslims and others Christians (see Husayn 1983, vol. 2: 148).[6] Some Coptic nationalists went beyond this, calling for the revival of the Coptic language to replace Arabic among the Copts and, it seems, non-Copts. One such writer expressed the view that, in the same way that a person cannot belong to two churches, a true Egyptian cannot be loyal to two languages (see Kilani, n.d.: 51–4). This view did not go unchallenged. Some Copts countered it by pointing out that Coptic should be restricted to the monasteries, and that the Copts should devote their attention to mastering the Arabic language as the national language of Egypt. Some writers of this persuasion believed that the danger to the Copts came not from Arabic but from European languages, which the missionaries used as a bait to convert the Copts to their churches.

The place of Arabic in Egyptian nationalism was a major issue in discussions of the kind of literature which the Egyptian writers must develop to reflect and mould the Egyptian national character and Egyptian national culture. The debate over this issue was based on four premises. The first stipulated that literature is the marker (*'unwān*) of a nation's culture and civilization (Haykal 1986: 112). The second stipulated that, although science and philosophy are the means of knowledge par excellence, literature represents the spirit or "nectar" of these two domains and all other domains of human knowledge (ibid.: 24). The third premise stipulated that the political and the literary-cum-cultural go hand in hand in all national movements, and that the latter provides a guarantee of survivability to the former. As Husayn points out, unlike political revolutions, literature cannot be easily eliminated in society (ibid.: 12). The fourth premise stipulated that while Egyptian national literature cannot and must not ignore its roots, it nevertheless must reflect and seek to develop the new national spirit. To do so, Egyptian literature must be rooted in its Egyptian environment, both physical and social. It must seek to describe the beauty of Egypt and the effect of the Nile environment on the Egyptian people. It must also mine the greatness of ancient Egypt for motivational effect. It must additionally seek to achieve this by espousing a realist and a naturalist approach which extols the virtue of the peasant and reflects the uprightness of his moral character as accurately as possible.

The debate about realism and naturalness brought to the fore the question of the kind of language which this literature must adopt. Some nationalists put forward the view that the desired realism and naturalness of the content of this new literature must be reflected in the realism and naturalness of its language. The point was made that the literary plausibility of the *fellah* (peasant) would be severely compromised if his normal speech was replaced by the formal register of the written language.[7] Niqula Yusuf raised this issue in 1929 in *al-Siyāsa al-usbū'iyya*, particularly with respect to the language of the theatre (see Muhammad 1996: 163). Some nationalists advocated the wholesale use of the colloquial in all literary genres as a solution to this problem. Witness the views put forward on this matter by Tawfiq 'Awwan which I mentioned earlier. Similar views were expressed by Ibrahim Jum'a, who was mainly interested in developing an Egyptian children's literature (ibid.: 162). Jum'a held the view that Egyptian writers must abandon their traditional attitude of favouring the standard form of the language over the colloquial, and that this change must go hand in hand with the rejection of the traditional styles and themes of Arabic literature. Egypt, it was pointed out by Niqula Yusuf (ibid.: 163), had its own environment which differed radically from the desert environment of the Arabs, and this difference was reflected in its language. Implicit in this view is the claim that, as a desert language, Arabic was and remains a Bedouin language, and as such it cannot be suitable for the modern needs of Egypt.[8]

Other writers were far less radical in their attitude towards the language issue. Haykal in particular did not condemn the use of the colloquial on the stage, although he did not wish to see it as the only medium in this literary genre. He believed that the use of the colloquial on the stage would prove to be a stopgap measure which, by analogy, would also be the case vis-à-vis the use of this variety for dialogue in the novel and the short story. The standard language, he believed, would eventually have the upper hand in the contest with the colloquial, owing to the spread of literacy and to the development of a simplified form of the written language. The fact that Haykal's prediction for the language of the stage has proved to be inaccurate is not the issue here. What matters is his attitude towards the standard, which was very favourable and rooted in an awareness that Arabic is not just a means of literary expression but also an instrument of cultural defence against foreign influences which may dilute the authenticity of the Egyptian national character. This fear was expressed most vociferously by a group of nationalist writers who called for a reduction in the reliance on translation and foreign literatures (Muhammad 1996: 164–6). Haykal believed that, although Arabic needed lexical, grammatical and stylistic modernization, it still represented the best link between the Egyptians and their literary and religious heritage. A national literature cannot ignore its literary past. It also cannot ignore the contribution made by the founding texts of its culture, including the Qur'an, to its evolution and development. Not even French, English or German literatures were able to sidestep their own heritage or history. Hence the continued relevance of Christianity, Greece and Rome to these literatures. Egypt must take heed of that.

The above discussion shows that, although language was not considered a definitional ingredient of Egyptian nationalism, it was nevertheless an issue of great importance for the Egyptian nationalists in the 1920s and the early 1930s. Some wished to bring to an end the identity association between Egypt and other Arabic-speaking countries by promoting the colloquial as the medium of writing and wider communication. In putting this forward, the proponents of this view invoked the environmentally determined character of this dialect. The majority of the nationalists, however, adopted a solution similar to that advocated by Lutfi al-Sayyid (see section 3). It consisted of modernizing the Arabic language by making it more receptive to lexical borrowings from the colloquial and foreign (mainly European) languages. The aim of this suggestion was to bridge the difference between the language of speech and writing by creating a middle language that can serve the two functions. It was envisaged that the new language would be closer to the standard than to the colloquial, and that the creation of an Arabic Language Academy would be a significant step in achieving this goal (see al-Jami'i 1983).[9] In addition to proposing new terminologies, it was suggested that such an academy would spearhead the compilation of dictionaries of a general and specialized nature. It was also thought that the Academy would bring forward suggestions for various language reforms, including those of the script (see Eliraz 1986).

By the late 1930s, the tide of Egyptian nationalism had started to turn in a more Arabist direction (see Gershoni and Jankowski 1995). The movement in this direction was gradual and, sometimes, mediated through an enhanced appreciation of the role Islam plays in the constitution of Egyptian society. Muhammad Husayn Haykal contributed to this by recanting most of his earlier views on Egyptian nationalism, particularly his earlier enthusiasm for the Pharaonic past of Egypt, which was now replaced as an object of study by Egypt's Islamic and Arab past (see Husayn 1983, vol. 2: 170–2).[10] A similar change occurred in the thinking of Muhammad 'Alluba, who declared that Egypt was an Arab country by virtue of, among other things, the Arabic language (ibid.:

173–5). This move was represented symbolically in the layout of *al-Siyāsa al-usbūʿiyya* itself (see Husayn 1983, vol. 2: 172). In its early years, the cover page of this newspaper appeared with Pharaonic decorations and the Common Era date only. The Islamic date was included in the inside pages only, alongside the Common Era date. Later, the newspaper omitted the Islamic dates completely. In the early 1930s, the Pharaonic decorations were dropped and replaced by caricatures. In its last stage, the newspaper had developed an Islamic visual identity, which it signalled by stating the Islamic date of publication only on the front page.

The strength of the Arabist idea as an alternative form of national identification did not, however, succeed in expunging Egyptian nationalism from the Egyptian cultural and political scene. My aim in the following three subsections is to show the sustained pull of this nationalism by examining the work of three Egyptian intellectuals who have contributed significantly to elucidating the relationship between language and nation in Egypt in the twentieth century: Salama Musa (1887–1958), Taha Husayn (1889–1973) and Luwis ʿAwad (1915–90).

4.1 The Arabic Language and Egyptian Nationalism: Salama Musa

Many of the ideas raised in the preceding section received the sustained attention of Salama Musa, whose hard-hitting style is characterized by a simplicity and clarity designed to motivate his Egyptian readers to espouse the ideals of modernization and nation-building he sought to promote. Salama Musa was a prolific writer who, like other Egyptian nationalists, understood the power of journalism in popularizing their nationalist cause. He wrote more than forty books, not all of which are directly relevant to the theme of the present work. Of these books, I will concentrate on *al-Yawm wa-l-ghad* (*Today and Tomorrow*, first published in 1928), *Miṣr aṣl al-ḥaḍāra* (*Egypt is the Source of Civilization*, first published in 1935) and *al-Balāgha al-ʿaṣriyya wa-l-lugha al-ʿarabiyya* (*Modern Rhetoric and the Arabic Language*, first published in 1945, with revised and expanded editions in 1953 and 1958). Although the ideas in these works show some slight variations, they are nevertheless consistent in ideology and zeal in spite of the thirty-year period separating the first publication above from the second revised edition of the last publication in the list.

Salama Musa conceives of the last chapter of *al-Yawm wa-l-ghad* as an investigation into the identity of the Egyptian nation; in particular, whether Egypt belongs to Europe and shares with it its culture, or whether it belongs to the East, to whose heritage it must remain true. He observes that, in the nineteenth century and the first two decades of the twentieth century, Egypt seemed to be unsure as to whether it belonged to Europe or to the East. Having considered the issue, Salama Musa dismisses out of hand the idea that Egypt belongs to the

East. He declares emphatically that the ascription of an Eastern identity to Egypt is an absurdity which must be resisted and ridiculed (*al-rābiṭa al-sharqiyya sakhāfa*, 1998: 660). Egypt belongs to Europe, not the East; and, if it belongs to the East, it does so only in the sense that it was once part of the Byzantine Empire, which to all intents and purposes is the bedrock of European civilization. He further points out that even Arabic, which might be thought of as an Asiatic and therefore Eastern language, contains well over 1,000 words from Greek and Latin. Similarly, al-Azhar, which is often considered the bastion of Islamic learning in Egypt and the rest of the Muslim world, was itself established by a European, Jawhar al-Siqilli, who was of Slav origin. Also, medieval Arabic culture was not different from ancient European culture, since both took their impetus from Greek philosophy. Salama Musa goes even further, claiming that Islam itself is almost a branch (*madhhab*) of Christianity (ibid.: 668). In *Miṣr aṣl al-ḥaḍāra*, Salama Musa declares that Egypt is the fountainhead of human civilization, and that European civilization and culture owe a great deal to Egyptian civilization and culture. Furthermore, the Egyptians are more biologically or racially related to the Europeans than to other Eastern nations. For all of these reasons, none of which Salama Musa substantiates, Egypt cannot be said to be part of the East. It should be noted here that the East which Salama Musa has in mind above is the Far East, as his references to China and Japan in *al-Yawm wa-l-ghad* indicate. In seeking to deny the claim that Egypt belongs to the East, Salama Musa sets out to counter the idea promoted by some Egyptian intellectuals to the effect that, by banding together, the nations of the East can resist European power and encroachment, and that they can enlighten Europe about the spirituality it had lost in its rush for industrialization.

Salama Musa is no less dismissive of the attempts to build Egyptian national identity on religious grounds. He declares that the religious bond in nation-building is a "gross impertinence" (*al-rābiṭa al-dīniyya waqāḥa shanīʿa*, ibid.: 662) which is unbecoming of civilized nations in the twentieth century. Religion clashes with science and offers views of the world that are antithetical to progress. Religion, points out Salama Musa, is a matter for the individual, who may not believe what others believe. In their attitude towards religion, the Egyptians should emulate the Turks, who discovered during the First World War that the Islamic bond is meaningless politically and otherwise. What is needed in Egypt is a secular outlook based on scientific socialism, a favourite concept of Salama Musa, rather than the futile harping on the religious bond which is ineffective and divisive as a form of national identification. As a Christian Copt, Salama Musa was aware that a religiously anchored national identity in Egypt was bound to split the Egyptian body politic along religious lines into, mainly, Muslims and Christians. To avoid this, a bond other than religion must be established as the basis of the national identity of Egypt.

In a manner reminiscent of the position in extreme forms of Egyptian nationalism, Salama Musa dismisses as misguided all the attempts to base Egyptian identity on Arab foundations. He declares that the Egyptians owe no loyalty to the Arabs. The Arabs are said to be less advanced than the Egyptians, thus making their culture unsuitable as a model for modern Egyptians, although it may be of archaeological interest similar to that which some people evince in the civilization of ancient Mesopotamia. In literature, Egyptian writers must eschew the temptation to emulate Arabic style and Arab themes. Interest in Arabic literature is time-wasting and leads to dissipating the creative energies of these writers. Arabic literature is said to contain obscene elements which can corrupt the morality of those Egyptians who may be exposed to it. This literature is also said to reflect the ethos of a society which was steeped in Bedouin life, bloodthirsty and dictatorial – so dictatorial, in fact, that even the Pope appears to be a model of democracy in comparison with Arab and Muslim rulers. Emulation of Arabic literature on the linguistic level may also lead to favouring form over content among Egyptian writers. It may also encourage the adoption of a style of writing in which linguistic pomposity and ornate rhetoric replace content as the standard by which an artwork can be judged. Should this happen, Egyptian literature would be shunted into the culture of the dark ages to which Arabic culture is said to belong.

Emulating classical Arabic literature is also dangerous because it bestows on the defective Arabic language the mantle of literary legitimacy which it does not deserve. As a lexically defective and grammatically unduly complex language, standard Arabic cannot serve as the medium of the national literature of Egypt. It should therefore give way to a refined colloquial language, which is living and authentic. Asserting this point, Salama Musa declares that standard Arabic is a dead language which cannot compete with the colloquial as the true mother-tongue of the Egyptians. What is, however, interesting is that Salama Musa himself did not use this language in his writings. In this respect, he is similar to the proponents of the standard language who hardly use it in everyday speech.

Salama Musa believes that the alternative to the Arab bond in the formation of national identity cannot be the link which the modern Egyptians have with their ancient ancestors, dubbed Pharaonism in the literature. In spite of this, Salama Musa believes that the Pharaonic legacy is far more beneficial to the modern Egyptians than the Arab legacy in the formation of their identity and the building of their nation. To begin with, the Pharaonic legacy belongs to the forefathers of the modern Egyptians, who still carry in their blood the genetic make-up of these ancestors. Modern Egyptians can take pride in this legacy which, Salama Musa declares, makes Egypt the source of human civilization (*Miṣr aṣl al-ḥaḍāra* being the title of one of his books). By studying ancient Egypt, modern Egyptians will provide their nationalism with the "nourishment" it needs (1947: 31 and 90). This is why every attempt should be made to train Egyptians in Egyptology, to write books on ancient Egypt in Arabic, to expand the Pharaonic history offerings in Egyptian schools, to make films which display the splendour that was Egypt, to erect Pharaonic-style statues in Cairo and to transport some of the Pharaonic monuments to the city to give it an ancient Egyptian atmosphere. Salama Musa is aware of the symbolism of these recommendations, which he exploits in his book *Miṣr aṣl al-ḥaḍāra* by including figures that display aspects of ancient Egyptian art and items of material culture. Being aware of the importance of language in nation-formation and nation-building, Salama Musa states that Coptic, the demotic partner of the ancient Egyptian language, is not dead but is embedded in features which it has injected into Arabic. Coptic is alive in the monasteries of the Coptic Church; all it needs to regain its authentic textual identity is for a patriotic monk to devise an ancient Egyptian script to replace the Greek alphabet used in writing it.

Armed with this spirit of renewal provided by the Pharaonic legacy, modern Egypt must seek its modern identity by aligning itself with European culture to which it properly belongs. This orientation carries with it certain obligations on the cultural and political level. By hankering after the East, points out Salama Musa, the Egyptians must accept that the Europeans have every right to be contemptuous of them, and that they have no right to hate the Europeans (*inna al-ajānib yaḥtaqirūnanā bi-ḥaqq wa-naḥnu nakrahuhum bi-lā ḥaqq*, 1998: 671). The way out of this is for the Egyptians to espouse European culture completely, as the Turks have done under Atatürk. Being aware of the power of symbols in nation-formation, Salama Musa calls on the Egyptians to replace the fez by the European cap, as the Turks had done. In addition, the Egyptians must seek to Egyptianize the foreigners living among them, thus giving them a stake in the future of the country which will help release their creative energies in the project of modernization. Egypt must also shed all the institutions of the past, including al-Azhar. Egypt must additionally develop its own literature and language to reflect its own unique national identity. And, in an obvious intertextual reference to the Qur'an, Salama Musa calls on the Egyptians to turn their faces towards Europe in fashioning for themselves a new identity: *fa-l-nuwalli wujūhanā shaṭr ūrūbā* ("Let us turn our faces in the direction of Europe", ibid.: 675), which recalls God's order to the Prophet Muhammad and to all his followers in the Qur'an to turn their faces in prayer in the direction of the Sacred Mosque in Mecca: *fa-walli wajhaka shaṭra al-masjid al-ḥarām wa-ḥaythu mā kuntum fa-wallū wujūhakum shaṭrah* ("Turn then thy face in the direction of the Sacred Mosque, and wherever you are turn your faces in that direction", Qur'an 2:144).

Clearly, Salama Musa believes that the modernization of Egypt along European lines should be the goal of Egyptian nationalism. In its broadest characterization, this modernization must have as its aim moving Egypt from an agricultural mode of life and the preoccupation with literature, to an industrial age in which science, not literature, has pride of place. Language is seen as an important element in this modernization, but this does not elevate it to the status of a defining marker of the nation. Most of Salama Musa's ideas on this issue are found in his book *al-Balāgha al-ʿaṣriyya wa-l-lugha al-ʿarabiyya* (*Modern Rhetoric and the Arabic Language*), which, by fronting modern rhetoric in the title, indicates where the author's interests and sympathies lie. This ordering of the two components of the title suggests an oppositional relation between them which the book seeks to resolve in favour of the "modern rhetoric".

Salama Musa's thesis in this work is that the Arabic language in Egypt is one of the most important factors behind the backwardness of the country in social and other spheres. The lexical poverty of the language in designating modern objects and concepts means that the Egyptians continue to live in a pre-industrial age of agricultural practices and habits, and that their mentality as a result is "ancient, fossilized, dull and backward-looking" (*ʿaqliyya qadīma, jāmida, mutaballida tanẓur ilā al-māḍī*, 1964: 8). This mentality is reflected in fossilized modes of expression, and the tendency to replace logical argumentation by linguistic gymnastics, in traditional Arabic rhetoric. Language in this case is the outcome of its social milieu. But it is also the case that the social milieu is the outcome of language. The reform of society and its modernization cannot therefore proceed without reforming and modernizing the language of the society concerned. Similarly, the reform and modernization of the language is bound to lead to the reform and modernization of the society to which it belongs. By explaining where the backwardness of Arabic lies, and by providing ideas for dealing with this backwardness, Salama Musa aims to contribute to the project of Egyptian modernization and nation-building.

Salama Musa states that traditional Arabic rhetoric (*al-balāgha al-taqlīdiyya*) pushes Arabic discourse towards sentimentality and emotionalism. It also encourages a kind of linguistic arrogance which leads to assigning the highest value in stylistic expression to linguistic artistry and the use of outlandish metaphors, ornate figures of speech and skilfully crafted but artificial metonymies. The application of this style in literature makes the writer a slave to these outmoded norms of rhetorical expression, thus yielding a literature of slavery (*adab ʿubūdiyya*, 1998: 559) and one full of hot air and linguistic bubbles (*adab al-faqāqīʿ*, ibid.: 560). What is needed in Egypt according to Salama Musa is a different kind of literature, a literature in which language is the means of rational expression rather than the end of artistic achievement. This new literature must also be able to address the ordinary people of Egypt in a language which they can understand and consider as their own. For this to happen, Egyptian writers must fashion a language in which words say what they are intended to say, a language in which vagueness is reduced to a minimum. To achieve this, an attempt must be made to purify this language from the over-abundance of synonyms and near-synonyms which are so characteristic of Arabic. In addition, the new language must be fit for expressing the modern needs of the Egyptians and capable of releasing their creative energies. Following the suggestion made by Sir William Willcocks in 1893 in a lecture he delivered at the Azbakiyya Club in Cairo (see Sa'id 1964: 32–40), Salama Musa held the view that this ideal language was the colloquial, not the standard.

Willcocks argued that the ornate style of standard Arabic works like a drug on the Egyptians, depriving them of their creativity and critical abilities. He also argued that, being a second language to the Egyptians, standard Arabic requires years of learning and formal instruction, and more often than not the process ends without the full mastery of the language. Very few writers in Egypt can write Arabic correctly, and many Egyptians cannot understand it at all. Some industrial accidents in Egypt were the result of this defective competence in the reception and processing of written documents. Egyptians live in a world of translation involving their mother-tongue and standard Arabic. This linguistic duality (or diglossia) slows the Egyptians down intellectually and mentally, and it is the single most important factor in the absence of scientific creativity and innovation among them. Having established the problem facing Egypt on the linguistic front, Willcocks argued that the solution to this problem is a simple one: it consists of turning the spoken language of Egypt into its language of science and culture. By adopting this course of action, Egypt would only be replicating the process in Europe which turned the vernaculars into the languages of writing, reading and high culture. And, in a manner reminiscent of this process in Europe, Willcocks produced a translation of the Bible into colloquial Egyptian. Salama Musa praises this translation, pointing out that the simplicity of its style and its rootedness in Egyptian life and culture make it superior to the translation of the Bible into standard Arabic. For all these reasons, Salama Musa believes that Egypt is indebted to Willcocks, who, by implication, provides an excellent argument for the call to Egyptianize foreigners in Egypt so that the nation can avail itself of their expertise and innovative spirit.

Salama Musa also argues that the artificiality of standard Arabic, its difficulty and the fact that its adoption dissipates the force of Egyptian nationalism in identity and modernization terms by creating links with other Arabic-speaking countries are but part of the problem facing Egypt on the linguistic front. In addition, the fact that the language is stamped by the indelible imprint of the desert environment which nurtured it in its early stages of development means that Arabic is unable to handle the needs of modern life. In the Arabic-speaking world, words have such a hold on speakers that they often base their linguistic and non-linguistic practices and behaviour on the effect these words have on them. We are told that by using the word *thuʿbān* (lit. snake) in Arabic to designate the eel, the Egyptians have deprived themselves of a great source of food because of the negative connotations of the word *thuʿbān* (1964: 36). Also, the absence of any poetry on the swan in Arabic – although it is the subject of fabulous poetic and musical compositions in other cultures – is said by Salama Musa to be the result of the ugly-sounding name, *bajaʿa*, it has in Arabic (ibid.). Arabic also contains a set of words which are said to have been responsible for many crimes, including the so-called crimes of honour, in Egypt. These are first and foremost "linguistic crimes" (*jarā'im lughawiyya lā akthar*, ibid.: 60). Salama Musa states that words of this kind have an intoxicating effect on their users, both speakers and hearers, owing to the fury (*junūn*, ibid.: 61) they generate in them. This set of words includes *damm* (blood), *tha'r* (revenge), *intiqām* (vengeance) and *ʿirḍ* (honour). These and similar words belong to a socially harmful archaeology of linguistic signification (*aḥāfir lughawiyya*, ibid.: 47), which further includes terms that designate and sanction superstitions, the abuse of others and the promotion of war and oppression in society. Salama Musa claims that the hypnotic effect of these words on their users (*tanwīm mighnāṭīsī*, ibid.: 63) is such that they correlate with the prevailing social conditions and practices of Arabic-speaking communities. Living under the spell of Arabic, the Egyptians are locked into a world of meanings which is inimical or, to say the least, not conducive to modernization. To argue the point, Salama Musa correlates the moral values of a society with the number of words it has to designate aspects of these values, the implication being that the larger the stock of words which designate these aspects in a language, the greater their preponderance in society. He presents his conclusions in a list format which I reproduce here to keep the visual effect (ibid.: 62):

> We are as virtuous as the number of words which designate virtue in our language.
> We are as depraved as the number of words that designate depravity in our language.
> We are as logical in our behaviour as the number of words that designate logic in our language.
> We are as muddleheaded as the the number of words that designate muddleheadedness in our language.

Egypt, points out Salama Musa, must take heed of the above correlations by acting in a way which can increase its fund of positive and morally uplifting terms while, at the same time, weeding out the negative and morally corrosive ones which act like a poison in society. By so doing, the Egyptians can purify their language, raise it to a higher status and harness its power in the modernization enterprise. Words are not just emblems (*shiʿār*, ibid.: 103), but a form of action which the Egyptians must exploit to move forward on the social, political and religious fronts. Clearly, language is the key to modernization and development in Salama Musa's thinking. But it also reflects this modernization and development on the lexical and other fronts. What Egypt needs, therefore, is a double movement whereby modernization and development in the linguistic and non-linguistic spheres can proceed together and aid each other. If so, the question arises as to the kind of modernization and reform which Arabic must undergo to be able to participate fully and positively in non-linguistic modernization.

As a first step towards answering this question, Salama Musa begins by outlining some of the problems which face the language lexically, stylistically, pedagogically and orthographically. On the lexical front, Salama Musa declares that Arabic as a means of scientific expression is dead (*lughatunā al-ʿarabiyya min nāḥiyat al-ʿulūm mayyita*, ibid.: 94). The answer to this problem lies in borrowing new terms from other languages, rather than coining equivalent terms from the native stock of the language itself. Borrowing can bring Arabic closer to other languages, which, in this case, are bound to be the European languages of learning and science. The injection of these borrowed terms will spread the spirit of modernity in the language. On the cultural level, this can be justified by the fact that other languages borrowed from Arabic in the past. On the stylistic front, the challenge facing Arabic is one of replacing the traditional Arabic rhetoric by modern rhetoric. In particular, the main task here is one of replacing the artificial artistry of the former by the precision of the latter. Salama Musa expresses this point by considering logic as the greatest quality in the modern rhetoric he is advocating. Meaning and the clarity with which it is conveyed must be promoted over form and whatever artistry may be moulded into it as per the traditional norms of expression. On the pedagogic front, grammar-teaching must be simplified, at least in the initial stages of the curriculum. This simplification may encompass eliminating those features of the language that are known to cause problems to the learners, for example the desinential inflections, the dual, and some forms of the broken plural. It may also take the form of promoting only reading at the primary-school level, leaving the far more complex skill of writing until later. This would equip the learners with the essential literacy skills they are most likely to need in their adult life. A more imaginative teaching approach than that practised in the schools is also needed. But this will require an organizational change of policy, whereby the traditional restriction of Arabic-language teacher-training to the conservative and Azhar-led Teacher Training College (Kulliyyat Dar al-ʿUlum) is lifted in favour of allowing other agencies to provide the needed teachers (see next section for a discussion of this point). To enrich the pool of available teachers, non-Muslim Egyptians must be allowed to teach the language in state schools, contrary to the practice in force at the time which restricted it to Muslims.

On the orthographic front, the Arabic script is charged with being too unwieldy to apply in teaching and learning the language in a grammatically correct manner, owing to the absence of the short-vowel diacritics in normal writing. It is also considered as one of the causes for the backwardness of Egypt in the pure and applied sciences, the acquisition of which is essential if Egypt is to enter the industrial age with confidence. To deal with these problems effectively, Egypt must, first, overcome its linguistic conservatism which ascribes to language a sanctity it does not merit. Second, Egypt must adopt the Roman alphabet in its capacity as a condition of modernity (1964, 1955). The advantages of adopting this solution are manifold. It will enable Egypt to shake off the legacy of the past and to orientate itself towards the future, as happened in Turkey, which took the initiative in this regard. The application of this solution will also ensure that the Arabic of Egypt will become truly Egyptian, thus taking Egypt outside the orbit of the Arab nationalist idea on the cultural and political spheres. The adoption of the Roman script will additionally have the effect of bringing Egypt closer to European culture by eliminating the psychological distance which the Egyptians feel exists between their culture and that of Europe. And, by virtue of the fact that European culture is the dominant culture of the modern world, the Egyptians will become part of this culture instead of continuing to stand outside it. As a result, the dichotomous distinction between East and West (*sharq wa-gharb*, 1964: 144) will lose its hold on the minds of the Egyptians.

As far as the sciences are concerned, the Roman alphabet will enable the Egyptians to borrow scientific terms from Europe more easily, and in a way which makes the internal composition of these terms transparent and more amenable to exploitation in generating new terminologies. The adoption of this alphabet is said by Salama Musa to be a condition for Arabizing and Egyptianizing the sciences. So, convinced of the validity of this assertion, he declares that without Romanizing Arabic writing the sciences will never be Arabized (*lan tastaʿrib al-ʿulūm illā idhā istaltan al-hijā' al-ʿarabī*, ibid.: 166). The borrowing of terms from European languages in all spheres of human knowledge will additionally have the effect of making the learning of these languages easier to accomplish by the Egyptians. For all these reasons, the adoption of the Roman alphabet would constitute an "enlightened leap into the future" (*wathba fī al-nūr naḥw al-mustaqbal*, ibid.: 145).

The above discussion shows the centrality of language in Salama Musa's thinking. Two features of this thinking are important from the perspective of the present work. First, language is not considered as a criterion of national self-definition on the Egyptian political or cultural scene. This precludes the possibility of launching a national identity for Egypt which exploits the affiliative bonds that Arabic may create on a pan-Arab level. To ensure that such a link could not be activated, Salama Musa calls for turning the colloquial into the national language of Egypt. Second, the importance of the language issue in the thinking of Salama Musa is part and parcel of the importance he attaches to modernization in all spheres of life in Egypt. Language here is the instrument through which modernization can be communicated. But it is also one of the instruments though which modernization can be induced and effected. To carry out this latter function, language itself must become the subject of modernization. And, since the modernization project Salama Musa advocates seeks to bring Egypt into the orbit of European culture, Arabic must be brought into this orbit by replacing the Arabic script by the Roman alphabet.

As has been said above, Salama Musa expresses his ideas in a hard-hitting style which reveals an unrivalled commitment and zeal for the modernization of Egypt as the national project par excellence. For him, modernity not tradition is the name of the game. However, tradition for Salama Musa is not the same thing as the past in all its accumulations, although the two are related. This explains his enthusiasm for the culture of ancient Egypt and its potential for taking the country outside the Arab and Islamic orbits into a terrain that is more sympathetic to European ideas.[11] Salama Musa reiterates these ideas in several of his publications, and in different places in each publication. Some of the articles setting out these ideas were initially published in the press over a long period of time. The net effect of these factors on the epistemological level is one of eclecticism rather than one of systematic treatment and thought. Salama Musa is not a theoretician of modernization but a popularizer of it. He is therefore not concerned if his ideas are not always consistent. Witness the fact that, although he calls for replacing standard Arabic by Egyptian colloquial as the national language of Egypt, he nonetheless seems to direct most of his linguistic-reform proposals towards the former. Witness also the fact that he himself does not use the colloquial in writing. This lack of consistency further characterizes his view of human language. On the one hand, he believes that language is not just a component of culture but is its creator. Most of his arguments about the harm which Arabic causes to Egyptian society (*ḍarar al-lugha*, ibid.: 51, 55) are based on this premise. However, when it suits him, Salama Musa (ibid.: 171) claims that language is no more than an instrument of communication, referring to it as *adā* (instrument) and *wasīla* (a means of). As such, language may be subjected to deliberate changes and modifications without infringing its cultural character and the system of symbolic values it serves in society (cf. section 5.2). One such modification is the use of the Roman alphabet in place of the Arabic script in writing.

Salama Musa shares with other Egyptian nationalists the belief that Egypt has its own national identity which it does not share with other countries surrounding it. Egypt is not Arab, although Arabic is its language and the language it shares with others in the Arabic-speaking world. Egypt is not Islamic, although Islam is the religion of the majority of its population and the faith they share with their co-religionists outside Egypt. Egypt is Egyptian and European. Its Egyptianness derives from its physical environment and the effect this has had on its people since the times of the Pharaohs. Its Europeanness derives from the long-lasting contacts it has had with Europe, and the fact that the culture of ancient Egypt informed the cultures of ancient Greece and Rome. Modernization in the linguistic and non-linguistic spheres must reflect the confluence of these factors. This will ensure its authenticity and sustainability. It will also ensure the revival and survival of Egypt as a worthy heir to its glorious past.

4.2 The Arabic Language and Egyptian Nationalism: Taha Husayn

Commonalities of thought exist between Taha Husayn and Salama Musa. Both writers believe that Egypt must form the focus of national loyalty and socio-political solidarity among all Egyptians, regardless of their religious beliefs or ethnic backgrounds, and that this is a precondition for achieving full national independence. Both writers also believe that European civilization and culture represent the standard by which other civilizations and cultures are judged in the modern world. Egypt therefore has no interest in staying outside the realm of European civilization and culture in its progress towards full independence. As a matter of fact, Egypt would betray its own history and civilizational legacy to the world if it were to stay outside the scope of modern European culture, owing to the fact that the very foundations of this culture were influenced by ancient Egypt itself (see sections 5.1–2 below for a similar view). Under this scheme of thought, espousing European culture on the personal and national level in Egypt is no more than a return to the roots of Egyptian culture itself. Finally, both Salama Musa and Taha Husayn agree that language is an important element in the national life of Egypt. They passionately believe that the modernization of Egypt must include the modernization of the language itself, if not actually begin with it. However, there are important differences between these two writers on this and other matters, as we shall see below.

In outlining Taha Husayn's thinking on the connection between language and Egyptian nationalism, I will base my argument principally on his key publication *Mustaqbal al-thaqāfa fī miṣr* (*The Future of Culture in Egypt* (1944), first published in 1938), which Hourani (1983: 327) describes as "his most important work of social thought [if not possibly] his only work of systematic thought". To understand the context for this work, it may be pointed out that it was written in the wake of the 1936 Anglo-Egyptian treaty which officially ended the British occupation of Egypt, and the 1937 Montreux Convention which ended the system of legal privileges given to foreigners in Egypt, known as the Capitulations. This context is highlighted in the opening sentence of *The Future of Culture* (1944: 5). Its implications for Egypt are set out in the introduction to the book as follows (cited in Hourani 1983: 327):

> I felt, as other Egyptians did ... that Egypt was beginning a new period of her life: she had obtained some of her rights, and must now set herself to important duties and heavy responsibilities ... We live in an age which can be defined as one in which freedom and independence are not an end to which peoples and nations strive, but a means to ends higher, more permanent, and more comprehensive in their benefits.

The first problem facing Taha Husayn in meeting this challenge is that of defining the national identity of a territorially distinct and officially independent Egypt. The starting point in this process consists of acknowledging that Egypt is linked to the countries surrounding it with ties of language, religion, geography and history. But this is soon followed by denying that unity of language and religion can serve as the basis of political unity. Taha Husayn declares this to be a historical truth which receives support from Islamic history itself. He points out that, beyond the initial stages of Islamic history, no attempt was made in the lands of Islam to base political unity on religion or language. The Muslims were divided between different polities which viewed each other with suspicion and which vied with each other for political and economic interests. Muslims (more accurately, Muslim rulers and elites), declares Taha Husayn, understood that "religion is one thing and politics is another" (1944: 21), and that the first basis for establishing political unity is common interests. Egypt absorbed this lesson well before other Muslim nations, and was quick to restore its status as an independent political entity in the first few centuries of Islam.

The second step in fashioning an Egyptian national consciousness on the part of Taha Husayn consists of rejecting the belief, held by some Egyptians, that Egypt is part of the East. In this respect, he is similar to Salama Musa, with whom he shares the view that Egypt belongs to Europe and not to the East in cultural terms. This similarity extends to the belief on the part of these two authors that talk about an Eastern identity for Egypt is an absurdity. Taha Husayn goes so far as to say that this talk represents the ultimate absurdity in the definition of the national character. To make this argument stick, Taha Husayn defines the East, as does Salama Musa, in terms of the paradigmatic cultures of China, Japan and India. Under this definition, Egypt and the countries of the Near East are said to belong to Europe culturally, since they share very little with these cultures. This linkage is justified by the interactive influences throughout history between Greek and Roman cultures, on the one hand, and the cultures of the Near East, including that of Egypt, on the other. Under this view, geography as a determining factor in nation-formation is subordinated to culture and common interests in shaping national identity. There is, however, some ambiguity in this position, for elsewhere in *The Future of Culture* (1944: 55) Taha Husayn fronts geography as a primary factor in defining the Egyptian national identity, alongside language and history. The influence of geography is further invoked by Taha Husayn to allay the fears of those among his compatriots who feel that, by aligning itself culturally with Europe, Egypt may end up losing its own cultural uniqueness. In response, Taha Husayn argues that this is unlikely to happen. The Egyptian character is known for its moderation, and this forms the ultimate guarantee that the espousal of European culture by the Egyptians will aim at integration and not assimilation. This moderation of the national character was formed by the moderate climatic conditions which Egypt enjoys (ibid.: 392), although we are not told how this was brought about. The Egyptians therefore have nothing to fear from European culture, especially as Egypt at the time of the publication of *The Future of Culture* in 1938 was moving in the direction of full independence.

Education is posited as the most secure basis for bringing about this cultural redefinition of the national identity in a manner which preserves and enhances the national unity of Egypt. But, to do so, the educational system in Egypt must be subjected to close scrutiny at all levels, and to targeted reforms which encompass structures, curricula and the provision of a teacher-training regime that is in step with the modern aspirations of the country. The issue of language is placed at the heart of this national project, which Taha Husayn sketches out with passion and bold determination. As a matter of fact, the predominance of the language issue in this project warrants considering *The Future of Culture* in part as a book about the modernization of Arabic and the teaching of Arabic language in the context of a project of national self-definition. The importance of language in this project springs from its being the medium of thought and socialization. In this capacity, language serves as a boundary-setter and as a criterion, among others, of inclusion and exclusion. Language is also important because it is the vehicle which creates the links between the present and the past, and between these two and the future, thus ensuring the continuity of the nation. Because of this, language education must be brought under the purview and control of the state, which must ensure that the language of the people is taught to the people in all schools in Egypt. In particular, Taha Husayn considers it as one of the duties of the state to insist that Arabic is taught in all the foreign schools in Egypt, and that this should be supported by putting in place a strict regime of inspection and assessment to guarantee that the policies set out by the state are vigorously pursued and implemented.[12] The importance of the national language in his thinking is further reflected in the call he made to eliminate all teaching of foreign languages in the primary stage in state schools. He argued that this step will ensure that maximum time is devoted to the teaching of Arabic, which is not an easy task owing to the diglossic nature of the language and the pedagogic burden this imposes on both learners and teachers. We are told that this step will have the additional virtue of (1) eliminating the competition which the foreign languages pose for the national language, and (2) removing the socially determined lure these languages have for Egyptians at such a young and impressionable age.

The success of this policy will ultimately depend on the kind of teaching of Arabic language offered in the schools. Taha Husayn points out that, for many learners, Arabic is a dreaded subject which excites a lot of antipathy and very little enthusiasm. The reason for this is partly located in the undue concentration on grammar as a means of teaching the language. Taha Husayn criticizes this approach as one which substitutes teaching *about* the language for teaching *of* the language *per se*. By turning grammar into the object of language-teaching and learning, the Egyptian schools dangerously confuse the means with the ends in this endeavour. Language-learning becomes a matter of parroting grammatical rules in artificial language settings. This fossilized attitude towards the language is said to be allied with a view of rhetoric which encourages the learners to imitate high style slavishly. Rhetoric under this scheme ceases to be an instrument of stylistic creativity and turns into an exercise in linguistic embellishment which pursues the sound of the word at the expense of its meaning. As a result, Taha Husayn points out, learners often say things which they do not understand, simply because what they say seems to satisfy the demands of this false rhetoric. As a form of "linguistic absurdity" (ibid.: 248), traditional rhetoric must therefore be assigned to the dustbin of history. In this respect, he is at one with Salama Musa.

Taha Husayn also argues that part of the problem of teaching Arabic is not the grammar of the language itself but the complex way it is set out in the manuals devoted to it. Making an implicit distinction between the grammar of the language in the *predescriptive* sense and its grammar in the *postdescriptive* sense, Taha Husayn assures his readers, who may be inclined to treat his ideas with suspicion, that simplifying the latter in no way infringes the linguistic integrity of the former. Grammar in the *predescriptive* sense is inherent in the language itself, whereas grammar in the *postdescriptive* sense is the creation of the grammarians, and as such it is open to critical evaluation and modification. The early Arabs understood this distinction, which is reflected in the differences between the various schools of grammar in the Arabic linguistic tradition. It is also reflected in some of the calls for simplifying or reforming this grammar. Taha Husayn points out that failure to reform the grammar, under the pretext that any reform of this kind would willy-nilly constitute an infringement of the integrity of the text of the Qur'an, will inevitably lead to depressing literacy in the schools and to heightening the danger which the colloquial poses to the standard form of the language in Egypt.

However, Taha Husayn is at pains to point out that his call to simplify Arabic grammar is intended not to bring the standard closer to the colloquial or to insinuate that the former should replace the latter – a position adopted by Salama Musa and other Egyptian nationalists – but to protect the standard against linguistic corruption and the challenge which the colloquial poses to it. As one of the most ardent supporters of the standard, in which he revelled as a student and as an accomplished writer, Taha Husayn never wavered in his support for it. Thus, he rejected the call to use the colloquial in writing in a most forceful manner, pointing out that its use in this domain will lead to destroying the cultural links which bind Egypt to other Arabic-speaking countries (1982). Later in his career, when the Arab nationalist idea started to be given official backing in Nasser's Egypt, Taha Husayn considered the above call as tantamount to an attack on the very basis which underlies the project of Arab unity (1957). This partly explains why he took strong exception to those critics from Syria who accused him of being more interested in Egypt's Pharaonic past than in its Arab heritage (1985). Taha Husayn's rejection of the colloquial is further motivated by his conviction that it is unfit for literary expression, and that its adoption would deprive the Egyptians of a link with their literary heritage. And, since literature is an important element in nation-building, Egypt cannot afford to let go of its standard language.

This protectionist attitude towards the standard extended into opposition to the proposals to replace the Arabic script by the Roman alphabet, as was suggested by Salama Musa and other radical Egyptian nationalists. However, Taha Husayn was careful not to let his support for the Arabic script be translated into a rejection of the much-needed reforms of the script concerned. Reforms were needed, but these should not aim at solving the problems of the desinential inflections by dropping them altogether from the language. Taha Husayn believed that this problem can be solved by combining orthographic reforms with grammatical reforms of the kind suggested by Ibrahim Mustafa in his book *Iḥyā' al-naḥw* (*The Revival of Grammar*), first published in 1937. In the introduction he wrote to this volume, Taha Husayn praises the author for his courage in tackling a subject which excites strong emotions among specialists and lay people alike. He also compliments him on equating the revival of grammar with a kind of reform whose aim is (1) to promote the correct use of the language in speech and writing, and (2) to encourage the interest in grammar as a scholarly enterprise. In *The Future of Culture*, Taha Husayn pushes these two arguments further, pointing out that the reform of grammar is needed to turn standard Arabic from a near-foreign language in Egypt to a fully functioning native one. It is also needed to ensure the survival of grammar itself as a living discipline of inquiry. The Egyptians, he says, have a choice: they either reform the sciences of the Arabic language to ensure its survival and the survival of these sciences; or they preserve these sciences as they are, thus causing their death and the death of the language they are intended to serve. The reform of grammar is also necessary because, without it, the reform of the system of education in Egypt itself will not be possible. And, since education constitutes the backbone of culture, it follows that the failure to reform grammar will compromise the very foundations upon which this culture is based. Furthermore, since the material progress of a society is dependent on the extent to which this progress is rooted in a strong and secure culture, it follows that the failure to reform grammar will compromise the very foundations upon which this progress is premised. This chain of arguments, exaggerated though it may be, demonstrates the extent to which Taha Husayn regards the language issue as a core ingredient in the life of Egypt and the modernization project it ought to follow. It also explains his conviction that Egypt has the right to reform its national language without formal consultation with, or the agreement of, other Arabic-speaking countries.

It is this centrality of the language in Taha Husayn's thinking which explains his aggressive attitude towards al-Azhar, the most famous institute of Islamic learning in the Muslim world. Taha Husayn considers it dangerous that al-Azhar, as one of the bastions of bigoted conservatism in Egypt, had acquired for itself the mantle of the guardian of Arabic, and that it had managed to promote itself as the body with sole authority over it in matters of grammatical reforms and teacher-training. The view of Arabic as the language of Islam underlies this acquisition of cultural and political hegemony on the part of al-Azhar. Taha Husayn considers the basis upon which this hegemony is based to be bogus: it is both historically unwarranted and out of touch with the modern conceptualization of the language. In arguing this point, Taha Husayn acknowledges that Arabic is the language of Islam par excellence, but he refuses to translate this fact into an admission that this is the sole or most important function of the language. Arabic is additionally the language of daily interaction, the vast intellectual heritage of the Arabs and the national language of Egypt in the modern world. Taha Husayn uses this to argue that there is no reason why al-Azhar should have the right of veto over any proposed reforms of Arabic grammar. There is also no reason why it should continue to have the final say in how the provision of Arabic-language teacher-training is delivered in the Egyptian schools. Control of these and other matters related to Arabic must therefore be wrested from the hands of al-Azhar and allocated to the state, where they properly belong.

To underpin this conclusion, Taha Husayn argues that the linking of Arabic to Islam, while doctrinally valid and culturally significant, obscures the fact that many nations operate with a linguistic duality in which the language of faith is different from the language of everyday life and culture. This is as much true of

Christianity as it is of Islam. The coincidence of the two linguistic functions in the case of Arabic must not therefore be used to outlaw its reform, since the reform concerned aims at the language in its capacity as the medium of culture, national identification and everyday life only. It follows from this that al-Azhar as a religious institution has no right to impose its authority on the speakers of the language. This is particularly true since the authority al-Azhar claims for itself is not historically sanctioned. Arabic was codified centuries before al-Azhar came into existence, with participation from scholars of different ethnic and linguistic backgrounds, most of whom came from outside Egypt. Attempts to reform the Arabic language in the early periods of Islam proceeded with little or no interference from the political authorities of the day. In addition, al-Azhar is not qualified to act as the authority in matters of language-maintenance and reform in the modern world. It lacks the freedom of opinion which the debate over these matters requires. It is out of touch with the modern sciences. It has no knowledge of historical and comparative linguistics. It has no knowledge of the Semitic languages. For all these reasons, Taha Husayn declares that the policy of assigning Arabic-language teacher-training to al-Azhar and its associated institutions, principally Kulliyyat Dar al-'Ulum, must be abandoned (compare section 4.1 above). Other institutions of higher education, including the University of Cairo, must be given a role in the delivery of this policy. Being modern and more attuned to the full range of the linguistic sciences, these institutions can serve as the channel of implementing the desired reforms. They can also serve to break the monopoly of power, functionally and symbolically, which the conservative al-Azhar holds over the cultural life of Egypt. In this new situation, al-Azhar will no longer be able to enforce its authority by accusing its opponents of being unbelievers and enemies of Islam. By denying it this coercive instrument, al-Azhar will learn to realize the limits of its power. In the long run, this will be to the benefit of al-Azhar and Egypt.

Arabic for Taha Husayn is the language of all the Egyptians, regardless of their religious affiliations. It is as much the national language of the Muslims as it is the language of the Christian Copts. He therefore believes that it is incumbent on the Coptic Church to ensure that its ministers are competent in the language, which is not always the case. It is also the duty of the Coptic Church to make sure that its followers have available to them worship materials in correct and elegant Arabic. Taha Husayn regrets the fact that the Arabic used in Coptic worship does not meet with this standard. He refers to the language used in this domain as "broken Arabic which is not in keeping with the dignity of Christianity" (ibid.: 360–1). He also regrets the fact that the Arabic translations of the Bible used in the Coptic churches do not rise to the standard attained in the English, French or German translations. This demands that this be rectified. So desperate was Taha Husayn to see this happen in Egypt and elsewhere in the Arabic-speaking world that he is reported to "have offered to help in rewriting [the liturgies] so that the Arab Christians could worship in good Arabic" (Hourani 1983: 334).

In assessing *The Future of Culture*, Hourani observes that "this book, while being a final statement of a certain type of purely Egyptian nationalism, marks the first step towards the merging of Egyptian in Arab nationalism" (ibid.: 335). This perceptive observation may help explain Taha Husayn's uncompromising support for the standard, and his dismissive attitude towards the colloquial as a corrupt variety which cannot be dignified with the term "language". It may also explain the fact that, although he once or twice calls Arabic the "Egyptian language" (1944: 68, for example), he generally refers to it as the Arabic language or, sometimes, as "our Arabic language" (ibid.: 197 for example). Thus, although Taha Husayn declares that Arabic is one of the defining features of Egyptian national identity, he does not seek to define it in such a way as to make it distinct from the same language in other Arabic-speaking countries, as did Salama Musa and other Egyptian nationalists (see section 3). The Egyptianization of Arabic called for by other Egyptian nationalists is definitely off the agenda for him, but its modernization is not. Also, unlike other Egyptian nationalists, Taha Husayn does not see Egypt as distinct from the surrounding countries. He believes that an independent Egypt has a duty towards its Arab neighbours, and that it can execute this by inviting Arab students to come to study in Egypt or by opening Egyptian educational institutes in these countries. This correlates with his pride in the literary heritage of the Arabs, and in the lip service he pays to the Pharaonic legacy of Egypt as a factor in defining its national identity (1985). The cumulation of these ingredients in his thinking does not, however, amount to an espousal of Arab nationalism, even when Egypt under Nasser championed this ideology. In spite of this, Taha Husayn's name is sometimes reviled by his opponents on the Islamic side. His statement that religion and the state are two different things, and his stinging attack on al-Azhar, have contributed to this in no small measure.[13]

4.3 *The Arabic Language and Egyptian Nationalism: Luwis 'Awad*

Although the 1920s and early 1930s constituted the heyday of Egyptian territorial nationalism, it would be wrong to conclude that articulations of this phenomenon disappeared from the Egyptian political and cultural scene as a result of the strengthening of the Islamic mood and the ties of Arabism towards the end of this period. In the latter sphere, Arabic started to emerge as the factor which binds Egypt in ties of identity with other Arabic-speaking countries. The idea that Egypt is Arab because its people speak Arabic assumed the same importance in this new vision of the nation, as did the environment in earlier articulations of Egyptian nationalism. The following statement by the writer

Ibrahim 'Abd al-Qadir al-Mazini (1890–1949), published in 1937, illustrates this vision (cited in Gershoni and Jankowski 1995: 118–19):

> Nationalism is nothing but language. Whatever the nature of a country may be, and however deeply embedded in antiquity its origins may be, as long as peoples have one language, they are only one people ... Every language has its own modes and methods, modes of thought and methods of conception ... In this regard, the sons of each language conform to and resemble each other and are distinguished from the sons of every other language.

In this context, it may be pointed out that the work of Luwis 'Awad (henceforth Lewis Awad) represents an attempt to challenge, or even deny, this link between language and national identity as the criterion of national self-definition for Egypt. He sets out his views on this topic in two books. The first, *Plutoland*, was published in 1947. In the introduction to this experimental collection of poetry, Lewis Awad advocates the adoption of Egyptian colloquial Arabic as the language of literature in Egypt. And he does so with a vehemence that is reminiscent of the forceful views on the topic expressed by Salama Musa two decades earlier (see section 4.1 above). The second work is *Muqaddima fi fiqh al-lugha al-'arabiyya*, (*Introduction to the Foundations of the Arabic Language*), which was published in Egypt in 1980. In 1981, this book was the target of censorship as a result of a court case which found against its author.[14] Its critics charged that Lewis Awad expressed views that were inimical to some of the deeply held beliefs of the Muslim community, mainly the inimitability of the Qur'an. The main point of interest for us in the present work, however, is the range of views which the author advances to decouple the language factor from that of national identity in the Egyptian cultural and, by implication, political sphere. It is not insignificant in this regard that the *Introduction* was published during the Sadat period (1970–81), when Egypt veered towards an "Egypt first" policy in response to the Arab boycott following its peace treaty with Israel in March 1979.

Let us consider the above two works, starting with *Plutoland*. In the first sentence of the introduction to this collection, Lewis Awad declares that Arabic poetry died a death in Egypt with the demise in 1931 of the Poet Laureate Ahmad Shawqi, whose neo-classical style was out of tune with Egyptian modernity and Egypt's sense of enduring identity. He later develops this theme by stating, triumphantly, that it would be more accurate to say that Arabic poetry in Egypt never died because it was never alive there. The evidence for this, he declares, lies in the fact that Egypt had failed to produce one poet of repute between what he refers to as the "Arab occupation" of Egypt in 640 and the "British occupation" of the country in 1882. The reason for this, we are told, is the status of Arabic as an external attribute and artificial tongue of the Egyptians, who failed to digest it in the way that living creatures naturally digest their food. Instead, the Egyptians developed a language which, in spite of its Arab roots, is different from pure Arabic in its phonology, morphology, syntax, lexicon and prosody. The problem for Egypt, however, is that its own sons do not seem to accord this language – the people's language – and the poetry produced in it the status and cultural significance they deserve. By equating the British occupation of Egypt with the Islamic conquest of the country, Lewis Awad aims to underline what he sees as the foreignness of Arabic in Egypt. He also aims to say, in a manner reminiscent of the claim made by Willcocks (see section 4.1 above), that the creativity of the Egyptians cannot be unlocked without their relying on their native tongue, this being the colloquial.

Behind this constellation of ideas is a clear political message: the struggle for full political independence in Egypt must proceed together with the struggle to rid the Egyptians of the hegemony which Arabic exercises over their cultural life. Hence the references to Arabic culture in Egypt as a colonizing culture whose language the Egyptians must seek to destroy and replace by what Lewis Awad calls, tongue in cheek, the "base" or "vulgar" language of Egypt (*munḥaṭṭa*, 1947: 9) which the colloquial epitomizes. This linguistic revolution is necessary if Egypt is to escape from the rotten cultural influences it has suffered for 4,000 years at the hands of successive foreign rulers, the Arabs included. It is only by returning to its Pharaonic past that Egypt can regain that sense of creativity which it so badly needs in the modern age. It is also by recognizing that Arabic and the colloquials will inevitably go the way of Latin and the Romance languages that the Egyptians will take the necessary steps to aid the progress of this development. As a contribution to this enterprise from someone whose feel and command of standard Arabic are very weak (1947: 19), Lewis Awad wrote his memoirs of his student days in Cambridge (*Mudhakkirāt ṭālib ba'tha*, 1965) in colloquial Arabic. In the introduction to *Plutoland*, Lewis Awad also relates how he promised himself never to use standard Arabic in writing, but points out with feelings of remorse and shame that he failed to keep this promise.[15] In the introduction to his memoirs, he adumbrates that he had not actually failed, for the promise he made was intended to refer to creative writing only (1965).

Lewis Awad considers the link between Arabic and Islam to be the main obstacle on the way to achieving the above goal of creating out of the colloquial an autonomous Egyptian language (*lugha miṣriyya*, 1947: 12). He argues that the creation of such a language will not undermine Islam as a religion, although it may help bring about the much-desired outcome of depriving orthodoxy of its linguistic power and authority in society. Also, the creation of an Egyptian language will not necessarily lead to the diminution in the status of standard Arabic. The two languages and their literatures can exist side by side. Being, however, aware of the religious significance of Arabic and of his status as a

Christian Copt, Lewis Awad considers it more appropriate and effective if the banner in this enterprise be carried by a Muslim Egyptian rather than himself. By putting forward this view, Lewis Awad displays a clear understanding of the role of Arabic in moulding Egyptian subjectivity. This view also highlights a clear understanding of the sectarian-based link between language and subjectivity, at least at the symbolic level, in the life of Egypt and among intellectuals of the same mindset and inclinations as Lewis Awad.

Let us now turn to the *Introduction*, which was published more than thirty years after *Plutoland*. In spite of the fact that the findings of this book – often speculative and controversial, as will be shown below – are radically different from those of any other work on Egyptian nationalism, it is still primarily dedicated to negating the link between Arabic and Egyptian national identity. The starting point for this work revolves around the assumption that most of the similarities between Arabic and other Indo-European languages are not the result of lexical borrowing, important though this was in the history of relations between them, but are the outcome of the genealogical relationship which holds between them. The same is also true of the similarities between Arabic and ancient Egyptian, which is a member of the Hamitic family of languages. If this is the case, then all of these languages are cognates. To support this conclusion, Lewis Awad applies what may be construed in very broad terms as a glottochronological approach, the aim of which is normally to calculate the point in time at which cognate languages have started to diverge from each other. The fact that Lewis Awad does not seem to be aware that this is more or less what he is trying to do – in spite of the fact that glottochronology is a highly controversial methodology in historical linguistics – should not detain us here. What matters from the perspective of the present research is the way in which Lewis Awad deploys the above assumption to argue (1) that the Arabs originated from outside the Arabian Peninsula, (2) that Arabic is not unique, and (3) that Arabic cannot be used as an instrument of national identification.

Concerning the first point above, Lewis Awad believes that the similarities between Arabic and the Indo-European languages, which he sets out at some length in his book (pp. 139–459), belong to the core of the language (*ṣulb al-aṣlāb*, 1993: 52) rather than to its periphery. And, in view of the fact that the recorded history of the Arabs goes back to between c. 800 BC (in Southern Arabia) and 328 BC (in Northern Arabia), it follows that, in comparison with the ancient Egyptians, the Arabs are a recent nation in the area. The combination of these two observations raises the question as to the origin of the Arabs. To answer this question, Lewis Awad rejects the traditional view which suggests Arabia as their original home, simply because it fails to account properly for the similarities he posits between Arabic and the Indo-European languages. Instead of asserting that the similarities concerned are genealogical in nature, this theory considers them as the outcome of linguistic contact. A more plausible interpretation of the above two observations therefore demands that the original home of the Arabs be placed elsewhere, outside Arabia itself. Lewis Awad specifies this home as the Caucasus, to which the Arabs arrived from Central Asia on their way to Arabia via the Caspian Sea area. This would help explain the linguistic similarities mentioned above as the outcome of a linguistic archaeology in which the deepest substratum is neither Semitic nor Indo-European, but a mixture of both. The spread of Arabic under this view can no longer be regarded as a matter of out-migration from the Arabian Peninsula, but as a matter of in-migration into it by people who preferred the nomadic existence – which they inherited from their ancient fathers – to settled life.

This is a highly speculative view, but it does serve the purpose of claiming that the Arabs lack the historical pedigree which other nations in the Middle East can claim for themselves. In comparison with these nations, the Arabs are said to be outsiders and not insiders in geographical terms. They are in this respect unlike the ancient Egyptians, or the Hebrews and the Phoenicians who receive mention in ancient Egyptian documents. However, coming into contact with these and other peoples, the Arabs absorbed aspects of their linguistic repertoire, thus adding further strata to the linguistic archaeology of their language which, Lewis Awad suggests, consists of seven layers. Under this interpretation, Arabic must be viewed as a mixture of core and acquired features. This hybrid structural compositionality must be taken to deny the claim of uniqueness attributed to the language in the Arabic intellectual tradition. It also suggests that Arabic did not emerge on the scene of human history fully formed and perfect, as is sometimes claimed to be the case in this tradition. Under this set of interpretations, Arabic is a language like all other languages. It is to this aspect of Lewis Awad's thinking that I will turn next.

The claims of uniqueness and superiority attributed to the language in the Arabic intellectual tradition derive primarily from the fact that Arabic was the medium of the Islamic revelation (cf. Chapter 3). And, since this revelation says of itself that it is inimitable, and since it also asserts that this inimitability lies in the linguistic domain, Arabic acquires connotations of doctrinally impregnated uniqueness. It is therefore claimed by some scholars that Arabic is the language of Heaven, that it was fully formed before its manifestation on earth came about or that the revelation did not contain any foreign terms – in spite of the fact that some of the words in the Qur'an patently belong to this category. Claims of this kind are said to be responsible for the almost complete lack of interest in the Arabic linguistic tradition in the history of Arabic or in its genealogical relationships to other languages. Moreover, if taken seriously, the above claims and their linguistic consequences would deny the conclusion, outlined above, that Arabic is a human phenomenon which is subject to the same forces of formation and change, and to the same methods of scholarly scrutiny, that apply to other languages.

Although the above views are not espoused by all Islamic scholars or schools of thought in Islam, as Lewis Awad himself avers, he nevertheless goes on to say that they serve a political agenda whose aim was to legitimize Arab hegemony over other races. The uniqueness of Arabic therefore was an instrument of power which allocated the authority of interpreting the revelation and that of conducting the affairs of state to the Arabs, or grudgingly to those among the non-Arab Muslims who mastered Arabic and therefore became Arabized. Under this scheme of things, Arabic became an instrument of inclusion and exclusion, in which the Arabs – *whose* language Arabic is – had the upper hand. The association of language, people and power in this context is said to have given the Arabs advantages that far outweighed their status among the other older and more distinguished nations in the area. The feeling of superiority this generated among the Arabs is therefore not only unjustified, but is also the "Semitic equivalent of Aryan racism in Europe" (*al-muqābil al-sāmī li-l-āriyya al-ūrūbiyya*, ibid.: 95). Under this view, Arabic must be branded an instrument of race and racial purity (ibid.).

Although not explicitly cast in *shuʿūbiyya*-orientated terms (see Chapter 3, section 5) or in an Egyptian nationalist framework (section 4), the arguments set out in the preceding paragraph build on these two ideological articulations. What matters for us here is the connection with the latter. As Gershoni and Jankowski (1986: 96–129) convincingly argue, constructions of Egyptian national identity in the 1920s and 1930s did invoke an anti-Arab feeling which sought to depict the Arabs as different and separate in personality and mentality from the Egyptians.[16] For some, the Arabs were depicted as aliens whose language and literature must be resisted in favour of an explicitly and uniquely Egyptian language and literature, as Lewis Awad himself did in the introduction to *Plutoland* which has been discussed above.

Although Lewis Awad declares that language cannot serve as the basis of racial identity, a view which most scholars would find unproblematic, he nevertheless undermines his case when he claims that the differences between Egyptian colloquial Arabic and standard Arabic are caused by the racially bound physical constitution of the Egyptian vocal tract. Without producing any evidence for it, he states that the use of the glottal stop in Egyptian Arabic instead of [q] in the standard – *'āl* = *qāl* (he said), or [g] instead of [j]: *gamal* = *jamal* (camel), or [t] instead of [th]: *tānī* = *thānī* (second), or [z] instead of [dh]: *izā* = *idhā* (if), and so on – reflects the peculiarities of the Egyptian vocal tract, including the shape of the tongue, the jaws, the hard and soft palates and the pharynx. Coupled with this physiologically induced racial difference in the production of speech sounds within the spectrum of Arabic phonetics, the theory of linguistic archaeology is implicitly employed to state that both ancient Egyptian and Coptic are important strata in the make-up of Arabic in Egypt. These two factors are said to give Egyptian Arabic a special character which distinguishes it from standard Arabic and other Arabic colloquials, although it may be pointed out in response that all the phonetic correspondences given above are attested elsewhere within the totality of the Arabic language. Lewis Awad expresses this special character of Egyptian Arabic by saying that its "skeleton is Arabic and its flesh is ancient Egyptian" (1993: 42). This view of Egyptian Arabic as a unique entity in the realm of Arabic varieties is consistent with the call in Egyptian nationalism to Egyptianize Arabic. It is, however, different from it in intent. Its aim is not to advocate a path of linguistic Egyptianization, a project whose realization Lewis Awad allocates to the future, but to assert that the Egyptian character of the colloquial in Egypt is a fact given by physiology and linguistic archaeology. Overt and interventionist Egyptianization would under this interpretation be no more than a reflection of the latent forces which have always conspired to make Egyptian Arabic truly Egyptian. If so, and since it is this variety of Arabic which is the mother-tongue of the Egyptians, Arabic cannot serve as a bond of identity with other Arabic-speaking peoples.

The above reading of Lewis Awad's views on language and national identity combines aspects of what he himself states explicitly and an element of construction in which what is implicit and inferred is made overt. There is, however, no doubt that these views, as I have tried to show above, are consistent with some of the major themes of Egyptian nationalism in the 1920s and 1930s. In some respects, these views are intended to push further the boundaries of these themes, or to excavate deeper into the foundations upon which they may be based. The problem with this project, however, is its lack of consistency and its highly speculative nature. Thus, while race and its identification with language are condemned in the *Introduction*, Lewis Awad does not hesitate to refer to the Egyptian race (ibid.: 41) and, as I have shown above, to the role played by the physiological features of this race in modifying Arabic phonology and phonetics among the Egyptians.

The highly speculative nature of Lewis Awad's ideas may be exemplified by his identification of *Remnen* in ancient Egyptian with *Lebanon* (ibid.: 23) via the intermediate derivative form *Lebnen*. This he does by applying a set of conversion rules which relate *r* and *m* in ancient Egyptian to *l* and *b* in *Lebanon* respectively. While this may be intuitively appealing, it cannot stand rigorous linguistic scrutiny. Thus we are not told under what conditions the above phonological conversions apply or what triggers them should such a trigger be involved. We are also not told whether these conversions between the two languages are obligatory or optional. We are also left in the dark as to the domain of the above conversion rules. Without this information, we cannot have any confidence in these conversions. They must therefore remain in the realm of speculation rather than that of assessable descriptive rules. There is indication, however, that Lewis Awad is aware of this serious shortcoming in his approach, although he fails to act on it. This is evidenced by the use of terms which signal the highly tentative nature of his findings: *rubbamā* (perhaps, ibid.: 26, 44, 46), *yajūz an* (it is possible, ibid.: 27), *naẓunn* (we believe, ibid.: 28), *yabdū anna* (it seems that, ibid.: 32), *'alā al-arjaḥ* (probably, ibid.: 36), *la'alla* (perhaps, ibid.: 36, 51), *qad* (it is possible that ..., ibid.: 54), and so on. These and other examples are used in connection with conclusions Lewis Awad draws from his investigation. Their utilization in this context lends further support to what has been said above concerning the speculative nature of his conclusions.

5. THE ARABIC LANGUAGE AND LEBANESE NATIONALISM: A GENERAL INTRODUCTION

There have been very few studies (at least in English) of the language situation in Lebanon, in spite of the enormous promise this subject holds for sociolinguists and the light it can shed on questions of colonialism and national identity in this country during the last half-century. The complexity and sensitivity of this issue in its political context is the main reason for this lacuna. It is not my intention in this research to rectify this deficiency or to consider the sociolinguistic reflexes of political conflict in Lebanon, a subject I hope to return to in a future project on language and sociopolitical conflict in the Middle East. Rather, my aim here will be to investigate how standard Arabic is used as a marker of Lebanese national identity by considering two contributions in this area, one based on historical and pragmatic advocacy and the other on philosophical grounds. However, before launching into this discussion, I will present a general sketch of the language situation in Lebanon in the context of the conceptualisation of national identity.

Broadly speaking, four languages share the linguistic space that makes up the Lebanese cultural scene. Two of these languages, English and Armenian, will not concern us here owing to the fact that they do not impact significantly on the conceptualizations of national identity *for* Lebanon. The spread of English in Lebanon is attributed to its role as the global language of business and international relations, although its presence in the country goes back to the nineteenth century. Armenian is restricted to the small Armenian community in Lebanon, who promote it as an instrument of keeping alive their cultural identity and their links with their country of origin. The other two languages, Arabic and French, are intimately interwoven with issues of national identity in Lebanon. Advocacy in favour of standard Arabic tends to be associated with pan-Arab nationalism, but not exclusively so, as I shall show below. It is generally believed that Muslims in particular are the main supporters of this variety and the nationalist ideology it underpins (cf. section 2). In contrast, promotion of colloquial Arabic as a marker of national identity tends to be associated with inward-looking Lebanese nationalism which sees in standard Arabic an instrument of pan-Arab cultural and, indirectly, political hegemony. A general perception exists that the supporters of this variety tend to be drawn from among the ranks of the Christian, particularly Maronite, segments of the population (cf. section 2). One of the strongest supporters of this variety is the poet Saʿid ʿAql who, after a long literary career in standard Arabic, published a collection of poems (*Yara*) in colloquial Lebanese using the Roman alphabet (see al-Naqqash 1988: 101). However, the use of the Roman alphabet is not universally advocated by the Lebanese nationalist colloquialists. Witness the fact that Saʿid ʿAql himself used the Arabic alphabet to render this dialect in his introduction to Michel Tarrad's collection of poems *Gulinnār* (see al-Hajj 1978: 242).

Support for French on the Lebanese cultural scene is generally linked to conceptualizations of Lebanese national identity which propel it outside the Arab orbit and lodge it in the sphere of a Western or non-Islamic Mediterranean culture. Under this interpretation, Lebanon is *in* the Middle East but is not exclusively *of* it. Lebanese national identity is therefore not purely Arab or purely Western, but must partake of both to remain genuinely authentic and true to its roots. The presence of French is seen now as part of a long-established multilingual tradition in Lebanon which takes the country back to the times of the Phoenicians, for whom multilingualism was a fact of life (see Skaf 1960). Educational and other contacts with France and the presence of French in Lebanon are said to predate the French Mandate (1918–43), although the language received a boost when the mandatory authorities declared it to be an official language alongside Arabic, and then proceeded to provide the resources to give effect to this policy through the educational system and the institutions of the state. The presence of French in Lebanon was also justified on what appeared to be pragmatic grounds. It was argued that, by arming itself with French, Lebanon can fulfil its civilizing mission in and to the East – read the Arab world – by interpreting the West to the Arabs and by advocating Arab causes in the West on behalf of the Arabs. Under this vision of Lebanon, the point is made that it is in the interest of those Lebanese who value Lebanon's connections to the Arabs to support the presence and spread of French in the country. Some proponents of French stressed its function as a medium of cultural, even spiritual, expression which enables the Christians, mainly the Maronites, to keep their contacts with the Christian West, mainly France.

It is clear from the above set of arguments that the presence of French in

Lebanon is endowed with political, religious and cultural connotations that bear directly on questions of the conceptualization of national identity, in spite of the fact that the official status of the language was dropped after independence in 1943. Politically, French underpins a concept of Lebanese national identity which sees it as irrevocably separate from Arab nationalism and Syrian Nationalism (see section 3 above). Religiously, French gives prominence to a specifically Maronite confessional identity within the Lebanese body politic, in spite of the fact that the language is used by Muslims and members of other Christian denominations for cultural and social interchange. Culturally, French signifies Lebanese linguistic and literary hybridity as a way of supplanting any monolinguistic or monoliterary articulations of the national self. Hence the use of this language as a medium of literary expression in Lebanon, and the pride shown by the Francophiles in literary works of this kind. These arguments, which are part of the cultural politics of Lebanon, have been given strong advocacy in a book on the subject by Selim Abou (1962). In an excellent review of this book and the wider issues it raises, Rosemary Sayigh summarizes its main conclusions – which at the same time serve as its implicit premises[17] – as follows (1965: 126–7):

1. French embodies the highest expression of Western civilisation, which is now to all intents and purposes world civilisation;
2. the renaissance of Arab civilisation depends on its openness to Western civilisation, and it is Lebanon's role to provide the channel through which Western ideas and techniques can pass to the Arab world;
3. Lebanon, geographically and traditionally, has two further functions: to interpret the Arabs to the West and the West to the Arabs, and to provide the site for the dialogue between Islam and Christianity;
4. [Arabic-French] bilingualism is essential to the fulfilling of these missions;
5. Lebanon has always been polyglot; French, historically speaking, has merely replaced Syriac as the "national" language of the Maronites;
6. Lebanese bilingualism must be studied anthropologically as an "existential" fact, not subject to scientific criteria, whether linguistic or sociological;
7. French is a "fundamental part of Lebanese reality", essential to the spiritual needs of the population; it is implicit in the National Pact, and to attack it implies an attack on the National Pact;[18] [and] far from creating problems, it is "the principle of solution to the problem of an already divided society";
8. Lebanon's possession of French has been the means of putting the country on the map culturally – or "inserting it in the historical present", as Abou puts it; if French is lost the country's relatively high educational and cultural level will decline, to the detriment not only of Lebanon but also of her Arab neighbours.

Although it is not the aim of this study to examine the above arguments in favour of the role of French, or those in favour of the Lebanese colloquial in constructing Lebanese national identity, it will be seen below that this role is questioned and rejected by other Lebanese nationalists. The fact that some of these nationalists are staunch supporters of standard Arabic, and that they are Maronites and French-educated, is very significant. First, the combination of these facts undermines the impression that the supporters of standard Arabic on the Lebanese cultural scene are from the Muslim segment of the population. Second, the association of standard Arabic with Lebanese nationalism provides an interesting case against the almost exclusive linkage of the language with Arab nationalism. This association shows that territorial or state nationalism does not have to distance itself from standard Arabic to be authentic or completely independent. Subscription to the one does not have to imply the negation of the other. The starting point for this argument, as will be seen below, is the acceptance of the state as the legal entity which gives legitimacy to Lebanese nationalism. Without it, the above linkage between language and national identity cannot proceed. To show how this is done, I will consider the contribution of two Lebanese nationalists, 'Abdalla Lahhud (1899–?) and Kamal Yusuf al-Hajj (1917–76).

5.1 *The Arabic Language and Lebanese Nationalism: 'Abdalla Lahhud*

Asserting his identity as a Christian and as a Maronite, Lahhud addresses himself to the colloquialists and Francophiles in Lebanon by declaring that support for Arabism in no way constitutes a denial of Lebanese nationalism or threatens the status of Lebanon as a fully independent state, for which – he says – he is prepared to die if necessary (1993). He points out that, being a cultural phenomenon and a loose association between the Arabic-speaking countries, Arabism poses no political threat to Lebanon or to the Lebanese national identity. The fear of Arabism among Christian Lebanese nationalists out of the belief that it is irrevocably and organically linked to Islam is therefore unjustified. To support this, he reminds his colleagues that the first stirrings of Arabism emerged and were promoted, culturally and otherwise, by the Christians of Lebanon in the nineteenth century. Also, the proponents of Arabism as a cultural idea among the Muslims were at pains to distance it, even dissociate it, from Islam. Arabism is not a licence to promote Islam, for had this been the case the proponents of this idea would have sought to forge links and bonds of identity with non-Arabic-speaking countries. The fact that this has not been done indicates the secular roots of Arabism, a secularism which Lahhud wishes to promote in Lebanon to counter the confessional basis of Lebanese politics and conceptualizations of national identity. Support for the Arabist idea would also enable Lebanon to fulfil its leading cultural role in the area, as well as to facilitate the discharge of its civilizing mission to the Arabs. This is important for Lebanon's own identity if it is to continue to be true to its distant and near past. Lebanon is a small country with little potential or ability to fashion for itself a similar mission to the West. Lahhud stresses that the Arabs have a role for Lebanon which the Lebanese would be ill-advised to forgo. Without the Arabs, Lebanon would be culturally and politically far smaller than it geographically is. It therefore behoves the colloquialists and Francophiles among the Lebanese nationalists to give up their ideological opposition to standard Arabic, because that would lead to a massive diminution in the stature of Lebanon among other nations. Enmity to standard Arabic in Lebanon, declares Lahhud, must therefore be regarded as a crime (*lawn min alwān al-ijrām*, ibid.: 52).

The above arguments in support of standard Arabic are mainly based on pragmatic grounds of national self-interest. But this is not the only basis for this support in Lahhud's thinking. He believes that a non-blinkered and fear-free reading of Lebanese history would unearth evidence which shows that Arabic and the Arabs are not recent newcomers to Lebanon. He points out that Arabic is a sister language to Phoenician and Aramaic, which dominated Lebanon before the final triumph of the language in the Levant. This linguistic triumph after Islam built on earlier contacts between the people of Lebanon and the Arabs through trade and emigration, and it was accomplished willingly and without subjecting the Lebanese to any coercion. This explains the fact that many of the leading families of Lebanon trace their origins to pre-Islamic Arab tribes which embraced Christianity before the rise of Islam. Lahhud concludes that the idea that Arabic was a foreign language to Lebanon is therefore ludicrous.

Furthermore, the idea that Arabic did not manage to supplant Syriac as the language of the Maronites in Lebanon until the end of the eighteenth century cannot withstand scrutiny. To begin with, Lahhud points out that history in Lebanon has not bequeathed any written documents in Syriac – apart from the liturgy – for over 1,000 years. Also, the fact that the main book of Maronite law, *Kitāb al-hudā*, was produced in Arabic in 1058/9, and that no other copies of this book exist in any other language, surely indicates that Arabic was the main language among the Maronites. This is acknowledged by the author of this book in the introduction he wrote to it, in which he states that he used Arabic in rendering the book because the language was widespread among the Maronites. Also, the existence of a set of major Maronite figures from the fourteenth century with Arabic names (for example, Khalid, Sinan, Qamar, Badr) shows that Arabic was deeply embedded in Maronite culture. The existence of popular poetry in dialect form supports this conclusion. In the sixteenth century, the Maronite cleric Jibrayil al-Qila'i from Lahfad in the Maronite hinterland composed a set of such poems in which he extols the virtues of the major families in the area, pointing out that they took pride in tracing their genealogy to the Arab tribe of Ghassan. Towards the end of the seventeenth century, an Italian cleric visited the Maronite areas and wrote in his account of his journey that Arabic was the language of literacy among them, and that the use of Syriac was restricted to the liturgy, as in the case of Latin in Europe.

Lahhud further points out that the relationship between the Maronite Church and Rome, which officially goes back to the sixteenth century, provides further evidence in support of the embeddedness of Arabic in Maronite society and culture. It is reported that, on the occasion of a visit by a Maronite envoy to Rome in 1515, the Pope ordered that the Maronite Patriarch's letters brought by the said envoy be read in public in their Arabic and Latin versions. Also, starting in the fifteenth century, the minutes of the council meetings between Rome and the Maronite Patriarchate were recorded in both Arabic and Latin. When disagreements occurred between the two parties, the Maronites used to invoke the Arabic version of the minutes in support of their position. This shows, Lahhud tells us, that Arabic was deeply rooted in Maronite culture and society. The same is true for other churches, for example the Greek Melchites, whose move to Arabic dates back to the beginning of the eighth century. History therefore shows that Arabic is not foreign to Lebanon, and that "he who serves Arabic serves Lebanon" (*man khadam al-ʿarabiyya fa-qad khadam lubnān*, ibid.: 41). Lahhud counts in this category of the servants of Arabic a galaxy of Maronite scholars, including Bishop Jermanus Farhat (1670–1732), who was instrumental in promoting grammatical literacy among the Maronites. He also points to the contribution of Islamic scholars from Lebanon in the development of Islamic law, in particular the jurist ʿAbd al-Rahman al-Awzaʿi (AD 707–74), whose reputation travelled far beyond his native town of Beirut.

Lahhud concludes that the above arguments show that the status of standard Arabic as the "national language of Lebanon" (ibid.: 42) is supported by history and justified by considerations of enlightened self-interest. Standard Arabic must therefore be protected against the colloquial. This will, however, require simplifying its pedagogic grammars and promoting it vigorously throughout the school and higher-education systems. Arabic must also be protected against French, which competes with it in this system. However, a protective policy of this kind should not discourage the learning of foreign languages. Any such policy would cripple Lebanon's ability to perform its civilizing mission to the East.

It is clear from the above discussion that Lahhud is not an ideologue of Lebanese nationalism. His comments on the subject tend to be journalistic and popularizing, rather than analytic or part of a fully worked-out ideology. He begins with the Lebanese state as the basis of this nationalism, and then seeks to construct a view of standard Arabic which treats it as an attribute of the Lebanese national self in the past, and promotes it as one in the present and the future. What makes Arabic serve in this capacity is therefore the existence of the state. There is no talk about the Lebanization of this language along the lines advocated for Arabic in the context of Egyptian nationalism (see section 3 above). The fact that the standard Arabic Lahhud is interested in is more or less the same as the Arabic of al-ʿAlayli, al-Husri and al-Arsuzi does not seem to bother him. What makes this language different in politico-linguistic terms is the existence of the Lebanese state. This takes precedent over everything else. A more systematic outlook on this issue of language and national identity from this angle is provided by Kamal Yusuf al-Hajj, to whom I shall turn next.

5.2 The Arabic Language and Lebanese Nationalism: Kamal Yusuf al-Hajj

Although the views of Kamal Yusuf al-Hajj (1917–76) on the link between standard Arabic and Lebanese nationalism are not devoid of a strong element of advocacy and intellectual justification of the status quo of the Lebanese political system, there is no doubt that he is the foremost proponent of this link in Lebanon, particularly among the Maronites. What makes him different from others who advocated the same position, for example Lahhud, is the systematic way in which he deals with this link and the attempt to premise his discussion of it on philosophical or semi-philosophical grounds. Al-Hajj is also different from these scholars in his total support for confessionalism in Lebanon,[19] treating it as the country's raison d'être in civilizational terms. If we add to this that he was thoroughly educated in French, then we have before us a character profile which – common wisdom about Lebanon would suggest – should show little sympathy for standard Arabic in national-identity terms. The fact that he is one of the staunchest defendants of this language in Lebanon, and that he treats it as one of the four ingredients – in conjunction with political geography, political economy and history – which mould the Lebanese national identity, makes his contribution to the debate about this identity a particularly significant intervention. From the perspective of the present work, al-Hajj is also important because his views about Lebanese nationalism emerged from his interest in the philosophy of language rather than the other way round. In the annals of the history of language and nationalism in the Arab Middle East, al-Hajj is therefore on par with al-Husri and al-Arsuzi, although the latter two are pan-Arab nationalists and he is a stalwart Lebanese nationalist who ignores the contribution of these two thinkers – in spite of the fact that he shares with al-Arsuzi a common fascination with the work of the French philosopher Henri Bergson (1859–1941). He is, however, different from al-Husri and al-Arsuzi in that he writes in a style which draws on the creative and evocative capacities of the language. The fact that he writes in such a style, emulating in this regard Bergson, on whom he wrote his doctorate at the Sorbonne, led some of his critics to deny him the title of philosopher of which he was very proud (see Nassar 1981, 1994).

The fundamental building block upon which al-Hajj erects his philosophy is the duality of essence (*al-jawhar*) and existence (*al-wujūd*), in which the latter is a manifestation or realization of the former, albeit not always in a completely perfect manner. Applying this duality to Lebanon, religion is a matter of the essence, whereas confessionalism is a matter of existence. Al-Hajj argues that the fact that confessionalism through blind fanaticism distorts religion is an argument not against religion *per se*, but against the faulty practice of confessionalism. And, since religion is a matter of doctrine, it follows that no society or nation can exist without doctrine, for the very denial of doctrinal belief is in itself doctrinal. Under this logic, atheism itself is doctrinal. There is therefore no escaping the fact in Lebanon that religion must be a core element of society and the state. This core element he calls *naṣlāmiyya*, a relative adjective that concatenates the first part of *naṣrāniyya* (Christianity) and *islām* (Islam). The challenge facing Lebanon therefore is not just how to defend itself against secularism, but how to construct a positive confessionalism (*tā'ifiyya bannā'a*) which can reflect the essence of religion that is common to both Christianity and Islam (al-Hajj 1966).

Linking the above dualism to another between the state and the government, whereby the former is declared to be a matter of essence and the latter one of existence, al-Hajj now associates religion with the state, and confessionalism (in its negative manifestations) with the government. This enables him to sanction the National Pact of 1943 in Lebanon as a matter of the state and therefore of the essence, and to condemn the excesses of confessionalism in Lebanon as a matter of government and therefore of existence. What is wrong in Lebanon therefore is not the formal structure of the state as envisaged in the National Pact, but the defective realization of this state in the negative confessional practices of the government in the administrative and political sphere. To put this right, the Lebanese must be motivated to practise positive confessionalism. But this requires an involvement in politics which can activate religion. Al-Hajj states that the Muslims have no problems with this, since Islam does not call for separating religion from the state. The Christians, however, have a problem because they have been exposed to the Western idea of the separation of the church and the state, which, he says, they tend to treat as a political doctrine. To counter this, al-Hajj sets up an elaborate argument to prove that Christianity cannot be separated from politics, drawing from this the conclusion that the Christians in Lebanon must always be politically involved if they are to resist secularism or Muslim dominance. Positive confessionalism now emerges as the moral equivalent of the philosophy of the National Pact, which is the main title of his book on the subject: *al-Ṭā'ifiyya al-bannā'a aw falsafat al-mīthāq al-waṭanī* (1961). The sub-title spells this connection out, declaring the book to be a "philosophical, theological and political study of confessionalism in Lebanon in the context of the National Pact": *mabḥath falsafī lāhūtī siyāsī ḥawl al-ṭā'ifiyya fī lubnān 'alā ḍaw' al-mīthāq al-waṭanī.*

The duality of greatest interest to us in the present work, however, is that between human language as a universal phenomenon that is inseparable from thought, and the mother-tongue (*al-lugha al-umm*) as an instantiation of that language. The former belongs to the world of the "essence" and the latter to that of "existence". Although the comparison is not directly made in al-Hajj's main book on the subject, *Fī falsafat al-lugha* (*On the Philosophy of Language*, first published in 1956), it is not unwarranted to equate "human language" with Saussure's *langage*, and the "mother-tongue" with his *langue*. Under this framework, standard Arabic is a realization of the phenomenon of human language. Both are abstract, but the former is a step more removed from the world of speech than the latter.

The second step in developing al-Hajj's thinking on the philosophy of language invokes the duality of *ma'nā* (meaning) and *mabnā* (linguistic structure). Although meaning is a matter of essence and, therefore, is universal, linguistic structure is a matter of existence through which meanings are realized or made manifest in a particular language. However, such is the duality of meaning and linguistic structure that the only way of getting at the former is through the latter. Meaning or thought, whenever we encounter them, are willy-nilly always localized in a particular language. Translators, more than others, are aware of this. And it is al-Hajj's struggle with translating Bergson from French into Arabic that led him to this set of conceptualizations and, ultimately, to his philosophy of the relationship between standard Arabic and the Lebanese national identity. Underlying this relationship, however, is the total belief in the givenness of the Lebanese state as envisaged in the National Pact. It is this state which legitimizes Lebanese national identity, for without it this identity cannot come into existence as a political or legal construct.

The mother-tongue for al-Hajj is more than just a means of communication. It is an end in itself by virtue of the fact that it is inseparable from thought and meaning, from humanity and from the construction of human society. The problem in Lebanon, points out al-Hajj, is that language is treated as a means of communication in the utilitarian sense of the term, thus depriving it of its true status as one of the forces that shape the Lebanese character and national identity (cf. section 4.1). Citing a number of psycholinguistic studies from the 1940s and early 1950s in France, and relying very heavily on his own experience and struggle to translate Bergson into Arabic, al-Hajj concludes that no-one can be truly bilingual across the full range of language functions served by the two languages he masters. Of the two or more languages that a person knows, one will dominate, and it is this language that qualifies for the status of mother-tongue. This applies to Arabic as it does to all other languages, particularly in the literary domain, where creativity of the highest order is the sought-after ideal. Evidence of this thesis can be derived from the fact that no creative writer who writes in a language other than his mother-tongue has ever been able to hit the highest notes of creativity achieved by indigenous writers writing in their mother tongues. Those who write in a language other than their mother-tongue rarely, if ever, enter the literary canon of the literature to which they seek to belong. Writers, says al-Hajj, have always understood this, and this is why they regard their mother-tongue as the most highly prized possession they have. It is true that meaning belongs to all humanity and that all languages are technically able to express it; but, when cast in a particular mother-tongue, at least in the literary domain, it so enters into an organic unity with the mother-tongue concerned that it is often impossible to separate the one from the other. Herein lies the genius of every language. And herein lies the enigma of the untranslatability of great works of verbal art. Shakespeare may be translated into Arabic, but his mother-tongue-based genius can never be. He will always remain an English writer, in both the linguistic and the national-identity sense.

There is no doubt as to who the target of this analysis in Lebanon is: it is the Francophiles who, in their advocacy of Arabic–French bilingualism, seem to behave as though language were the outer garment of meaning, its fez (*ṭarbūsh*), rather than of its very essence. Al-Hajj argues that, since complete bilingualism is an impossibility, the Lebanese have a choice: they either opt for French or they choose Arabic. Rational consideration of this matter makes it clear that French cannot function as the mother-tongue of the Lebanese. First, it is a foreign language in Lebanon, which the French mandatory authorities imposed on the Lebanese to weaken Arabic and to create a situation of unidirectional dependence between them and the French. The imposition of the French on the Lebanese is a case of "linguistic colonization" (*istiʿmār lughawī*, 1978: 156). In this context, al-Hajj lists the coercive measures which the French authorities adopted to impose French on Lebanese children in the schools. A system of naming and shaming was put in place to punish and ostracize those who dared to use Arabic, or who used it by mistake. Being unable to express themselves with complete facility in French, Lebanese children studied in a linguistically deprived environment. Second, being unable to achieve native fluency in French, Lebanese children, and adults for that matter, developed an inferiority complex towards the French, who could speak their language naturally. Third, the Arabic–French bilingualism advocated by the Francophiles is more of a dream than a reality. Very few Lebanese had near-native mastery of French, and some of those who did achieved this at the expense of a reduction in fluency in Arabic.

Later studies confirmed this observation by al-Hajj. They showed the defective use of French by the Lebanese, in newspapers and in news broadcasts, in shop signs and in other printed materials. Instead of developing a full facility in French, the Lebanese injected Arabic elements into it, creating what had come to be known in Lebanon as *franbanais*, although this term is not used by al-Hajj. The call to espouse Arabic–French bilingualism has led not to achieving it, but to promoting a state of linguistic hybridity which dilutes the creative impulses of the Lebanese, who, al-Hajj argues, have no choice but to stick to Arabic as their mother-tongue. Being known by almost all the Lebanese, Arabic alone qualifies for this role. Thus, where French can divide the Lebanese, Arabic can unite them. And, where French can stunt the creative impulses of the Lebanese, Arabic can release these impulses and give full rein to them. This way, Lebanon and the Lebanese can fulfil their civilizing mission to the Arab world. Granted, knowledge of French and other foreign languages can help in this, but not in the way the Francophiles stipulate. They can help as foreign languages, but not as mother-tongues.

Being aware of the emotive and motivating power of language in task-orientation and rational persuasion, al-Hajj sets out his main thesis of the unique linkage between a particular nation and its mother-tongue by using aphoristic expressions that tap into aspects of Lebanese and Arab culture. The following are a few examples: "For each heart there is a single language" (*lā majāl fi-l-qalb illā li-lisān wāḥid*, 1978: 122); "A genius takes care of his language as a virgin does of her chastity" (*yaḥriṣ al-ʿabāqira ʿalā lughātihim kamā taḥriṣ al-ʿadhrāʾ ʿalā ʿafāfihā*, ibid.: 128); "When the tongue commits adultery, thought does so too" (*matā zanā al-lisān zanā al-fikr*, ibid.: 131); "It is not possible for more than one tongue to live under the same roof without fighting each other" (*inna alsina ʿadīda lā yumkin an taskun taḥt saqf wāḥid bi-dūn an tatanāḥar*, ibid.: 132); "The mother-tongue does not accept a co-wife under its roof" (*inna al-lugha al-umm lā taqbal lahā ḍarra taḥt saqf baytihā*, ibid.: 139); and "A mature, alert, honourable and moral people extol the standing of their national language" (*inna al-shaʿb al-wāʿī al-sharīf al-ʿafīf yukbir sha'n lughatih al-qawmiyya*, ibid.: 151). Al-Hajj also points out that great leaders understand the emotional basis of the link between language and nation, which, in the last three statements above, is signalled by the use of the emphatic *inna* in Arabic. Witness also the utilization of the purity metaphor in setting out the relationship between language and nation.[20] Hence, we are told, the refusal by Antun Saʿada, the leader of the Syrian National Party, to speak to the court in French when he was tried by the French authorities in Lebanon in 1936. Al-Hajj tells us that although Saʿada did not treat language as a defining feature in his nationalist ideology, he understood that Arabic was his mother-tongue and that French was not. This is also the reason why he refused to respond to the French judge when he called him Antoine rather than by the Arabic form of his name, Antun (cf. Chapter 4, section 2).

However, the idea that "the nation and its national language are inseparable" (*al-lugha al-qawmiyya wa-l-umma sharṭān mutalāzimān*, ibid.: 154) may be thought to be negated by the Swiss example, where three major languages are believed to live under the same state roof. Al-Hajj considers the Swiss example a red herring. First, Switzerland is a loose confederation of self-governing entities, each with its own language. Second, the creative writers in each of these entities use their mother-tongue as the medium of literary expression. Third, the speakers of each language feel the bonds of unity which link them to the speakers of the same language outside the Swiss borders: the French-speaking with France, the German-speaking with Germany and the Italian-speaking with Italy. But this raises the question as to why Switzerland continues to enjoy political unity. Al-Hajj answers this by saying that although the three languages mentioned above are related to the languages of the surrounding countries, nevertheless they have their own special flavour which gives them their own nuanced identities (cf. section 2 above). Differences of this kind also apply to British English and American English. Furthermore, Swiss political unity would have crumbled had it not been for the fact that it is more or less guaranteed by the enlightened self-interests of the surrounding countries whose languages are represented inside Switzerland. For all these reasons, the Swiss case cannot be taken as a refutation of the thesis that to every state nationalism there is one language.

As I have said earlier, the above arguments are directed at the Francophiles in Lebanon. There is, however, another constituency, the colloquialists, who need to be addressed. The arguments used by the colloquialists in support of their favoured variety are well rehearsed in the Lebanese linguistic scene. They include the difficulty of standard Arabic, the absence of good learner-orientated pedagogic grammars to teach it and the claim that standard Arabic instils in the learners a conservative and old-fashioned value system, which is out of step with the values of modernity Lebanon wishes to absorb and promote. However, the main argument against the standard springs from the diglossic nature of the Arabic language situation. Standard Arabic is no-one's mother-tongue. The colloquial is. It therefore makes more sense to promote the latter in Lebanon. The argument goes that the adoption of this variety of Arabic as Lebanon's national language would give the Lebanese a language that is unquestionably theirs, and theirs alone.

Supporters of the standard would respond by saying that the difference between their favoured variety and the colloquial in Lebanon is not as big as the colloquialists claim (see Abu Sa'd 1994). The difficulty of standard Arabic is not linguistically but pedagogically induced. Pedagogic problems require pedagogic solutions, not linguistic or sociolinguistic ones. These solutions can be provided by simplifying Arabic grammars for language-teaching and learning purposes, and by modernizing the language lexically. Enhanced literacy levels and the increasing contacts between Arabic-speakers will help solve the problem of inter-dialect communication in due course. It is also not in the interests of the speakers of Arabic to dismantle the linguistic unity that exists between them on the standard-language front. The loss of this unity will lead to a diminution in the cultural exchange between these speakers. Furthermore, if it is true that Lebanon has a civilizing mission to the Arabs, which is a recurrent theme in Lebanese cultural politics, it will be well-nigh impossible for it to deliver this mission under this scenario.

Important as these arguments are, they fail in al-Hajj's view to provide the ultimate, philosophically grounded argument in favour of standard Arabic. He points out that these arguments are born out of a concern with utility, and the attendant limited understanding of language as a means to something else. If language is a tool, an instrument or a means to something else, it should in principle be possible to introduce changes in it without affecting the system of symbolic values it carries and signifies. But, since this is not possible, language must be treated as more than just a system of communication. What is needed, therefore, is a philosophical engagement with the problem of diglossia. To achieve this, al-Hajj devotes the last chapter of *Fī falsafat al-lugha* (1978: 210–93) to this task. Rather than arguing in favour of standard Arabic against the colloquial or vice versa, al-Hajj states that each of these two forms of the language requires the existence of the other. By failing to grasp this idea, the supporters both of the standard and of the colloquial fail to appreciate the ontology which binds the two forms of the language together.

Al-Hajj believes that those who think of diglossia in Arabic as a problem fail to understand that it is the result of a more fundamental duality which is of the very essence of man. Man's inner psyche (*wijdān*) consists of sense (*ḥiss*) and mind (*ʿaql*), without which man cannot be complete. Each of these two components has its own domain. Feelings in the widest sense of the term constitute the domain of sense. The intellect in its widest sense constitutes the domain of the mind. Sense is related to sensibility, while the mind is related to rationality. Each has its own mode of operation. Sense is raw and spontaneous. The mind is reflective, deliberate and calculating. Each therefore requires its own medium of expression. The colloquial acts as that medium to sense. The standard acts as the medium of the mind, which deploys it in the service of rationality. The colloquial partakes of the properties of sense: it is "spontaneous and impulsive" (*lugha tilqā'iyya [wa] infiʿāliyya*, ibid.: 226). It is also ungrammatical and full of loose ends. The standard reflects the measured and methodical workings of the mind: it is controlled and regulated. It is structured and systematic. Diglossia therefore is nothing but a reflection of the sense–mind duality in man. And, since this duality is universal, diglossia itself must be universal. All human languages are therefore diglossic to one extent or another. A language which does not exhibit diglossia cannot be a human language, and if such a language existed it must be a primitive or impoverished language. Arabic is no exception to this rule. This is why it makes no sense to argue against the standard in favour of the colloquial, or against the colloquial in favour of the standard. The one is the ontological counterpart of the other. It is therefore natural that they should exist next to each other, and that each would have its own functional domain into which the other does not and should not stray. Unsanctioned boundary-crossings between the two would result in dissonance and the disintegration of meaning, as happened, we are told, in Sa'id 'Aql's musings on aesthetic sensibility in literature which he penned in the colloquial in his introduction to Michel Tarrad's collection of poems *Gullinār* (al-Hajj 1978: 242).

Under this analysis, diglossia is not and should not be seen as a problem in Lebanon. It is a fact of life from which there is no escape. The colloquialists should therefore cease to undermine the standard. Even if the Lebanese colloquial is adopted as a national language for Lebanon, there will soon emerge another colloquial to fill its place. This will lead to replacing one form of diglossia with another. Supporters of the standard should also stop their attacks on the colloquial. Even if they succeed in eliminating the colloquial by bringing it closer to the standard, there will inevitably develop another colloquial to fill its place. Diglossia responds to a basic human need, emerging out of the sense–mind duality. Failure to understand this fact has led to sterile and needlessly antagonistic debates between the supporters of the colloquial and those of the standard in Lebanon. Rather than working against each other, they must work together to fill the lexical gaps that exist in the standard by taking on board some of the terminological innovations existing in the colloquial. What, however, should not happen is to camouflage the modification of grammar in the descriptive sense (*taghyir*, ibid.: 250) as a simplification of grammar in the pedagogic sense (*taysir*, ibid.) in the calls to simplify standard Arabic. The call to eliminate the desinential inflections made by some reformers of Arabic is one such example of ill-conceived simplification, whereby what is definitional of the standard is presented as an attribute which can be dispensed with. This is not possible, says al-Hajj, without interfering with the ontological structure of diglossia and the sense–mind duality that underlies it.

It is not my aim to evaluate the validity or otherwise of the philosophical basis upon which the diglossic nature of Arabic is valorized in *On the Philosophy of Language*. Such an evaluation would belong more to philosophy than to an investigation of the relationship between language and national identity. What matters from the perspective of this study is the fact that al-Hajj uses philosophy to produce a rationalization and justification for the linguistic status quo in Lebanon in the same manner he did for confessionalism. In the process, he produced a novel argument that transcends the polarization between the supporters of the colloquial and those of the standard. Each party can have its cake and eat it. But there is no doubt as to where al-Hajj's real sympathies lie.

As an intellectual and, as he constantly reminds us, a philosopher, he is more concerned with rationality and the mind than with sense and sensibility. His enthusiasm on the linguistic scene is therefore mainly reserved for the standard.

But this enthusiasm is motivated by something far greater than the imperatives of the subjectivity of al-Hajj as an individual. It is motivated by a deep concern for Lebanon as a beacon of civilization in the East. In the past, Lebanon acted as a "teacher" (*ustādh*, ibid.: 284) in the Arab world. Lebanon had a mission to the East where it is geographically located, and it can have none in the West which has no need for the genius of the Lebanese. Al-Hajj therefore believes that Lebanon must be linguistically Arab in order to deliver its mission. And, since the language which can help it do so is standard Arabic, Lebanon has no choice but to adopt it as its national language. This is also incumbent upon it because it is a fact of life that no one nation or individual can master the genius of two languages. The Lebanese must therefore stop taking pride in the fact that they do not know Arabic as well as they do French or English. They must realize that Lebanese culture is inseparable from Arabic. They should not fear Arabic, since the meanings of Lebanese culture remain intrinsically Lebanese in spite of the Arabic linguistic structure which envelops them ([*thaqāfat lubnān*] *lubnāniyyat al-ma'nā 'arabiyyat al-mabnā*, ibid.: 258). Although al-Hajj does not believe that meaning and linguistic structure can be separated from each other, as I have explained above, the kind of separation he envisages here is justified by him on the flimsy grounds that the same words in the Arabic-speaking world do not necessarily mean the same things across the whole language community. Geography and history take care of that by adding their own localized connotations to these words. In response to this, it may be argued that while it is true that variations of this kind do exist, it is even more true that far more constancies of meaning exist among Arabic-speakers. But, in a philosophy of advocacy, it is what proves one's point that matters. The exception, which may be the rule, gets sidelined. Al-Hajj is certainly guilty of this contrivance in the present context.

So, in what sense is standard Arabic a component of Lebanese nationalism for al-Hajj? The idea that standard Arabic in Lebanon has its flavour and unique meanings is part of the answer, since it makes of standard Arabic in Lebanon a construct that is in one way or another uniquely related to it (Lebanon). But the association of standard Arabic and Lebanese national identity goes deeper, taking the form of a series of spiralling moves which interlace argument with argument. The first move starts with the view that language is inseparable from thought, and that language is a factor that shapes the national character. Arabic is declared to be the operative language in these domains. The second move builds on this by invoking the psycholinguistic fact that no one individual or nation can be truly bilingual. Wherever two languages exist, one of them tends to be dominant in one functional domain or another. In Lebanon, this language is Arabic and not French, which is actually foreign to the country and is a relic of French colonialism. The third move consists of legitimizing diglossia and sanctioning the Arabic language situation in Lebanon. The fourth move invokes an argument from internal colonialism concerning Lebanon's civilizing mission to the Arabs, the purpose of which is to instil in the Lebanese a moral imperative which turns the adoption and promotion of standard Arabic in Lebanon as one of the highest forms of virtue. Finally, all of these moves are rooted in a political philosophy which treats nationality as the correlate of the state. The fact that there is a Lebanese state must therefore mean that there is a Lebanese nationalism and a Lebanese national identity. And, since language is traditionally thought of as an ingredient, marker or attribute of national identity, Arabic is the only candidate – for philosophical, linguistic, moral and pragmatic reasons – which can fulfil this function. It is this web of ideas that al-Hajj reworks in his other publications on Lebanese nationalism (1959a, 1959b, 1959c, 1966, 1978). These publications contain further elaborations, but they add little that is new or not implied in what he says in *On the Philosophy of Language* about the relationship between the Arabic language and the Lebanese national identity.

6. CONCLUSION

In this chapter, I have discussed two types of territorial nationalism: regional nationalism, represented by Antun Saʿada's Syrian Nationalism, and state-orientated nationalism, represented by Egyptian and Lebanese nationalism. In dealing with these two types of territorial nationalism, I was interested in the way they construct the relationship between Arabic and their own brand of national identity. Different strategies are adopted for this purpose. The first consists of denying the thesis that language is a criterion of national identity. This is explicitly stated by Saʿada, who prefers to give primacy in his nationalist ideology to the role the environment plays in shaping the national character of the nation. The fact that language is not a definitional marker of the nation does not, however, mean that it can be dispensed with in nation-formation. The existence of one language in the nation helps communication between members of the nation concerned, and this in turn can enhance the cohesiveness with which the nation acts and imagines itself. When two or more languages exist in the same nation – as in Switzerland, for example – the unity of that nation may come under pressure and could, with time, lead to political fragmentation. Language for Saʿada, therefore, is first and foremost a means to something else: it is relevant insofar as it can aid or hinder achieving the ends it is intended to serve in the national domain.

This unashamedly instrumentalist view of language is the antithesis of the Arab nationalist idea wherein language, in both its functional and symbolic dimensions, is projected as a definitional criterion of the national self. It is this idea which Sa'ada wishes to oppose, and whose validity he sets out to deny, on the analytical and historical level. He accepts that language is functionally important in nation-formation; and, judging by his insistence on using Arabic and the Arab version of his name when he was tried by the French in Lebanon on 23 December 1936 (section 5.2 above), we may even say that he fully understood the symbolic significance of language in signalling both his Syrian National identity and his resistance to the French occupation. However, he had no choice but to deny that language is a criterion of Syrian Nationalism, because without such a denial it would have been hard to distinguish between this Nationalism and Arab nationalism which was the dominant ideology at the time. Furthermore, since without this denial Sa'ada would have brought himself perilously close to Arab nationalism, thus ringing the alarm bells among the Maronites of Lebanon, he had little choice but to reject the idea that Arabic is a criterion of the Syrian National identity. However, this rejection had to be watered down somewhat to avoid antagonizing the Muslims of Greater Syria, for whom any diminution in the status of Arabic would have rung alarm bells of a different kind. Sa'ada knew he had to walk a tightrope, and he did so with consummate ideological agility.

Sa'ada could, however, have followed the second strategy in territorial nationalism – for dealing with the connection between language and national identity – to get out of his dilemma. This consists of claiming that Arabic is a criterion of national self-definition, coupling it with the statement that although standard Arabic shares a common set of features across the Arabic-speaking lands, it is nevertheless the case that the Arabic of each nation is characterized by a unique flavour which brands it as that nation's mother-tongue alone. This view is advocated by Kamal al-Hajj (section 5.2) and other Lebanese nationalists who were dealt with indirectly above (section 5 and sub-sections). It is also adopted by some Egyptian nationalists who called for Egyptianizing Arabic, thus creating an Egyptian language that is not the same as the Arabic of the other parts of the Arabic-speaking world. One of the earliest advocates of this strategy in Egypt was Lutfi al-Sayyid (section 3). However, the difficulty of creating a standard Arabic that is specifically Egyptian must have convinced some Egyptian nationalists that the real solution lies in discarding standard Arabic in favour of the Egyptian colloquial (section 4.1). This solution was also advocated in Lebanon. The ultimate aim behind it was the break-up of Arabic linguistic unity, thus depriving the Arab nationalists of the very foundations upon which their nationalism is built. This aim was sometimes admitted openly. At other times, it was camouflaged as a measure aimed at promoting literacy, enhancing realism in literature or unleashing the scientific creativity of the sons and daughters of the nation.

A third strategy for dealing with language and national identity in territorial nationalism consists of obfuscation, whether deliberate or not. Here, language is dealt with at some length, explaining how important it is in the national literature and in keeping the links between the past and the present. This may be coupled with informal statements to the effect that the language of a nation is one of its emblems, but without raising this informal statement to the status of a nationalist principle. This is the strategy adopted by most Egyptian nationalists (section 4 and sub-sections). It is also the practice in ʿAbdalla Lahhud's statements on the topic. Being a compromise between competing positions, this strategy tends to be associated with journalistic articulations of territorial nationalism. In this context, the focus is not on theoretical coherence but on persuasion as dictated by the needs of the moment and the kind of arguments the opposition brings into play. What principally matters here is not ideology *per se*, but deploying ideological positions for task-orientation purposes. This explains the recourse to reiteration and the reliance on emotive language as spurs to action under this strategy. Ideological shifts are tolerated as long as the ultimate aims of a particular nationalism are preserved. These shifts and changes of focus are also inevitable owing to the fact that this strategy is applied by individuals working on their own or as a part of a loose association of intellectuals who share a broad vision that is not fully worked out in its details. This is particularly true of the group of Egyptian journalists and intellectuals who worked around *al-Siyāsa al-usbūʿiyya* (section 4).

The fourth strategy for dealing with language and national identity in territorial nationalism consists of stressing the needs of linguistic or extralinguistic modernization in a particular nationalism. Although linguistic modernization, in one form or another, was called for by almost all Lebanese nationalists, extralinguistic modernization receives little or no attention in this nationalism. Admitting that extralinguistic modernization is a primary concern for Lebanon was not seriously entertained because such an admission would have meant that Lebanon was not qualified to discharge its civilizing, and hence modernizing, mission to the Arab world. The situation in Egyptian nationalism was different in that linguistic and extralinguistic modernization were thought to be two sides of the same coin. In some cases, this modernization was read emblematically into the modernization of Arabic in its capacity as an ingredient that defines the Egyptian nation. This is the position adopted by Taha Husayn (section 4.2). Salama Musa does not see modernization in these terms. His instrumental view of language means that he does not establish it as a criterion of national self-definition. But it also means that he can be more daring and radical in the kind of modernization he proposes.

The discussion in this chapter shows that territorial nationalism is broader than state nationalism in scope and orientation. Thus, while Syrian Nationalism is regional in scope, Lebanese nationalism is state-orientated in character. Egyptian nationalism acknowledges the existence of the state but without giving it the ideological visibility it has in Lebanese nationalism. This difference between Lebanese and Egyptian nationalism – insofar as it is constructed from the perspective of language and national identity – makes Lebanese nationalism more political than Egyptian nationalism. However, both culture and politics interact in both nationalisms, as they also do in Syrian Nationalism which, nevertheless, labours under the strong disadvantage of not having its own state with its own legally recognized territory.

Although both Egyptian and Lebanese nationalism make reference to the past in constructing their vision of the nation, there is no doubt that this appeal to the past has greater importance in the former than it does in the latter. Much of Egyptian nationalism is built around constructing a "golden age" which shifts the centre of cultural definition and popular influence from the Arabo-Islamic heritage to that of the Pharaohs.[21] This attempt to reroot the nation in a different space and time puts strain on the claims of continuity which are necessary to make the "golden age" usable and capable of interpretation in a way that serves the present goals of Egypt and its future aspirations. Egypt's Pharaonic "golden age" is punctured by another, the Arabo-Islamic "golden age", which resonates with a large segment of the country's Muslim population. To overcome this, environmental determinism is injected into the nationalist ideology to make the discontinuous look continuous. By locking the Egyptian character into a capsule moulded by geography, the claim is made in Egyptian nationalism that the transition from the Pharaonic "golden age" – when the Egyptian national character exhibited its genius to the full and achieved its highest point of grandeur – to the present was almost seamless. Instead of being assimilated into the culture of its foreign rulers, Egypt assimilated them into its own culture. A similar position is taken by Antun Saʿada in his exposition of Syrian Nationalism.

Lebanese nationalism envisages Lebanon as Janus-like. In one direction, it looks to France and the West. In the other direction, it looks to the Arab world. Its relationship to the West is characterized by a feeling of inferiority (*dūniyya*), as al-Hajj points out when he says that Europe has no need for the cultural wares of Lebanon (1978: 283). In contrast, the relationship of Lebanon to the Arab world is characterized by a feeling of superiority, expressed in terms of the civilizational mission which the former has to the latter. This feature of Lebanese nationalism is based on a "myth of election" which endows Lebanon with a sense of moral virtue not available to other Arabic-speaking countries. As a case of intra-Arab cultural imperialism, this "myth of election" in Lebanese nationalism is but a reflection of the cultural imperialism exercised by France in

Lebanon itself.[22] In this context of cultural dependence and double dependence, Lebanese nationalism envisages the role of Lebanon to the Arabs as one of interpretation and translation. This is exactly what Pierre Gemayel says when he articulates the Phalangist viewpoint of Lebanese nationalism (1968: 109): "Lebanon is necessary to the West. It is the interpreter of its ideas, of its spiritual values to the Arabs." This is why the maintenance of Arabic and the promotion of French and other European languages, particularly English, is thought by him to be so important for Lebanon.

7

Conclusion: Looking Back, Looking Forward

1. THE ARABIC LANGUAGE AND NATIONAL IDENTITY: LOOKING BACK

The major aim of this book has been to show the dominance of language in ideological formulations of national identity in the Arab Middle East. Formulations of Arab nationalism, whether embryonic or fully fledged in character, are invariably built around the potential and capacity of Arabic in its standard form to act as the linchpin of the identity of all those who share it as their common language. A positive and indissoluble link is therefore established between language and national identity in discourse of this type. This was the case in the Arab Middle East in the last few decades of the Ottoman Empire, and in post-First World War discussions of the topic. The names of al-Husri, al-Arsuzi and, to a lesser extent, al-Yaziji, al-ʿUraysi, al-ʿAlayli and al-Bitar are all connected with identitarian formulations in this mode. The nation in this mode is cultural in character, although in practice culture cannot be separated from politics, particularly in the high sense.

So dominant was this mode of defining the Arab national self that (alternative) territorial modes of imagining the nation in the Arab Middle East could not but respond to it. Antun Saʿada's answer was to argue that language cannot play a defining role in conceptualizing the Syrian nation. Instead, he proposed environmental determinism as the principle which acts in this capacity, with language playing no more than an assisting role in this regard. Similar formulations existed in Egyptian and Lebanese nationalism. Other territorial strategies of responding to the emphasis on standard Arabic in Arab nationalism did exist. One such strategy consisted of accepting the definitional role of the language in the formation of national identity, but locking it into an understanding of the nation which conceives of it as a construct that is inseparable from the state as the focus of loyalty and solidarity. Under this strategy, the fact of sharing a common language by people living under the jurisdiction of different states or in different countries cannot function as the basis for a common national identity between them. Egyptian and Lebanese nationalism provide examples of this kind. In these examples, Arabic is given a role in defining the nation, but it is presented as a factor among other definitional factors which operate within the orbit of the state as the focus of the nation in question. Taha Husayn and Kamal al-Hajj conceive of the role of Arabic in the formation of national identity in these terms. A second strategy consists of accepting the view that language is a factor in nation-formation, but assigning this role to the colloquial as the true mother-tongue of the people who speak Arabic. This vernacularizing strategy is designed to create for the state and the putative nation associated with it a language that is uniquely its own. Examples of this kind exist in Egyptian and Lebanese nationalism. A variation on this strategy consists of calling for the creation of a middle language between the standard and the colloquial, with strong input from the latter to deliver the same territorially particularizing function for the envisaged language. The call to Egyptianize Arabic by some Egyptian nationalists – notably Lutfi al-Sayyid – is an example of this kind. A third strategy consists of promoting a linguistic duality in a particular nationalism in which the bilingual partners are Arabic in its generic form and a foreign language, typically French. This is the situation in some articulations of Christian Lebanese national identity, the best-known example being Abou's views on the subject. A variation on this theme consists of anchoring the linguistic duality in question to the standard and the colloquial in their diglossic setting. This strategy is embedded, but not fully exploited, in Kamal al-Hajj's analysis of the language situation in Lebanon. A fourth strategy consists of highlighting the role of language in the formation of national identity, but without specifying whether this role is definitional or not. Typically in this strategy, a fudge is provided whereby language is at times conceived of as no more than an instrument of communication, and at others as that medium which is inseparable from thought and which, additionally, is directly responsible for undesirable behavioural patterns in society. Salama Musa's views on Arabic in Egypt provide a good example of this strategy. This and the other strategies listed above are all associated with a political vision of the nation and nationalism in the Arab Middle East. However, this vision is embedded in a keen appreciation of the role culture plays in this enterprise.

Whether directly or indirectly, the past – a resonant past – is always present in constructions of national identity. This is true of articulations of cultural and political nationalism in the Arab Middle East. The role of the past in these articulations is one of valorization of a particular ideological position, or of conferring authenticity on what a particular nationalism claims for itself. Thus, Arab nationalism invokes in a variety of ways the traditional esteem with which Arabic is held in Arab societies, the aim being to promote the thesis that the language is the marker par excellence of Arab national identity. What makes an Arab Arab in this nationalism is his or her membership in an Arabic-speaking community that is as much defined by its attitude of reverence towards the language as it is by actual linguistic behaviour. This attitude towards Arabic is also found in some articulations of territorial national identity, as exhibited by Lahhud's statements on the topic. However, being tied to the state as an existing or imagined entity, the past here is read in a territorial fashion which invokes factors of political history, economy and geography as forces that imbue the language with a local flavour. This is more or less the position taken by Taha Husayn and Kamal al-Hajj in Egyptian and Lebanese nationalism respectively.

In some articulations of territorial nationalism, the past is excavated to derive ideas which may be used to characterize Arabic as a construct that is symptomatic of cultural backwardness. This is the case in those examples of Egyptian nationalist discourse where *shu'ūbiyya*-type ideas are deployed to characterize Arabic as a Bedouin language that is unfit for application in the sciences or for use in other domains of modern life. Other ideas from the same source are resurrected to argue that a language-based Arab national identity is a form of linguism which echoes and recreates in modern times the "chauvinistic" or "racist" feelings the Arabs held towards the non-Arabs in the first few centuries of Islam. The past may also be deployed or manipulated to argue against deeply held attitudes towards Arabic, for example the doctrinally sanctioned thesis of the uniqueness of the language as a factor in the esteem in which it is held by its speakers. This is particularly present in some of the arguments offered by Lewis Awad in his book *Muqaddima fī fiqh al-lugha al-'arabiyya*. In other cases, one past is pitted against another to press the claim that Arabic cannot be treated as a marker of a particular national identity. Examples of this strategy abound in Egyptian nationalism. Here, the Pharaonic past is declared as the genuine and authentic past of Egypt, using this as a prelude to launching the argument that all the pasts that had succeeded this original past were more or less marginal in their influence on the already formed Egyptian character. The intended effect of this argument was to deny that the Arabs and Arabic had any formative effect on the Egyptian national character in the modern period. This is often accompanied by references to the presumed ability of Egypt throughout its history to assimilate into its character those who came to settle on its land. On the linguistic front, this assimilative power means that Egypt was able to stamp Arabic with the indelible imprint of its imperishable soul, thus fashioning out of it a language that is structurally and stylistically Egyptian in character. Being so shaped and defined, the Arabic of Egypt cannot serve as the basis of a national bond involving other Arabic-speakers.

Nationalism is Janus-like. It looks towards the past, a usable past, for valorization and authentication. And it looks towards the future for modernization on all fronts: social, economic, political, cultural and linguistic. Modernization is part and parcel of the mission of all nationalisms in the Arab Middle East, be they cultural or territorial in nature, although some nationalist discourses tend to place more emphasis on modernization than others. An example of this kind of discourse is provided by Salama Musa, who treats the modernization of Egypt as the most pressing task facing the Egyptians. Broadly speaking, the modernizing mission of nationalism in the Arab Middle East may therefore be outlined as one of bringing about a significant change in the structure of society and in the way in which the individual relates to it and to other individuals. In this respect, nationalism aims to transcend the present by moving towards a different kind of future. In so doing, it invokes aspects of the past to respond to the deeply felt needs of the community it addresses. Following Smith, these needs may be characterized as follows (Smith 1991: 163):

> Transcending oblivion through posterity, the restoration of collective dignity through an appeal to a golden age; the realisation of fraternity through symbols, rites and ceremonies, which bind the living to the dead and fallen of the community: these are the underlying functions of national identity and nationalism in the modern world, and the basic reasons why the latter have proved so durable, protean and resilient through all vicissitudes.

It is not my intention here to discuss the domains in which modernization as an objective of nationalism is to take place in the Arab Middle East. Rather, my aim is to comment on one aspect of modernization that is directly relevant to the theme of this book: linguistic modernization. There is a commonly held belief in the nationalist discourses I have examined in this work that Arabic is in need of modernization grammatically, lexically, stylistically and pedagogically to make it better able to participate in the nationalist project in an effective manner. Grammatical modernization should have as its aim the use of a syntax that is unencumbered by the outmoded and dead rules of the past. Lexical modernization should aim at increasing the stock of new terminologies available to the language-users. It should also aim at culling the excesses of synonymy in the language, thus freeing some lexical slots for use in designating new meanings. Stylistic modernization should encourage the development of a new rhetoric in which meaning is not neglected in favour of linguistic virtuosity, but in which the latter is made to serve the functions of the former. Pedagogic modernization should aim at developing new ways of setting out the facts of grammar for the effective nurturing of grammatical competence in the learners. Some demanded that a daring approach be adopted in this area, consisting, among other things, of dropping the desinential inflections. Others considered any such so-called pedagogic simplification of grammar to be an unwarranted intrusion into the very structure – even the soul – of the language. Some nationalist thinkers additionally argued for reforming the Arabic script. Others called for its wholesale abandonment as the Turks had done.

Behind the above calls for linguistic modernization, there existed an immediate aim and an ulterior motive. On the one hand, the modernization of Arabic was thought to make the language more able to deliver the fruits of the extralinguistic modernization which nationalism wishes to promote as part of its programme. This dimension of modernization, its immediate aim, targets the functional capacities of the language as a medium of communication. On the other hand, the modernization of Arabic is intended to signal through the language-as-medium the extralinguistic dimensions of modernization. In this respect, the modernization of Arabic becomes symbolic of modernization as a whole – this symbolism being the ulterior motive referred to above. By tapping into these two roles of Arabic, the functional and the symbolic, nationalism in the Arab Middle East uses the power of language in society to the full. The fact that the functional sometimes dominates the symbolic or vice versa does not invalidate this conclusion.

2. THE ARABIC LANGUAGE AND NATIONAL IDENTITY: LOOKING FORWARD

Having established in this work the broad outlines of the role of language in nationalism as ideology in the Arab Middle East, a basis now exists for launching studies of an empirical nature to investigate how linguistic behaviour and nationalism as movement or action interact with each other in the Arabic-speaking world. I will suggest below some areas in which this kind of research may be pursued. However, before doing this, I would like to highlight two issues of language and national ideology which this study has not dealt with, and to which I hope to return in the future. The first concerns the attempts by some state nationalists to construct fully fledged ideologies which treat language, history and culture in a manner that is definitionally inseparable from the state. A good example of this, which comes from outside the Middle East proper, is provided by al-Bashir bin Salama in his book *al-Shakhṣiyya al-tūnisiyya: khaṣā'iṣuhā wa-muqawwimātuhā* (*The Tunisian Character: Its Properties and Formative Elements*, 1974). The main thrust of this book is to argue that the Tunisians form a nation proper (*umma*), not a people (*sha'b*) as would be envisaged under Arab nationalism. This state ideology is inscribed in discursive practices which ascribe the term "nation" and its derivatives to all aspects of life in Tunisia, including language but excepting religion. On the empirical level, this ideology responds to practices in whose creation the state in the Arab world is wittingly or unwittingly an active participant; hence the symbolic significance to the state of the national flag, the national flag-carrier, the national anthem, national festivals, national holidays, national museums and galleries, passports, stamps and so on. So pervasive has been the influence of the state in creating its own self-perpetuating dynamic that, even in the field of high culture, Arab intellectuals now speak about the Syrian novel, the Iraqi short story, the Egyptian theatre and cinema, Palestinian poetry, the Jordanian or Kuwaiti song, Lebanese cuisine and so on. In Jordan and Kuwait, the Parliament is called *majlis al-umma* (lit. the Nation's Council), but in Syria and Egypt it is called *majlis al-sha'b* (lit. the People's Council). In the constitutions of some Arab countries, Arabic is declared as the national language (*al-lugha al-waṭaniyya*); in the constitutions of other countries, it is described as the official language (*al-lugha al-rasmiyya*) of the state (see Suleiman 1999d). The term *'arab* or its derivative *(al-)'arabiyya* is included in the names of some Arab states, for example Syria and Egypt, but it is absent from the names of others, for example Lebanon and Jordan. Other manifestations of the state in the nationalist field are present, but these will not concern us here. The point to be made here, however, is that the all-pervasive nature of the state in the Arab world can no longer be regarded – as was assumed by al-Husri and other Arab nationalists in the middle of the twentieth century – as a temporary phenomenon that is doomed to extinction on the way to establishing political unity between the Arabic-speaking countries. The state in the Arab world is here to stay, and this is bound to have a significant effect on how Arabic will be ideologized in various state nationalist projects. While building on nationalist ideologies of the territorial kind we have examined above, modern state nationalisms are better equipped to pursue their self-centred aims in what seem to be more propitious circumstances internally and externally (cf. Tarabishi 1982). This is why state nationalism in its modern manifestations in the Arabic-speaking world must be regarded as a more advanced realization of the territorial idea examined earlier. As such, it deserves further study and analysis to establish how Arabic may be cast as an ingredient, marker or emblem in state-orientated national-identity formulations.

Let us now consider the second issue of language and ideology which has not been dealt with in this study. This is the connection between (what may be called) Islamic nationalism and Arabic insofar as the language relates to Arab and territorial nationalism (cf. Vatikiotis 1987). Most expressions of the latter nationalisms tend to be secular in nature, thus giving little visibility to the Islamic and doctrinal significance of the language. Islamic nationalism opposes this secularizing attitude towards Arabic. It also opposes the attempt by Arab and territorial nationalists to appropriate the language in their ideological enterprises, arguing in response that the high status of Arabic in sociolinguistic terms is part and parcel of its association with Islam. The argument continues that, without this association, Arabic would never have attained the prestige it enjoys in the modern world, and could even lose it in the future (cf. al-Bishri 1998, al-Ghazali 1998, Husayn 1979, al-Jundi 1982, Khalafalla 1990). It follows from this that the use of Arabic as a marker of secular national identities, or of ones that are not infused with the spirit and mission of Islam, is considered by Islamic nationalists to be an aberration and an unwarranted distortion of history. According to these nationalists, it is therefore not possible to equate

Arabic with any national identity in which Islam is not an operative ingredient. This is an absolutist position. In practice, however, some Islamic nationalists are prepared to tolerate expressions of Arab and territorial nationalism as long as these view themselves as transitory stages on the way to achieving Islamic unity. This would make it possible to create a rapprochement between Islamic and other nationalists, as long as the latter are prepared to disavow secularism and to incorporate Islam as a constitutive element in their nationalist thinking. How this relates to Arabic is a matter worthy of study in the future.

Let us now highlight other areas of the connection between language and national identity that are worthy of future study. One such area is the description and analysis of the sociolinguistic reflexes of interethnic conflict in the Arabic-speaking world. These reflexes may be realized dialectally, as I have tried to show for Jordan (Suleiman 1993, 1999b; El-Wer 1999). They may also be realized through the interplay between Arabic and another language within the state, for example Berber in Algeria or Kurdish in Iraq. Another area is the description and analysis of the sociolinguistic reflexes of inter-nation conflict in the Middle East. Typically, conflicts of this kind involve another language in relation to Arabic in the context of existing or emerging states, for example Hebrew as in Palestine and Israel (cf. Amara and Spolsky 1996, Ben-Rafael 1994, Ibrahim 1980, Spolsky and Cooper 1991, Spolsky and Shohamy 1999, Suleiman 1999f), or Turkish as in south-western Turkey. Sociolinguistic reflexes of conflicts of the latter kind may also be played out through the media of international languages, typically via translations of place and other types of name in English (cf. Suleiman 1999b). Future studies of language as a marker of national identity in the Arabic-speaking world may also involve the attempts to exploit the colloquial for this purpose; they may also involve the tug-of-war between this variety and the standard language. Studies of the manner in which the standard is defended against the colloquial would provide an excellent example of the principle in some nationalist discourses that "language is worthier than territory", the implication being that a nation must defend its language at least as vehemently as it does its territory. As the site of stereotypical representations of national identity, Arabic may be studied from the perspective of social psychology. At times, it would be necessary to refute the unwarranted conclusions offered by studies conducted from this perspectives (cf. Patai 1973, Shouby 1951, Suleiman 1999e). Studies of code-switching between dialects or languages may yield valuable insights into issues of language and national identity, as would the eliciting of language attitudes among Arabic-speakers. We may also add to this list studies of (1) the grammatical and lexical reform proposals; (2) the use of foreign languages as the media of teaching in schools and universities; (3) the use of these languages in shop signs and advertising generally; (4) the position of Arabic in such Arab countries as Somalia,

Djibouti and Mauritania that have recently joined the Arab League and in which Arabic is not very well rooted (cf. Abuhamdia 1995); and (5) the Arabicization/Arabization efforts in these countries as well as in the countries of North Africa and Sudan. The above are but some of the themes which future research on Arabic and national identity may tackle. That they represent a rich field for cross-disciplinary research from the perspective of identity is not in doubt. What is required, therefore, is collaboration between scholars from different disciplinary backgrounds to deliver the rich yield this research does promise the students of nationalism.

Notes

CHAPTER 1

1. This statement by Anthony Smith is clearly aimed at Benedict Anderson (1991), Hobsbawm (1990) and Gellner (1983).
2. The term "attribute" (*ṣifa* in Arabic) is used in a specific sense by Antun Sa'ada (see Chapter 6, section 2) to distinguish it from "ingredient". To the best of my knowledge, this is the only context where the term "attribute" is used in this sense.

CHAPTER 2

1. Max Weber (1968: 395) expresses a similar view in connection with the two related terms "ethnic group" and "nation": "The concept of 'ethnic group', which dissolves if we define our terms exactly, corresponds in this regard to one of the most vexing, since emotionally charged, concepts: the *nation*, as soon as we attempt a sociological definition".
2. The differences between languages in conceptualizing the nation are dealt with by 'Amr Ibrahim (1981/2), although the main emphasis is placed on Arabic and French.
3. The term "ethnicity" is used in the literature to cover communities exhibiting four levels of ethnic incorporation (Handelman, in Hutchinson and Smith 1996: 6): (1) "*ethnic category* … where there is simply a perceived cultural difference between the group and outsiders"; (2) "*ethnic network* [where] there is interaction between ethnic members such that the network can distribute resources among its members"; (3) "*ethnic association* [where] the members develop common interests and political organizations to express these at a collective, corporate level"; and (4) "*ethnic communities*, which possesses a permanent, physically bounded territory, over and above its political organization".
4. This mode of defining the nation is prevalent in the literature on Arab nationalism. See al-'Alayli (1996), al-Jundi (1968), al-Kharbutli (n.d.), Khalafalla (1990) and Nuseibeh (1956).
5. Smith (1991: 12) points out that "every nationalism contains civic and ethnic elements in varying degrees and different forms", and that "sometimes civic and territorial elements predominate, [while] at other times it is the ethnic and vernacular components that are emphasized". However, ethnic nationalism has not always been respected in the West (see Fishman 1972: 25).
6. A good example of this tendency may be illustrated by the arguments which surrounded the design and building of the new Museum of Scotland, opened on 30

November 1998, St Andrew's (Scotland's patron saint) Day. In an article in *Scotland on Sunday* (29 November 1998, p. 9), Alan Taylor explains how at "one stage it was seriously suggested that the [new] museum should not have its own entrance and that visitors should approach it through the old museum [Royal Museum of Scotland]", commenting: "such was the fear of turning it into a nationalist shrine".

7. Kedourie's attack on this aspect of nationalism reveals a serious lack of appreciation of its sociohistorical context in which literature plays a role in developing group identity. In the context of Arab nationalism, this role was crucial, as Tibi (1997: 104) observes: "Arab nationalism in its early phase took the form of a literary renaissance not based on political theories, which was generated exclusively by linguists and men of letters. This was because neither the subjective nor the objective conditions for a political movement existed in the Middle East in the nineteenth century. Thus the early Arab nationalists confined themselves to emphasising the existence of an independent Arab cultural nation without demanding a national state."
8. Kedourie expresses this as follows (1966: 101): "Nationalist movements are children's crusades; their names are manifestos against old age: Young Italy, Young Egypt, the Young Turks, the Young Arab Party". This generational dimension of nationalism is characteristic of Africa and Asia. Singhal (in Fishman 1972: 33) writes: "An outstanding common feature of Asian nationalism has been the remarkable role of its student communities. Both in Burma and in Indonesia the major strength of the nationalist forces was provided by their student populations. In Burma even the principal leadership came straight from the University." The same is to some extent true of the early stages of Arab nationalism: "On the eve of World War I the Arab [nationalist] movement was already, by and large, a movement of the young" (Tauber 1993: 294).
9. The defence of the national or ethnic language is a feature of all nationalist movements in which language is a defining feature (see Chapter 7 for Arabic). The following example may illustrate this point: "In Assam, when Bengalis and hill people opposed making Assamese the official language of the state, a placard in their procession read 'Assamese is a donkey's language'. An Assamese counter-procession declared Bengali to be 'a goat's language'" (Horowitz 1985: 219).

CHAPTER 3

1. The term "manifesto" is used by Sylvia Haim in translating the title of the declaration/statement of the conference. This may give the wrong impression, particularly of a political programme adopted by a cohesive movement, which the Conference of the Arab Students in Europe could hardly be said to represent. Haim gives the title of the declaration/statement as *al-qawmiyya al-ʿarabiyya: ḥaqīqatuhā, ahdāfuhā, wasāʾiluhā* (Arab Nationalism: its tenets, objectives and methods).
2. The term "inventing traditions" is borrowed from Hobsbawm (1983). It is used by him to mean "a set of practices, normally governed by overtly or tacitly accepted rules of a ritual or symbolic nature, which seek to inculcate certain values and norms of behaviour by repetition, which automatically implies continuity with the past" (ibid.: 1). Invented traditions are not, strictly speaking, subject to evaluation

on grounds of empirical truth or falsity, that is, on whether they relate to a mythic or real past, but on the efficacy of the role they play in achieving the aims they are intended to realize. Failure to appreciate this qualification of the term "invented" in the above phrase can lead to fruitless debate in the literature on nationalism.

3. See 'Amara (1984), *Fajr al-qawmiyya al-'arabiyya* (*The Dawn of Arab Nationalism*), al-Duri (1960), *al-Judhūr al-tārīkhiyya li-l-qawmiyya al-'arabiyya* (*The Historical Roots of Arab Nationalism*) and al-Kharbutli (n.d.), *al-Qawmiyya al-'arabiyya min al-fajr ilā al-ẓuhr* (*Arab Nationalism from its Dawn to its Zenith*), who place the origins of Arab nationalism in pre-Islamic times. A similar attempt is made by Sharara (1988), who traces the unity of the Arabs to pre-Islamic times through poetry. The attempt to trace the origins of Arab nationalism to formative impulses in premodern times is a central thesis in Nuseibeh's *The Ideas of Arab Nationalism* (1956). Referring to the role of language in forming group identity in pre-Islamic Arabia, Nuseibeh says (ibid.: 12): "Pre-Islamic Arabia was not a political entity, and yet it developed a high degree of social and cultural consciousness, akin to nationality, largely on account of its community of language". Nuseibeh adds (ibid.: 13): "The poems, the proverbs, the traditions, the legends and mythologies, expressed in spoken literature and transmitted by oral tradition, greatly influenced the development of an Arab national consciousness; they moulded the minds of the Arabs, fixed their character, and made them morally and spiritually a nation long before Muhammad welded the various conflicting groups into a single organism animated by one purpose". Nuseibeh (ibid.: 13) sums up the "Islamic contribution to modern Arab nationalism" as follows (ibid.: 13–14): "To Islam is due the birth of a nation, the birth of a state, the birth of a national history, and the birth of a civilization. These events moulded the structure of Islamic Arabism in new and unique ways ... Whereas the pre-Islamic period had witnessed the emergence of an Arab nationality, the Islamic ... carried the Arabs far toward the development of a full fledged national consciousness." Although the above factors are important to any understanding of the construction of Arab nationalist discourse in the modern period, they are in themselves not sufficient to put forward the view that nationalism or even nationality in the modern sense was a feature of pre-Islamic and Islamic societies.
4. Evidence for this retrospective Arab nationalism is found in Qunstantin Zurayq's work, in spite of the fact that he is fully aware of the rootedness of this notion in modernity (1962: 170): "We do know that nationalism, in its true sense, is the offspring of the modern age, and of the political, economic and social factors which it has brought to birth. However, even in spite of this we still find a strong Arab feeling in the first age [of Islam], when the Islamic religious emotion was still in full effervescence. The Muslims treated the Banu Taghlib and other Arab Christians quite differently from the way they treated non-Arab Christians; some Christian tribes took part in the early conquests and fought side by side with the Muslims. This Arab feeling grew in strength with the introduction of the foreigners and the growth of *shu'ūbiyya*; the Arabs became more united in order to fend off the attacks of the Persians, the Turks and others." See section 5.
5. The following quotations cited in Fishman (1972) illustrate the general tendency to eulogize the group's language; they are given here to contextualize the claims made

about Arabic in this chapter. Bonald (cited in Fishman 1972: 63) describes French as "a language which is simple without baseness, noble without bombast, harmonious without fatigue, precise without obscurity, elegant without affection, metaphorical without conscious effort; a language which is the veritable expression of a perfected nature". Fichte declares that the Germans were "honest, serious, sober and speak a language which is shaped to express the truth" (ibid.: 65). Writing in Latin in 1751, Ribinyi extols the virtues of his native Hungarian as follows: "Italian is pleasant, French beautiful, German earnest; but all these qualities are so united in Magyar that it is difficult to say wherein its superiority consists" (ibid.). The Greek scholar Korai has the following to say about his language: "It is a rare thing for one to submit to ... slavery if one has once managed to drink to the full the charm of the Hellenic language" (ibid.).

6. This is reflected in the *ḥadīth* literature. Shu'ba (a *ḥadīth* transmitter, d. 160/776) relates that the Prophet likened a *ḥadīth* specialist who does not devote himself to the study of Arabic grammar to a hooded cloak (*burnus*) without a hood, or to a donkey with a nosebag but without fodder (al-Tufi 1997: 248–9). It is also related in the *ḥadīth* literature that some of the Prophet's companions said that they would not hesitate to travel forty days and nights to learn the correct vowelling of a verse of the Qur'an (ibid.: 243).
7. See 'Arafa (1985) and al-Rafi'i (1974) for a general discussion of the inimitability of the Qur'an.
8. Ibn al-Qayyim (n.d.: 3) expresses this point as follows: "*anzalahu bi-lisān al-'arab li-yakūn ḥujja 'alayhim*".
9. Hourani (1983: 260) expresses this linkage as follows: "In the history of Islam, and indeed in its essential structure, the Arabs had a special part. The Qur'an is in Arabic, the Prophet was an Arab, he preached first to Arabs, who formed the 'matter of Islam', the human instrument through which the religion and its authority spread; Arabic became and has remained the language of devotion, theology and law."
10. For a general discussion of al-Khafaji's views on this and related topics, the reader may refer to Suleiman (1996a).
11. This view of the superiority of Arabic is opposed by al-Khafaji's contemporary and compatriot, the Andalusian scholar Ibn Hazm (456/1064), in the first volume of his book *al-Iḥkām fī uṣūl al-ahkām* (1984: 32–7). As a Zahirite (literalist), Ibn Hazm believes that the superiority-of-Arabic thesis cannot be supported by a careful interpretation of the surface – and therefore legitimate – meaning of the text of the Qur'an. He goes even further, claiming that a literalist interpretation of the text of the Qur'an with respect to the superiority thesis of Arabic can lead to conclusions which contradict this thesis. Ibn Hazm also refuses to assign any superiority to any language over another. It is this linguistic egalitarianism which causes Ibn Hazm to reject deprecating references to other languages by the Greek philosopher Galen. He also decries the practice among some Jews of swearing falsely in languages other than Hebrew because of the belief that the angels speak Hebrew only.
12. For a general treatment of the principle of lightness, the reader may refer to Suleiman (1999c).
13. See al-Tufi (1997: 243).

14. Ibid.: 250.
15. Ibid.
16. Ibid.: 251.
17. See Suleiman (1999c: 75–80) for an extensive discussion of these arguments.
18. The term *laḥn* has a multiplicity of meanings. It is used to refer to (1) singing and chanting, (2) allusion, (3) solecism, incorrect or corrupt speech, (4) dialect or sociolect, (5) gist of an utterance or a text, and (6) acumen or intelligence (cf. Matar 1967: 19–28). The reader may also refer to al-Qali (1978, vol. 1: 6–9) and Matlub (1987, vol. 3: 166–9).
19. For a general survey of the major works on *laḥn* and the general aims which these works set out to serve, the reader may refer to Matar (1967: 29–70).
20. See Ibn ʿAbd Rabbih (1928, vol. 1: 18) for further reports of this kind.
21. See Blau (1963) for the role of the Bedouins as arbiters in linguistic disputes.
22. The term "status-planning" refers to the allocation of languages to functional domains which, on a more practical level, involves the setting up of "laws and norms for when to use a language" (Spolsky 1998: 125). See also Cooper (1989) and Suleiman (1999d).
23. See Ibn ʿAbd Rabbih (1928, vol. 2: 18).
24. See *Naqd al-nathr* – which is wrongly, but famously, attributed to Qudama Ibn Jaʿfar (1982: 143) – for this and other stories.
25. See Anis (1960: 17).
26. See Fück (1980: 38) for this and other reports on solecism.
27. See Lewis (1970) for a discussion of the meaning of the term "Arab" in history.
28. See *al-Iḥkām fī uṣūl al-aḥkām* (1984, vol. 1: 36) for Ibn Hazm's views.
29. See Gabrieli (1979: 206) for a similar treatment; see also the entry on *ʿajam* in Lane (1980, Part 5) for the meaning of this term in Arabic.
30. An example of this attitude in pre-Islamic discourse is the reference to the Persian and Christian monks as "stuttering barbarians" because of their language (Goldziher 1966, vol. 1: 99). In the Islamic period, a Bedouin is reported to have referred to Persian as "*kalām al-khurs*, the language of the dumb" (ibid.). The bodyguards of the Umayyad rulers of al-Andalus (known usually as the *Ṣaqāliba*) were also called *khurs* because of their inability to speak Arabic properly (I am grateful to Carole Hillenbrand for pointing this out to me).
31. Not all instances of this phenomenon are framed in the context of contrastive self-identification at group level (cf. Ibn Hazm 1984, vol. 1: 34).
32. Anis (1970: 198–201) argues that the *ḥadīth* upon which this view is based – *anā afṣaḥ man naṭaq bi-l-ḍād* (I am the most eloquent speaker of *ḍād*) – is apocryphal. However, what matters in this connection is not the factual truth of this *ḥadīth* but the fact that it is consistent with a trend which considers eloquence in pure Arabic (*ḍād*) as a mark of distinction. Anis further argues that the term *lughat al-ḍād* is a fourth/tenth-century invention, and that it came to signal group difference between the Arabs on the one hand and the Persians and Turks on the other.
33. See *Sharḥ dīwān al-Mutanabbī* (1938, vol. 2: 56). See also vol. 4: 230, in which al-Mutanabbi declares that the Arabs can never succeed if they are ruled by *ʿajam*. Other references to Arabs and *ʿajam* exist in al-Mutanabbi's *Dīwān*, but these will not detain us here.

34. One of the anonymous readers of the book suggested that "Another explanation of why [Arabic] is called *lughat al-ḍād* is that this consonant originally had a lateral release (which still survives in some Yemeni dialects), and this really is pretty unusual". I am grateful to this reader for this suggestion and for other useful comments on the text.
35. For our purposes here, the term *mawālī* is taken to designate "people descended from foreign families whose ancestors, or even they themselves, on accepting Islam, have been adopted into an Arab tribe, either as freed slaves or free-born aliens" (Goldziher 1966, vol. 1: 101).
36. The fact that *ḍ* is often mixed with *ẓ* by putative Arabic-speakers (cf. al-Hariri, Maqama 46, in al-Suyuti 1986, vol. 2: 288; and 'Abd al-Tawwab 1971) is not considered falsifying evidence of the role of *ḍ* as a group-identity symbol. This shows the extent to which the linguistic criterion as a signifier of identity is rooted in the Arabic intellectual tradition.
37. The term *'arab* was used to cover both people of Arab lineage and Bedouin (*a'rāb*) in Bukhari's *Saḥīḥ*. Although the veracity of the tradition, ascribed to the caliph 'Umar, in which the term *'arab* is used in this sense may be in doubt, the lexical meaning of the term concerned is not in question. This must reflect a much earlier usage. See al-Sayyid (1990) for a discussion of this tradition.
38. See Anis (1970), Gibb (1962), Goldziher (1966, vol. 1), Norris (1990) and Qaddura (1972) for more information on this movement.
39. Cited in Anis (1970: 198).
40. The reader may also refer to the following works by al-Jahiz: *al-Ḥayawān* (1938–45), *al-Bayān wa-l-tabyīn* (1932), *Rasā'il* (1964) and *al-Maḥāsin wa-l-aḍdād* (1969), although there is some doubt as to whether the latter was written by al-Jahiz. The reader may also refer to Ibn Qutayba's two works *Adab al-kātib* (n.d.) and *Kitāb al-'arab* (1913).
41. Goldziher (1966, vol. 1: 193) points out that the interest in names during the fourth century was strong in the *shu'ūbiyya* camp. He mentions a Persian contemporary of Ibn Durayd, Hamza Ibn al-Hasan al-Isfahani (350/961), whose philological work included investigating "the original forms of the Muslim-Persian nomenclature ... to establish its etymological and historical relations; to reconstruct and explain etymologically the original Persian forms of geographical names which Arab national philology had explained from Arab etymologies; and in general to recover the original Persian forms from the shape they had acquired in the mouths of the conquering Arabs".
42. These may be called homo-antonyms on account of their combining homonyms with antonyms.
43. It is quite interesting that, in spite of his anti-*shu'ūbiyya* position, al-Zamakhshari is claimed by Turkists (advocates of Turkish nationalism) as a *Turkish* Arabic grammarian.
44. See al-Bazzaz (1962), al-Duri (1968, 1982), al-Husri (1962), al-Kawakibi (1962), al-Kharbutli (1968), Nuseibeh (1956), Rida (1962), Zabadiya (1982) and Zurayq (1962).
45. The term *shu'ūbiyya* appears in the title of Bayhum's book *al-'Urūba wa-l-shu'ūbiyyāt al-ḥadītha*, published in Beirut in 1957. In her *Arab Nationalism: An*

Anthology (1962), Sylvia Haim includes a translation of a portion of this book (pp. 145–71) under the title "Arabism and Jewry in Syria" (pp. 128–46). The choice of the word "Jewry" in the title of this selection is unfortunate because of the loss of the historical reference to the concept of *shu'ūbiyya*, not to mention the fact that Haim's title deviates from the original in an ideologically motivated manner. Al-Bazzaz's piece in Haim's anthology was first published in Baghdad in 1952. Al-Fikayki's reference to *shu'ūbiyya* occurs in the title of his book *al-Shu'ūbiyya wa-l-qawmiyya al-'arabiyya*, first published in Beirut in 1961. It is clear from the translated extract from this book in Karpat (1968: 80–6) that al-Fikayki uses *shu'ūbiyya* in a wide sense to refer to all the movements which, in his view, are anti-Arab, including the Turkification movement in the Ottoman empire and in Turkey (see Chapter 4), Arab communism, Antun Sa'ada's Syrian Social Nationalist Party (see Chapter 5), Egyptian nationalism (see Chapter 6) and Lebanese nationalism (see Chapter 6). He sums up his views on this topic as follows (1968: 86): "If we were to summarize the objectives of anti-Arabism (*shu'ūbiyya*) we find that it concentrates [on] attacking Arab nationalism, perverting history, emphasising Arab regression, denying Arab culture, being hostile to everything Arab, and being in league with all the enemies of Arab nationalism. In all its various roles, anti-Arabism has adopted a policy of intellectual conquest as a means of penetrating Arab society and combating Arab nationalism."

46. Cited in al-Sayyid (1990: 19).
47. The term *umma* in Arabic discourse ranges over a wide terrain of meaning. Broadly speaking, this term signifies the following meanings: (1) a group of people, (2) religion, (3) an individual who follows the right path (in religious terms), (4) a period of time and (5) body part. See Farhat (1983) for discussion of these meanings.
48. The contingency of nations (as post-eighteenth-century creations) is a fundamental principle of the modernist approach to the study of nationalism. As Halliday points out in his study of the formation of Yemeni nationalism (1997: 27–8), this approach "carries with it the implication of the modernity of nations, i.e. that they cannot be identified prior to the existence of the ideological and social conditions that give them meaning, namely in the early nineteenth century. Identifiable linguistics and cultural groups, peoples, or, in a clear pre-nationalist sense, "nations" can be accepted, but these are not nations in the contemporary sense, nor, it is emphasized, was it inevitable that they should become so." One term which may therefore be suggested as an equivalent of the term *umam* (plural of *umma*) used by al-Mas'udi is "communities", although this term would fall short of the much wider collective groupings that al-Mas'udi seems to have in mind when he talks about *umam*.
49. See Nassar (1992: 41).
50. The term "myth" is used by Ferguson (1972: 375) to cover three types of attitude: (1) those that are true by virtue of corresponding well to "objective reality", (2) those that are "involved with aesthetic or religious notions the validity of which cannot be investigated empirically", and (3) those which are "partly or wholly false". It should be clear from this that Ferguson does not use the term "myth" entirely in its dictionary meaning.

CHAPTER 4

1. This is the first hemistich of a well-known ode by the poet Fakhri al-Barudi which runs as follows: (Line 1) *bilādu al-ʿurbi awṭānī, mina al-shāmi li-baghdāni* (The lands of the Arabs are my homeland, from Greater Syria to Baghdad/Iraq). (Line 2) *wa-min najdin ilā yamanin, ilā miṣra fa-taṭwāni* (And from Najd to Yemen, to Egypt and Tetuan/North Africa). (Line 3) *fa-lā ḥaddun yubāʿidunā wa-lā khulfun yufarriqunā* (Borders do not separate us, and differences do not divide us). (Line 4) *lisānu al-ḍādi yajmaʿunā, bi-qaḥṭānin wa-ʿadnāni* (The Arabic language unites us with the ancient Arabs of Qahtan and ʿAdnan).
2. Periodization of political and cultural movements is a hazardous procedure in history. It is therefore not surprising that objections are made to the anchoring of modernity in the Arabic-speaking countries to Napoleon's invasion of Egypt in 1798. The following quotation from Tibawi (1969: 39) illustrates the general thrust of this kind of objection: "There is really no decisive point at which we can say that the old world changed itself into the new world in the near East and elsewhere. Long before 1798 the movement that is variously called modernisation or reform was under way in different parts of the Muslim world. Long after 1798 'medieval' ideas held undisputed sway and their supremacy was not fundamentally in question. The change, modernisation, reform or renaissance was first inspired by native and internal forces; only its more obvious and later development was in response to foreign and external challenge."
3. See Feroz Ahmad (1969) for a detailed study of the politics of the Young Turks.
4. Turkism or Pan-Turkism must be distinguished from Turanism. Landau (1981: 1) identifies as the guiding objective of the former the attempt to "strive for some sort of union – cultural or physical, or both – among all peoples of proven or alleged Turkic origins, whether living both within and without the frontiers of the Ottoman Empire (subsequently of the Republic of Turkey)". "Turanism", he explains, "is … a far broader concept than Pan-Turkism, embracing such peoples as the Hungarians, the Finns and Estonians" (ibid.).
5. The list consists of the following sources (Kushner 1977: 75): "(1) The Turkish vocabulary prevalent among all classes of population in Istanbul, including even old women. (2) The vocabulary of the inhabitants of Anatolia and Rumelia. (3) The creation of several new words through the use of existing roots. (4) Old Ottoman words. (5) The old and new vocabularies of Eastern Turkish which [is called] Chagatay. (6) The vocabulary of Azerbayjan. (7) The dialects of the Crimea and Kazan. (8) The vocabulary of Uigur. (9) The vocabulary of Uzbek. (10) The vocabulary of Kalmuk. (11) Dialects of other Turkish peoples. (12) Creation of new words through the use of roots, from the dialects … mentioned in items … 4–11. (13) Arabic. (14) Persian. (15) European languages."
6. The attitude of the Turkists of the Committee of Union and Progress (CUP) and the Young Turks towards the Arabs is dealt with, albeit briefly, by Hanioğlu (1991: 31): "In their publications, the Young Turks claimed that all ethnic groups of the Ottoman Empire were equal, that there was no difference between Arabs and Turks, and that it was normal for all groups to desire to develop their ethnic cultures. But in the confidential correspondence of some of the important members

of the Committee of Union and Progress (CUP) the opposite attitude can be seen through the use of such derogatory phrases for Arabs as 'the dogs of the Turkish nation' in private letters of two key members of the Central Committee of the CUP, Dr Nazım Bey, one of the reorganisers of the CUP in 1906, and Ishak Süküti, one of its five founding members." And (ibid.: 32): "although Arabs were of the same religion as the Turks, the Young Turks viewed them as the most inferior ethnic group of the empire".

7. See Landau (1993b) for the euphoria with which the Young Turk Revolution was met in Egypt. See also Jurji Zaydan's novel *al-Inqilāb al-'uthmānī* (*The Ottoman coup d'état*, n.d.) for an expression of this euphoria in literature. For a more historical account of the impact of the Young Turk Revolution on the Arabic-speaking provinces, see Kedourie (1974b).
8. See Antonius (1938: 31–4) and Zeine (1966: 40–1) for a general discussion of this issue.
9. In dealing with this issue, Tibawi (1969: 88) writes: "In the literary field the Egyptian impact [in Syria] was more profound [than in the field of formal education]. Preserved in the Egyptian archives are cumulative lists of books printed in Cairo and supplied to various centres in Syria ... The lists include books on science, mathematics, medicine, theology, mysticism, language, history, geography and travel. They were ordered not by civil servants, physicians, chemists and army officers, but also by religious functionaries, members of consultative councils, notables, teachers and private individuals of all communities, Muslim, Christian and others." See also Antonius (1938: 38) on this point.
10. Antonius (1938: 39) assesses Ibrahim Pasha's contribution in this area in more positive and upbeat terms: "The scholastic system introduced by Ibrahim, although short-lived, gave a powerful stimulus to national education, particularly among the Muslim community; and the start he gave it was all the more far-reaching as his system aimed deliberately at awakening Arab national consciousness among pupils". Tibawi (1969: 87–8) offers a different and more reliable assessment of Ibrahim Pasha's input in the field of education, which gives no hint of any deliberate nationalist objectives behind it.
11. In assessing the role of missionary education, attention must be paid to aspects of its negative impact. A representative view of this impact is given by Antonius (1938: 92): "In a country [Lebanon] which was ... a prey to internal division, [the] very diversity [of the missionary schools] was an added mischief, as some of the missions had become the tools of political ambitions and brought in their trains the evils of international rivalry as well as the benefits of education". Tibi (1997: 100) shares this view in the context of the French missionary schools: "In the French mission schools, Arab Christians, mainly Maronites, were taught that they could only emancipate themselves under the protection of France, which meant French colonial rule. In the beginning, instruction in the French schools was in French alone, and it was only in the face of competition from the Protestants that they began to use more Arabic, although even then only occasionally." See also Hawi (1982) on this point.
12. Butrus al-Bustani (1819–83) was a pioneer in this field. His contribution to the development of Arabic culture, journalism and the Arabic language in the nineteenth century was widely acknowledged, as was his call for unity between Christians

and Muslims, whom he urged to love their fatherland. For his contribution to the formation of Syrian nationalism in the second half of the twentieth century, see Abu-Manneh (1980). See Tibawi (1963) for the relationship between Butrus al-Bustani and the American missionaries in Beirut.

13. See Tibawi (1966) for a detailed study of the American interests in Syria in the nineteenth century.
14. It is interesting to note here that the establishment of the college was championed by locally based American missionaries who wanted to avoid the universal prescription of the use of the "vernacular" as a medium of instruction in missionary schools. At the time (early 1880s), the American schools were facing tough competition from other missionary schools which taught foreign languages or used them as the medium of instruction. Tibawi (1969: 143) refers to this obliquely in the following quotation: "By the order of their superiors in Boston, the Americans were debarred from teaching foreign languages, even English. This was one of the common considerations which led the American mission in Beirut to seek the establishment of a Protestant high school independent of Boston's control. The result was the establishment in 1866 of the Syrian Protestant College."
15. Kedourie (1974a) suggests that the decision to use the "vernacular" in the work of the American mission was based on the experience of missionaries in India and Ceylon. Reflecting on their work among the Mahrattas in India, the missionaries concluded that "experience has seemed to show that such schools are not the most efficient instruments in forwarding the great work of the missions – that of making known the gospel to the heathen, and saving souls. The vernacular of any people … is believed to be the most suitable language in which to communicate truth, and through which to affect the heart" (quoted in Kedourie, ibid.: 70). The missionaries in Ceylon encouraged the use of the "vernacular" for the same reason, but they additionally pointed out that by depriving their graduates of English-language proficiency they made them less able to pursue careers in government administration, commerce and business and, therefore, more available for use in propagating the work of the mission itself among the indigenous population: "too often the graduate [with English-language proficiency] went into the more lucrative service of the government, or of some merchant planter, and thus his labours and influence were lost to the mission and to his native village. Were our object merely to educate and civilise the people … this might do; but the churches cannot afford to prosecute their work in this manner" (ibid.: 71). By contrast, the situation in the Levant developed in the opposite direction, in spite of the early preference for Arabic in the American mission schools. Increased contact with Europe created a demand for foreign languages (mainly English and French), as did emigration to North America by native Lebanese. This demand was met by other missions, leading to a reduction in the number of students enrolled in the American mission schools. To reverse this trend, English was later (1882) adopted as the medium of instruction in the Syrian Protestant College to challenge the Jesuits' promotion of French. In this connection, Henry Harris Jessup, a member of the mission, remarked: "Was [the teaching of foreign languages] to be left to the Jesuits, those enemies of a pure Gospel, those masters of intrigue and duplicity and perverters of the human conscience? This must not be" (quoted in Kedourie, ibid.).

16. Considering this policy on the part of the American missions, Tibi (1997: 100) argues that it is "significant that the early Arab nationalists emerged not from the French but from the American Protestant mission schools, whose activities were less directly tied to colonial aims". The same assessment is offered of the work of the Russian Orthodox schools, especially the Nazareth School in Palestine. Tibawi (1969: 172) states that in the Russian Orthodox schools "instruction was through the medium of Arabic, and this language was taught very thoroughly throughout the system. Russian was taught only as a foreign language." See Hopwood (1969: 137–58) for further information on the role of the Russian Orthodox Church schools in the Levant (particularly in Palestine) towards the end of the nineteenth century and the beginning of the twentieth century. The reader may also consult al-Husri's *Muḥāḍarāt fī nushū' al-fikra al-qawmiyya* (1985: 126–9) for some interesting remarks on this topic.
17. Eli Smith (1801–57) was a pioneer in this respect. He came to Beirut in 1827, but started to learn Arabic in Malta before actually moving to Beirut. Another member of the mission, the famous physician Cornelius van Dyck (1818–95), followed in Smith's footsteps. He came to Beirut in 1840, learned Arabic to a very high standard and "wrote text-books in it on various scientific subjects, some of which remained in use for two or three generations" (Antonius 1938: 48). The titles of some of these books (twenty-five in total), which he wrote in Arabic, are listed in al-Zarakli's biographical dictionary *al-A'lām* (1995, vol. 5).
18. George Post came to Lebanon as a member of the American mission in 1863. He learned Arabic to a very high standard, worked as a staff member at the Protestant College for forty-one years (since its inception) and published many books in Arabic on medicine, biology and botany. He also published the magazine *Majallat al-ṭabīb* (*The Doctor/Physician*) before relinquishing its editorship to Ibrahim al-Yaziji (see section 3). His missionary zeal landed him in trouble with Muslim students at the College, who refused to attend his lectures (see al-Zarakli 1995, vol. 2).
19. A fourth placard or handbill, dated 17 Rabi' al-Thani 1298/19 March 1881, was distributed in Algeria, Egypt, Greater Syria, Iraq and Sudan in the name of the little-known Society for Watching over the Rights of the Arab Millet (*Jam'iyyat ḥifẓ huqūq al-milla al-'arabiyya*). The placard attacks the Turks as a corrupt nation and addresses Muslims and Christians as members of the Arab nation, calling on them to unite against the Turks in the struggle for liberty and independence. This bill makes no reference to the Arabic language, restricting itself mainly to Turkish misrule in the levying of war taxes and the conscription of Arab soldiers. See Landau (1993a: 141–53) for the text, a translation and a discussion of this handbill.
20. Dozy, vol. 2, 159: includes in the cluster of meanings he lists for this word the following item: "a coarse and unbridled man who yields to his brutal passions", and adds that it is applied to apostates, whether they renege to Christianity from Islam or the other way round. I am grateful to Carole Hillenbrand for pointing this out to me.
21. Faris Nimr graduated from the American Protestant College in 1874. He worked with Cornelius van Dyck at the University's observatory and later became its director. He established with Ya'qub Sarruf (see n. 40 below) *al-Muqtaṭaf* magazine in 1876. In 1884, he emigrated to Egypt and resumed the publication of *al-Muqtaṭaf* a year later. He established *al-Muqaṭṭam* magazine in Cairo in 1889. He co-

translated with Ya'qub Sarruf a number of books into Arabic. He served as a member of the Egyptian Senate and as a member of the Arabic Language Academy in Cairo.

22. Shaykh Tahir al-Jaza'iri was one of the prominent men of letters in Syria in his time. He had more than twenty publications to his name on various aspects of Arabic and Islamic culture. He was instrumental in establishing the famous Zahiriyya library in Damascus and the Khalidiyya library in Jerusalem.
23. It is also reported that a Christian Armenian was appointed to teach Islamic religion in a Beirut school against his will (see al-Afghani 1971: 24).
24. These and other terms were cited by 'Abd al-Rahman al-Kawakibi in his book *Umm al-qurā* (see al-Afghani 1971: 33).
25. See Tauber (1993: 197–8) for information on this congress.
26. For a translation of this proclamation, see Sylvia Haim (1962: 83–8).
27. Sylvia Haim (1962: 88) translates the word *'ulūj* as "contemptible creatures". Like Tibawi (1969), Haim misses the relevant connotations of this term in this context, mainly those of being unbelievers and non-Arabs by virtue of their not knowing Arabic or their speaking it with a foreign accent. See the discussion of this issue earlier in this section.
28. In extreme cases, the use of Turkish was frowned upon. Tauber (1993: 337) tells us that a French diplomat writing in 1880 noted how, at a public meeting in Damascus, a speaker warned against the use of Turkish – "Anyone who will use a Turkish word to indicate 'bread' will be beaten to death" – and how he did not encounter the "slightest protest".
29. Rida expresses his views on this topic in the following manner (see Hourani 1983: 300): "One of the religious and social reforms of Islam was to bring about linguistic unity, by making its common language that of all the peoples who adhered to it. The religion preserved the language and the language preserved the religion. But for Islam, the Arabic language would have changed like others, as it had itself changed previously. But for Arabic, the different interpretations of Islam would have grown apart from each other, and it would have split into a number of faiths, with the adherents of each accusing the others of infidelity; when they wished to give up following their passions and return to the truth, they would have found no general principles to invoke. Thus the Arabic language is not the private property of the descendants of Qahtan [original Arabic-speakers], it is the language of all Muslims."
30. Khalidi sums up the contribution of *al-Mufid* as follows (1981: 46–7): "Without question the most important theme in *al-Mufid*, indeed in a sense the paper's very *raison d'être*, is Arab nationalism, whose basic ideas: political, cultural and linguistic, are forcefully hammered home either directly or indirectly in virtually every leading article. This overriding preoccupation with Arab nationalism is also frequently evident in the choice of articles reprinted from other papers, in the items carried from all over the Arab world, and in the political developments in the capital [Istanbul] which are reported."
31. In this connection, al-'Uraysi once said (1981: 48) that "all affiliative bonds may disintegrate except that of religion".
32. This article is attributed to al-'Uraysi by Naji 'Allush on the basis, it seems, of

similarity of content with another article (1981: 3–5) written by the author, whose authorship is not in dispute and for which he was taken to court and punished.

33. Amin Abu Khatir was born in Zahla, Lebanon. He studied medicine at the American Protestant College in Beirut before moving to Egypt, where he died. He published many articles on a variety of topics in *al-Muqtaṭaf* and other Egyptian newspapers.
34. Ibrahim al-Yaziji was born in Beirut in 1847. He worked in journalism and on a new translation of the Bible into Arabic before leaving for Egypt in the 1880s to take advantage of the atmosphere of freedom available there at the time. Al-Yaziji published three journals – *al-Ṭabīb*, *al-Ḍiya'* and *al-Bayān* – in which he set out his ideas on a host of issues, including the revitalization of the Arabic language, which occupied him most. In addition, he published two Arabic lexica and a volume of poetry. He died in Egypt in 1906. His remains were brought back to Beirut in 1913.
35. Antonius describes the content of this poem and its diffusion in the Levant as follows (1938: 54–5): "In substance, the poem was an incitement to Arab insurgence. It sang of the achievements of the Arab race, of the glories of Arabic literature, and of the future that the Arabs might fashion for themselves by going to their own past for inspiration. It denounced the evils of sectarian dissensions, heaped abuse on the misgovernment to which the country was a prey, and called upon the Syrians to band together and shake off the Turkish yoke. It was all the more seditious as it was couched in stirring terms, and it was recited in a hushed voice to eight members of the [Syrian Scientific Society in 1868] who had assembled in a private house one night and were known to one another to be of the same way of thinking. The poem had a wide circulation. It was too treasonable to be safely committed to anything but memory ... It made a particular appeal to the students and stamped their minds in their receptive years with the impress of racial pride. The poem did much to foster the national movement in its infancy. It owed its vogue to its easy cadence and the neatness of its rhymes, and above all to the fact that, echoing sentiments unconsciously felt, it could awaken true emotion in the people for whom it was intended. With its utterance the movement for political emancipation sang its song." The place of this poem in the history of the Arab nationalist idea meant that it was taught in schools in parts of the Arab world as late as the 1960s. The present writer remembers being taught it at school in Jerusalem in the mid-1960s.
36. Whether the Druze identify themselves as Muslims or not, or whether they are identified by other Muslims as Muslim or not, is not something that concerns us here. The labels Christian, Druze and Muslim are used here in conformity with the relevant literature on the subject.
37. In carrying out this task, I base my argument on the two collections of magazine articles by al-Yaziji edited by Yusuf Qazma Khuri (1993a, 1993b). I also refer to one of the articles in Jeha's (1992) introduction to al-Yaziji's life and works.
38. Cooper (1989: 31) characterizes corpus-planning as a sub-field of language planning which refers to "activities such as coining new terms, reforming spelling, and adopting a new script. It refers, in short, to the creation of new forms, the modification of old ones, or the selection from alternative forms in a spoken or written code."
39. Status-planning refers to the "allocation of languages or language varieties to given functions, e.g. medium of instruction, official language, vehicle of mass communication, etc." (ibid.: 32).

40. Ya'qub Sarruf was born in Lebanon. He studied at the American Protestant College. He was an accomplished translator and writer of both poetry and fiction.
41. It may actually be argued that exaggerations in this sphere are functionally relevant because they serve to highlight the strength of the posited connection between language and nation.
42. See Antonius (1938: 92–5) for an assessment of the effect of the foreign schools on the progress of the Arab national movement. In the course of this assessment, Antonius makes the following point, as if to give credence to al-Yaziji's views: "The French Government, anxious to strengthen their influence, subsidised the French ecclesiastical missions; and these, entering into an alliance with the Maronite and Melchite clergy, strove to give the rising generation an education which, although well-enough in itself, aimed also at shaping their minds in a French mould and turning their outlook and their mental allegiance towards France. The Russians, through the agency of an ecclesiastical mission and a richly-endowed pedagogic society, cultivated the Orthodox Arab population and the Orthodox Patriarchates of Antioch and Jerusalem with similar ulterior aims." Evidence for this penetration may be derived from a debate run by the weekly *al-Nashra al-usbū'iyya* in 1881 on the use of Arabic or foreign languages for instruction in schools in the Levant. One of the claims made by Antonius about the influence of Western education on the Arab national movement deals with the transfer of the leadership of this movement from the hands of the Christians to the Muslims (1938: 92): "It [Western education] did this mainly by its indirect attack on the position of the Arabic language as the instrument of the national culture". This is an extremely interesting point whose substantiation requires further research. To illustrate the extent to which foreign languages had penetrated Levantine society, the editors of this weekly mention that a man had insisted that one of the essential requirements in his wife-to-be was that she should know English or French (in Khuri 1991: 7).
43. Tibawi believes that educational Westernization in Greater Syria in the latter part of the nineteenth century had a negative impact on its sociopolitical environment (1969: 178): "The westernisation in material life may be dismissed as superficial, but that in speech indicates mental attitudes built up through a long process of education in foreign schools ... All these foreign influences tended to retard movements towards a Syrian Arab entity; they militated even more against any form of Ottoman unity. Within the Syrian Arab house, foreign cultural influences heightened and aggravated religious divisions by giving them a cultural stamp. An observer who might have seen the country around the year 1890 thus tossed from one ideology to another could hardly have resisted asking the question: whither Syria?"

CHAPTER 5

1. This is the second hemistich of a well-known poem by the Lebanese poet Anis al-Khuri al-Maqdisi (1885–1977), in which he says that language in national-identity terms overrides the divisions which differences in faith may produce: (1) *in farraqa al-īmānu bayna jumū'inā, fa-lisānunā al-'arabiyyu khayru muwaḥḥidi* (Should differences in faith divide us, our Arabic language is the thing which first and foremost unites us); (2) *qarubat bihi al-aqṭāru wa-hiya ba'īdatun, wa-tawaḥḥadat min ba'di fattin*

fi al-yadi (Arabic shortens the distances between the Arabic-speaking lands, and it unites the Arabs when division threatens to fragment them).

2. 'Umar 'Abd al-Rahman al-Fakhuri was born in Beirut. He studied law in Paris and served as a member of the Damascus Academy (al-Majma' al-'Ilmi al-'Arabi). He worked in broadcasting and published many books, essays and translations (from French into Arabic).
3. Salah al-Din al-Qasimi graduated in medicine from Damascus in 1914, a profession he practised in Hijaz until his death in al-Ta'if in 1916. He championed the cause of the Arabic language against the Turkification policies of the Young Turks and was a founder member of the Arab Renaissance Society (1906) in Damascus.
4. The question as to whether or not Arab nationalism is need of definition was hotly contested in the 1960s (see Nazik al-Mala'ika 1993a, 1993b, al-Naqqash 1993, al-Basir 1993a, Budur 1993, al-Dahhan 1993, 'Abd al-Da'im 1993).
5. For a recent appreciation of Sati' al-Husri, see *Sāṭi' al-Ḥuṣrī: thalāthūn 'ām 'alā al-raḥīl* (1999). See also Choueiri (2000).
6. Cleveland's comments (1971: 90–1) on the issue of style in al-Husri's writings highlight its interactive qualities with the intended audience: "al-Husri possessed a spare but forceful literary style, one which was quite direct in its approach to the issues which he raised, but which was also capable of occasional imagery. He most often presented his arguments in self-contained essays which employed the following organisation: he stated a premise which he favoured, buttressed it with 'historical scientific facts,' and then said that these facts proved the irrefutable validity of the initial premise which was forcefully repeated as a conclusion. Another device which al-Husri often used was to recognise and predict the doubts his audience might have concerning a statement which he had just made, and then to demolish those rhetorical doubts with even more facts. It was an effective and convincing method when combined with his wide reading and his ability to grasp and manipulate what he had read."
7. In his book *Mulūk al-'arab*, Amin al-Rihani (1929, vol. 2: 402) refers to this fact: "[al-Husri] is an Arab; his Arabic is beyond reproach, except for his accent". The original text, which reads "*huwa 'arabiyy lā ghubār 'alā 'arabiyyatih ghayr lahjatihā*", was mistranslated by Cleveland into (1971: 66): "He [al-Husri] is an Arab, irreproachable in his Arabism except for his accent". Cleveland misread *'arabiyyatih* for *'urūbatih*, the latter meaning *Arabism*, but not the former.
8. See Sa'd (1979) for a study of al-Husri's educational thought.
9. See Cleveland (1971: 32–3) for this debate.
10. The urgency of modernization is summed up in al-Husri's exhortation to the Arabs to adopt as their slogan "modernization at all times, in all places and in everything" (*Ārā' wa-aḥādīth fi al-tārīkh wa-l-ijtimā'*, 1985e: 19: *al-tajdīd fi kull zamān, wa-fi kull shay' wa-fi kull makān yajib an yakūn shi'āranā al-'āmm*).
11. See the following publications by al-Husri for these views: *Ārā' wa-aḥādīth fi al-waṭaniyya wa-l-qawmiyya*, 1984a: 21; *al-'Urūba bayn du'ātihā wa-mu'āriḍīhā*, 1985a: 73; and *Muḥāḍarāt fi nushū' al-fikra al-qawmiyya*, 1985b: 21.
12. Had al-Husri been aware of the fact, he would undoubtedly have pointed out how "language was part of the national heritage strenuously appealed to by the dictionary-maker Noah Webster" (Honey 1997: 68) who, "in the immediate aftermath of

American Independence ... was at pains to emphasize the distinctiveness of standard American English" (ibid.: 81) against standard British English.
13. See Faysal (1971) for al-Husri's views on language education in Syria.

CHAPTER 6

1. The Syrian and secular nature of Sa'ada's nationalist thinking is embedded in the Constitution of the Syrian National Party (see Makdisi 1960: 173–4).
2. See Thomas (1991) for a discussion of the notion of purity in language.
3. See Muhammad (1996) and Zalat (1988) for a general discussion of Haykal's work.
4. The potential of this discovery in linking the present with the past was exploited to the full by Egyptian nationalists. Pilgrimages to the tomb site were organized by these nationalists, with Muhammad Husayn Haykal taking the lead. Pharaonic motifs were used on stamps, banknotes, the coat of arms of the Egyptian University and the coats of arms of each of its faculties. In 1928, a statue (*Nahḍat Miṣr*/The Revival of Egypt), containing a Sphinx-like figure by the sculptor Mahmud Mukhtar (1891–1934), was unveiled in a grand ceremony (see Baron 1997). Also in 1928, the Egyptian government authorized the building of a Pharaonic-style mausoleum to inter the remains of the Egyptian leader Sa'd Zaghloul (1857–1927), although the reburial did not take place until 1936. Name-giving practices reflected the national mood of the period. This mood was also reflected in literature: Ahmad Shawqi alone composed four poems on the topic (see Khouri 1971 for the role of poetry in the making of modern Egypt). This pride in the Pharaonic past of Egypt has led some nationalist poets to adopt *shu'ūbiyya*-style themes, pointing out that the greatness of the Arab past pales into insignificance when compared with that of the Egyptians (see Gershoni and Jankowski 1986: 185).
5. See Abu Sayf (1987) for the history of the Arabic language in Egypt.
6. See Abu Sayf (1987), al-Bishri (1982), Carter (1986), al-Fiqqi (1985), Hanna (1994), Kilani (n.d.) and al-Mi'dawi (1978) for discussions of the role of the Copts in the national life of Egypt.
7. See Cachia 1990 (59–73) for a discussion of the use of the colloquial in modern Arabic literature.
8. See Anis (1969) for a discussion of the issue of the Bedouin nature of Arabic.
9. The idea of establishing a language academy was mooted as early as 1892. Several attempts were made to establish it, but it was finally established in 1932 and took as its name *Majma' al-Lugha al-'Arabiyya al-Malakī* (The Royal Arabic Language Academy). Its name was changed to *Majma' Fu'ād al-'Awwal li-l-Lugha al-'Arabiyya* (King Fu'ad's Arabic Language Academy). Its name was finally changed to *Majma' al-Lugha al-'Arabiyya* (The Arabic Language Academy) in 1954. See al-Jami'i (1983).
10. For the history of the Arabist idea in Egypt, see 'Abdalla (1975), 'Amara (1997), al-Barri (1992), Burj (1992), Coury (1998), Gershoni and Jankowski (1995), Jalal and al-Mutawalli (1997), Khatir (1985), Muhammad (1978), Nassar (1980), Qarqut (1972) and Zaki (1983).
11. See 'Amara (1995) for an attack on this dimension of Salama Musa's thinking. For a more balanced assessment of Salama Musa's thinking, the reader may refer to Shukri (1983).

12. Taha Husayn states that the same must apply to the teaching of the geography and history of Egypt as the two other components which make up the Egyptian national identity on the cultural level. The teaching of Islam and Christianity must also be provided to their followers in all schools, whether state or non-state schools.
13. For criticism from this angle, see al-Jundi (1977, 1984) and al-Muhtasib (1980). See Rukaybi (1992) for a more balanced assessment of Taha Husayn's thinking.
14. For views on this matter, see al-Alfi (1990), 'Ayyad (1992), Faraj (1992), Hashim (1992), Khalafalla (1992), Mijli (1995), Qandil (1992), Salim (1992), al-Tawil (1992) and Zahran (1985). For some of the court documents, see the appendix to 'Awad (1993).
15. Lewis Awad's bold pronouncements on this and other matters in the introduction to *Plutoland* have made him the subject of vitriolic attacks by a band of critics. Shakir (1972) describes him as "wicked charlatan, impostor, transgressor, puppet, trash, insane, odious, rotten, depraved, useless thing, missionary errand boy" (cited in Suleiman 1997: 130). 'Attar (1965) refers to him as "a communist and Christian zealot, an enemy of Islam, the Qur'an, Islamic culture and heritage, and the Arabic language and literature" (ibid.). 'Attar also refers to him as an "atheist Marxist Leninist Stalinist radical communist lefty" (ibid.). For a more balanced evaluation of Luwis 'Awad's ideas, see al-Naqqash (1988) and Raghib (1989).
16. Views to this effect were voiced during the Sadat regime (1970–81), when *Muqaddima fi fiqh al-lugha al-'arabiyya* was first published.
17. For a criticism of the conceptual framework of this book, see Shahin (n.d.: 175–84).
18. The National Pact (1943) was an unwritten understanding between Bishara al-Khury, a Maronite Christian, and Riyad al-Sulh, a Sunni Muslim, to regulate the division of political power among the various confessional communities in Lebanon. Under this understanding, the presidency was allocated to the Maronites and the office of prime minister to the Sunnis.
19. For a discussion of confessionalism in Lebanon, see 'Amil (1989), Dahir (1986), Ghalyun (1979), Hallaq (1988), Khalifa (1985), Nassar (1981), Phares (1995), Rondot (1984) and Shahin (n.d.).
20. See Douglas (1966) and Thomas (1991) for an analysis of the concept of purity in social practices. The latter is devoted to this concept in discussions of language reform.
21. See Smith (1997) for an excellent discussion of the notion of the "golden age" in national renewal.
22. See Schöpflin (1997) for other contexts in which what he calls the "myth of election" obtains.

Bibliography

WORKS IN ARABIC CITED IN THE TEXT

ʿAbd al-Dāʾim, ʿAbdalla (1993), "al-Qawmiyya al-ʿarabiyya bayn al-shuʿūr wa-l-ʿaql", in *Qirāʾāt fī al-fikr al-qawmī*, vol. 1: *al-Qawmiyya al-ʿarabiyya, fikratuhā wa-muqawwimātuhā* (Beirut: Markiz Dirāsāt al-Waḥda al-ʿArabiyya), pp. 455–63. (First published in *al-Ādāb*, 9 (1960): 4–6, 76–8.)

ʿAbd al-Malik, Anwar (1983), *Nahḍat miṣr* (Cairo: al-Hayʾa al-Miṣriyya al-ʿĀmma li-l-Kitāb).

ʿAbd al-Muʾmin, Muḥammad al-Saʿīd (1990), "al-Shuʿūbiyya al-ḥadītha", in *Waqāʾiʿ al-nadwa al-qawmiyya li-muwājahat al-dass al-shuʿūbī* (Baghdad: Dār al-Ḥurriyya li-l-Ṭibāʿa), vol. 3, pp. 31–50.

ʿAbd al-Tawwāb, Ramaḍān (1971), "Mushkilat al-ḍād wa-turāth al-ḍād wa-l-ẓā'", *Majallat al-majmaʿ al-ʿilmī al-ʿirāqī*, 21: 214–40.

—— (1990), "al-Shuʿūbiyyūn al-judud wa-mawqifuhum min al-ʿarabiyya al-fuṣḥā", in *Waqāʾiʿ al-nadwa al-qawmiyya li-muwājahat al-dass al-shuʿūbī* (Baghdad: Dār al-Ḥurriyya li-l-Ṭibāʿa), vol. 1, pp. 353–73.

ʿAbdalla, Nabīh Bayyūmī (1975), *Taṭawwur fikrat al-qawmiyya al-ʿarabiyya fī miṣr* (Cairo: al-Hayʾa al-Miṣriyya al-ʿĀmma li-l-Kitāb).

Abū-Khāṭir, Amīn (1913), "al-Jinsiyya wa-l-lugha", in Yūsuf Qazmā Khūrī (ed.), *Najāḥ al-umma al-ʿarabiyya fī lughatihā al-aṣliyya* (Beirut: Dār al-Ḥamrāʾ, 1991), pp. 136–43.

Abū Saʿd, Aḥmad (1994), "al-Lahja al-lubnāniyya fī uṣūlihā al-ʿarabiyya", *al-Fikr al-ʿArabī*, 277: 7–19.

Abū Sayf, Yūsuf (1987), *al-Aqbāṭ wa-l-qawmiyya al-ʿarabiyya: dirāsa istiṭlāʿiyya* (Beirut: Markiz Dirāsāt al-Waḥda al-ʿArabiyya).

al-Afghānī, Saʿīd (1971), *Min ḥāḍir al-lugha al-ʿarabiyya* (Damascus: Dār al-Fikr). (Second printing.)

ʿAflaq, Michel (1993a), "Fī al-qawmiyya al-ʿarabiyya", in *Qirāʾāt fī al-fikr al-qawmī*, vol. 1: *al-Qawmiyya al-ʿarabiyya, fikratuhā wa-muqawwimātuhā* (Beirut: Markiz Dirāsāt al-Waḥda al-ʿArabiyya), pp. 78–80. (First published in 1940.)

—— (1993b), "al-Qawmiyya ḥubb qabl kull shay'", in *Qirāʾāt fī al-fikr al-qawmī*, vol. 1: *al-Qawmiyya al-ʿarabiyya, fikratuhā wa-muqawwimātuhā* (Beirut: Markiz Dirāsāt al-Waḥda al-ʿArabiyya), pp. 74–5. (First published in 1940.)

—— (1993c), "al-Qawmiyya qadar muḥabbab", in *Qirāʾāt fī al-fikr al-qawmī*, vol. 1: *al-Qawmiyya al-ʿarabiyya, fikratuhā wa-muqawwimātuhā* (Beirut: Markiz Dirāsāt

al-Waḥda al-ʿArabiyya), pp. 76–7. (First published in 1940.)
Aḥmad, Khalīl (1981), *Dawr al-lisān fī binā' al-insān ʿind Zakī al-Arsūzī* (Damascus: Dār al-Su'āl).
ʿAlā' al-Dīn, Bakrī (1971), "Tajrubat al-lugha ladā al-Arsūzī", *al-Maʿrifa*, 13: 127–45.
al-ʿAlāylī, ʿAbdalla (1938), *Muqaddima li-dars lughat al-ʿarab* (Cairo: al-Maṭbaʿa al-ʿAṣriyya).
—— (1954), *al-Muʿjam* (Beirut: Dār al-Muʿjam al-ʿArabī).
—— (1963), *al-Marjiʿ* (Beirut: Dār al-Muʿjam al-ʿArabī).
—— (1996), *Dustūr al-ʿarab al-qawmī* (Beirut: Dār al-Jadīd). (First published in 1938.)
al-Alfī, ʿAlī (1990), "Luwīs ʿAwaḍ widāʿan", *Adab wa-naqd*, 65–75.
ʿAlī, Saʿīd Ismāʿīl (1995), *Dawr al-taʿlīm al-miṣrī fī al-niḍāl al-waṭanī zaman al-iḥtilāl al-barīṭānī* (Cairo: al-Hay'a al-Miṣriyya al-ʿĀmma li-l-Kitāb).
al-ʿAlī, Ṣāliḥ Aḥmad (1986), "al-Shuʿūr al-qawmī al-ʿarabī ʿabr al-tārīkh: muqawwimāt al-qawmiyya al-ʿarabiyya wa-maẓāhiruhā ʿabr al-tārīkh", in *Taṭawwur al-fikr al-qawmī al-ʿarabī* (Beirut: Markiz Dirāsāt al-Waḥda al-ʿArabiyya), pp. 19–51.
ʿAmāra, Muḥammad (1976), *al-Jāmiʿa al-islāmiyya wa-l-fikra al-qawmiyya ʿind Muṣṭafā Kāmil* (Beirut: al-Mu'assasa al-ʿArabiyya li-l-Dirāsāt wa-l-Nashr).
—— (1984), *Fajr al-qawmiyya al-ʿarabiyya* (Beirut: Dār al-Waḥda).
—— (1995), *Salāma Mūsā: ijtihād khāṭi' am ʿamāla ḥaḍāriyya?* (Cairo: Dār al-Ṣaḥwa).
—— (1997), *ʿIndamā aṣbaḥat miṣr ʿarabiyya islāmiyya* (Cairo: Dār al-Shurūq).
ʿĀmil, Mahdī (1989), *Fī al-dawla al-ṭā'ifiyya* (Beirut: Dār al-Fārābī). (First published in 1988.)
al-Anbārī, Abū al-Barakāt Kamāl al-Dīn ʿAbd al-Raḥmān Ibn Muḥammad (n.d.), *Lumaʿ al-'adilla fī ʿuṣūl al-naḥw*, ed. ʿAṭiyya ʿĀmir (Stockholm: Almqvist and Wiksell).
al-Anbārī, Muḥammad Ibn al-Qāsim (1987), *Kitāb al-Aḍdād*, ed. Muḥammad Abū al-Faḍl Ibrāhīm (Sidon and Beirut: al-Maktaba al-ʿAṣriyya).
Anīs, Ibrāhīm (1960), *Mustaqbal al-lugha al-ʿarabiyya al-mushtaraka* (Cairo: The Arab League).
—— (1969), "Hal al-lugha al-ʿarabiyya lugha badawiyya?", *Majallat majmaʿ al-lugha al-ʿarabiyya*, 24: 172–80.
—— (1970), *al-Lugha bayn al-qawmiyya wa-l-ʿālamiyya* (Cairo: Dār al-Maʿārif).
ʿArafa, ʿAbd al-ʿAzīz ʿAbd al-Muʿṭī (1985), *Qaḍiyyat al-iʿjāz al-qur'ānī wa-atharuhā fī tadwīn al-balāgha al-ʿarabiyya* (Beirut: ʿĀlam al-Kutub).
Arslān, Shakīb (1994), "Al-ʿUrūba jāmiʿa kulliya", in Muḥammad Kāmil al-Khaṭīb (ed.), *Al-Qawmiyya wa-l-waḥda* (Damascus: Wazārat al-Thaqāfa), vol. 1, pp. 287–311. (First published in 1940.)
al-Arsūzī, Zakī (1972–6), *al-Mu'allafāt al-kāmila*, 6 vols (Damascus: Maṭābiʿ al-Idāra al-Siyāsiyya li-l-Jaysh wa-l-Quwwāt al-Musallaḥa).
ʿAṭṭār, Aḥmad ʿAbd al-Ghafūr (1965), *al-Zaḥf ʿalā lughat al-Qur'an* (Beirut: no publisher).
ʿAwaḍ, Luwīs (1947), *Plutoland* (Cairo: Maṭbaʿat al-Karnak).

—— (1965), *Mudhakkarāt ṭālib ba'tha* (Cairo: al-Kitāb al-Dhahabī).
—— (1993), *Muqaddima fī fiqh al-lugha al-'arabiyya* (Cairo: Dār Sīnā). (First published in 1980.)
'Awn, Mīkhā'īl (1983), "Ibrāhīm al-Yāzijī wa-l-'urūba", *al-Bāḥith*, 26: 137–45.
al-'Aysamī, Shiblī (1994), "al-Tārīkh fī khidmat al-umma", in *Qirā'āt fī al-fikr al-qawmī*, vol. 3: *al-Qawmiyya al-'arabiyya wa-l-islām wa-l-tārīkh wa-l-insāniyya* (Beirut: Markiz Dirāsāt al-Waḥda al-'Arabiyya), pp. 130–3. (First published in *al-Ādāb*, 4 (1956): 17–19.)
'Ayyād, Shukrī (1992), "Munāqashat al-afkār lā i'dāmuhā", *al-Qāhira*, 119: 29.
'Āzūry, Najīb (n.d.), *Yaqẓat al-umma al-'arabiyya*, trans. from the French *Le Réveil de la nation arabe dans l'asie turque* by Aḥmad Abū Milḥim (Beirut: al-Mu'assasa al-'Arabiyya li-l-Dirāsāt wa-l-Nashr).
Ba'albakī, Ramzī (1984), "al-Naẓariyya al-lughawiyya 'ind al-'Alāylī", in *al-Shaykh 'Abdalla al-'Alāylī mufakkiran wa-lughawiyyan wa-faqīhan: dirāsāt wa-shahādāt* (Beirut: Ittiḥād al-Kuttāb al-Lubnāniyyīn wa-Dār Ibn Khaldūn), pp. 9–26.
Barakāt, Salīm (1977/8), *al-Fikr al-qawmī wa-ususuh al-falsafiyya 'ind Zakī al-Arsūzī* (Damascus: University of Damascus).
al-Barrī, 'Abdalla Khūrshīd (1992), *al-Qabā'il al-'arabiyya fī miṣr fī al-qurūn al-thalātha al-ūlā li-l-hijra* (Cairo: Al-Hay'a al-Miṣriyya al-'Āmma li-l-Kitāb).
al-Baṣīr, 'Abd al-Razzāq (1993a), "Ḥawl 'al-qawmiyya al-'arabiyya wa-l-ḥayā'", in *Qirā'āt fī al-fikr al-qawmī*, vol. 1: *al-Qawmiyya al-'arabiyya, fikratuhā wa-muqawwimātuhā* (Beirut: Markiz Dirāsāt al-Waḥda al-'Arabiyya), pp. 439–41. (First published in *al-Ādāb*, 7 (1960): 64–5.)
—— (1993b), "Tasmiyat al-khalīj bi-l-khalīj al-'arabī", in *Qirā'āt fī al-fikr al-qawmī*, vol. 3: *al-Qawmiyya al-'arabiyya wa-l-islām wa-l-tārīkh wa-l-insāniyya* (Beirut: Markiz Dirāsāt al-Waḥda al-'Arabiyya), pp. 351–4. (First published in *Majallat al-aqlām*, 1/8 (1965): 64–7.)
Bayhum, Muḥammad Jamīl (1957), *al-'Urūba wa-l-shu'ūbiyyāt al-ḥadītha* (Beirut: Dār al-Kashshāf).
al-Bazzāz, 'Abd al-Raḥmān (1956), *al-Tarbiya al-qawmiyya* (Baghdād: Maṭba'at al-'Ānī). (Pages 9–47 are reproduced in *Qirā'āt fī al-fikr al-qawmī*, vol. 1: *al-Qawmiyya al-'arabiyya, fikratuhā wa-muqawwimātuhā* (Beirut: Markiz Dirāsāt al-Waḥda al-'Arabiyya), pp. 259–79.
—— (1993), "Taḥrīr al-qawmiyya wa-ta'rīfuhā", in *Qirā'āt fī al-fikr al-qawmī*, vol. 1: *al-Qawmiyya al-'arabiyya, fikratuhā wa-muqawwimātuhā* (Beirut: Markiz Dirāsāt al-Waḥda al-'Arabiyya), pp. 524–55. (First published in 1964.)
bin Salāma, al-Bashīr (1974), *al-Shakhṣiyya al-tūnisiyya: khaṣā'iṣuhā wa-muqawwimātuhā* (Tunis: Mu'assasat 'Abd al-'Azīz bin 'Abdalla).
al-Bishrī, Ṭāriq (1982), *al-Muslimūn wa-l-aqbāṭ fī iṭār al-jamā'a al-waṭaniyya* (Beirut: Dār al-Waḥda).
—— (1998), *Bayn al-islām wa-l-'urūba* (Cairo: Dār al-Shurūq).
al-Bīṭār, Nadīm (1979), *Min al-tajzi'a ilā al-waḥda* (Beirut: Markiz Dirāsāt al-Waḥda al-'Arabiyya).
—— (1981), *Ḥudūd al-iqlīmiyya al-jadīda* (Beirut: Ma'had al-Inmā' al-'Arabī).

—— (1982), *Ḥudūd al-huwiyya al-qawmiyya* (Beirut: Dār al-Waḥda).
—— (1993), *Fī al-qawmiyya al-'arabiyya* (Baghdad: Maktabat al-Shabāb al-Qawmī), first published in 1948. (Pages 7–68 are reproduced in *Qirā'āt fī al-fikr al-qawmī*, vol. 1: *al-Qawmiyya al-'arabiyya, fikratuhā wa-muqawwimātuhā* (Beirut: Markiz Dirāsāt al-Waḥda al-'Arabiyya), pp. 182–208.)
Budūr, 'Alī (1993), "Min ẓalām al-tajzi'a ilā fajr al-waḥda", in *Qirā'āt fī al-fikr al-qawmī*, vol. 2: *al-Waḥda al-'arabiyya* (Beirut: Markiz Dirāsāt al-Waḥda al-'Arabiyya), pp. 219–33. (First published in *al-Ādāb*, 1 (1963): 3–4, 74–8.)
Būluṣ, Jawād (1973), *Lubnān wa-l-buldān al-mujāwira* (Beirut: Mu'assasat Badrān wa-Shurakāh li-l-Ṭibā'a wa-l-Nashr).
al-Bundāq, Muḥammad Ṣāliḥ (1980), *al-Mustashriqūn wa-tarjamat al-qur'ān al-karīm* (Beirut: Dār al-Āfāq al-Jadīda).
Burj, Muḥammad 'Abd al-Raḥmān (1992), *Miṣr wa-l-ḥaraka al-'arabiyya* (al-Hay'a al-Miṣriyya al-'Āmma li-l-Kitāb).
al-Dahhān, Ṣāliḥ 'Abdu (1993), "Ḥawl 'al-qawmiyya al-'arabiyya wa-l-mutashakkikūn'", in *Qirā'āt fī al-fikr al-qawmī*, vol. 1: *al-Qawmiyya al-'arabiyya, fikratuhā wa-muqawwimātuhā* (Beirut: Markiz Dirāsāt al-Waḥda al-'Arabiyya), pp. 442–5. (First published in *al-Ādāb*, 7 (1960): 64–5.)
Ḍāhir, Mas'ūd (1986), *al-Judhūr al-tārīkhiyya li-l-mas'ala al-ṭā'ifiyya al-lubnāniyya: 1697–1861* (Beirut: Ma'had al-Inmā' al-'Arabī). (First published in 1981.)
Dhihnī, Maḥmūd al-Ḥanafī (1990), "al-Dass al-shu'ūbī 'alā al-lugha al-'arabiyya wa-ādābihā", in *Waqā'i' al-nadwa al-qawmiyya li-muwājahat al-dass al-shu'ūbī* (Baghdad: Dār al-Ḥurriyya li-l-Ṭibā'a), vol. 3, pp. 189–214.
Dimashqiyya, 'Afīf (1984), "al-Shaykh 'Abdalla al-'Alāylī lughawiyyan", in *al-Shaykh 'Abdalla al-'Alāylī mufakkiran wa-lughawiyyan wa-faqīhan: dirāsāt wa-shahādāt* (Beirut: Ittiḥād al-Kuttāb al-Lubnāniyyīn wa-Dār Ibn Khaldūn), pp. 45–53.
Ḍūmaṭ, Jabr (1991), "al-'Arabiyya wa-l-madrasa al-kuliyya", in Yūsuf Qazmā Khūrī (ed.), *Najāḥ al-umma al-'arabiyya fī lughatihā al-aṣliyya* (Beirut: Dār al-Ḥamrā'), pp. 97–103.
al-Dūrī, 'Abd al-'Azīz (1960), *al-Judhūr al-tārīkhiyya li-l-qawmiyya al-'arabiyya* (Beirut: Dār al-'Ilm li-l-malāyīn).
—— (1981), *al-Judhūr al-tārīkhiyya li-l-shu'ūbiyya* (Beirut: Dār al-Ṭalī'a). (Third printing.)
—— (1982), "al-Islām wa-intishār al-lugha al-'arabiyya wa-l-ta'rīb", in *al-Qawmiyya al-'arabiyya wa-l-islām* (Beirut: Markiz Dirāsāt al-Waḥda al-'Arabiyya), pp. 61–90.
Fākhūrī, 'Umar (1981), *Kayfa yanhaḍ al-'arab?* (Beirut: Dār al-Āfāq al-Jadīda).
Faraḥ, Ilyās (1994), "al-Qawmiyya al-'arabiyya wa-l-tārīkh", in *Qirā'āt fī al-fikr al-qawmī*, vol. 3: *al-Qawmiyya al-'arabiyya wa-l-islām wa-l-tārīkh wa-l-insāniyya* (Beirut: Markiz Dirāsāt al-Waḥda al-'Arabiyya), pp. 118–27. (First delivered as a lecture in Aleppo in 1955 and published in Baghdad in 1973.)
Faraj, Nabīl (1992), "Luwīs 'Awaḍ amām maḥākim al-taftīsh", *al-Qāhira*, 119: 21–3.
Farḥāt, Aḥmad Ḥasan (1983), *al-Umma fī dalālatihā al-'arabiyya wa-l-qur'āniyya* (Amman: Dār 'Ammār li-l-Nashr wa-l-Tawzī').

Fayṣal, Shukrī (1971), "Tajrubat al-lugha ladā al-Ḥuṣrī", *al-Ma'rifa*, 13: 109–26.
al-Fiqqī, Muṣṭafā (1985), *al-Aqbāṭ fī al-siyāsa al-miṣriyya* (Cairo: Dār al-Shurūq).
Fück, Johan (1980), *al-'Arabiyya: dirāsāt fī al-lugha wa-l-lahajāt wa-l-asālīb*, trans. from the German by Ramaḍān 'Abd al-Tawwāb (Cairo: Maktabat al-Khānjī).
Ghalyūn, Burhān (1979), *al-Mas'ala al-ṭā'ifiyya wa-mushkilat al-aqaliyyāt* (Beirut: Dār al-Ṭalī'a).
al-Ghazālī, Muḥammad (1998), *Ḥaqīqat al-qawmiyya al-'arabiyya wa-usṭūrat al-ba'th al-'arabī* (Cairo: Nahḍat Miṣr).
al-Ḥājj, Kamāl Yūsuf (1959a), *Difā'an 'an al-'arabiyya* (Beirut: Manshūrāt 'Uwaydāt).
—— (1959b), *Fī al-qawmiyya wa-l-insāniyya* (Beirut: Manshūrāt 'Uwaydāt).
—— (1959c), *al-Qawmiyya laysat marḥala* (Beirut: Manshūrāt 'Uwaydāt).
—— (1966), *Fī ghurrat al-ḥaqīqa* (Beirut: Manshūrāt al-Nadwa al-Lubnāniyya).
—— (1978), *Fī falsafat al-lugha* (Beirut: Dār al-Nahār li-l-Nashr). (Second printing; first published in 1956.)
Ḥallāq, Ḥassān (1988), *al-Tayyārāt al-siyāsiyya fī lubnān: 1943–52* (Beirut: al-Dār al-Jāmi'iyya).
Hāshim, Ḥāzim (1992), "Asrār jadīda ḥawl *muqaddima fī fiqh al-lugha al-'arabiyya*", *al-Qāhira*, 119: 194–7.
Ḥāwī, Khalīl (1982), "al-Nahḍa wa-l-baḥth 'an al-huwiyya", *al-Fikr al-'arabī al-mu'āṣir*, 17: 30–45.
Haykal, Muḥammad Ḥusayn (1986), *Thawrat al-adab* (Cairo: Dār al-Ma'ārif). (First published in 1933.)
Ḥusayn, Muḥammad Muḥammad (1979), *al-Islām wa-l-ḥaḍāra al-gharbiyya* (Beirut: al-Maktab al-Islāmī).
—— (1983), *al-Ittijāhāt al-waṭaniyya fī al-adab al-mu'āṣir*, 2 vols (Beirut: Mu'assasat al-Risāla). (Sixth printing.)
Ḥusayn, Ṭāha (1944), *Mustaqbal al-thaqāfa fī miṣr* (Cairo: Maṭba'at al-Ma'ārif). (First published in 1938).
—— (1957), "al-Lugha al-fuṣḥā wa-ta'līm al-sha'b", *Majallat al-majma' al-'ilmī al-'arabī*, 32: 44–56.
—— (1982), *Khiṣām wa-naqd* (Beirut: Dār al-'Ilm li-l-Malāyīn). (Eleventh printing.)
—— (1985), *Kalimāt* (Beirut: Dār al-'Ilm li-l-Malāyīn). (Fifth printing.)
al-Ḥuṣrī, Sāṭi' (1984a), *Ārā' wa-aḥādīth fī al-waṭaniyya wa-l-qawmiyya*, vol. 1 (Beirut: Markiz Dirāsāt al-Waḥda al-'Arabiyya).
—— (1984b), *Aḥādīth fī al-tarbiya wa-l-ijtimā'*, vol. 2 (Beirut: Markiz Dirāsāt al-Waḥda al-'Arabiyya).
—— (1985a), *al-'Urūba bayn du'ātihā wa-mu'āriḍīhā*, vol. 4 (Beirut: Markiz Dirāsāt al-Waḥda al-'Arabiyya).
—— (1985b), *Muḥāḍarāt fī nushū' al-fikra al-qawmiyya*, vol. 5 (Beirut: Markiz Dirāsāt al-Waḥda al-'Arabiyya).
—— (1985c), *Ārā' wa-aḥādīth fī al-'ilm wa-l-akhlāq wa-l-thaqāfa*, vol. 6 (Beirut: Markiz Dirāsāt al-Waḥda al-'Arabiyya).
—— (1985d), *Ārā' wa-aḥādīth fī al-qawmiyya al-'arabiyya*, vol. 7 (Beirut: Markiz Dirāsāt al-Waḥda al-'Arabiyya).

—— (1985e), *Ārā' wa-aḥādīth fī al-tārīkh wa-l-ijtimā'*, vol. 8 (Beirut: Markiz Dirāsāt al-Waḥda al-'Arabiyya).

—— (1985f), *al-'Urūba awwalan*, vol. 9 (Beirut: Markiz Dirāsāt al-Waḥda al-'Arabiyya).

—— (1985g), *Difā' 'an al-'urūba*, vol. 10 (Beirut: Markiz Dirāsāt al-Waḥda al-'Arabiyya).

—— (1985h), *Fī al-lugha wa-l-adab wa-'alāqatihimā bi-l-qawmiyya*, vol. 11 (Beirut: Markiz Dirāsāt al-Waḥda al-'Arabiyya).

—— (1985i), *Ḥawl al-waḥda al-thaqāfiyya al-'arabiyya*, vol. 12 (Beirut: Markiz Dirāsāt al-Waḥda al-'Arabiyya).

—— (1985j), *Ḥawl al-qawmiyya al-'arabiyya*, vol. 14 (Beirut: Markiz Dirāsāt al-Waḥda al-'Arabiyya).

Ibn 'Abd Rabbih, Shihāb al-Dīn Aḥmad (1928), *al-'Iqd al-farīd*, 4 vols (Cairo: al-Maṭba'a al-Azhariyya).

Ibn al-Qayyim, Shams al-Dīn Abū 'Abdalla Muḥammad Ibn Abū Bakr Ibn Ayyūb al-Zar'ī (n.d.), *al-Fawā'id al-mushawwiq ilā 'ulūm al-qur'ān wa-'ilm al-bayān* (Beirut: Dār al-Kutub al-'Ilmiyya).

Ibn al-Sarrāj, Abū Bakr Muḥammad Ibn Sahl (1985), *al-Uṣūl fī al-naḥw*, 2 vols, ed. 'Abd al-Ḥusayn al-Fatlī (Beirut: Mu'assasat al-Risāla).

Ibn Durayd, Abū Bakr Muḥammad Ibn al-Ḥasan (1958), *al-Ishtiqāq*, ed. 'Abd al-Salām Muḥammad Hārūn (Cairo: Maktabat al-Khānjī).

Ibn Fāris, Abū al-Ḥusayn Aḥmad (1993), *al-Ṣāḥibī fī fiqh al-lugha wa-masā'ilihā wa-sunan al-'arab fī kalāmihā*, ed. 'Umar Fārūq al-Ṭabbā' (Beirut: Maktabat al-Ma'ārif).

Ibn Ḥazm, Abū Muḥammad 'Alī Ibn Aḥmad (1984), *al-Iḥkām fī uṣūl al-aḥkām*, 6 vols (Cairo: Dār al-Ḥadīth).

Ibn Ja'far, Qudāma (1982), *Naqd al-nathr* (Beirut: Dār al-Kutub al-'Ilmiyya).

Ibn Jinnī, Abū al-Fatḥ 'Uthmān (n.d.), *al-Khaṣā'iṣ*, 3 vols, ed. Muḥammad 'Alī al-Najjār (Beirut: Dār al-Kitāb al-Lubnānī).

—— (1993), *Sirr ṣinā'at al-i'rāb*, 2 vols, ed. Ḥasan Hindāwī (Damascus: Dār al-Qalam).

Ibn Qutayba, Abū Muḥammad 'Abdalla Ibn Muslim (n.d.), *Adab al-kātib*, ed. Muḥammad Muḥyī al-Dīn 'Abd al-Ḥalīm (Beirut: Dār al-Maṭbū'āt al-'Arabiyya).

—— (1913), *Kitāb al-'arab*, in *Rasā'il al-Bulaghā'*, ed. Muḥammad Kurd 'Alī (Cairo: Dār al-Kutub al-'Arabiyya al-Kubrā).

Ibrāhīm, 'Amr (1981/2), "Mafhūm al-umma bayn lugha wa-ukhrā", trans. from the French by Adūnīs al-'Akr, *al-Fikr al-'arabī al-mu'āṣir*, 17: 64–77.

Jabbūr, 'Abdalla (1991), "Muḥibbū al-taqaddum li-l-'arab hum yufaḍḍilūn ta'līmahum bi-l-lugha al-'arabiyya 'alayh fī mā siwāhā", in Yūsuf Qazmā Khūrī (ed.), *Najāḥ al-umma al-'arabiyya fī lughatihā al-aṣliyya* (Beirut: Dār al-Ḥamrā'), pp. 17–19.

al-Jābirī, Muḥammad 'Ābid (1995), *Mas'alat al-huwiyya: al-'urūba wa-l-islām wa-l-gharb* (Beirut: Markiz Dirāsāt al-Waḥda al-'Arabiyya).

al-Jāḥiẓ, Abū 'Uthmān Ibn Baḥr (1932), *al-Bayān wa-l-tabyīn*, 3 vols, ed. Ḥasan al-Sandūsī (Cairo: al-Maṭba'a al-Raḥmāniyya).

—— (1938–45), *al-Ḥayawān*, 6 vols, ed. ʿAbd al-Salām Muḥammad Hārūn (Cairo: Maktabat Muṣṭafā al-Bābī al-Ḥalabī wa-Awlādih).

—— (1964), *Rasāʾil al-Jāḥiẓ*, ed. ʿAbd al-Salām Muḥammad Hārūn (Cairo: Maktabat al-Khānjī).

—— (1969), *al-Maḥāsin wa-l-aḍdād*, ed. Fawzī ʿAṭawī (Beirut: al-Sharika al-Lubnāniyya li-l-Kitāb).

Jalāl, Muḥammad Nuʿmān and Majdī al-Mutawallī (1997), *Huwiyyat miṣr* (Cairo: al-Hayʾa al-Miṣriyya al-ʿĀmma li-l-Kitāb).

al-Jamīʿī, ʿAbd al-Munʿim al-Dasūqī (1983), *Majmaʿ al-lugha al-ʿarabiyya: dirāsa tārīkhiyya* (Cairo: al-Hayʾa al-Miṣriyya al-ʿĀmma li-l-Kitāb).

Jeha, Michel (1992), *Ibrāhīm al-Yāziji* (London: Riyad El-Rayyes Books Ltd).

al-Jundī, Anwar (1977), *Ṭāha Ḥusayn: ḥayātuh wa-fikruh fī mīzān al-islām* (Cairo: Dār al-Iʿtiṣām).

—— (1982), *al-Fuṣḥā lughat al-Qurʾān* (Beirut: Dār al-Kitāb al-Lubnānī).

—— (1984), *Muḥākamat fikr Ṭāha Ḥusayn* (Cairo: Dār al-Iʿtiṣām).

al-Khafājī, Ibn Sinān Abū Muḥammad ʿAbdalla Ibn Muḥammad Ibn Saʿīd (1982), *Sirr al-faṣāḥa* (Beirut: Dār al-Kutub al-ʿIlmiyya).

Khalafalla, Muḥammad Aḥmad (1981), "al-Takwīn al-tārīkhī li-mahāfīm al-umma, al-qawmiyya, al-waṭaniyya, al-dawla wa-l-ʿalāqa fīmā baynahā", in *al-Qawmiyya al-ʿarabiyya wa-l-islām* (Beirut: Markaz Dirāsāt al-Waḥda al-ʿArabiyya), pp. 17–29.

—— (1990), *ʿUrūbat al-islām* (Rabat: al-Majlis al-Qawmī li-l-Thaqāfa al-ʿArabiyya).

—— (1992) "al-Turāth al-islāmī shahid al-ikhtilāf al-fikrī", *al-Qāhira*, 119: 30–1.

Khalīfa, ʿIṣām Kamāl (1985), *Fī muʿtarak al-qaḍiyya al-lubnāniyya* (no place of publication or publisher).

al-Kharbūṭlī, ʿAlī Ḥusnī (n.d.), *al-Qawmiyya al-ʿarabiyya min al-fajr ilā al-ẓuhr* (Cairo: ʿĪsā al-Bābī al-Ḥalabī wa-Shurakāh).

al-Khaṭīb, Muḥammad ʿAlī (1983), *al-Ṣirāʿ al-adabī maʿ al-shuʿūbiyya: al-Jāḥiẓ [wa-] al-shāʿir al-Qarawī* (Beirut: Dār al-Ḥadātha).

Khāṭir, Fuʾād al-Mursī (1985), *Ḥawl al-fikra al-ʿarabiyya fī miṣr: dirāsa fī tārīkh al-fikr al-miṣrī al-muʿāṣir* (Cairo: al-Hayʾa al-Miṣriyya al-ʿĀmma li-l-Kitāb).

Khūrī, Raʾīf (1984), "Marjiʿ al-ʿAlāylī wa-l-muʿānā al-ījābiyya li-mashākil al-ʿarabiyya", in *al-Shaykh ʿAbdalla al-ʿAlāylī mufakkiran wa-lughawiyyan wa-faqīhan: dirāsāt wa-shahādāt* (Beirut: Ittiḥād al-Kuttāb al-Lubnāniyyīn wa-Dār Ibn Khaldūn), pp. 171–83.

Khūrī, Yūsuf Qazmā (ed.) (1991), *Najāḥ al-umma al-ʿarabiyya fī lughatihā al-aṣliyya* (Beirut: Dār al-Ḥamrāʾ).

—— (ed.) (1993a), *al-Shaykh Ibrāhīm al-Yāzijī: Abḥāth lughawiyya* (Beirut: Dār al-Ḥamrāʾ).

—— (ed.) (1993b), *Asʾila ilā majallat al-bayān wa-l-ḍiyāʾ wa-ajwibat al-Shaykh Ibrāhīm al-Yāzijī ʿalayhā (1897–1906)* (Beirut: Dār al-Ḥamrāʾ).

Kīlānī, Muḥammad Sayyid (n.d.), *al-Adab al-qibṭī qadīman wa-ḥadīthan* (Cairo: Dār al-Farajānī).

Laḥḥūd, ʿAbdalla (1993), *Lubnān: ʿarabī al-wajh, ʿarabī al-lisān* (Beirut: Dār al-ʿIlm li-l-Malāyīn).

Luṭfī al-Sayyid, Aḥmad (1945), *al-Muntakhabāt*, 2 vols (Cairo: Maktabat al-Anglū al-Miṣriyya).

Maḥāfẓa, 'Alī (1980), *al-Ittijāhāt al-fikriyya 'ind al-'arab fī 'aṣr al-nahḍa, 1789–1914: al-ittijāhāt al-dīniyya wa-l-siyāsiyya wa-l-ijtimā'iyya wa-l-'ilmiyya* (Beirut: al-Ahliyya li-l-Nashr wa-l-Tawzī'). (Third printing.)

al-Malā'ika, Nāzik (1993a), "al-Qawmiyya al-'arabiyya wa-l-ḥāya", in *Qirā'āt fī al-fikr al-qawmī*, vol. 1: *al-Qawmiyya al-'arabiyya, fikratuhā wa-muqawwimātuhā* (Beirut: Markiz Dirāsāt al-Waḥda al-'Arabiyya), pp. 414–22. (First published in *al-Ādāb*, 5 (1960): 1–4, 67–8.)

—— (1993b), "al-Qawmiyya al-'arabiyya wa-l-mutashakkikūn", in *Qirā'āt fī al-fikr al-qawmī*, vol. 1: *al-Qawmiyya al-'arabiyya, fikratuhā wa-muqawwimātuhā* (Beirut: Markiz Dirāsāt al-Waḥda al-'Arabiyya), pp. 423–31. (First published in *al-Ādāb*, 7 (1960): 1–5.)

al-Marrākishī, Muḥammad Ṣāliḥ (1985), *Muḥammad Rashīd Riḍā min khilāl majallat al-manār (1898–1935)* (Tunis: al-Dār al-Tūnisiyya li-l-Nashr).

al-Marṣafī, Ḥasan (1982), *Risālat al-kalim al-thamān*, ed. Khālid Ziyāda (Beirut: Dār al-Ṭalī'a).

—— (1984), *Risālat al-kalim al-thamān*, ed. Aḥmad Zakariyyā al-Shilq (Cairo: al-Hay'a al-Miṣriyya al-'Āmma li-l-Kitāb).

Maṭar, 'Abd al-'Azīz (1967), *Laḥn al-'āmma fī ḍaw' al-dirāsāt al-lughawiyya al-ḥadītha* (Cairo: Dār al-Kātib al-'Arabī li-l-Ṭibā'a wa-l-Nashr).

Maṭlūb, Aḥmad (1987), *Mu'jam al-muṣṭalaḥāt al-balāghiyya wa-taṭawwurihā*, 3 vols (Baghdad: al-Majma' al-'Ilmī al-'Irāqī).

al-Mi'dāwī, Hānī (1978), "al-Aqbāṭ wa-qaḍiyyat al-'urūba", *al-Fikr al-'arabī*, 54–5: 352–65.

Mijlī, Nasīm (1995), *Luwīs 'Awaḍ wa-ma'ārikuh al-adabiyya* (Cairo: al-Hay'a al-Miṣriyya al-'Āmma li-l-Kitāb).

Mruwwa, Ḥusayn (1984), "al-Shaykh 'Abdalla al-'Alāylī faqīhan", in *al-Shaykh 'Abdalla al-'Alāylī mufakkiran wa-lughawiyyan wa-faqīhan: dirāsāt wa-shahādāt* (Beirut: Ittiḥād al-Kuttāb al-Lubnāniyyīn wa-Dār Ibn Khaldūn), pp. 115–54.

Muḥammad, 'Abd al-'Āṭī (1978), "Taṭawwur al-fikra al-'arabiyya fī miṣr", *al-Fikr al-'arabī*, 54–5: 295–318.

Muḥammad, Laṭīf Karīm (1990), "al-Shu'ūbiyya al-ḥadītha: al-wasā'il wa-l-ahdāf", in *Waqā'i' al-nadwa al-qawmiyya li-muwājahat al-dass al-shu'ūbī* (Baghdad: Dār al-Ḥurriyya li-l-Ṭibā'a), vol. 3, pp. 9–30.

Muḥammad, Sayyid Muḥammad (1996), *Haykal wa-l-siyāsa al-usbū'iyya* (Cairo: al-Hay'a al-Miṣriyya al-'Āmma li-l-Kitāb).

al-Muḥtasib, 'Abd al-Majīd (1980), *Ṭāha Ḥusayn mufakkiran* (Amman: Maktabat al-Nahḍa al-Islāmiyya).

Mūsā, Salāma (1947), *al-Balāgha al-'aṣriyya wa-l-lugha al-'arabiyya* (Salāma Mūsā li-l-Nashr wa-l-Tawzī'). (First published in 1945.)

—— (1964), *Miṣr aṣl al-ḥaḍāra* (Salāma Mūsā li-l-Nashr wa-l-Tawzī'). (First published in 1935.)

—— (1998), *al-Yawm wa-l-ghad* (Salāma Mūsā li-l-Nashr wa-l-Tawzī'). (First published in 1928.)

Muṣṭafā, Ibrāhīm (1959), *Iḥyā' al-naḥw* (Cairo: Lajnat al-Ta'līf wa-l-Tarjama wa-l-Nashr). (First published in 1937.)

al-Mutanabbī, Abū al-Ṭayyib (1938), *Sharḥ dīwān al-Mutanabbī*, 4 vols, ed. 'Abd al-Raḥmān al-Barqūqī (Cairo: Maṭba'at al-Istiqāma).

al-Naqqāsh, Rajā' (1988), *al-In'izāliyyūn fī miṣr* (Riyadh: Dār al-Marrīkh).

—— (1993), "al-Qawmiyya al-'arabiyya wa-l-khayāliyyūn", in *Qirā'āt fī al-fikr al-qawmī*, vol. 1: *al-Qawmiyya al-'arabiyya, fikratuhā wa-muqawwimātuhā* (Beirut: Markiz Dirāsāt al-Waḥda al-'Arabiyya), pp. 446–54. (First published in *al-Ādāb*, 8 (1960): 1–4.)

Naṣr, Naṣr al-Dīn 'Abd-l-Ḥamīd (1984), *Miṣr wa-ḥarakat al-jāmi'a al-islāmiyya: 1882–1914* (Cairo: al-Hay'a al-Miṣriyya al-'Āmma li-l-Kitāb).

Naṣṣār, Ḥusayn (1980), *Miṣr al-'arabiyya* (Beirut: Iqra').

Naṣṣār, Nāṣīf (1981), *Naḥw mujtama' jadīd: muqaddimāt asāsiyya fī naqd al-mujtam' al-ṭā'ifī* (Beirut: Dār al-Ṭalī'a). (First published in 1970.)

—— (1992), *Mafhūm al-umma bayn al-dīn wa-l-tārīkh: dirāsa fī madlūl al-umma fī al-turāth al-'arabī wa-l-islāmī* (Beirut: Dār Amwāj). (First published in 1978.)

—— (1994), *Taṣawwurāt al-umma al-mu'āṣira: dirāsa taḥlīliyya li-mafāhīm al-umma fī al-fikr al-ḥadīth wa-l-mu'āṣir* (Beirut: Dār Amwāj). (First published in 1986.)

Nūḥ, 'Alī (1994), "Ishkāliyyat al-lugha al-falsafiyya 'ind Zakī al-Arsūzī", *al-Fikr al-'arabī*, 76: 67–84.

al-Nuṣṣ, 'Izzat (1994), "al-Tārīkh bayna al-qawmiyya wa-l-insāniyya", in *Qirā'āt fī al-fikr al-qawmī*, vol. 3: *al-qawmiyya al-'arabiyya wa-l-islām wa-l-tārīkh wa-l-insāniyya* (Beirut: Markiz Dirāsāt al-Waḥda al-'Arabiyya), pp. 193–211. (First published in *al-Ādāb*, 6 (1961): 69–72.)

Qaddūra, Zāhiya (1972), *al-Shu'ūbiyya wa-atharuhā al-ijtimā'ī wa-l-siyāsī fī al-ḥayāt al-islāmiyya fī al-'aṣr al-'abbāsī al-awwal* (Beirut: Dār al-Kitāb al-Lubnānī).

al-Qālī, Abū 'Alī Ismā'īl Ibn al-Qāsim (1978), *al-Amālī fī lughat al-'arab*, 2 vols (Beirut: Dār al-Kutub al-'Ilmiyya).

Qandīl, Bayyūmī (1992), "Nanquduh lā nuṣādiruh", *al-Qāhira*, 119: 32–8.

Qarqūṭ, Dhūqān (1972), *Taṭawwur al-fikra al-'arabiyya fī miṣr* (Beirut: al-Mu'assasa al-'Arabiyya li-l-Dirāsāt wa-l-Nashr).

al-Qāsimī, Ṣalāḥ al-Dīn (1959), *Āthāruh: ṣafaḥāt min tārīkh al-nahḍa al-'arabiyya fī awā'il al-qarn al-'ishrīn*, ed. Muḥibb al-Dīn al-Khaṭīb (Cairo: al-Maṭba'a al-Salafiyya).

al-Qaysī, Nūrī Ḥamūdī (1986), "al-Fikr al-qawmī wa-iḥyā' al-turāth", in *Taṭawwur al-fikr al-qawmī al-'arabī* (Beirut: Markiz Dirāsāt al-Waḥda al-'Arabiyya), pp. 73–87.

al-Qirnī, 'Izzat (1995), *Fī al-fikr al-miṣrī al-ḥadīth* (Cairo: al-Hay'a al-Miṣriyya al-'Āmma li-l-Kitāb).

al-Rāfi'ī, Muṣṭafā Ṣādiq (1974), *Taḥt rāyat al-Qur'ān* (Beirut: Dār al-Kitāb al-'Arabī). (Seventh printing.)

Rāghib, Nabīl (1989), *A'lām al-tanwīr al-mu'āṣir* (Cairo: al-Hay'a al-Miṣriyya al-'Āmma li-l-Kitāb).

Ra'ūf, 'Imād 'Abd al-Salām (1986), "al-Jam'iyyāt al-'arabiyya wa-fikruhā al-qawmī: malāmiḥ al-fikr al-qawmī 'ind al-'arab mundh maṭla' al-qarn al-tāsi' 'ashar ḥattā qiyām al-ḥarb al-ʿālamiyya al-ūlā", in *Taṭawwur al-fikr al-qawmī al-ʿarabī* (Beirut: Markiz Dirāsāt al-Waḥda al-ʿArabiyya), pp. 103–34.

al-Rīḥānī, Amīn (1929), *Mulūk al-ʿarab* (Beirut: al-Maṭbaʿa al-ʿIlmiyya).

Rondot, Pierre (1984), *al-Ṭawāʾif fī al-dawla al-lubnāniyya* (Beirut: Mu'assasat Dār al-Kitāb al-Ḥadīth). (Translated from the French *Les Communautés dans l'Etat libanais*.)

Rukaybī, ʿAbdalla (1992), *al-Frankūfūniyya mashriqan wa-maghriban* (Beirut: Dār al-Ruwwād).

Saʿāda, Anṭūn (1976), *al-Inʿizāliyya aflasat* (Manshūrāt ʿUmdat al-Thaqāfa fī al-Ḥizb al-Sūrī al-Qawmī al-Ijtimāʿī).

—— (1993), *Mukhtārat fī al-qawmiyya al-ijtimāʿiyya* (Beirut: Dār Fikr li-l-Abḥāth wa-l-Nashr).

—— (1994), *Nushūʾ al-umam* (no place of publication or publisher).

Saʿd, ʿAlī (1984), "al-Buʿd al-siyāsī wa-l-ijtimāʿī fī kitābāt al-Shaykh ʿAbdalla al-ʿAlāylī", in *al-Shaykh ʿAbdalla al-ʿAlāylī mufakkiran wa-lughawiyyan wa-faqīhan: dirāsāt wa-shahādāt* (Beirut: Ittiḥād al-Kuttāb al-Lubnāniyyīn wa-Dār Ibn Khaldūn), pp. 55–114.

Saʿd, Nihād Ṣabīḥ (1979), *al-Fikr al-tarbawī ʿind Sāṭiʿ al-Ḥuṣrī: taḥlīluh wa-taqwīmuh* (Basra: Maṭbaʿat Dār al-Kutub, University of Basra).

Saʿīd, Naffūsa Zakariyyā (1964), *Tārīkh al-Daʿwa ilā al-ʿāmiyya wa-āthāruhā fī miṣr* (Cairo: Maṭbaʿat Dār Nashr al-Thaqāfa).

Ṣalībā, Jamīl (1993), "al-Ṭābiʿ al-insānī li-l-qawmiyya al-ʿarabiyya", in *Qirāʾāt fī al-fikr al-qawmī*, vol. 1: *al-Qawmiyya al-ʿarabiyya, fikratuhā wa-muqawwimātuhā* (Beirut: Markiz Dirāsāt al-Waḥda al-ʿArabiyya), pp. 499–514. (First published in 1962.)

Sālim, Ḥilmī (1992), "Lughat al-samāʾ wa-lughat al-arḍ", *al-Qāhira*, 119: 10–20.

Sāṭiʿ al-Ḥuṣrī: thalāthūn ʿām ʿalā al-raḥīl (symposium) (1999) (Beirut: Markiz Dirāsāt al-Waḥda al-ʿArabiyya).

al-Sayyid, Raḍwān (1990), "al-ʿArab wa-l-ʿurūba wa-lʿarabiyya: min mafāhīm al-huwiyya wa-l-umma wa-l-dawla fī al-fikr al-ʿarabī al-islāmī", in *Waqāʾiʿ al-nadwa al-qawmiyya li-muwājahat al-dass al-shuʿūbī* (Baghdad: Dār al-Ḥurriyya li-l-Ṭibāʿa), vol. 1, pp. 5–26.

al-Shaḥḥādh, Aḥmad Muḥammad (1990), "Khaṭar al-shuʿūbiyya ʿalā huwiyyat al-lugha al-ʿarabiyya", in *Waqāʾiʿ al-nadwa al-qawmiyya li-muwājahat al-dass al-shuʿūbī* (Baghdad: Dār al-Ḥurriyya li-l-Ṭibāʿa), vol. 1, pp. 337–51.

Shāhīn, Fu'ād (n.d.), *al-Ṭāʾifiyya fī lubnān: ḥāḍiruhā wa-judhūruhā al-tārīkhiyya wa-l-ijtimāʿiyya* (Beirut: Dār al-Ḥadātha).

Shākir, Maḥmūd Muḥammad (1972), *Abāṭīl wa-asmār* (Cairo: Maṭbaʿat al-Madanī). (First published in 1965.)

Sharāra, ʿAbd al-Laṭīf (1988), *Waḥdat al-ʿarab fī al-shiʿr al-ʿarabī: dirāsa wa-nuṣūṣ shiʿriyya* (Beirut: Markiz Dirāsāt al-Waḥda al-ʿArabiyya).

al-Shayyāl, Jamāl al-Dīn (1951), *Tārīkh al-tarjama wa-l-ḥaraka al-thaqāfiyya fī ʿaṣr Muḥammad ʿAlī* (Dār al-Fikr al-ʿArabī).

Shukrī, Ghālī (1983), *Salāma Mūsā wa-azamat al-ḍamīr al-ʿarabī* (Beirut: Dār al-Āfāq al-Jadīda).

Shūmalī, Qusṭandī (1996), *Madkhal ilā 'ilm al-tarjama* (Jerusalem: Jam'iyyat al-Dirāsāt al-'Arabiyya).
Skāf, George (1960), *Ḥaqā'iq lubnāniyya* (Beirut: Dār Maktabat al-Ḥayāt).
al-Suyūṭī, 'Abd al-Raḥmān Jalāl al-Dīn (1986), *al-Muzhir fī 'ulūm al-lugha wa-anwā'ihā*, 2 vols, ed. Muḥammad Aḥmad Jād al-Mawlā, 'Alī Muḥammad al-Bajāwī and Muḥammad Abū al-Faḍl Ibrāhīm (Sidon and Beirut: al-Maktaba al-'Aṣriyya).
al-Ṭahṭāwī, Rifā'a Rāfi' (1981), *al-A'māl al-kāmila*, vol. 5: *Fī al-dīn wa-l-lugha wa-l-adab*, ed. Muḥammad 'Amāra (Beirut: al-Mu'assasa al-'Arabiyya li-l-Dirāsāt wa-l-Nashr).
Ṭarābīshī, George (1982), *al-Dawla al-quṭriyya wa-l-naẓariyya al-qawmiyya* (Beirut: Dār al-Ṭalī'a).
—— (1993), *Madhbaḥat al-turāth fī al-thaqāfa al-'arabiyya al-mu'āṣira* (London and Beirut: Dār al-Sāqī).
Tarḥīnī, Fāyiz (1985), *al-Shaykh 'Abdalla al-'Alāylī wa-l-tajdīd fī al-fikr al-mu'āṣir* (Beirut and Paris: Manshūrāt 'Uwaydāt).
al-Ṭawīl, Rizq (1992), "al-Muḥāwara aqwā min al-muṣādara", *al-Qāhira*, 119: 24–8.
al-Tha'ālibī, Abū Manṣūr (1938), *Fiqh al-lugha wa-sirr al-'arabiyya*, ed. Muṣṭafā al-Saqqā, Ibrāhīm al-Abyārī and 'Abd al-Ḥafīẓ Shalabī (Cairo: Sharikat Maktabat wa-Maṭba'at Muṣṭafā al-Bābī al-Ḥalabī wa-Awlādih bi-Miṣr).
al-Ṭūfī, Abū al-Rabī' Najm al-Dīn Sulaymān Ibn 'Abd al-Qawiyy Ibn 'Abd al-Karīm (1997), *al-Ṣa'qa al-ghaḍabiyya fī al-radd 'alā munkirī al-'arabiyya*, ed. Muḥammad Ibn Khālid al-Fāḍil (Riyadh: Maktabat al-'Ubaykāt).
'Umar, Aḥmad Mukhtār (1970), *Tārīkh al-lugha al-'arabiyya fī miṣr* (Cairo: al-Hay'a al-Miṣriyya al-'Āmma li-l-Ta'līf wa-l-Nashr).
al-'Uraysī, 'Abd al-Ghanī (1981), *Mukhtārāt al-mufīd*, ed. Nājī 'Allūsh (Beirut: Dār al-Ṭalī'a).
'Uways, Muḥammad (1977), *al-Mujtama' al-'abbāsī min khilāl kitābāt al-Jāḥiẓ* (Cairo: Dār al-Thaqāfa li-l-Ṭibā'a wa-l-Nashr).
Zabādiya, 'Abd al-Qādir (1982), "Dawr al-islām wa-l-'arabiyya (lugha wa-thaqāfa) fī takwīn muqawwimāt al-qawmiyya al-'arabiyya wa fī ba'th al-wa'y al-qawmī al-'arabī", in *al-Qawmiyya al-'arabiyya wa-l-islām* (Beirut: Markiz Dirāsāt al-Waḥda al-'Arabiyya), pp. 111–18.
Zahrān, al-Badrāwī 'Abd al-Wahhāb (1985), *Daḥḍ muftarayāt ḍidd i'jāz al-Qur'an wa-lughatih wa-abāṭīl ukhrā ikhtalaqahā al-ṣalībī al-mustaghrib al-duktūr Luwīs 'Awaḍ* (Mecca: Rābiṭat al-'Ālam al-Islāmī).
al-Zajjājī, Abū al-Qāsim (1959), *al-Īḍāḥ fī 'ilal al-naḥw*, ed. Māzin al-Mubārak (Cairo: Dār al-'Urūba).
Zakī, Ṣalāḥ (1983), *Miṣr wa-l-mas'ala al-qawmiyya: baḥth fī 'urūbat miṣr* (Cairo: Dār al-Mustaqbal al-'Arabī).
Zalaṭ, Aḥmad (1988), *al-Duktūr Muḥammad Ḥusayn Haykal bayn al-ḥaḍāratayn al-islāmiyya wa-l-gharbiyya* (Cairo: al-Hay'a al-Miṣriyya al-'Āmma li-l-Kitāb).
al-Zamakhsharī, Abū al-Qāsim Maḥmūd Ibn 'Umar (1840), *al-Mufaṣṣal fī al-naḥw*, ed. J. P. Broch (Christianiae: Libraria P. T. Mallingii).

al-Zaraklī, Khayr al-Dīn (1995), *al-Aʿlām* (Beirut: Dār al-ʿIlm li-l-Malāyīn). (Fifth printing.)

Zaydān, Jurjī (n.d.), *al-Inqilāb al-ʿuthmānī* (Cairo: Dār al-Hilāl).

Ziyāda, Niqūlā (1950), *al-ʿUrūba fī mīzān al-qawmiyya* (Beirut: Dār al-ʿIlm li-l-Malāyīn).

Zurayq, Qunsṭanṭīn (1959), *Naḥnu wa-l-tārīkh* (Beirut: Dār al-ʿIlm li-l-Malāyīn).

WORKS IN OTHER LANGUAGES CITED IN THE TEXT

Abou, S. (1962), *Le Bilinguisme arabe-français au Liban: essai d'anthropologie culturelle* (Paris: Presses Universitaires de France).

Abuhamdia, Zakaria (1995), "Orthography Policy-making by Fiat: The Policy to Romanise Somali", *Journal of King Saud University*, 7: 49–69.

Abu-Manneh, Butrus (1980), "The Christians between Ottomanism and Syrian Nationalism: The Ideas of Butrus al-Bustani", *International Journal of Middle Eastern Studies*, 2: 287–304.

Ahmad, Feroz (1969), *The Young Turks: The Committee of Union and Progress in Turkish Politics, 1908–1914* (Oxford: Clarendon Press).

Ahmed, Jamal Mohammed (1960), *The Intellectual Origins of Egyptian Nationalism* (London: Oxford University Press).

Allen, Irving Lewis (1983), *The Language of Ethnic Conflict: Social Organisation and Lexical Culture* (New York: Columbia University Press).

Amara, Muhammad and Bernard Spolsky (1996), "The Construction of Identity in a Divided Palestinian Village: Sociolinguistic Evidence", in Yasir Suleiman (ed.), *Language and Identity in the Middle East and North Africa* (Richmond, Surrey: Curzon Press), pp. 81–99.

Anderson, Benedict (1991), *Imagined Communities* (London and New York: Verso).

Antonius, George (1938), *The Arab Awakening: The Story of the Arab National Movement* (London: Hamish Hamilton).

Arab Baʿth Party (1962), "Constitution", in Sylvia G. Haim (ed.), *Arab Nationalism: An Anthology* (Berkeley, CA: University of California Press), pp. 233–41.

Armbrust, Walter (1996), *Mass Culture and Modernism in Egypt* (Cambridge: Cambridge University Press).

Armstrong, John A. (1982), *Nations before Nationalism* (Chapel Hill, NC: University of North Carolina Press).

Badawi, M. M. (1985), *Modern Arabic Literature and the West* (London: Ithaca Press).

Balibar, Étienne (1991), "The Nation Form", in Étienne Balibar and Immanuel Wallerstein (eds), *Race, Nation, Class* (London and New York: Verso).

Balibar, Étienne and Immanuel Wallerstein (eds) (1991), *Race, Nation, Class* (London and New York: Verso).

Baron, Beth (1997), "Nationalist Iconography: Egypt as a Woman", in James Jankowski and Israel Gershoni (eds), *Rethinking Nationalism in the Arab Middle East* (New York: Columbia University Press), pp. 105–24.

Barth, Fredrik (ed.) (1969), *Ethnic Groups and Boundaries* (Boston, MA: Little, Brown).

Bartlett, Robert (1994), *The Making of Europe: Conquest, Colonisation and Cultural Change (950–1350)* (Harmondsworth: Penguin).

Bayhum, Muḥammad Jamīl (1962), "Arabism and Jewry in Syria", in Sylvia G. Haim (ed.), *Arab Nationalism: An Anthology* (Berkeley, CA: University of California Press), pp. 128–46.

al-Bazzāz, ʿAbd al-Raḥmān (1962), "Islam and Arab Nationalism", in Sylvia G. Haim (ed.), *Arab Nationalism: An Anthology* (Berkeley, CA: University of California Press), pp. 172–88.

Bengio, Ofra (1998), *Saddam's Word: Political Discourse in Iraq* (Oxford: Oxford University Press).

Ben-Rafael, Eliezer (1994), *Language, Identity and Division: The Case of Israel* (Oxford: Clarendon Press).

Blau, Joshua (1963), "The Role of the Bedouins as Arbiters in Linguistic Questions", *Journal of Semitic Studies*, 8: 42–51.

Blau, Joyce and Yasir Suleiman (1996), "Language and Ethnic Identity in Kurdistan: An Historic Overview", in Yasir Suleiman (ed.), *Language and Identity in the Middle East and North Africa* (Richmond, Surrey: Curzon Press), pp. 153–64.

Bohas, Georges, J.-P. Guillaume and D. E. Kouloughli (1990), *The Arabic Linguistic Tradition* (London and New York: Routledge).

Boon, J. A. (1982), *Other Tribes, Other Scribes: Symbolic Anthropology in the Comparative Study of Cultures, Religions and Texts* (Cambridge: Cambridge University Press).

Bourdieu, Pierre (1992), *Language and Symbolic Power* (Oxford: Polity Press).

Brass, Paul (1991), *Ethnicity and Nationalism: Theory and Comparison* (New Delhi/Newbury Park/London: Sage Publications).

Breuilly, John (1993), *Nationalism and the State*, 2nd edn (Manchester: Manchester University Press).

Brubaker, Rogers (1992), *Citizenship and Nationhood* (Cambridge, MA: Harvard University Press).

Cachia, Pierre (1990), *An Overview of Modern Arabic Literature* (Edinburgh: Edinburgh University Press).

Cameron, Deborah (1997), "Demythologizing Sociolinguistics", in Nikolas Coupland and Adam Jaworski (eds), *Sociolinguistics: A Reader and a Coursebook* (New York: St Martin's Press, Inc.), pp. 55–67. (First published in 1990.)

Carter, Barbara Lynn (1986), *The Copts in Egyptian Politics* (London: Croom Helm).

Chejne, Anwar G. (1969), *The Arabic Language: Its Role in History* (Minneapolis, MN: University of Minnesota Press).

Choueiri, Youssef M. (2000), *Arab Nationalism: A History* (Oxford: Blackwell Publishers).

Cleveland, William L. (1971), *The Making of an Arab Nationalist: Ottomanism and Arabism in the Life and Thought of Satiʿ al-Husri* (Princeton, NJ: Princeton University Press).

—— (1997), "The Arab Nationalism of George Antonius Reconsidered", in James

Jankowski and Israel Gershoni (eds), *Rethinking Nationalism in the Arab Middle East* (New York: Columbia University Press), pp. 65–86.

Cohen, Anthony P. (1994), *Self Consciousness: An Alternative Anthropology of Identity* (London and New York: Routledge).

Connor, Walker (1978), "A Nation is a Nation, is a State, is an Ethnic Group, is a ...", *Ethnic and Racial Studies*, 1: 377–400.

—— (1990), "When is a Nation?", *Ethnic and Racial Studies*, 13: 92–103.

—— (1994), *Ethnonationalism: The Quest for Understanding* (Princeton, NJ: Princeton University Press).

Cooper, Robert L. (1989), *Language Planning and Social Change* (Cambridge: Cambridge University Press).

Coury, Ralph M. (1998), *The Making of an Egyptian Arab Nationalist: The Early Years of Azzam Pasha* (Reading: Ithaca Press).

Davison, Roderic H. (1963), *Reform in the Ottoman Empire, 1856–1876* (Princeton, NJ: Princeton University Press).

Dawn, Ernest C. (1991), "The Origins of Arab Nationalism", in Rashid Khalidi, Lisa Anderson, Muhammad Muslih and Reeva S. Simon (eds), *The Origins of Arab Nationalism* (New York: Columbia University Press), pp. 3–30.

Deutsch, Karl (1966), *Nationalism and Social Communication: An Inquiry into the Foundations of Nationality*, 2nd edn (Cambridge, MA: MIT Press).

Douglas, Mary (1966), *Purity and Danger: An Analysis of the Concepts of Pollution and Taboo* (London: Routledge & Kegan Paul).

al-Dūrī, ʿAbd al-ʿAzīz (1968), "The Historical Roots of Arab Nationalism", in Kemal H. Karpat (ed.), *Political and Social Thought in the Contemporary Middle East* (New York: Frederick A. Praeger), pp. 33–7.

Eastman, Carol and Thomas C. Reese (1981), "Associated Language: How Language and Ethnic Identity are Related", *General Linguistics*, 21: 109–16.

Edwards, John (1988), *Language, Society and Identity* (Oxford: Basil Blackwell).

Eliraz, Giora (1986), "Tradition and Change: Egyptian Intellectuals and Linguistic Reform, 1919–1939", *Asian and African Studies*, 20: 233–62.

Enderwitz, S. (1996), "Shuʿūbiyya", *Encyclopaedia of Islam*, 2nd edn, vol. 9, pp. 513–16.

Ferguson, Charles A. (1972), "Myths about Arabic", in Joshua A. Fishman (ed.), *Readings in the Sociology of Language* (The Hague: Mouton), pp. 375–81.

al-Fikāykī, ʿAbd al-Hādī (1968), "The Shuʿubiyya and Arab Nationalism", in Kemal H. Karpat (ed.), *Political and Social Thought in the Contemporary Middle East* (New York: Frederick A. Praeger), pp. 80–6.

First Arab Students' Congress (1962), "Arab Pledge, Definitions, Manifesto", in Sylvia G. Haim (ed.), *Arab Nationalism: An Anthology* (Berkeley, CA: Berkeley University Press), pp. 100–2.

Fishman, Joshua A. (1972), *Language and Nationalism: Two Integrative Essays* (Rowley, MA: Newbury House Publishers).

—— (1980), "Social Theory and Ethnography: Language and Ethnicity in Eastern Europe", in P. Sugar (ed.), *Ethnic Diversity and Conflict in Eastern Europe* (Santa Barbara, CA: ABC-Clio), pp. 69–99.

Freitag, Ulrike (1994), "Writing Arab History: The Search for the Nation", *British Journal of Middle Eastern Studies*, 21: 19–37.

Gabrieli, F. (1979), "'Ajam", *Encyclopaedia of Islam*, 2nd edn, vol. 1, p. 206.

Gellner, Ernest (1964), *Thought and Change* (London: Weidenfeld and Nicolson).

—— (1983), *Nations and Nationalism* (Oxford: Basil Blackwell).

Gemayel, Pierre (1968), "Lebanese Nationalism and its Foundations: The Phalangist Viewpoint", in Kemal H. Karpat (ed.), *Political and Social Thought in the Contemporary Middle East* (New York: Frederick A. Praeger), pp. 107–10.

Gershoni, Israel and James Jankowski (1986), *Egypt, Islam and the Arabs: The Search for Egyptian Nationalism 1900–1930* (New York and Oxford: Oxford University Press).

—— (1995), *Redefining the Egyptian Nation: 1930–1945* (Cambridge: Cambridge University Press).

—— (1997), "Introduction", in James Jankowski and Israel Gershoni (eds), *Rethinking Nationalism in the Arab Middle East* (New York: Columbia University Press), pp. ix–xxvi.

Gibb, H. A. R. (1962), *Studies on the Civilization of Islam*, ed. Stanford J. Shaw and William R. Polk (London: Routledge & Kegan Paul).

Goldziher, Ignaz (1966), *Muslim Studies*, 2 vols, ed. Samuel M. Stern and trans. from the German by G. R. Barber and Samuel M. Stern (London: George Allen & Unwin).

Greenfeld, Liah (1992), *Nationalism: Five Roads to Modernity* (Cambridge, MA: Harvard University Press).

Grew, Raymond (1986), "The Construction of National Identity", in Peter Boerner (ed.), *Concepts of National Identity: An Interdisciplinary Dialogue* (Baden-Baden: Nomos Verlagsgesellschaft), pp. 31–43.

Haim, Sylvia G. (1953), "*The Arab Awakening*: A Source for the Historian?", *Welt des Islam*, 2: 237–50.

—— (ed.) (1962), *Arab Nationalism: An Anthology* (Berkeley, CA: University of California Press).

Halliday, Fred (1997), "The Formation of Yemeni Nationalism: Initial Reflections", in James Jankowski and Israel Gershoni (eds), *Rethinking Nationalism in the Arab Middle East* (New York: Columbia University Press), pp. 26–41.

Hanioğlu, M. Sükrü (1991), "The Young Turks and the Arabs before the Revolution of 1908", in Rashid Khalidi, Lisa Anderson, Muhammad Muslih and Reeva S. Simon (eds), *The Origins of Arab Nationalism* (New York: Columbia University Press), pp. 31–49.

Hanna, Milad (1994), *The Seven Pillars of the Egyptian Identity* (Cairo: General Egyptian Book Organisation).

Hayes, Carlton J. H. (1960), *Nationalism: A Religion* (New York: Macmillan Press).

Hechter, Michael (1986), "Rational Choice Theory and the Study of Race and Ethnic Relations", in John Rex and David Mason (eds), *Theories of Race and Ethnic Relations* (Cambridge: Cambridge University Press), pp. 264–79.

Heyd, Uriel (1950), *Foundations of Turkish Nationalism: The Life and Teachings of Ziya Gökalp* (London: Luzac/Harvill Press).

Hobsbawm, Eric (1983), "Inventing Traditions", in Eric Hobsbawm and Terence Ranger (eds), *The Invention of Tradition* (Cambridge: Cambridge University Press), pp. 1–14.

—— (1990), *Nations and Nationalism since 1780* (Cambridge: Cambridge University Press).

Holes, Clive (1993), "The Uses of Variation: A Study of the Political Speeches of Gamal Abdul-Nasir", in Mushira Eid and Clive Holes (eds), *Perspectives on Arabic Linguistics V* (Amsterdam: John Benjamins), pp. 13–45.

Holt, Mike (1996), "Divided Loyalties: Language and Ethnic Identity in the Arab World", in Yasir Suleiman (ed.), *Language and Identity in the Middle East and North Africa* (Richmond, Surrey: Curzon Press), pp. 11–24.

Honey, John (1977), *Language is Power: The Story of Standard English and its Enemies* (London: Faber and Faber).

Hopwood, Derek (1969), *The Russian Presence in Syria and Palestine 1843–1914: Church and Politics in the Near East* (Oxford: Clarendon Press).

Horowitz, Donald (1985), *Ethnic Groups and Conflict* (Berkeley, CA: University of California Press).

Hourani, Albert (1981), *The Emergence of the Modern Middle East* (Berkeley, CA: University of California Press).

—— (1983), *Arabic Thought in the Liberal Age: 1789–1939* (Cambridge: Cambridge University Press).

Hudson, Michael C. (1977), *Arab Politics: The Search for Legitimacy* (New Haven, CT and London: Yale University Press).

al-Ḥuṣrī, Sāti' (1962), "Muslim Unity and Arab Unity", in Sylvia G. Haim (ed.), *Arab Nationalism: An Anthology* (Berkeley, CA: University of California Press), pp. 147–53.

—— (1968), "The Historical Factor in the Formation of Arab Nationalism", in Kemal H. Karpat (ed.), *Political and Social Thought in the Contemporary Middle East* (New York: Frederick A. Praeger), pp. 55–9.

Hutchinson, John (1987), *The Dynamics of Cultural Nationalism* (London: Allen and Unwin).

Hutchinson, John and David Aberbach (1999), "The Artist as Nation-Builder: William Butler Yeats and Chaim Nachman Bialik", *Nations and Nationalism*, 5: 501–21.

Hutchinson, John and Anthony D. Smith (eds) (1996), *Ethnicity* (Oxford: Oxford University Press).

Ibrahim, Muhammad H. (1980), "Language and Politics in Modern Palestine", *Arab Journal for the Humanities*, 1: 323–41.

al-Jundī, Darwish (1968), "The Foundations and Objectives of Arab Nationalism", in Kemal H. Karpat (ed.), *Political and Social Thought in the Contemporary Middle East* (New York: Frederick A. Praeger), pp. 42–8.

Karpat, Kemal H. (ed.) (1968), *Political and Social Thought in the Contemporary Middle East* (New York: Frederick A. Praeger).

al-Kawakibi, Abd al-Rahman (1962), "The Excellences of the Arabs", in Sylvia G.

Haim (ed.), *Arab Nationalism: An Anthology* (Berkeley, CA: University of California Press), pp. 78–80.

Kedourie, Elie (1966), *Nationalism* (London: Hutchinson University Library).

—— (1974a), "The American University of Beirut", in *Arab Political Memoirs and Other Studies* (London: Frank Cass), pp. 59–72.

—— (1974b), "The Impact of the Young Turk Revolution in the Arabic-Speaking Provinces of the Ottoman Empire", in *Arab Political Memoirs and Other Studies* (London: Frank Cass), pp. 124–61.

Khadduri, Majid (1970), *Political Trends in the Arab World: The Role of Ideas and Ideals in Politics* (Baltimore and London: Johns Hopkins Press).

Khalidi, Rashid (1981), "'Abd al-Ghani al-'Uraisi and *al-Mufid*: The Press and Arab Nationalism before 1914", in Marwan R. Buheiry (ed.), *Intellectual Life in the Arab East, 1890–1939* (Beirut: American University of Beirut), pp. 38–61.

—— (1991), "Ottomanism and Arabism in Syria before 1914: A Reassessment", in Rashid Khalidi, Lisa Anderson, Muhammad Muslih and Reeva S. Simon (eds), *The Origins of Arab Nationalism* (New York: Columbia University Press), pp. 50–69.

Khalidi, Tarif (1975), *Islamic Historiography: The Histories of Mas'ūdī* (Albany: State University of New York Press).

al-Kharbūṭlī, 'Alī Ḥusnī (1968), "The Qur'an and Arab Nationalism", in Kemal H. Karpat (ed.), *Political and Social Thought in the Contemporary Middle East* (New York: Frederick A. Praeger), pp. 38–41.

Khouri, Munah (1971), *Poetry and the Making of Modern Egypt (1882–1922)* (Leiden: E. J. Brill).

Kirk, George (1962), "*The Arab Awakening* Reconsidered", *Middle Eastern Affairs*, 13: 162–73.

Kohn, Hans (1945), *The Idea of Nationalism* (New York: Macmillan).

Krejcí, Jaroslav and Vítezslav Velímsky (1981), *Ethnic and Political Nations* (London: Croom Helm).

Kushner, David (1977), *The Rise of Turkish Nationalism: 1876–1908* (London: Frank Cass).

Labov, William (1966), *The Social Stratification of English in New York City* (Washington, DC: Centre for Applied Linguistics).

—— (1972), *Sociolinguistic Patterns* (Philadelphia: University of Pennsylvania Press).

Landau, Jacob (1981), *Pan-Turkism in Turkey: A Study of Irredentism* (London: C. Hurst & Co.).

—— (1993a), "An Arab Anti-Turk Handbill, 1881", in *Jews, Arabs, Turks: Selected Essays* (Jerusalem: The Magness Press), pp. 141–53.

—— (1993b), "A Note on the Egyptian Response to the Young Turk Revolution", in *Jews, Arabs, Turks: Selected Essays* (Jerusalem: The Magness Press), pp. 164–8.

Lane, Edward (1980), *An Arabic English Lexicon* (Beirut: Librairie du Liban).

Lefevere, André (1992), *Translation, History, Culture: A Sourcebook* (London and New York: Routledge).

Lewis, Bernard (1968), *The Emergence of Modern Turkey*, 2nd edn (Oxford: Oxford University Press).

—— (1970), *The Arabs in History*, 5th edn (London: Hutchinson University Library).
Lukitz, Liora (1984), "The Antonius Papers and *The Arab Awakening*, Over Fifty Years On", *Middle Eastern Studies*, 30: 883–95.
Maalouf, Amin (2000), *On Identity*, trans. from the French by Barbara Bray (London: Harvill Press).
Makdisi, Nadim K. (1960), *The Syrian National Party: A Case Study of the First Inroads of National Socialism in the Arab World* (unpublished doctoral thesis: The American University).
Mazraani, Nathalie (1997), *Aspects of Language Variation in Arabic Political Speech-Making* (Richmond, Surrey: Curzon Press).
Miller, David (1995), *On Nationality* (Oxford: Clarendon Press).
Muhawi, Ibrahim (1996), "Language, Ethnicity and National Identity in the Tunisian Ethnic Joke", in Yasir Suleiman (ed.), *Language and Identity in the Middle East and North Africa* (Richmond, Surrey: Curzon Press), pp. 39–59.
Mūsā, Salāma (1955), "Arabic Language Problems", *Middle Eastern Affairs*, 6: 41–4.
Nash, Manning (1989), *The Cauldron of Ethnicity in the Modern World* (Chicago and London: University of Chicago Press).
Norris, H. T. (1990), "Shu'ūbiyya in Arabic Literature", in Julia Ashtiany, T. M. Johnstone, J. D. Letham, R. B. Serjeant and G. Rex Smith (eds), *The Cambridge History of Arabic Literature: 'Abbasid Belles-Lettres* (Cambridge: Cambridge University Press), pp. 31–47.
Nuseibeh, Hazem Zaki (1956), *The Ideas of Arab Nationalism* (Ithaca, New York: Cornell University Press).
Overing, Joanna (1997), "The Role of Myth: An Anthropological Perspective, or: 'The Reality of the Really Made-up'", in Geoffrey Hosking and George Schöpflin (eds), *Myths and Nationhood* (London: Hurst), pp. 1–18.
Patai, R. (1973), *The Arab Mind* (New York: Charles Scribner's Sons).
Phares, Walid (1995), *Lebanese Christian Nationalism: The Rise and Fall of an Ethnic Resistance* (London: Lynne Reinner Publishers).
Reynolds, Susan (1984), *Kingdoms and Communities in Western Europe (900–1300)* (Oxford: Clarendon Press).
Riḍā, Rashīd (1962), "Islam and the National Idea", in Sylvia G. Haim (ed.), *Arab Nationalism: An Anthology* (Berkeley, CA: University of California Press), pp. 75–7.
Sayigh, Rosemary (1965), "The Bilingualism Controversy in Lebanon", *The World Today*, 21: 120–30.
Schöpflin, George (1997), "The Functions of Myth and a Taxonomy of Myths", in Geoffrey Hosking and George Schöpflin (eds), *Myths and Nationhood* (London: Hurst), pp. 19–35.
Seton-Watson, Hugh (1981), *Language and National Consciousness. Proceedings of the British Academy*, lxvii (Oxford: Oxford University Press).
Sharāra, 'Abd al-Laṭīf (1962), "The Idea of Nationalism", in Sylvia G. Haim (ed.), *Arab Nationalism: An Anthology* (Berkeley, CA: University of California Press), pp. 225–8.

Shivtiel, Shraybom Shlomit (1999), "Language and Political Change in Modern Egypt", *International Journal of the Sociology of Language*, 137: 131–40.

Shouby, E. (1951), "The Influence of the Arabic Language on the Psychology of the Arabs", *The Middle East Journal*, 5: 284–302.

Smith, Anthony D. (1991), *National Identity* (Harmondsworth: Penguin Books).

—— (1997), "The 'Golden Age' and National Renewal", in Geoffrey Hosking and George Schöpflin (eds), *Myths and Nationhood* (London: Hurst), pp. 36–59.

Snyder, L. Louis (1954), *The Meaning of Nationalism* (New Brunswick, NJ: Rutgers University Press).

Spolsky, Bernard (1998), *Sociolinguistics* (Oxford: Oxford University Press).

Spolsky, Bernard and Robert Cooper (1991), *The Languages of Jerusalem* (Oxford: Clarendon Press).

Spolsky, Bernard and Elena Shohamy (1999), *The Languages of Israel: Policy, Ideology and Practice* (Clevedon: Multilingual Matters Ltd).

Stalin, Joseph (1994), "The Nation", in John Hutchinson and Anthony D. Smith (eds), *Nationalism* (Oxford: Oxford University Press), pp. 18–21.

Suleiman, Yasir (1990), "Sībawayhi's 'Parts of Speech' According to al-Zajjājī", *Journal of Semitic Studies*, 35: 245–63.

—— (1991), "The Methodological Rules of Arabic Grammar", in Kinga Dévényi and Támas Iványi (eds), *Proceedings of the Colloquium on Arabic Grammar: The Arabist: Budapest Studies in Arabic* 3–4, pp. 351–64.

—— (1993), "The Language Situation in Jordan and Code-Switching: A New Interpretation", *New Arabian Studies*, 1: 1–20.

—— (1994), "Nationalism and the Arabic Language: An Historical Overview", in Yasir Suleiman (ed.), *Arabic Sociolinguistics: Issues and Perspectives* (Richmond, Surrey: Curzon Press), pp. 3–24.

—— (1996a), "The Concept of *Faṣāḥā* in Ibn Sinān al-Khafājī", *New Arabian Studies*, 3: 219–37.

—— (1996b), "Language and Identity in Egyptian Nationalism", in Yasir Suleiman (ed.), *Language and Identity in the Middle East and North Africa* (Richmond, Surrey: Curzon Press), pp. 25–37.

—— (1997), "The Arabic Language in the Fray: A Sphere of Contested Identities", in Alan Jones (ed.), *University Lectures in Islamic Studies I* (London: Altajir World of Islam Trust), pp. 127–48.

—— (1999a), "Autonomy versus Non-Autonomy in the Arabic Grammatical Tradition", in Yasir Suleiman (ed.), *Arabic Grammar and Linguistics* (Richmond, Surrey: Curzon Press), pp. 30–49.

—— (1999b), "Language and Political Conflict in the Middle East: A Study in Symbolic Sociolinguistics", in Yasir Suleiman (ed.), *Language and Society in the Middle East and North Africa: Studies in Identity and Variation* (Richmond, Surrey: Curzon Press), pp. 10–37.

—— (1999c), *The Arabic Grammatical Tradition: A Study in Ta'līl* (Edinburgh: Edinburgh University Press).

—— (1999d), "Language Education Policies: Arabic-speaking countries", in Bernard

Spolsky (ed.), *Concise Encyclopedia of Educational Linguistics* (Oxford: Elsevier/ Pergamon), pp. 106–16.

—— (1999e), "Under the Spell of Language: Arabic between Linguistic Determinism and Linguistic Relativity", in Ian Netton (ed.), *Hunter of the East I*, Studies in Honour of C. E. Bosworth (Leiden: Brill).

—— (1999f), "Sociolinguistic Reflexes of Political Conflict: The Case of Jerusalem", in *Beyond the Border: A New Framework for Understanding the Dynamism of Muslim Society*, international symposium (Tokyo: Islamic Area Studies), pp. 399–415.

Tauber, Eliezer (1993), *The Emergence of the Arab Movements* (London: Frank Cass).

Thomas, George (1991), *Linguistic Purism* (London and New York: Longman).

Thompson, John Alexander (1956), *The Major Arabic Bibles: Their Origin and Nature* (New York: American Bible Society).

Tibawi, A. L. (1963), "The American Missionaries in Beirut and Buṭrus al-Bustānī", in Albert Hourani (ed.), *Middle Eastern Affairs, 3* (London: Chatto & Windus), pp. 137–82. (St Antony's Papers, Number 16.)

—— (1966), *American Interests in Syria, 1800–1901: A Study of Educational, Literary and Religious Work* (Oxford: Clarendon Press).

—— (1969), *A Modern History of Syria including Lebanon and Palestine* (London: Macmillan).

Tibi, Bassam (1997), *Arab Nationalism between Islam and the National State*, 3rd edn (London: Macmillan).

Tilmatin, Mohamed and Yasir Suleiman (1996), "Language and Identity: The Case of the Berber", in Yasir Suleiman (ed.), *Language and Identity in the Middle East and North Africa* (Richmond, Surrey: Curzon Press), pp. 165–79.

Tonkin, Elisabeth, Maryon McDonald and Malcolm Chapman (eds) (1989), "Introduction", in *History and Ethnicity* (London: Routledge), pp. 1–21.

Tütsch, Hans E. (1965), *Facets of Arab Nationalism* (Detroit, MI: Wayne State University Press).

'Umar, Aḥmad Mukhtār (1998), "The Establishment of Arabic in Egypt", *The Arabist (19–20), Proceedings of the Arabic and Islamic Sections of the 35th International Congress of Asian and North African Studies, Part 1*, ed. K. Dévényi and T. Iványi (Budapest), pp. 37–50. (Author's name rendered as Ahamad Mokhtar Omer.)

Vatikiotis, P. J. (1987), *Islam and the State* (London and New York: Routledge).

Versteegh, Kees (1995), *The Explanation of Linguistic Causes: al-Zajjājī's Theory of Grammar* (Amsterdam/Philadelphia: John Benjamins).

Walters, Keith (2002), "Review of Niloofar Haeri, *The Sociolinguistic Market of Cairo: Gender, Class and Education* (London and New York: Kegan Paul International, 1997)", *Journal of Sociolinguistics*, 6: 152–5.

Weber, Max (1948), *From Max Weber: Essays in Sociology*, trans. and ed. H. H. Gerth and C. Wright Mills (London: Routledge and Kegan Paul).

—— (1968), *Economy and Society: An Outline of Interpretative Sociology*, ed. Guenther Roth and Claus Wittich (New York: Bedminster Press).

Wendell, Charles (1972), *The Evolution of the Egyptian National Image: From its Origins to Aḥmad Luṭfī al-Sayyid* (Berkeley, CA: University of California Press).
El-Wer, Enam (1999), "Why Do Different Variables Behave Differently?", in Yasir Suleiman (ed.), *Language and Society in the Middle East and North Africa: Studies in Identity and Variation* (Richmond, Surrey: Curzon Press), pp. 38–57.
Wild, Stefan (1981), "Negib Azoury and his Book *Le Réveil de la nation arabe*", in Marwan R. Buheiry (ed.), *Intellectual Life in the Arab East, 1890–1939* (Beirut: American University of Beirut), pp. 92–104.
Zeine, N. (1966), *The Emergence of Arab Nationalism: With a Background Study of Arab–Turkish Relations in the Near East* (Beirut: Khayats).
Zurayq, Qunsṭanṭīn (1962), "Arab Nationalism and Religion", in Sylvia G. Haim (ed.), *Arab Nationalism: An Anthology* (Berkeley, CA: University of California Press), pp. 167–71.

Index